☽ INSIGHT GUIDES

CARIBBEAN CRUISES

DISCOVERY CHANNEL

APA PUBLICATIONS
Part of the Langenscheidt Publishing Group

L

INSIGHT GUIDE
CaRIBBean CRUISES

Editorial
Managing Editor
Lesley Gordon
Editorial Director
Brian Bell

Distribution

UK & Ireland
GeoCenter International Ltd
The Viables Centre, Harrow Way
Basingstoke, Hants RG22 4BJ
Fax: (44) 1256 817988

United States
Langenscheidt Publishers, Inc.
36–36 33rd Street 4th Floor
Long Island City, NY 11106
Fax: 1 (718) 784 0640

Canada
Thomas Allen & Son Ltd
390 Steelcase Road East
Markham, Ontario L3R 1G2
Fax: (1) 905 475 6747

Australia
Universal Publishers
1 Waterloo Road
Macquarie Park, NSW 2113
Fax: (61) 2 9888 9074

New Zealand
Hema Maps New Zealand Ltd (HNZ)
Unit D, 24 Ra ORA Drive
East Tamaki, Auckland
Fax: (64) 9 273 6479

Worldwide
Apa Publications GmbH & Co.
Verlag KG (Singapore branch)
38 Joo Koon Road, Singapore 628990
Tel: (65) 6865 1600. Fax: (65) 6861 6438

Printing

Insight Print Services (Pte) Ltd
38 Joo Koon Road, Singapore 628990
Tel: (65) 6865 1600. Fax: (65) 6861 6438

©2006 Apa Publications GmbH & Co.
Verlag KG (Singapore branch)
All Rights Reserved

First Edition 2003
Revised 2004
Updated 2006

CONTACTING THE EDITORS
We would appreciate it if readers
would alert us to errors or out-
dated information by writing to:
Insight Guides, P.O. Box 7910,
London SE1 1WE, England.
Fax: (44) 20 7403 0290.
insight@apaguide.co.uk

www.insightguides.com

ABOUT THIS BOOK

This guidebook combines the interests and enthusiasms of two of the world's best-known information providers: Insight Guides, whose titles have set the standard for visual travel guides since 1970, and Discovery Channel, the world's premier source of nonfiction television programming.

The editors of Insight Guides provide both practical advice and general understanding about a destination's history, culture and people. Discovery Channel and its popular website, www.discovery.com, help millions of viewers explore their world from the comfort of their own home and encourage them to explore it firsthand.

Insight Guide: Caribbean Cruises is structured to convey an understanding of sea travel by cruise ship as well as to guide readers through the sights and activities on dry land.

◆ The **Features** section, indicated by a yellow bar at the top of each page, covers the cultural history of the Caribbean and cruising tips in a series of informative essays.

◆ The main **Places** section, indicated by a blue bar, is a complete guide to all the shore excursions and sights worth visiting. Places of special interest are coordinated by number with the maps.

◆ The **Travel Tips** listings section, with an orange bar, provides a handy point of reference for information on travel, hotels, shops, restaurants and more.

The contributors

This book was produced by **Lesley Gordon**, who is Insight Guides'

London-based managing editor in charge of Caribbean titles.

The first writer on board was **Lisa Gerard-Sharp**, a contributor to many Insight Guides. Her contributions here include *Tall Ships*, *The Secret Life of a Cruise Ship*, *Glamour, Glitz and Games*, *Topical Talks*, *Caribbean under Sail*, *The Deep Sea*, *Private Hideaways*, *Dominica*, *St Lucia* and *The Tourism Dollar*.

Pam Barrett refined the Caribbean Cruises narrative, paying close attention to *Bermuda* and *The Bahamas*, and wrote *Sailing the East*. Barrett is co-author of *Compact Guide Antigua & Barbuda*.

The book's introduction was written by **Douglas Ward**, the highly respected author of the cruise industry's "bible", the *Berlitz Guide to Ocean Cruising and Cruise Ships*.

Based in Miami, Florida's cruise gateway, journalist **Joann Biondi**, was well placed to contribute a profile of a serving cruise ship captain, *The Changing Face of Cruising*, *Choosing a Route*, *Sailing the Western Shores*, *Florida, Mexico and Central America*, *Panama Canal, Cayman Islands* and *Cuba*. Biondi is also the author of Insight Pocket Guide *Cayman Islands*.

Tony Peisley, a journalist and cruise specialist, plotted the history chronology, and wrote *Cruising Through History*, *Southern Sailing*, *San Juan, US Virgin Islands*, *St Vincent and The Grenadines*, and *Grenada and Carriacou*.

Maria Harding, another seasoned cruise writer and journalist, wrote *The A to Z of Cruising*, *Cruising with Children*, *Spas at Sea*, *St Maarten*, *British Virgin Islands*, *St Kitts*, *Guadeloupe, Aruba and Curaçao*.

Sue Bryant, editor of *Cruise Traveller* magazine, wrote *Cruise Cuisine*, *Cruise-and-Stay*, *Shore Excursions*, *Barbados* and *Jamaica*. Bryant also compiled the comprehensive Travel Tips section.

James Ferguson, author of many books including the *Traveller's History of the Caribbean*, wrote *The Caribbean Character* and *Pirates*.

Martha Ellen Zenfell, editor of Insight Guides' North American titles, wrote *The Art of Cruising* and *The Big Time*.

David Howard, a Latin America specialist, wrote about Antigua. **Simon Lee** guided travellers through Trinidad, his home for many years.

Journalist and author **Polly Pattullo** analysed the impact of cruising on the Caribbean. **Deby Nash**, provided text for Nassau and Grand Bahama.

Map Legend

—— ‥	International Boundary
_ _ _ _	State/Province Boundary
⊖	Border Crossing
▬•▬	National Park/Reserve
─ ─ ─ ─	Ferry Route
✈ ✈	Airport: International/Regional
🚌	Bus Station
❶	Tourist Information
✉	Post Office
⌂ † ⛪	Church/Ruins
†	Monastery
☾	Mosque
✡	Synagogue
🏰 ⛰	Castle/Ruins
🏠	Mansion/Stately home
∴	Archaeological Site
∩	Cave
🏛	Statue/Monument
★	Place of Interest

The main places of interest in the Places section are coordinated by number with a full-colour map (e.g. ❶), and a symbol at the top of every right-hand page tells you where to find the map.

INSIGHT GUIDE
CaRIBBEan CRUISES

CONTENTS

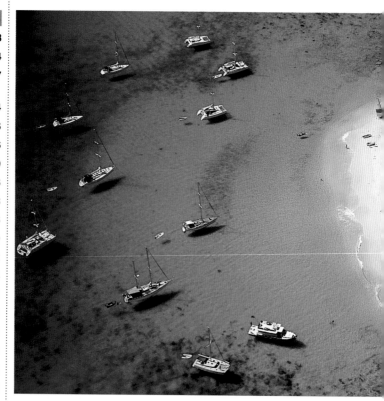

Noise disturbs
Wildlife Please
be quiet

Sandy Cay, British
Virgin Islands

Information panels

Travel Tips

Places

ISLAND HOPPING

Douglas Ward, the world's leading authority on cruise ships,
considers why many people choose to cruise the Caribbean

White sandy beaches, deep blue waters, bougainvillaea and passion flowers, tropical fruits, glowing sunshine, vibrant music and friendly, laid-back people place the islands of the Caribbean among the world's most popular holiday destinations. And there is no better way to experience the Caribbean, certainly for first-time visitors, than on a cruise. It enables visitors to be as lazy or as active as they wish and combines the pleasures of life in a luxury, floating hotel – which offers a wide range of accommodation, sports facilities, health spas, restaurants and entertainment – with the enjoyment of trouble-free, well-organised shore excursions that enable people to experience a taste of life on very different islands. On shore, they can take part in activities that range from sightseeing in historic ports, to mountain biking, snorkelling or swimming with dolphins, or just shopping and trying exotic foods.

The Caribbean basin, a vast area, contains thousands of islands, stretching from Bermuda in the north to Venezuela in the south, Barbados in the east, and Costa Rica in the west. With many cruises beginning in Florida or in San Juan, Puerto Rico, much of this huge area is accessible on relatively short trips by sea, and the value for money is unbeatable.

Cruising has come a long way since the "booze cruises" of the 1930s, designed chiefly to escape Prohibition laws in the United States. The industry launched the revival of fortunes for many islands in the Caribbean, but World War II intervened and it was only in the 1960s that cruising was reborn, with passengers being flown to embarkation ports, and a working relationship emerging between cruise lines and airlines.

The worldwide cruise industry has grown enormously since then; the concept hasn't changed much but it has been vastly improved, refined, expanded and packaged. Six companies operating large ships (defined as ships carrying between 1,000 and 3,000 passengers) dominate the market, but smaller vessels (carrying fewer than 300 passengers) also have a place, and are capable of entering the tiny, uncrowded harbours where their larger sisters cannot venture.

These days, cruising is not just for the elderly or for the wealthy and indolent few – passengers come from all age groups and walks of life, and cruises are designed to suit their many different needs. Read on, and see if you would like to join them. ❑

PRECEDING PAGES: a waterfront view in Montego Bay, Jamaica; at the pool on *Club Med 1*; a ship at anchor in George Town, Grand Cayman. **LEFT:** an aerial view of Tobago Cays, The Grenadines.

THE CARIBBEAN CHARACTER

Centuries of foreign domination, slavery and migration have forged
local cultures that are strong, proud and creative

Arrive in any Caribbean port, from the Bahamas down to Trinidad, and the first thing you will see will probably be a fortress. Havana's harbour mouth, for instance, is guarded by three formidable castles, the oldest of which was completed in 1630. The seaward approach to Martinique's capital, Fort-de-France, is watched over by the grim-looking Fort St Louis, continuously occupied by the French military for almost four centuries. Even a tiny island like St Kitts, no more than a dot on the map, has nine impressive forts, one of which proved so impregnable it was dubbed the "Gibraltar of the West Indies".

These scattered vestiges of military power, some ruined and others restored, remind us that the Caribbean has always been fought over. Its history is, to a large extent, one of conquest and conflict. Its landscapes are marked not only by fortifications, but by the memory of battles, uprisings and massacres. The surrounding seas have witnessed countless naval engagements and the waters of the Caribbean conceal a wealth of sunken warships and rusting cannons. Not only did competing European nations go to war over this rich and desirable region, but pirates preyed on its ports, and enslaved Africans rose up in violent bids for freedom. Only in more recent times has this archipelago of islands discovered peace and left behind its turbulent history.

Early invaders

The first invaders were the people who gave their name to this part of the world. The Caribs arrived in around AD 1000, pushing up the island chain from their homelands in the Amazon Basin and conquering each territory they reached. Their victims were the peaceful Taínos, the first people to settle in the region, who also originated from South America. Fierce, fearless and reputedly inclined to cannibalism, the Caribs overwhelmed the Taínos, killing men and capturing women.

The Carib invasion may have been violent, but it was mild in comparison to the horrors inflicted by the first European invaders. Believing himself to be somewhere near China, Christopher Columbus landed on a flat, scrubby

island in the Bahamas on 12 October 1492, unleashing the conquest of the New World by the Old. The Genoese adventurer, backed by the Spanish monarchy, made a first permanent settlement in what is now the Dominican Republic, founding a fledgling colony among the normally placid Taínos on the island he called Hispaniola.

Such was the brutality inflicted by the colonists on the Taínos, as they forced them to search for gold, that the indigenous people revolted. As uprisings were followed by reprisals and the Taínos succumbed to European diseases, a community of 300,000 on Hispaniola was reduced to a mere handful within three decades.

PRECEDING PAGES: a painting depicts the sugar cane harvest in Cuba, 1874.
LEFT: Carib Amerindians.
RIGHT: Columbus lands on Watling Island, the Bahamas.

From this unpromising foothold, the Spanish empire strengthened and spread. Cuba, Puerto Rico and Jamaica were conquered, and *conquistadores* set sail from Santo Domingo to seize the vast territories of Mexico and Central America. The smaller Eastern Caribbean islands, sighted and named by Columbus, were not colonised, largely because of the presence of the ferocious Caribs. When it became apparent that the Caribbean islands had only limited supplies of gold, the emphasis shifted to a new form of wealth: sugar.

BUCCANEERS

When on-shore, pirates grilled their meat over "boucans" (a Carib word) or barbecues, from which the name "buccaneer" derived.

interest. Protestant England claimed religious motivations for its hostility towards Catholic Spain, but money and military competition were equally important grounds for animosity. Pirates from England, France and Holland began to prey on Spanish galleons and ports. Sir Francis Drake attacked and occupied Santo Domingo in 1585, destroying the pride of the Spanish empire. In response, the Spanish fortified their towns and protected their treasure fleets with warships. Gradually, other European nations began to settle in the region,

King Sugar

It had been discovered that sugar cane, brought by Columbus on his second expedition in 1493, flourished in the fertile Caribbean soil. So began the reign of "King Sugar", the cruel ruler of the Caribbean economy for five centuries. But sugar plantations required labour, and with the Taínos almost extinct and the Spanish disinclined to sweat in the fields, a workforce was needed. The colonists accordingly turned to the African slave trade, which had been practised since the 1450s. The first slaves arrived in 1518, but soon the trickle turned into a flood.

Other European nations watched the expansion of the Spanish Caribbean with keen choosing the smaller islands of the Eastern Caribbean, which the Spanish had claimed but not occupied. The English claimed St Kitts in 1624 and Barbados in 1627. The French took Martinique and Guadeloupe in 1635. The Dutch took possession of islands like Curaçao and St Maarten between 1630 and 1640.

Throughout the 17th and 18th centuries, the European powers fought among themselves for control of the Caribbean and its rich sugar industry. The British took Jamaica from the Spanish in 1655 and from then on did their utmost to weaken the Spaniards' dominance of the larger islands. At the same time, conflicts between the British, French and Dutch reflected

Pirates

For almost 200 years, from the 16th century, pirates, privateers and buccaneers terrorised the Caribbean, wreaking havoc among the Spanish treasure fleets and earning notoriety for their spectacular brutality. Fiction has been kind to pirates, painting them as dashing desperadoes, but the truth was rather different. For the most part, they were driven by a mixture of religious hatred and greed. Tolerated and even supported by European governments hostile to Spain, they were eventually banished by those same governments after they had outlived their usefulness.

The first pirates were independent operators, mixing attacks on Caribbean shipping and harbours with smuggling and slave-trading. Soon they were sponsored by their rulers at home (and known as privateers rather than pirates), with Queen Elizabeth I of England a staunch supporter of Sir Francis Drake. He and others attacked shipping and towns throughout the Caribbean and Central America, forcing the Spanish to build expensive fortifications and reinforce the fleets that carried gold and silver from South America back to Europe. Yet all these precautions couldn't stop Piet Heyn, a Dutch privateer, from capturing 31 bullion-laden ships off the coast of Cuba in 1628.

As wars raged between European nations in the 17th century, deserters, shipwrecked sailors and escaped slaves formed runaway communities in the Caribbean. The favourite haunts of these buccaneers were isolated Tortuga off Haiti and the empty cays of the Bahamas. They enticed ships onto reefs or attacked them from their own long canoes, capturing cargoes and murdering crews.

Life was short and brutish, with violent death or disease ever present. They lived in basic shacks, wore rough clothes of cotton and rawhide and were reportedly filthy with the blood of slaughtered cattle. Even so, the buccaneers developed deep bonds of affection among themselves and even entered into a sort of same-sex marriage, called *matelotage*, although this was probably a means of dealing with an individual's assets in the event of his death. In return for weapons, tobacco and rum, the buccaneers traded hides and meat with the passing ships that they did not choose to attack.

LEFT: slaves working in the fields in Cuba.

RIGHT: Henry Morgan, the fearsome Welsh buccaneer who became the Governor of Jamaica.

The heyday of the pirates came in the 1680s, when Port Royal in Jamaica achieved infamy as the "wickedest town in Christendom", a decadent boomtown of taverns, brothels and gambling dens. It was here that Henry Morgan, fiercest of all seafarers, ruled as Lieutenant-Governor after a bloody career raiding Spanish ports. In 1692 Port Royal was destroyed by an earthquake and tidal wave in what many deemed an act of divine retribution.

Around that time, European leaders were tiring of their former pirate friends, as they now had their own Caribbean possessions and were afraid of such lawless elements. Some pirates retired gracefully, others were hunted down. The golden age of

Caribbean piracy was over by the end of the 17th century, even though a few individuals, such as Edward "Blackbeard" Teach, carried on into the next.

The pirates have left traces throughout the Caribbean, mostly in the form of forts and look-out posts used by their victims. They left few buildings of their own, but the ruins of Port Royal give an idea of what life was like.

Under the sea, however, lie literally hundreds of wrecks, many the result of pirate attacks. Most are still undiscovered, but there are thought to be many off the coasts of Florida and Bermuda and around the Bahamas. Are they full of gold doubloons? Crowds of treasure hunters, professional and amateur, who flock to the islands think so. ❑

wider hostilities in Europe. No sooner were peace treaties signed than a new outbreak of fighting shook the region. Between 1660 and 1814, the island of St Lucia changed hands between the British and French 14 times. Throughout this period, millions of enslaved Africans were brought to the islands to ensure the flow of sugar to Europe was not interrupted.

Seeds of destruction

The heyday of the sugar industry was the second half of the 18th century, the age of luxurious "great houses" and fantastically rich West Indian planters. Fabulous fortunes were made,

republic of Haiti. Here, in 13 years of civil war and foreign intervention, an army of ex-slaves beat Napoleon's military machine and freed themselves by force. Men such as Toussaint Louverture and Jean-Jacques Dessalines turned their fellow slaves into a lethal fighting force, capable of beating the French and British. The other Caribbean societies watched with horror as the region's richest colony disintegrated.

Another blow to King Sugar came with the development of a rival beet sugar industry in Europe. European farmers and manufacturers began to compete with the vested interests of the old "plantocracy". Within the islands them-

both by planters and manufacturers and traders in Europe. The wealth generated by sugar and slavery fuelled the industrial revolution first in Britain, then in the rest of Europe. But the system also carried the seeds of its own destruction. Huge plantations became breeding grounds for resistance and revolt among the slaves, who had nothing to lose but a life of overwork and cruelty. Uprisings ravaged almost every island and, although bloodily repressed, caused terror among the white minority.

The single event that changed the course of Caribbean history was the slave revolution of 1791–1804, which destroyed the French colony of Saint Domingue and created the independent

selves, grotesquely unequal societies were increasingly under strain. A small minority of white landowners, backed by military force, lorded it over a mixed-race population and a much greater number of black slaves. Hatreds ran deep, and conflict was commonplace.

Abolition

Slavery ended in the mid-19th century (it took longest to disappear in the Spanish colonies) through a combination of economic and political pressures. In short, the system was costly and inefficient as well as barbarous. Planters feared a repeat of the Haitian revolution, while liberals at home in Europe campaigned for abolition. Eventually, slavery was outlawed, the planters were compensated for their losses, and the slaves found themselves faced with freedom – of a sort. Few options were open to them and many continued to work for paltry wages on the plantations, while others left, establishing small farms or seeking work in the towns.

Abolition spelt the downfall of the Caribbean sugar industry, although vestiges of it clung on on many islands. Contract labourers arrived from India and other countries to fill the gaps left by the departing slaves. But the industry went through hard times, and gradually the European powers lost interest in their subsequent interventions in Haiti and the Dominican Republic, where political chaos and economic mismanagement irritated Washington. The completion of the Panama Canal in 1914, together with hostilities against Germany in World War I, made the US especially protective of its strategic interests in the Caribbean.

What most of the Caribbean islands wanted was independence. Haiti had led the way in 1804, but had been plagued by instability and poverty. The Dominican Republic finally threw out the Spanish in 1864; Cuba and Puerto Rico followed suit in 1898. But American influence remained strong, creating resentment among

Caribbean possessions, turning instead to imperial adventures in Africa and Asia.

The American century

The 20th century was the American century in the Caribbean. The new superpower was opposed to any remaining European interference in its "backyard" and moved to fill the void left by the colonial forces. In 1898, the US ousted the Spanish from Cuba and Puerto Rico, ending 400 years of Hispanic rule. There were

LEFT: proclaiming emancipation to slaves on a sugar plantation.
ABOVE: French and patriots battle in Haiti (1802–04).

INTERNAL CHANGES

While the post-slavery Caribbean islands slipped off the map as far as Europe was concerned, it was a period of great social change. The power of the white minority dwindled, although Europeans still remained firmly in control. The contrast between their lifestyles and those of the black and coloured communities encouraged the latter to seek improvements through education and social reform. Churches of all denominations were active in redressing old inequalities and providing new opportunities. The Moravian church (a Protestant sect that originated in Bohemia) was particularly insistent that people of all races should receive education.

those who wanted to be free of outside interference. Afraid of communism, the US supported conservatives, including such unsavoury dictators as Rafael Leonidas Trujillo, who ran the Dominican Republic like a family business from 1930 to 1961. Washington's worst fears were realised when another dictator, Fulgencio Batista of Cuba, was ousted in 1959, and replaced by the revolutionary government of Fidel Castro, who has remained in power ever since.

Independence

In most instances, independence took a more peaceful form. In the British colonies, greater

self-government and universal suffrage was followed by complete independence from the 1960s onwards. Jamaica, Barbados and Trinidad and Tobago all severed colonial ties with London after the failure of a short-lived federation of English-speaking islands. They were followed by smaller territories, from Antigua to St Vincent. But some islands preferred to maintain their links with Europe. In 1946, Martinique and Guadeloupe voted to become *départements* of France, while the Dutch islands formed a federation with the Netherlands. A few tiny territories, such as Montserrat and Anguilla, opted to remain British colonies rather than face the economic uncertainty of independence.

In many respects, the modern Caribbean is something of a success story. With the exception of Cuba, the region enjoys democratic government and a steadily growing standard of living. Haiti remains politically volatile and stubbornly poor, but elsewhere human rights and a modest prosperity are now taken for granted. Barbados, for instance, has some of the best quality-of-life statistics outside Europe and North America, while the Dominican Republic, once a poverty-stricken dictatorship, is now reaping the benefits of democratic government and sustained economic growth.

There are still social and political flashpoints in the Caribbean. Cuba's future remains uncertain, and Haiti's deep-seated problems seem no closer to a solution. There is occasional trouble in the tough inner-city ghettos of Kingston, Jamaica, and elections in Trinidad have been tense. But, for the most part, the Caribbean is a region of stability and social tolerance, where people of all backgrounds live together.

The threats facing the Caribbean are now more economic than political. As a cluster of small states, the islands are especially vulnerable to developments beyond their control. These range from the hurricanes that regularly ravage communities, to the onward march of globalisation and the threatened loss of export markets to cheaper producers around the world.

The European heritage

This history of colonialism and conflict has left an indelible mark on today's Caribbean. Four European languages (English, French, Spanish and Dutch) are spoken across the region, together with many local dialects and creoles – a mixture of European, African and other languages. Colonial rule has left behind the architecture, habits and the tastes of the European mother country, whether in the shape of croissants in Guadeloupe, cricket in Antigua or gabled roofs in Curaçao.

Each island bears the imprint of its colonial past, but often this past is as culturally mixed as the people it has produced. Where more than one European power ruled an island at different times, distinctly different influences become obvious. The smaller islands of the Eastern Caribbean, for instance, are a fascinating blend of French and British influences, where French-built Catholic churches rub shoulders with solidly Anglo-Saxon town halls. Towns like

Castries in St Lucia or St George's in Grenada reveal a subtle blend of Gallic and British influences, reflected in the French-based, musical *patois* spoken by many islanders.

Elsewhere, a particular European model is dominant. Barbados, affectionately known as "Little England", was never occupied by any other colonial power and exudes Englishness in its parish churches, cricket grounds and Victorian architecture. The great cities of Havana and San Juan, on the other hand, are unmistakably Spanish, with colonnaded streets, plazas and fountains. The warehouses of Willemstad, Curaçao, look like a canal-side section of Amsterdam, while small towns in Martinique are reminiscent of provincial France with their war memorials and *tricolores*.

pean migration, and the descendants of migrants from Andalucia and the Canary Islands can still be seen in the lighter-skinned peasant farmers of Cuba and Puerto Rico. In these islands slavery was less dominant than in Haiti or Jamaica, where today's majority population is of African descent.

Where Africans arrived in great numbers, their cultural and religious practices remained strong despite attempts by white slave masters to drive out "superstition". The *voodoo* religion of Haiti, much maligned and distorted by outsiders for centuries, is the living connection between this Caribbean nation and the West

Migrants and settlers

But the European heritage is only part of the story. Each Caribbean island is also the product of a long history of migration and settlement, in which Africa, Asia and the Americas have all played vital roles. In the Spanish Caribbean, there was always a greater tradition of Euro-

LEFT: a young Fidel Castro.
ABOVE: farm labourers hitching a ride after a hard day's work in the cane field, Cuba.

MIXTURE OF RELIGIONS

The Caribbean is a place where religion is taken seriously and where religious values look back to the pivotal role played by churches in the post-slavery period. Christian churches of every sort co-exist with other religious faiths, mostly derived from Africa or India and transplanted with the slaves and labourers to the Caribbean. In Haiti and Cuba, traditional African spirits are worshipped by followers of *vodou* and *santería*. In Trinidad and the French islands Hindu temples and Muslim mosques are testimony to the importation of religious ideas from the Indian subcontinent, brought by the labourers who became the new workforce in the 19th century.

African societies from which millions of slaves were forcibly removed. In agricultural techniques, in food and drink, in dance, music and ritual, almost every Caribbean island remains linked to the distant African point of departure.

In some instances, there is another strong connection. Trinidad, for instance, has a majority population descended from the Indian labourers who were shipped from the subcontinent in the second half of the 19th century to work on the sugar plantations. Today, parts of rural Trinidad resemble Hindustan, as *dhoti*-clad labourers tend buffaloes among coconut groves. In the towns, meanwhile, the sounds

and smells of India are evident in contemporary *chutney* music and Trinidad's favourite fast food, the curry-filled *roti*. Elsewhere, in Jamaica especially, a strong Chinese influence is detectable. Throughout the region the descendants of migrant traders from the Middle East play an important role in retailing and finance.

A Caribbean cocktail

Jamaica's motto "Out of many, one people" contains the key to understanding the Caribbean character. This is a part of the world, perhaps more than anywhere else, where people and cultures from every continent have been brought together into hybrid and mixed societies. The mixture of European, African, Asian and American has created what is known as a creole culture, a cocktail of differing influences and traditions. The term creole used to apply to a white individual born in the region, but now means the distinctive blend of the parts that make the Caribbean whole.

So what are the defining characteristics of "creoleness"? Generalisations are dangerous, and clearly each island has its own particular traits, but firmly at the heart of the region's collective identity lies creativity. Creole culture is enormously inventive, producing some wonderful music, literature and visual arts. For a relatively small area of fewer than 20 million people, the Caribbean has been disproportionately fertile in creating new artistic forms.

The region is the birthplace not only of reggae, calypso and salsa, but also of world-class writers such as Trinidad's V.S. Naipaul, Cuba's Alejo Carpentier and St Lucia's Derek Walcott. In painting, sculpture and dance, the Caribbean can confidently compete with any other part of the world. Its sportsmen and women, too, are often world-beaters, ranging from champion Cuban boxers to Jamaica's footballing "Reggae Boyz" heroes.

Above all, the creole character is formed by a love of freedom and a respect for the individual. The Caribbean has undergone the traumatic experience of slavery and, in many cases, dictatorship, and this bitter history has taught its people to value freedom. Independence and self-reliance are valued qualities in a region where economic conditions are often harsh, and many people are deeply attached to a small patch of land that they can call their own.

There is little affection for authority in the Caribbean, and pompous politicians or overbearing bureaucrats are likely to face well-deserved mockery. Few people enjoy taking orders – perhaps another legacy of slavery – and that is why visitors are sometimes frustrated by what they view as inefficiency or insolence. The only solution is to recognise that taking one's time is not necessarily a bad thing, and that patience and a sense of humour go a long way towards breaking down barriers.

A changing economy

A child born today in the Caribbean is more likely to end up serving drinks in a hotel or driving a taxi than cutting sugar cane or growing vegetables. Agriculture is still the lifeblood of many Caribbean economies, and King Sugar still holds some vestiges of power in Cuba and several other islands, but the economic landscape is changing rapidly.

Sugar never really recovered from the downturn of the late 19th century and continued to decline throughout the 20th. Some governments looked for agricultural alternatives, and in the 1950s the banana industry was encouraged to displace sugar across the Eastern Caribbean. The advent of low-cost air transport meant that fruits, flowers and other exotic exports could be flown fresh to New York or London.

baseballs. With advances in technology came new opportunities such as data processing and offshore banking.

Tourism

The real economic trump card has been tourism. Since Victorian times, the islands have attracted the wealthy from colder climates, who wintered in the first hotel resorts to be built in Barbados and Cuba. With Prohibition in the US came floods of thirsty Americans to Cuba and the Bahamas, in search of rum cocktails and a good time. From the 1950s onwards, jet planes transported growing numbers of tourists from

But many farmers simply gave up commercial agriculture and found work in towns, or migrated. Big estates sometimes prospered, but small farmers faced tough times.

The islands looked for other livelihoods. Some, like Trinidad, were fortunate in having natural resources such as oil and gas. Others built up light manufacturing, taking advantage of their proximity to the huge US market and cheap labour rates. The Caribbean soon began to develop a reputation for low-cost assembly plants, making everything from T-shirts to

Europe and North America to the region, and almost every island, from mighty Cuba to tiny Saba, developed a tourism industry.

The 1990s witnessed new peaks in Caribbean tourism as all-inclusive resorts and cruising became increasingly popular with holidaymakers. Large all-inclusive chains such as Sandals spread throughout the islands, offering a guaranteed price for an entire vacation but frustrating local restaurant owners and others who depend on tourists spending money outside their hotels.

From hubs in Miami, Puerto Rico and Mexico, cruise ships criss-crossed the region, bringing millions of visitors each year to the

LEFT: a woman in traditional Garífuna costume, Belize.
ABOVE: discussing the topic of the day in Jamaica.

islands. There is no sign that this vibrant industry is liable to slow down, although governments and investors know that tourism is a notoriously fickle business.

The economic importance of tourism to the Caribbean cannot be exaggerated. Some three million jobs depend on the industry; in 2004, tourist spending in the region amounted to US$40.3 billion and this is expected to rise to US$58.5 billion by 2014. And for every "official" tourism worker there are many others – taxi drivers, farmers and artisans – who depend on the influx of visitors.

Caribbean cruising

The attractions of the Caribbean need no introduction: a year-round warm climate, blue seas, and some of the best beaches in the world are just a few reasons to visit. Add to that impressive waterfalls and mountains, an eclectic range of architectural styles and some fascinating historic sites, and it is easy to see why people return time after time.

Cruise ships offer a particularly inviting way into this rich and varied part of the world. In a week, for instance, it is possible to explore half a dozen entirely different islands, getting a tantalising taste of the Caribbean's diversity. In some cases, a day may be long enough to gain

an impression of an island, especially if it's a small one. More probably, a brief visit will leave you wanting to see more. Many people return for a longer stay in a place they first visited, fleetingly, from a cruise ship.

The beauty of Caribbean cruising is that each day offers an entirely different cultural experience. At first sight, some of the islands may look similar, with wooded hills surrounding the harbour and mountains stretching into the interior. But on closer inspection, you will discover that each port, and each island, has its own distinctive identity and flavour.

There is no mistaking the French feel of Pointe-à-Pitre, Guadeloupe, for instance, where ships moor next to the bustling Place de la Victoire, with its cafés, war memorial and colourful market traders. But just to the north, you'll find Antigua, where memories of Admiral Lord Nelson, an Anglican cathedral and a cricket ground are all resolutely British in atmosphere.

Most Caribbean islands have done a great deal to upgrade and modernise their cruise terminal facilities and visitors can normally expect an array of shops, bars and restaurants on shore. But it would be a mistake to stay in the terminal and not take a look at the island beyond.

The heart of the islands

With a few exceptions, cruise ships moor close to the centre of the major Caribbean ports, such as in Havana, San Juan and Santo Domingo. In the smaller islands it is normally only a brief walk or taxi ride from ship to town. This means visitors are quickly at the heart of things – and ports are the heart of Caribbean islands. Usually the capital or main town, the port is also the commercial centre, and has been since the height of the sugar trade. As a result, the ports are full of historic interest, revealing ancient warehouses, colonnaded arcades and imposing buildings as well as the ubiquitous fortifications.

Each, of course, is different, but all evoke a shared history of maritime trade and bitter-sweet sugar wealth. Take a taxi or bus to the surrounding countryside or nearby beaches, but remember that the history of the Caribbean, both good and bad, is most clearly seen in the streets and buildings around the waterfront. ❑

LEFT: a couple enjoy the romance of a cruise.
RIGHT: a ship dwarfs the cruise terminal in Pointe-à-Pitre, Guadeloupe.

CARTA
de las Costas de
TIERRA FIRME
Desde el rio Orinoco hasta Yucatan
y de las islas Antillas y Lucayas
CON LAS DERROTAS QUE SIGUIÓ
D. CRISTOBAL COLON
en sus descubrimientos por
estos mares.

LUCAYAS

SANTO DOMINGO

Pto Rico

Guadalupe

Domini

Ma

ISLAS ANTILLAS

Granada

I. Trinidad

Gº de Venezuela

Maracaybo

Laguna de Maracaybo

Caracas

Cumaná

Barcelona

TIERRA FIRME

Rio

Decisive Dates

1835 Arthur Anderson co-founds the Peninsular Steam Navigation Company; by the 1840s it offers Mediterranean cruises and has become the Peninsular & Oriental Steam Navigation Company (P&O).

1881 Oceanic Yachting Company buys the *Ceylon* from P&O; it becomes first full-time cruise ship.

1900 Orient Line operates the first Caribbean cruises, round-trips from the UK.

1910 Cunard Line, which had been founded in 1840 to operate transatlantic services, introduces its first cruise ships, *Laconia* and *Franconia*.

1920–33 US Prohibition creates a demand for "booze cruises". Non-US ships head into international waters, where they can supply alcohol.

1938 The first million-dollar cruise (based on total fares paid), by French Line (Compagnie Générale Transatlantique) on *Normandie* from New York to Rio.

1949 *Caronia* is built for Cunard as a transatlantic liner, but becomes a full-time cruise ship known as the Green Goddess and the most popular postwar cruise ship with UK passengers.

1955 Epirotiki Line begins the first Greece-based Greek islands cruises, which are booked as fly-cruises by North American and British passengers.

1962 French Line introduces *SS France* to transatlantic service between Le Havre and New York. At 1,035 ft (945 metres), it was the longest passenger ship ever built.

1965 Princess Cruises is founded and begins cruising from the US West Coast.

1966 Norwegian Caribbean Lines (NCL) is set up to operate *Sunward* out of Miami on the first regular, year-round Caribbean cruise programme.

1967 Cunard Line withdraws its transatlantic liner *Queen Mary* from service and announces that *Queen Elizabeth* will follow suit in 1968, making way for the new *QE2*.

1969 Royal Caribbean Cruise Line is created by Scandinavian shipping companies I.M.Skaugen, Anders Wilhelmsen and Gotaas-Larsen to compete with NCL. The first two of a fleet of three ships are ordered for delivery over the next two years.

1970 Another trio of Scandinavian companies – Bergen Line, A.F.Klaveness and Nordenfjeldske – combine to form Royal Viking Line. Each funds one new ship (*Royal Viking Sea/Star/Sky*) which begin worldwide five-star cruising in 1972–73.

1972 Carnival Cruise Lines (CCL) is formed by Ted Arison after he leaves NCL. The first cruise of the *Mardi Gras* is a disaster as it runs aground.

1974 Arison buys loss-making CCL from AITS for US$1 and assumption of US$5m debts. It becomes the most successful Caribbean cruise line. P&O buys Princess Cruises. Greek-owned Royal Cruise Line, founded three years earlier, takes delivery of *Golden Odyssey*, the first cruise ship designed for fly-cruising. Its 400-passenger capacity mirrors that of one of the new Boeing jets.

1975 US television show, *The Love Boat*, becomes the first soap opera set aboard a cruise ship. Princess Cruises' *Pacific Princess* stars in the show.

1976 Thomson Cruises, an offshoot of the UK's leading tour operator, Thomson, is wound up, signalling the end of direct involvement in cruising by UK tour operators for the next 20 years.

1978 RCCL's *Song of Norway* is the first cruise ship to be "stretched" – cut in half and a new central section inserted. The same happens to RCCL's *Nordic Prince* two years later and to all three RVL ships between 1981 and 1983.

1979 Knut Kloster, owner of Kloster Redeerei, gambles on buying the decaying laid-up *SS France* to convert into the *Norway* for Caribbean cruising.

1980 Sea Goddess Cruises formed by a Norwegian consortium.

1982 The UK cruise market hits an all-time low when the UK government requisitions three cruise ships – *QE2*, P&O's *Canberra* and British India's *Uganda* – to help the Falklands War Task Force.

1983 Trafalgar House, Cunard's owner, buys Norwegian America Cruises and tries to take over P&O.
1984 The first major cruise industry use of TV advertising comes with a major campaign launched by CCL across the US networks.
1986 Seabourn Cruise Line (originally named Signet Cruise Line) is formed to provide luxury cruises.
1987 Norwegian Caribbean Lines changes its name to Norwegian Cruise Line, expanding its operations to other regions.
1988 P&O buys Sitmar Cruises and merges it with its Princess Cruises in North America; Carnival prevented from buying into RCCL by Hyatt Hotels which becomes joint owner of RCCL with one of the original owners, Anders Wilhelmsen. Instead, Carnival buys Holland America Line and Windstar Cruises.
1989 The Greek-owned Chandris Group creates a new and more upmarket cruise brand, Celebrity Cruises. The Panama Canal celebrates its 75th birthday.
1993 Three cruise lines designed to appeal specifically to niche markets are launched: Fiestamarina (by Carnival) for the Latin American market to the Caribbean; American Family Cruises; and Festival Cruises for pan-European passengers. The first two don't last one year but Festival Cruises becomes a major operator.
1994 The second largest UK tour operator, Airtours (MyTravel), sets up Sun Cruises, and for the first time a UK tour operator buys rather than charters ships – one each from RCCL and NCL. From 1995, the ships go to the Mediterranean in summer and the Caribbean in the winter.
1996 Thomson Cruises is revived, operating ships on charter. The number of passengers doubles in just three years to more than half a million. The first-ever passenger ship to exceed more than 100,000 tons – *Carnival Destiny* – begins cruising; too large to transit the Panama Canal, it cruises the Caribbean year-round.
1997 Carnival Corporation and Airtours jointly buy the leading European operator, Costa Cruises (Carnival later buys out the Airtours share). In the same year Royal Caribbean International (RCI) acquires Celebrity Cruises for US$1.3 billion.
1998 Carnival buys Cunard Line and NCL buys Orient Line, which operates one ship on world itineraries, including Antarctica.
1999 The world's largest cruise ship is introduced:

Royal Caribbean's 137,300-ton *Voyager of the Seas* is not only the largest but is also the first to have an ice rink and a rock-climbing wall among the passenger facilities. Asian company Star Cruises acquires the majority share of NCL and Orient Line in a joint deal with Carnival.
2000 Worldwide, the number of cruises booked tops 10 million for the first time. Nearly 7 million are from North America, with three-quarters of a million from the UK. Star Cruises takes full control of Norwegian Cruise Line (NCL) after buying out Carnival's share of the company.
2001 Carnival sells its shareholding in UK tour operator, Airtours (MyTravel).

2002 SeaDream Yacht Club begins operating with two small, luxury ships, *SeaDream I* and *SeaDream II*, calling mainly at small ports.
2003 The Carnival Corporation merges with P&O Princess Cruises, forming the largest cruise company in the world, with 13 cruise brands operating worldwide. Oceania Cruises is set up.
2004 Festival Cruises and Royal Olympia Cruises cease operations. A record 1 million Britons book a cruise. Cunard Line launches the world's biggest passenger ship to date, the 150,000-ton Queen Mary 2.
2005 Sun Cruises (MyTravel) goes out of business. Hurricane Katrina devastates the Port of New Orleans, a popular embarkation point for cruises to the Western Caribbean and Mexico. ❏

PRECEDING PAGES: a map showing Columbus' travels.
LEFT: Thomas Cook, package holiday pioneer.
RIGHT: a ship docks in Fort-de-France, Martinique.

L'AMAZONE, LES ANTILLES
L'AMÉRIQUE DU NOR
PAR LE N.M. «MILWAUKEE» 10 JANVIER 1938 DE BOULOGNE
HAMBURG-AMERIKA LINI

CRUISING THROUGH HISTORY

The pursuit began as a novelty and developed, after a number of setbacks,
into one of the most popular ways of seeing exotic places

Cruising really began in the early part of the 20th century as an adjunct to the steamship companies' main business, which was getting passengers, mail and other goods to their destinations on line voyages. As the Hollywood blockbuster *Titanic* demonstrated, these ships were unashamedly class-conscious, divided into as many as four classes depending on the ticket price paid.

Most early cruising was on ships built for line voyages, and the ocean was not seen as something to be enjoyed. It was not until the mid-1930s that people were able to travel on ships designed to reflect the revolutionary concept of the sea as a positive attraction. The enclosed liners were being opened up so that passengers could see the sea from inside as well as outside and cruise itineraries were being geared to avoid rough seas and bad weather.

Prohibition

It was during the mid-1920s and early 1930s that cruising really took off, when itineraries from the United States were being devised for a very specific reason. Prohibition, which was in force from 1920 to 1933, created a demand for alcohol, exaggerated by its lack of availability. The shipping lines saw their opportunity. By cruising from New York into international waters, they could offer a legal way of circumventing the ban. "Cruises to nowhere" were advertised and quickly became known as "booze cruises".

Prohibition played a major part in stimulating the initial post-World War I cruise boom, but it was the keen pricing, increasingly lavish on-board facilities and stylish way of life that soon enhanced cruising's popularity. Across a broad (and relatively prosperous) spectrum of US and British society, as the Roaring Twenties turned into what became the Depression-hit Thirties, cruising was established as a fashionable thing to do.

LEFT: a poster promoting an early sea voyage.
RIGHT: playing volleyball on Great Stirrup Cay, a private island near the Bahamas operated by NCL.

Big spenders

Value for money has always been one of cruising's most important aspects and a reason for its continued popularity through the decades, but there has always been a place for conspicuous consumption, too. Thus, French Line (CGM) was only too happy to promote the 1938 New

York to Rio cruise of its transatlantic liner, the *Normandie* (at 79,280 tons, the largest French passenger ship yet built), as the first "million dollar cruise". The company arrived at that figure by calculating the revenue it received from the 975 passengers who paid between $395 and $8,600 for the 22-day round-trip.

The *Normandie*'s passengers timed their escapism well – the outbreak of World War II ensured that it would be another decade before cruising was back on the international agenda, with the arrival of the "Green Goddess". Cunard's *Caronia* got its name because it was painted in three shades of green to increase its heat resistance in the tropics. The Green

Goddess caught the imagination of high society on both sides of the Atlantic and quickly became known as the "millionaires' ship", with Cunard line deliberately targeting high-rolling passengers.

In 1955, the Greek Epirotiki Line scheduled its ship *Semiramis* for the first Greek islands cruises to start and finish in Greece – a formula that became hugely popular when sold as "fly cruises" from North America and the UK in the late 1960s.

Coping with the jet age

The 1960s were a time of tumultuous change for the shipping industry. The first commercial jet flight across the North Atlantic took off in 1958 and heralded the end of the transatlantic liner business. Only Cunard Line continues the tradition today with the 150,000-ton *Queen Mary 2*, which took over the transatlantic run from QE2 in 2004.

Change was rapid. Speed mattered. Within a couple of years, airlines had the bulk of the transatlantic business and by the end of the 1960s, just one in every 25 transatlantic travellers was choosing to go by sea. With other liner business to the Mediterranean, India and Australia gradually going the same way, the shipping companies found themselves with fleets of ships but nowhere to operate them profitably. Inevitably, many of the vessels were switched to cruising, but they met with mixed success.

Cunard was one of the lines trying to move with the cruising times but, having tried and failed with the two *Queens* (*Mary* and *Elizabeth*), it had to lay them up, along with the *Caronia* and two other ships, in 1967–68. It had more success converting *Saxonia* and *Ivernia* into the cruise ships *Carmania* and *Franconia*, but the most successful and best-remembered British cruise ships of the period were *Andes* and *Reina del Mar*.

Towards the end of that decisive decade, though, the focus in cruising switched firmly to North America, where a number of developments coincided to spark a new boom. Here, a new style of cruising was emerging that would lead to an era of unprecedented growth – and the Caribbean was to be at the heart of it.

The Caribbean was not always seen as an ideal area for sea cruises. It was considered too far away from big cruising base ports such as New York. Although there had been some cruises from New York, and later Miami, to the Bahamas, Cuba and other Caribbean islands since the 1920s, the breakthrough only came towards the end of the 1960s.

Scandinavians lead the way

The innovators were the Norwegian shipping family, Kloster Redeerei, which branched out from tankers and cargo ships and ordered the construction of a vessel that would open up a route from the United Kingdom to Spain via Gibraltar. By the time the *Sunward* was delivered, however, stringent UK currency restrictions had been imposed and Britain and Spain were at loggerheads over the status of Gibraltar.

Action had to be taken. Kloster's contacts included the Arison Group in Miami and, with its help, *Sunward* was positioned there to test the market for Caribbean cruises. It would be the first ship to operate regular weekly cruises from Miami to the Caribbean islands.

The hunch paid off and the operations of the company, now known as Norwegian Cruise Line (NCL), expanded fast. Three more new ships were built between 1968 and 1971 and became known as the "White Fleet" as their bright, white livery made *Skyward, Starward* and *Southward* stand out against the blue of the Caribbean sea and skies.

Almost immediately other Scandinavian companies saw the potential, and three of them grouped together to form Royal Caribbean Cruise Line (RCCL). It, too, swiftly built three ships, the *Song of Norway, Nordic Prince* and *Sun Viking*, all introduced in the early 1970s.

All six ships were about the same size, at 16,000–18,000 tons and capable of carrying between 700 and 800 passengers. They were

Teething troubles

After a disagreement with Kloster, the Arison Group's owner, Ted Arison, left and in 1972 set up Carnival Cruise Lines. This got off to an inauspicious start when its first ship, the *Mardi Gras*, went aground on its first "shakedown" cruise carrying hundreds of travel agents.

After two loss-making years, Arison had to buy out the company from its original backers for a derisory US$1 plus the assumption of a $5 million debt, but it became profitable almost immediately. In its early days, though, its success was based on low-cost cruises operated on secondhand ships which their owners were

all based in Miami, which suddenly became a leading cruise port to rival New York and Southampton. Cunard also built a couple of similar-sized ships to cruise in the Caribbean (*Cunard Countess* and *Cunard Princess*).

Initially, all the lines restricted their operations to one-week cruises. Then, as now, North Americans had a shorter holiday entitlement than Europeans, and few people could commit more than a week of that valuable time to this new, untried style of vacation.

LEFT: no expense was spared in order to keep the wealthy cruise ship passengers amused.

ABOVE: elegance was a must for an evening on board.

selling off cheaply as the liner business disappeared. A dramatic policy change at the end of the 1970s was to change Caribbean cruising again and turn Carnival into the largest mass-market cruise line in the Caribbean and the largest cruise company in the world.

In ordering new ships in the early 1970s, NCL and RCCL were followed by the new, worldwide cruise company Royal Viking Line (RVL), also set up by Scandinavians. After that, however, there was a long gap to the end of the decade when no line dared to order any more. During much of that time, the oil crisis caused by OPEC disputes threatened the viability of much passenger shipping. But the demand for Caribbean cruising continued to grow and so RCCL compromised by "stretching" two of its ships.

This was a not-uncommon procedure with cargo ships, but the 1978 stretching of *Song of Norway* was the first time a cruise ship had ever been cut in half and had a new centre section added to increase its capacity by nearly 50 per cent. *Nordic Prince* went through the same process in 1980 and all three RVL ships were stretched over the next three years.

But, by then, Carnival had surprised the industry by ordering *Tropicale* for delivery at the end of 1981. This was not only the company's first new ship but the first for the industry

Fleet and RCCL's first three ships and carried double the number of passengers (1,400–1,500) that those first ships had been designed to carry.

The cost of these first mega cruise ships – US$100 million for *Tropicale* and $140 million for *Song of America* – also showed that the lines were prepared to gamble that Caribbean cruising was here to stay. NCL had already made this gamble, adding the former classic transatlantic liner, *France* (renamed *Norway*), to its fleet in 1980. The ship, laid up in France since being withdrawn from service in 1974, was in a shocking state, which is how NCL could acquire it for a knockdown $18 million in 1979. It cost another

in eight years. It marked a breakthrough, and the cruise industry – not to mention the Caribbean – has never looked back.

Size matters

Almost immediately, RCCL ordered *Song of America* and Home Lines ordered the *Atlantic*. This new confidence was mirrored in Europe, where a couple of German ships were also under construction. Lines were not just ordering new ships, they were ordering them big.

The Carnival and RCCL ships were both about 37,000 tons – not an unusual size for a liner but then considered huge for a purpose-built cruise ship. They were twice the size of the White

THE LOVE BOAT

In the 1960s, Stanley MacDonald, a Canadian-born, Seattle-based entrepreneur, set up Princess Cruises to run winter cruises from the US West Coast to the Mexican Riviera and summer ones from Vancouver to Alaska. In 1975, a year after it was bought by P&O, the company received a boost when the seagoing TV soap opera, *The Love Boat* began. As the scripts had been started on board a Princess ship, the line was chosen for location filming. Not only did the popular nine-year series boost Princess Cruises, the entire industry benefited, and *The Love Boat* undoubtedly played a key part in the enormous increase in the popularity of cruising in the United States.

$130 million to convert, but it was money well spent as the ship sailed full until it was withdrawn in 2003 following a boiler explosion.

New ways of cruising

The *Norway*'s initial cruise pattern was typical of the classic one-week routes taken by Caribbean cruise ships over the next two decades. From Miami, it headed for the duty-free port of Charlotte Amalie on St Thomas in the US Virgin Islands. The next stop was Nassau in the Bahamas and finally there was a call at a private island (Great Stirrup Cay) also in the Bahamas, where the ship anchored.

But Caribbean cruises were developing in different ways. There were short cruises, of three and four days, to the Bahamas (Nassau and Freeport). At first, these all started from Miami but gradually other Florida ports turned to cruising – Fort Lauderdale/Port Everglades, Port Canaveral, Jacksonville, Tampa and Palm Beach all became starting points.

The classic Eastern Caribbean itinerary operated by companies such as NCL could also include San Juan, Puerto Rico. Then the lines developed Western Caribbean cruises which included calls at the exotic Mexican ports of Cozumel and Playa del Carmen as well as Grand Cayman and sometimes Jamaica.

The problem with operating just one-week cruises was that there was only so far into the Caribbean that ships could travel from Florida in that length of time. It was a logical move, therefore, to start home-porting ships in the Caribbean itself, to save time. Within a week's cruising range of attractive islands like Grenada and the Grenadines, San Juan has become a major cruise hub as well as a port of call. Barbados, St Maarten and Guadeloupe, too, have become regular home ports for cruise ships.

Life on board

While views from outside the ships have been changing fast, the views inside have been undergoing even faster change. The "mega-ships" of the early 1980s would be dwarfed by those now cruising the Caribbean. During the 1980s and 1990s, vessels grew larger and larger until the first 100,000-ton ship, *Carnival Destiny*, arrived.

LEFT: St George, Bermuda is a regular port of call.
RIGHT: a cruise ship in the Port of Miami at night, the most popular starting point of a Caribbean cruise.

Since then, all the major lines – Carnival, P&O Princess, and Royal Caribbean International (formerly RCCL) – have built even larger ships, which spend most of their time in the Caribbean region.

The five largest – RCI's 137,000-ton *Adventure of the Seas, Explorer of the Seas, Mariner of the Seas, Navigator of the Seas* and *Voyager of the Seas* – spend all year there. However, in 2006 *Voyager* will be offering Mediterranean cruises out of Barcelona for the first time as Royal Caribbean launches its biggest ship to date – the 160,000-ton *Freedom of the Seas* – in the Caribbean.

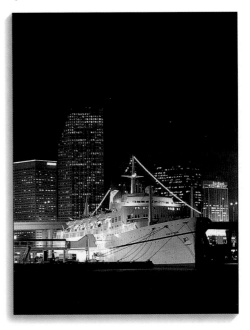

These are not just ships, they are entire resorts. They are the culmination of a process that began in the 1980s, when those first large vessels were created to resemble resort hotels, with the emphasis firmly on fun, food and endless entertainment. Bars became "themed" while show lounges and nightclubs were given the latest sound and lighting effects.

NCL was the first to stage on-board versions of major Broadway musicals of the time, such as *Hello Dolly*. Casinos became larger and more exciting, with higher limits. Carnival now has its own gamblers' club and runs horse-racing simulcasts, so fans can have a bet on the ponies, too.

Soon it became the norm for all cabins to have private bathrooms, televisions with closed circuit, interactive and then satellite programming. Some of the more expensive cabins and suites also have DVDs or VCRs and music centres. Private balconies have now been added to most cabins that have outside views.

On land, the cruise lines – led by a hard-selling television campaign by Carnival for its "Fun Ships" fleet – sold their ships as holidays that happened to be at sea rather than as cruises. They wanted to dispel the anxieties of people who had never been to sea before and, to a great extent, it has worked.

Some seagoing statistics

The number of North Americans going on cruises every year has increased from 500,000 in 1970 to 9.1 million in 2004. The rest of the world contributes another 4 million-plus passengers, a quarter of them British.

The Caribbean has been a major beneficiary. In 2005, it still had a 46 per cent share of all the booked "bed nights" (as they are known in the business). The total of 31.5 million bed nights represents roughly 6 million of the world's 14.4 million cruise passengers. The world's second most popular region – the Mediterranean – had around 13 per cent.

The terrorist attacks of 2001 prompted North Americans to take their vacations closer to home, and cruise lines have put even more ships into the Caribbean and extended the choice of US home ports, such as Galveston, Jacksonville, Houston, New Orleans, New York, Philadelphia and Tampa, to make it easier for more Americans to join a cruise.

Younger cruisers

The average age of cruise ship passengers has been getting progressively lower. In the 1970s, the average age was approaching 60; today, on short Bahamas cruises, the average passengers are 30-somethings while, for trips of one week or longer, the average age for Caribbean cruise passengers is the mid-40s. This is partly due to the increasing number of families taking cruises. Most of the mega-ships run fully supervised activity programmes for children, who have designated swimming pools, playrooms, video arcades, clubs and discos.

Carnival carries the greatest number of children (more than 400,000) but Disney's two ships are the most family-friendly vessels, with parents provided with pagers so that they can be contacted by the youth counsellors.

Caribbean pros and cons

The bigger ships – and most of them are very big – have not always been popular within the Caribbean. There have been problems with hoteliers who are worried that cruise lines are stealing their business; and from island authorities who have understandable anxieties about pollution and overcrowding. For their part, the cruise lines have for a long time resisted increases in charges levied by ports and complained about facilities at the terminals and services on some of the islands.

Increasingly, however, the Caribbean islands have come to recognise that the revenue and the jobs created on the islands by cruising are invaluable to their economies. It is estimated that about one-seventh of all tourist revenue comes from cruise ship passengers and crews.

The higher quality of technology on board the newest ships is also solving problems of pollution and waste disposal. What is more, there is also clear evidence that passengers who like an island they visit briefly on a cruise often do return for longer holidays. The Caribbean therefore needs the cruise lines as much as the cruise lines need the Caribbean. ❑

Tall Ships

The seafaring poet, John Masefield wrote: "All I ask is a tall ship and a star to steer her by". If tall ships still tug at the heart it is because they tap into the romance of the great age of sail, when tea clippers such as the *Cutty Sark* plied the seven seas. The quintessential tall ship is the clipper, which enjoyed mastery of the seas from 1850–75. Compared with its rounded, low-masted predecessors, the sleek clipper had a long waterline and narrow design build, allowing it to sail faster and closer to the wind.

In 1866 the *Thorbecke*, a fast Dutch merchant clipper, sailed from the Netherlands to the Dutch East Indies in a record 71 days. Braving the perils of shipwreck, pirates or enemy fleets, the clippers transported cargoes of sugar, spices, rum and coffee from the Caribbean colonies to Europe. Although the clippers struggled to survive the age of steam and the opening of the fast Suez Canal route, tall ship replicas still sail Caribbean waters.

Set against the bleached Caribbean light, these square-rigged windjammers conjure up an era of buccaneers and buried treasure, exotic cargoes and distant ports of call. These latter-day tall ships, often lofty four-masted barquentines, make voyages similar to those by ships following the spice routes of several centuries ago, while other majestic replica clippers, such as *Stad Amsterdam*, can be chartered by wealthy modern adventurers.

The sense of seafaring continuity is most apparent in Antigua's picturesque English Harbour, where Nelson was based from 1784–87 as Captain of HMS *Boreas*, a three-masted fully-rigged frigate. In Nelson's day, life on board a tall ship was one of considerable hardship. Space was at a premium, given that the ship had to carry provisions to last the entire voyage, as well as weapons and up to 100 cannon on the gun deck. While officer's quarters were acceptable, the crew slept in hammocks strung into netting around the deck; these formed a protective barrier during battle, and could be used as a life raft. On a typical tall ship's voyage, lunch was fish stew or salted pork or beef while supper consisted of weevil-infested biscuits and red worm-infested cheese. Depending on supplies, drink was beer, brandy and rum, which, if mixed

with four parts of water as stipulated, was called "grog". To combat scurvy, the British sailors were given fresh fruit, lemon or lime juice, hence the nickname "limeys" given them by the Americans.

In the British navy, punishment for drunkenness was a flogging with the cat-o'-nine tails, a punishment abolished only in 1879. Since 12 lashes would normally remove the flesh from a man's back, the ship's surgeon was required to apply salt or vinegar as an antiseptic. For a serious offence, such as desertion or striking an officer, the seaman would be "flogged around the fleet": after being tied in a crucifix position, the hapless culprit was flogged on every ship in the fleet.

A more romantic way of recalling the era of tall ships is to try a day's sailing on one of the replica windjammers that ply the Caribbean ports. The *Brig Unicorn* was the distinctive sailing ship featured in *Roots*, the epic film about slavery, but the vessel now takes visitors on day trips between Castries and Soufrière in St Lucia. As the 12-man crew goes aloft to unfurl the sails, the hardships of the seafaring life pale into insignificance beside the grace of this fully-rigged brig.

And if you fancy a taste of how life on the ocean wave once was under sail, but without the hardship, you can opt for a tall ship cruise with Windstar Cruises, Star Clippers or Windjammer Barefoot Cruises *(see pages 90, 93–98)*. ❑

LEFT: fun at the tables.
RIGHT: a *Windstar* sailing ship at sunset.

THE IMPACT OF CRUISING

*Cruise ship passengers are essential to the economy of most Caribbean islands,
but there are social and environmental problems that need to be addressed*

Cruise ship passengers get a big welcome when they step onto the dockside of a Caribbean port. The reception committee lined up to welcome them is anticipating a good day's business, for the cruise industry is crucial to the region – even if the sea-based tourists spend only a few hours in each place. Many

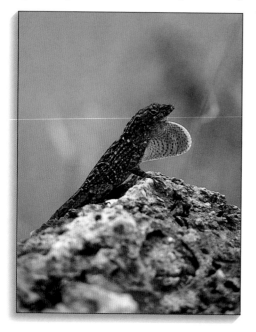

livelihoods depend on cruise ship passengers and crews.

Leading destination

The Caribbean is the world's leading cruise destination. There were a record 12.4 million cruise arrivals in one recent year, with cruise ships making nearly 9,000 visits to 22 ports of call. The Bahamas is by far the most popular, with some 2,000 cruise ship visits a year. Not far behind are Cozumel, (Mexico), the Cayman Islands, Puerto Rico and the British Virgin Islands. Over the past decade, most of the islands have experienced an enormous increase in cruise arrivals. Dominica welcomed 6,800

cruise ship passengers in 1990; less than a decade later it had 221,000.

This increase is due to new cruise-ship terminals and more ships but also, and most importantly, larger ships. Of those built since 1995, nearly 80 per cent have 1,500 or more berths. The largest in the region, the 160,000-ton *Freedom of the Seas*, is being built for Royal Caribbean International.

What are the implications of these great numbers of visitors? For a start, the Caribbean ports must be modern, services first-class and excursions efficient and dependable. The logistics of providing such facilities is an enormous challenge for small and under-resourced islands. The port at Ocho Rios in Jamaica is now considered inadequate for the forthcoming mega-liners, while in nearby Montego Bay there is bad congestion. Complaints about hygiene at St Vincent's capital, Kingstown, have led to cruise cancellations, while cruise officials have told the Puerto Rico government that arriving there is "very unappealing". The Caribbean is constantly addressing such problems – many of which require massive investment.

Big spenders?

Another concern is the issue of tourist "spend". Critics say that because the cruise ships provide everything for their customers there is no need for them to spend at the ports of call. Some ships are such fun that many passengers do not even disembark. Cruise industry officials point to their own 1998 survey of 10 Caribbean ports: each passenger spent an average of US$104 in each port visited, with the US Virgin Islands topping the chart with $174 per person. Most of this, however, is on duty-free shopping, most of whose outlets are foreign-owned. Local tour operators also benefit. Restaurants and hotels do not.

Another criticism of the cruise ship industry is that it does not buy enough local produce. Passengers drink orange juice from Florida and enjoy bananas from South America rather than the island produce. While some successful land-to-cruise suppliers do exist – St Kitts, for example, provides Royal Caribbean International with tomatoes; Barbados supplies ice cream; Trinidad and Jamaica provide beverages – everyone agrees that the islands have been slow to take up opportunities to sell to the cruise lines. Local manufacturers complain of unrealistic standards and the cruise ships' lack of interest in providing a "Caribbean flavour" for their customers.

The cruise lines claim that their industry also provides jobs, not just on the islands (where some 60,000 jobs are created) but also on the ships. Not enough, according to Caribbean

destination to try a land-based holiday was Cozumel, followed by the US Virgin Islands.

Environmental impact

The impact of hundreds of thousands of tourists a year on a particular beauty spot is hard to measure but it certainly creates challenges. The costs of protecting the environment, while providing facilities, are steep. Tourists also create a huge amount of waste and in the early days ships offloaded their solids onto the islands. An environmental levy of US$1.50 per head has been in place since 1998 in the eight islands that make up the Organisation of Eastern Caribbean States.

trades union officials. One survey reported that only 7 per cent of cruise employees are from the Caribbean, with most jobs going to workers from Asia and eastern Europe, while officers are mainly European. The numbers of Caribbean nationals on board the ships are, however, showing a gradual increase.

The cruise industry also points out that it provides a "taster" to millions who gain their first experience of the Caribbean on a cruise. Statistics suggest an average of 53 per cent would return as land-based tourists. The most popular

Apart from the impact of cruise visitors on land, environmentalists have long drawn attention to the way cruise ships pollute the sea. The bigger, modern ships, with built-in waste management systems and recycling centres, now conform to international law, which bans dumping food waste and sewage in coastal waters and plastics anywhere at sea.

Whatever the arguments about the benefits and costs, there is a growing recognition that land and sea must work together. Although cruise lines are powerful, a more conciliatory atmosphere now prevails. A proper partnership will benefit everyone – including the traveller (*see Responsible Cruising page 358*). ❑

LEFT: at Ding Darlings Wildlife Refuge, Florida, USA.
ABOVE: a sign at Trunk Bay, US Virgin Islands.

THE ART OF CRUISING

Old hands know how to get the best out of a cruise. Here are their top tips on how to stay ahead of the crowd

Gazing out across the waves at sunset during the cocktail hour, the trials of everyday life drift away across the deep blue water. Life aboard a cruise ship is so much more civilised, congenial, elegant. So much more of what life should be.

A cruise is a floating fantasy, and so great is the choice, it can be anything you want it to be. The ports of call and excursions may be memorable, but they are side shows; the ship itself is the destination. Travellers who visit every port, take every available excursion and shop until it's time to sail, still spend about 60–70 percent of their voyage on board. More important than the route is the choice of cruise line, and which particular liner offers the style most suitable for your taste.

Spoilt for choice

At the upper end of the scale, dining standards compare well with the finer restaurants on land, with impeccable service and menus designed by celebrity chefs. There are lavish productions in the theatres, plus cabaret acts. On the party ships, the emphasis is on fun. Wine, beer and champagne flow, parties run back to back, and nights melt into days and back to nights again.

Several generations travelling together are usually best-served by a large liner, where grandma and the teenagers will be safely and sufficiently entertained, giving the parents a chance to get to the salsa lessons. Entrepreneurs with money to burn often choose a small, "boutique" cruise, where shore excursions are big and beefy, and cuisine is Californian and lean. Sociable sea-dogs might try joining the Caribbean leg of an around-the-world cruise. Passengers – well-heeled and often somewhat bored – lean over the railings and avidly scan the faces on the gangway; new kids on the floating block can, if they choose, make a different friend every day.

For a first-time cruiser, the choice of ship is

bewildering: the floating skyscrapers can be cavernous rather than cosy, while small ships force them into an uncomfortably small pool of passengers, whether flamenco fanatics or "harpoon-that-whale" adventurers. The best option may be a mid-sized ship with a touch of elegance and a wide range of activities (such as

Oceania Cruises' *Insignia* and *Regatta*). These ships have enough nooks and crannies for luxurious privacy, but with spas, pools, casinos and art auctions, plenty to engage the mind.

Despite brochure promises, cruise lines do not guarantee visits to specific destinations. Ships are huge moving objects subject to wind, weather, mechanical surprises and passenger emergencies. There is always the possibility that destinations will be deleted from the schedule with no obligation for financial compensation; as with all shipboard life, the Captain's decision is final. If the Maya ruins of Mexico's Chichén Itzá are central to your dream, perhaps you should consider a fly/drive package instead.

LEFT: Celebrity's *Infinity* sails the Caribbean.
RIGHT: on the promenade of *Voyager of the Seas.*

The simple answer to the question "How long should you go for?" is "How long can you afford?" Cruise ships offer such a variety of activities that the first week is often spent running from spa to bridge lesson to wine-tasting class, living the same high-octane life a small fortune has been spent to escape. A 10-day cruise is ideal: one week for exploring both on- and off-shore, then three days doing what cruising does best: providing an opportunity to watch the waves as they change from navy blue to emerald green to aquamarine, and to discuss matters of marginal importance or complete irrelevance.

5am, and 10 hours in a stuffy bus to spend two hours in a temple at high noon can take the gloss off. Thinking ahead about excursions also allows you to pack accordingly. If you're going to be hurling a jeep through the jungle, you'll be glad of combat-strength insect repellent, a hat, sunscreen and your driver's licence.

The magic of a cruise is the cruise itself; a sense of purposefully losing touch with the out-side world. Some shore excursions can wipe that equanimity right off the compass, and per-petual tour-takers miss out on one of the most delightful benefits – a port day spent aboard ship when all is serene, solitary and calm.

Excursions ashore

Excursions get snapped up quickly, so savvy travellers are likely to have researched destina-tions – and booked – along with their tickets. Think carefully beforehand: is a port small enough to enjoy wandering around without a guided tour? Might a museum be more easily reached just by grabbing a taxi, rather than waiting with everyone else to get on a bus?

Caribbean excursions can sound wonderful, especially if reading about them in a cold, unforgiving climate, but take care not to over-book on them. A crowded schedule can be pun-ishing on the pocket, as well as physically strenuous. Assembly times can be as early as

Dress to impress

If in doubt – pack it. Haute couture and the high seas were made for each other, and the sheer act of transformation is part of the allure of sail-ing. Surrounded by mysterious strangers, you can be whoever you always wanted to be.

The formality associated with cruising was thought to deter some neophytes and so, even on the most luxurious ships, "formal nights" are now limited to two evenings per week-long cruise. Nevertheless, if you choose to uphold the tradition of dressing to the hilt, fellow pas-sengers will have seen enough black-and-white movies to appreciate the effect. And, perhaps, to adopt it for themselves.

Knowing the score

Old hands at cruising know how to get the best out of a stay at sea. Checking in can be a lengthy process, but regular voyagers of the same cruise line often score club-member style perks. As well as cabin upgrades, these can include swifter check-ins. Old hands know they must give a credit card number on embarkation to pay for on-board extras; this "cashless cruising" is usually achieved with a "cabin card", to which everything can be charged.

PASSPORT PRECAUTIONS

Be warned, non-American passport holders will have their passports retained at check-in, so make photocopies; a photo ID must be produced at the gangway to reboard the ship after a trip out.

appointments, such as hair appointments just before the Captain's Cocktail Party, and spa and beauty treatments on "at sea" days, rather than "in-port" days.

Seasoned cruisers also stake out prime locations by the outdoor pool, draping towels (preferably crumpled) on chairs and loungers, knowing that accommodation in the shade is like gold-dust.

Old hands also check which dining tables they have been assigned to. Many ships now offer a range of bistros and buffets

Savvy cruisegoers know to arrive at the harbour early and to embark as soon as possible. While novices are waiting for their luggage to reach the stateroom (which takes hours) or lamenting the size of the cabin (they're almost all tiny), well-practised cruisers are moving from deck to deck, swiftly securing the best of everything. First they book any outstanding shore excursions – by the time the ship sails, vacancies will be few, if any. Then they head for the spa and beauty salon to snap up coveted

where passengers can eat at any time, dressed as they please, but some ships still offer two seatings for dinner each evening. The first tends to be populated by the very young and the very old; the second is for more worldly diners. Guests are seated at tables for two (rare), four, six or eight, and retain these arrangements for the duration. Before the ship sails is the time to change tables, if you can, because sitting next to someone uninspiring night after night can make a journey very, very long indeed.

LEFT: working off the effects of the ship's cuisine at the gym on Carnival's *Sensation*.

ABOVE: time to relax on the Miami to Nassau leg.

Life at sea

The Purser's Office (also called Guest Relations or the Information Desk) is the nerve centre of the ship for general passenger information and minor problems. This is the place to pick up videos for in-cabin entertainment and ship-compiled newspapers of the day's "real world" events. The ship's programme – slipped under the door of each cabin – is usually a well-produced, multi-page document with information on activities, the next port of call, the cocktail of the day, and that all-important question "What time is sunset?"

The latter might lead to another high-seas tradition: romance. The easiest way to achieve this is to bring your own – i.e. travel as a couple – but although it's true that women passengers

to merchants as "rich cruise passengers". One potential perk, however, is that some cruise lines have "quality assurance" deals with particular shops. These mean that the line will offer guarantees, including price promises, for products bought from these stores.

When in doubt, bargain, bargain, bargain. And research the ports as much as possible in advance, so you know what to look for. Ships sailing out of the US, for instance, don't carry Cuban cigars or rum, but those from Caribbean and Mexican ports may do. As a general rule only the rum can be taken back on board, and must be consumed there, not brought back to

well outnumber males and that crew found fraternising with passengers can be dismissed, a certain amount of staff and guest activity does take place. Anyone contemplating an "updeck, downdeck" liaison would be advised to remember, however, that the phrase "a girl in every port" is only two words away from "a girl on every cruise".

Shopping

Practically all pre-paid excursions, even those to museums, leave a couple of hours free for shopping. Tour guides have been known to give their charges badges, ostensibly to identify them in a crowd, but this can also identify them

the US. A good time to read up would be while at sea, but ship's libraries tend to be woefully lacking in good reference books.

Disembarkation

To make departure as painless as possible, pack on the last evening and place your luggage outside the cabin door. Don't forget to leave a change of clothing for the next day. Then slip into your most glamorous glad rags and retire to the SkyDeck. Cocktails will be cool, dinner tasty, and life in general all the sweeter for having had a smooth and successful sailing. ❑

ABOVE: there's plenty of space on deck.

Spas at Sea

Dedicated dieters will be appalled to hear that for every week's holiday aboard a cruise ship, the average passenger gains 5 lbs (2.3 kg) in weight. It's all that food, drink and sea air, and in the old days – short of a sprightly walk around deck and the occasional game of quoits – there wasn't much you could do about it.

But on today's ships you can return home fitter rather than fatter, by taking advantage of the gyms, jogging tracks, ball courts, golf ranges and health spas you'll find on board. You can even have your fitness level and body fat assessed (for around US$60) and a health regime designed specifically for you by a personal trainer ($20 to $35 an hour), who will put you through your paces. And you don't have to pound away on a treadmill or stepper; you can experiment with yoga, boxercise and aerobics classes geared to every age and ability level. Most of these are free, though some ships charge a small fee for specialist classes.

If you're *really* into self-improvement, you can join a lifestyle themed cruise and learn about t'ai chi, feng shui, nutrition, herbalism and aromatherapy. P&O Cruises, Cunard Line and Crystal Cruises, among others, offer a broad programme of themed cruises, so check brochures.

Sea spas now rival land-based health farms in terms of facilities, and the latest fad is for Asian-based decor as an aid to relaxation, with warm woods, gently flowing water and staff dressed in Eastern attire. Also, designers are doing their bit to create serenity by not situating the massage rooms directly beneath, say, a basketball court.

Celebrity Cruises' fleet is known for its high-tech spa facilities; its newest ships (all but the *Horizon* and *Zenith*) have imaginative gyms equipped with virtual reality machines. And their spa facilities – modelled on gardens with a huge thalassotherapy pool as the centrepiece – are a sight to behold. Use of these pools costs around US$30 per day and also covers steam and sauna rooms, though on most ships these are available for free.

The mega-ships owned by Carnival Cruise Lines, Royal Caribbean, Princess Cruises and Norwegian Cruise Line have the most substantial spas – often with bars selling juice and health drinks and even cafés with their own spa menus.

Prettiest of the big-ship spas are on Princess Cruises' *Grand Princess* and *Golden Princess*. Spread over several decks they have lovely relaxation areas with sunken, jet-powered lap pools. Disney Cruise Line is another contender; its spas aboard *Disney Magic* and *Disney Wonder* include a series of aromatherapy scented "rain" showers – heaven after a stint in the sauna.

Not surprisingly, luxury ships such as those operated by Crystal Cruises, Silversea Cruises and Yachts of Seabourn have spas to match. Penthouse guests aboard the Crystal ships can have massages and other treatments in the privacy of their own suites, while Silversea (along with Norwegian Cruise Line) offers unusual treatments like

hot basalt lava rock massages. Travel with Seabourn and you can enjoy "random massage moments" – free mini-massages.

Before you head off for some pampering, remember that spa treatments can leave you with a hefty bill at the end of your trip (expect to pay upwards of US$100 for a facial, a 50-minute massage, or a reflexology session – plus tip) and beware of therapists pushing lotions and potions, which can cost an astonishing amount. Don't be intimidated by a snooty atmosphere; always ask the price before committing, and don't be afraid to take the product list back to your cabin and think about it. Lastly, do set a maximum budget and stick to it, then you'll enjoy the experience and not regret it later. ❏

RIGHT: opt for a pampering treatment on a day at sea.

THE CHANGING FACE OF CRUISING

If you want to give up smoking, sample gourmet food, learn to play bridge,
try stargazing or just lie around in the nude, there's sure to be a cruise to suit you

What is a typical Caribbean cruise passenger? At one time, that would have been an easy question to answer – an older person, relatively wealthy, and white. But today, it would be difficult to categorise typical cruise passengers because they are as diverse as the world we live in.

They can be any age, from elderly, retired people to the toddlers who are brought along on family holidays. They may belong to any nationality or ethnic group or any kind of multi-cultural mix. They may be single, married or divorced; high-income executives or call-centre employees; forecourt mechanics or professors of philosophy. They are born-again Christians, Reformed Jews, devout Catholics, Buddhist converts, moderate Muslims, and devotees of Transcendental Meditation. Some wear ortho-paedic shoes, others sport thong bikinis. They drink dry Martinis and bottled lager. They eat rare roast beef and grilled tofu burgers. They have a variety of physical handicaps that do not prevent them getting the most out of life. They include Olympic athletes, and prima ballerinas. Some fly their own planes, others ride bicycles to work. There are World War II veterans and committed pacifists. Some are straight, some are gay, some think this matters, others don't.

Passenger statistics

According to demographic studies conducted by Cruise Lines International Association (CLIA), there are a few statistics to consider. The average American cruise passenger's age is 50, but 27 per cent are under 40. The average British passenger is aged 53. About 75 per cent of all cruisers are married, and more than a third have children under 18. Their average house-hold income is US$68,000 (around £40,000) a year. More than half are college or university educated, and many spend seven hours a week surfing the internet. One out of four cruisers travels with friends rather than a spouse or other family members. Women outnumber men, but only by 1 per cent. On longer cruises – of three weeks or more – passengers tend to be older and wealthier, reflecting the amount of free time they have available, and fewer family

demands on their income. On shorter cruises, of one week or less, passengers tend to be more varied. Note, however, that statistics provided are only from the 24 member lines of the US-based CLIA and do not represent the inter-national cruise industry.

Tricks of the trade

While they probably don't want clients to know this, many cruise lines divide their passengers – or prospective passengers – into market segments and then create advertising campaigns geared just for them. Among these market segments are "family folks" – people described as family orientated, traditional and cautious;

LEFT: the *Monarch of the Seas* docked in St John's harbour, Antigua.
RIGHT: a young girl and two friendly green parrots in Costa Rica, which has an amazing variety of birds.

"baby boomers" – middle-age professionals who want to inject a sense of adventure into their everyday lives; "luxury seekers" – people who take great pleasure in being pampered; "want-it-alls" – people who are not necessarily wealthy, but have high aspirations and tend to spend beyond their means; "consummate shoppers" – travellers who look for the best value, rather than the lowest price, when choosing a holiday; "explorers" – well educated, well travelled people who are interested in the history and culture of the places they visit; and, last of all, "ship buffs" – elderly, repeat passengers who just love being on cruise ships.

Simply put, theme cruises are dedicated to a particular interest and allow passengers to immerse themselves in whatever passion tugs at their hearts. Sometimes, all the passengers on a ship participate in the particular theme; at others, only a proportion of them get involved. If two people travel together, and one wants to take part in the theme activities and the other doesn't, that is quite feasible. Occasionally theme cruises are connected in some way to the region they are sailing through, but most of the time they aren't. Best of all, theme cruises feature all the standard amenities of regular cruises and usually don't cost any more money.

Theme cruises

What does all this mean to "average passengers" trying to pick a cruise that will suit them best? It means that the choice is theirs, because the industry has accepted that the concept of a generic, one-size-fits-all cruise is obsolete, and that they must cater to a wider, cross-section of the population. As in other areas of society, consumers have become more demanding, and are seeking cruises that reflect their personal values and interests. In order to satisfy this, cruise lines have turned to specially designed theme cruises that cater to a huge range of interests, lifestyles, hobbies and niche markets. You name it and there's probably a cruise for it.

Of the hundreds of theme cruises offered each year, only some are organised by the cruise lines themselves, while many are arranged by cruise organisers – individuals, small companies, special interest groups, and non-profit organisations that work hand-in-hand with the cruise companies to make it all happen. On some occasions, ships are chartered – or "hired out" – by the cruise lines to the specific groups. Rarely advertised publicly, such cruises usually attract their clientele by word-of-mouth or by small, highly targeted marketing campaigns.

The most popular theme cruises today focus on food and wine. So-called culinary voyages, they range from those that offer cookery demonstrations by acclaimed master chefs, such as Wolfgang Puck and Jacques Pépin, to those with an emphasis on a regional cuisine such as Taste of the Islands cruises that highlight French West Indian or Latin Caribbean food.

Some of the better-known culinary cruises include the Michel Roux Culinary Cruise, Relais Gourmands Series, and Le Cordon Bleu Culinary Workshops.

On most culinary cruises, distinguished wine authorities provide wine-tasting demonstrations of select vintages and lectures devoted to the noble grape to go along with the gourmet food. Because they are smaller and more intimate, Windjammer Cruises tend to offer some of the best culinary voyages.

Music is another major focus for theme cruises, with choices that range from jazz, classical, opera, soul, salsa, gospel, country and western, dixieland, 1950s retro rock 'n' roll, and big band orchestras. Whatever the musical theme may be, live music is the main component of shipboard entertainment.

Taking a hard line

Since some (mainly American) cruise passengers have objected to passive smoking on ships for many years, Carnival's decision to introduce the first non-smoking ship, *Paradise*, in 1999 was greeted with delight by hardline anti-smokers, who welcomed its tough stance. Passengers and crew were banned from smoking anywhere on board, and also threatened with a US$250 fine and instant enforced disembarkation if they were caught in possession of smoking materials. But while the health police rejoiced, industry critics were sceptical – and they were proved right; Carnival quietly abandoned the concept after it proved an impediment to attracting group business.

However, the cruise line continues with its attempts to help passengers improve their health with "Quit Smoking Caribbean Cruises". On these, as well as being forbidden to smoke, passengers have to attend lectures, group therapy sessions, and behaviour modification training to help them kick the habit. It's a good way to do it, as there is nowhere a desperate smoker could buy tobacco for the duration of the voyage.

American passengers must also attend orientation sessions offered by the American Lung Association before they start the cruise.

Cruise to health

The emphasis on health goes a long way beyond non-smoking. There are speciality cruises devoted to yoga, body building, martial arts, meditation, stress reduction, aerobics, massage, tai chi and weight loss – for the latter, US diet guru Richard Simmons is a great favourite, with his Cruise To Lose voyages. All of these have experts on board who offer classes and demonstrations throughout the journey.

LEFT: making the most of a massage on Royal Caribbean's *Explorer of the Seas*.

RIGHT: more strenuous activity on Carnival *Sensation*.

Cruise and Stay

The cruise lines have coined the term "cruise and stay" for the practice of adding a land-based stay to a cruise to extend a holiday. From a traveller's point of view, this can offer the best of both worlds. It could mean combining a fairly active cruise itinerary with a spell on a beach. For example, a 12-night Panama Canal cruise might include Costa Rica, Nicaragua, the Panama Canal, Curaçao and the US Virgin Islands, plus a day in the Bahamas, which could be the only lazy beach day of the entire cruise.

In contrast, a nine-night Western Caribbean cruise from Florida might include Grand Cayman, Jamaica and Cozumel, so a week's touring in Florida would make a good combination.

Alternatively, you could create a contrast between types of accommodation. A spell on an enormous, glitzy ship like Royal Caribbean's *Voyager of the Seas*, packed with action, might be followed by a quick hop from Miami to the Bahamas to chill out on a remote beach in the Out Islands.

Most cruise lines don't allow passengers to jump ship halfway through a cruise, so an extended holiday must be planned around one of the Caribbean gateways. Generally speaking, cruise lines are not very imaginative about options. One exception is Disney, which offers seamless combinations of Disney World in Orlando and its twin ships, *Disney Wonder* and *Disney Magic*, which operate three-, four- and seven-night cruises from Port Canaveral in the same polished, Disney style as the park.

The main reason for booking land-based accommodation through a cruise line is financial, as many of them have set up good deals with hotels, and will also include transfers to the port. Passengers arriving from Europe will usually incur an overnight stay, which should be included in the cruise package and can be extended at low cost.

Princess Cruises, for example, has some good deals in Orlando, Miami Beach and San Juan, and will also arrange car hire with Hertz. Royal Caribbean features hotels in Miami Beach, Fort Lauderdale and San Juan.

For the more adventurous traveller, there are endless opportunities for island hopping from Miami. An intricate network of regional flights links most of the Caribbean islands, using the services of 15 tiny airlines. American Airlines, LIAT and BWIA all offer air passes, although a private charter may be cost-effective if you are travelling as a group.

Miami and Fort Lauderdale work well as jumping-off points for the Bahamas, with plenty of flights to Nassau and onward connections to the Out Islands. Cruises that start and finish offshore are harder to find. Fred Olsen's fly-cruise programme is based in Barbados, as is the winter programme of Star Clippers (alongside St Maarten), with good hotel deals in Barbados and St Maarten. P&O Cruises uses Barbados as a departure point for some cruises, while the luxury line, Seabourn, features Barbados, San Juan and even Costa Rica.

Barbados is an excellent base for touring the Windward islands, just a short flight from St Lucia, St Vincent, the Grenadines and Grenada. San Juan, meanwhile, is close to the Virgin Islands.

Joining a cruise in a more remote location is much harder. Windjammer Barefoot Cruises has an innovative programme of island hopping, its six ships roaming the Virgin Islands, the Windward and Leeward islands, the ABC islands and the Caribbean coast of Venezuela. But to combine a mainstream Caribbean cruise with a less visited island will require advance planning, a willingness to put up with the vagaries of the inter-island flights (so go easy on the luggage) and the services of a good travel agent. ❑

LEFT: laying out in Key West, Florida, a convenient place for a pre- or post-cruise stopover.

Sporty cruises

Sport is another magnet for theme cruises, with golf being one of the favourites. Royal Caribbean is the official cruise line of the PGA Tour, and has developed a following for its Golf Ahoy programme. There are on-board lessons by golf pros, and cruises stop near famous Caribbean golf courses and offer passengers the opportunity to play a few rounds.

Norwegian Cruise Line is noted for its Sports Illustrated Afloat cruises that include well-known football and baseball players on the guest list. Carnival Cruise Lines has specially designed NASCAR Cruises that feature motor racing activities and the chance to rub shoulders with world-famous drivers. There are even companies that offer Olympic Gold Cruises where Olympic champions take part in question-and-answer sessions, and preside over competitions. And, of course there are numerous cruises with a focus on diving that offer passengers a chance to become scuba-certified.

Natural affinity

Affinity groups are a natural market for niche cruises. Singles Cruises that make it easier for unattached people to meet members of the opposite sex, are growing rapidly. Also increasing in popularity are Family Cruises, focusing on wholesome activities for children.

One of the biggest US organisations that caters to the family market is Sail with the Stars (www.sailwiththestars.com, tel: 818-991 5611). Teaming up with Disney Cruise Line and Crystal Cruises, Sail with the Stars puts together Caribbean cruises geared especially for children and teenagers that include encounters with television and movie celebrities, MTV personalities, authors of children's books and costumed cartoon characters.

Another growing segment of the affinity market are cruises catering to African-American travellers. One company in particular, Blue World Travel (www.festivalatsea.com, tel: 415-882 9444), has earned a stellar reputation for its Festival at Sea Cruises. These cruises (usually on Carnival ships) run several times a year

FESTIVE FUN
All the lines sailing in the Caribbean create festive Holiday Cruises for Christmas and New Year, complete with roving Santas, presents for children, and champagne and fireworks at midnight.

and feature lectures on African-American culture, Motown music nights and African-attire dinner parties. They also raise money for the United Negro College Fund, and donate thousands of children's books annually to Caribbean island libraries.

Cruising with pride

Wanting to make sure they will feel comfortable in their cruise environment, many gays and lesbians turn to travel organisations that arrange packages just for them. This usually means

groups of 200 or 300 gay people, singles and couples, joining an existing cruise.

Some of the more respected US companies that arrange these trips include Atlantis Events (www.atlantisevents.com, tel: 310-859 8800), Gay Cruise Vacations (www.gay cruisevacations.com, tel: 314-838 8880) and Cruising with Pride (www.cruisingwithpride. com, tel: 714-540 7400). Along with fostering a comfortable shipboard environment, these companies also stop at islands known to be tolerant and friendly towards gay people – the conservative Cayman Islands turned away a gay cruise in the 1990s and has since been boycotted by many gay and lesbian cruise groups.

RIGHT: shore diving at Parrot's Landing in the Cayman Islands.

Accessibility for all

Travellers with disabilities are catered for by the industry. Some of the options are escorted Caribbean cruise packages for wheelchair users, organised in the US by Accessible Journeys (www.disabilitytravel.com, tel: 610-521 0339); cruises for the hearing impaired (www.deafcruises.com, tel: 870-339 4086); and cruises for the blind and partially sighted (find a list of these at www.access-able.com, tel: 303-232 2979). In the UK Accessible Travel and Leisure (www.accessibletravel.co.uk, tel: 01452 729 739) and Tourism for All (Holiday Care, tel: 08451 249971), both provide practical travel advice.

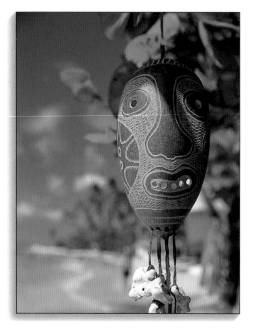

For free-spirited adults who want to feel the salty sea breezes on their skin and socialise with like-minded passengers, Nude Cruises are offered by several groups, usually on smaller ships. Some of the more established include Bare Necessities Tours (www.bare-necessities.com, tel: 1 800-743 0405); and Travel Au Naturel (www.travelaunaturel.com, tel:1 800-728 0185).

From education to geeks

Part of the growing trend for combining education with travel, an organisation called University at Sea (www.universityatsea.com, tel: 1 800-926 3775) runs an innovative series of fully-accredited, continuing education courses, with several designed for the harried US medical professional. Among these programmes are: anaesthesiology, addiction counselling, emergency medicine, dentistry, geriatrics and ageing, pediatrics, pharmacology and veterinary medicine. It also offers cruise programmes on financial planning, computers and the internet and organisational management. Many of these cruises are tax-deductible in the US.

The Comedy Cruise, offered by Norwegian Cruise Lines, hosts an evening line-up of well-known comedians – most of them better known to American than to European passengers. Princess Cruises have Soap Opera cruises that include daily discussions about US afternoon television programmes, with guest appearances by the actors who star in them. One cruise line used to put on a Sailing with Noah Cruise that ran from New Orleans to the Caribbean and featured bible study, bible trivia contests, and gospel music. On these cruises there was no gambling and no alcohol. Alcohol-free cruises are currently offered by Alcoholics Anonymous.

Narrowing their focus and target audience, some theme cruises offer offbeat specialities. For instance, California-based Geek Cruises (www.geekcruises.com, tel: 650-327 3692) offers cruises for techno-buffs and chess fiends, covering everything from advanced use of Photoshop and Macintosh to web design and digital photography (the company's website also features "Convincing Your Boss" and "Convincing Your Spouse" sectors to help geeks justify the trip). There's something for everyone. ❑

LEFT: a hand-crafted mask on sale on the beach, Tobago.
RIGHT: diving in the Caribbean can be very rewarding.

Cruise Cuisine

L ike restaurant food, cruise cuisine can be very good, very bad or somewhere in between, although every brochure will portray meal times as a gourmet extravaganza. In general, the maxim that you get what you pay for applies. A budget ship will serve bland food in generous portions, with endless buffets. On a big, modern cruise ship expect a choice of restaurants (some applying a service charge for the premier ones), together with a traditional two-sitting or eat-when-you-please main dining room with silver service and some themed

evenings, for example Italian or French Night. On ultra-luxurious ships such as those of the all-inclusive Silversea Cruises, SeaDream Yacht Club and Seabourn, champagne is available at any time and caviar on request.

It is possible to eat around the clock – and many do – hence the joke that you board as a passenger and leave as freight. Some passengers munch their way through a huge, cooked breakfast, then it's mid-morning burgers on deck and a plate piled high from the lunch buffet. Next, a few cocktails by the pool, ice cream, afternoon tea with cakes, room service sandwiches, canapés at Happy Hour, full seven-course dinner and the final nail in the coffin, the midnight buffet. Some cruise lines make a big

event of this. NCL is famous for its chocolate-themed buffets, while Costa Cruises lays on a "buffet safari" through its kitchens.

Equally, though, you could enjoy a bowl of fruit on deck at sunrise, a fresh salad for lunch and a perfectly grilled sea bass or lobster in the evening, interspersed with visits to the gym. In fact most ships include low sodium and low fat options on the menu.

Changing styles

Cruising used to be one of very few types of holiday where guests would be assigned a specific table and dine at a fixed time every night. Happily for the gregariously challenged, the modern trend is towards open seating and multiple-choice dining. Even budget-priced ships like Ocean Village and Island Cruises' Island Breeze offer à la carte restaurants, while modern "floating resorts" have up to 10 restaurants apiece, ranging from French and Italian to Japanese and even Indian (service charges for these alternative restaurants vary from US$10–30 a head, while some ships apply prices to individual dishes).

However, most ships still include a free-to-use main dining room for those who enjoy a traditional five-course dinner and like to make friends with their fellow passengers across the dining table. Several lines – such as Princess – have made their dining rooms open seating (or "Freestyle" on NCL ships), whereby you turn up when you like for meals, while others retain a more formal two-sitting system. Pick the early sitting and you'll be able to enjoy a whole evening of entertainment and have room, if you are so inclined, for the midnight buffet. American passengers tend to prefer this. Choose the late sitting and you can sunbathe until sunset, spend time dressing for dinner and still have time for a cocktail and the late show.

Tables for two can be hard to come by on a cruise ship, so ask early if you wish to dine à deux. You may want to choose a big table if you're travelling alone. If you are unhappy with your table (or your dining partners), ask the maitre d' to move you; a discreet tip will do the trick, provided the ship is not full.

What to wear

Although it is possible to cruise for a week without dressing up, most cruises will feature a mix of casual nights (smart casual "resort wear"), informal nights (confusingly, this means cocktail dress and jacket and tie), and one formal night – full black tie. If you are invited to dine at the captain's table on the formal night, it should be regarded as an honour. There is no real knack to securing your place – invited guests include past passengers, VIPs, dignitaries or people celebrating a special occasion.

Dress code is interpreted very differently from ship to ship. Passengers on Celebrity, Crystal, Silversea, Seabourn and Windstar ships tend to be very smartly dressed, with no shortage of jewellery. Carnival, P&O, Princess, Holland America Line and NCL passengers are less ostentatious, while SeaDream Yacht Club passengers are too rich to worry about formal dress and you won't see a tie all week. For the ultimate shorts and T-shirt lifestyle, try Windjammer Barefoot Cruises.

Caribbean Princess, which has its own free-to-use Caribbean speciality restaurant.

Economies of scale dictate that most provisions are bought in bulk; Carnival Corporation, for example, keeps an entire county in Iowa in business, raising beef cattle for its ships. While you will find fresh local fruit and vegetables on the buffet, there is rarely more than a token dish or two to indicate that you are in the Caribbean. Even the mix for the rum punch may be from a tin.

Special diets

Cruise lines are used to accommodating special diets, within reason. Even the most basic of lines

What to expect

Given that the vast majority of Caribbean cruise passengers are American, the food on most ships will be geared to their tastes – generous portions, salads with rich dressings, a fair amount of meat and not much spice. This means that you'll have no problem finding burgers or pizza, but a spicy Jamaican patty, a bowl of freshly made conch chowder or a snack of flying fish with chips will have to wait until you get ashore, that is unless you are travelling aboard Princess Cruises'

LEFT: flavours of the Caribbean: mango and papaya crêpe in Tequila, with butterscotch sauce, San Juan.
ABOVE: seafood specialities can be found in port.

offers a vegetarian option – although interpretation of the word "vegetarian" may vary on ships that are not British- or American-owned. If you are not happy, have a word with the maître d' and ask for something else. On some ships it is possible to order "off menu" in the main dining room, although the service will not be advertised.

Getting kosher food on a ship can be difficult (except for Holland America Line), although some kosher charters can be found. Ask a specialist cruise travel agent about what is available.

US lines offer healthy options, too, or a "light" alternative, which is a step in the right direction – as long as you're not tempted by the midnight chocoholic buffet afterwards. ❏

THE SECRET LIFE OF A CRUISE SHIP

A good cruise should appear effortless, but an enormous amount of skill goes into making it seem so. Here's what goes on behind the scenes

In a headlong rush to cruise around the globe, many passengers overlook the extraordinary floating world they are privileged to participate in. The occasional "fly on the wall" documentary claims to present life behind the scenes of a cruise ship but tends to sacrifice truth to sensationalism: rampant affairs, aggressive outbursts and sinking ships make better television than social harmony at sea.

The reality is that the crew, as diverse as a United Nations delegation, spend up to eight months at sea, sharing this potential powder keg with passengers. During a classic voyage, constellations of islands are visited and shipboard life runs like clockwork, from the delivery of thousands of meals to a dazzling array of on-board activities, culminating in dancing under the stars. It is an extraordinary achievement, and a testament to the skill and professionalism of the crew, that each voyage seems to pass so smoothly.

What about the workers?

The days of crew being treated as galley slaves have long since gone. Company loyalty is paramount but, in such a highly competitive industry, there is a high staff turnover. The cruise industry faces an unprecedented demand for seagoing staff, with each new mega-ship employing a 1,000-strong workforce. Since a contented staff provides better service and therefore encourages more repeat business, it is in the cruise companies' interests to recruit, train and retain the best crews.

As turnover can be as high as 80 per cent in the hospitality business, the most successful cruise companies are delighted to have reduced staff turnover to around 25 per cent. The marine department is less problematic since it comprises only 15 per cent of the seagoing workforce. Moreover, the perceived glamour of sailing a passenger liner rather than a cargo ship

LEFT: cruise staff keep the ship spick-and-span.
RIGHT: on many ships the cabin, dining and waiting staff tend to be predominantly Asian.

means that there is no shortage of officers eager to clock up the nautical miles.

It is not uncommon to find over 40 nationalities working on a ship together. Hotel staff, who account for 70 per cent of cruise personnel, used to be Europeans, but since the late 1980s land-based hotels have been offering

better wages so this labour market has evaporated, or at least shrunk to Eastern European nationals. Staff from developing countries, who are more prepared to accept lower wages, are filling the gap. North Americans, Canadians, Australians and English-speaking Europeans tend to be found on the entertainment or guest relations side, as well as in marine positions.

Equal opportunities

While all the cruise companies are equal opportunities employers, certain nationalities gravitate towards similar positions. The cabin, dining and waiting staff are predominantly Asian, which hotel directors attribute to the politeness, discretion, grace and unobtrusiveness of the Asian temperament. Exceptionally among major cruise lines, NCL recruits primarily from the Caribbean basin, even though the navigational officer class are Norwegian.

The cruise lines' junior officers are drawn from the best international marine academies, with other officers coming from cargo ships and ferries, and from rival cruise lines. Certain companies traditionally recruit particular nationalities. On the navigational side, the Norwegians, British, Greeks and Italians predominate on European-style lines, with Americans, Canadians and Scandinavians popular on

mixed nationality officer class, believing that there is more to be learned in a spirit of international co-operation. On *Brilliance of the Seas*, for instance, the Swedish captain is supported by Norwegian, North American and Canadian officers.

Attracting the best

The high turnover of staff and the vast geographical spread of recruitment contribute to the cruise companies' headaches. Staff loyalty cannot be assured by anything other than constantly improving career prospects and conditions on board, as well as increased shore leave

the more international-style lines. English may be the international language at sea, but this is no barrier to a smattering of Mexicans, Argentines, Dutch and Poles working their way around the fleets. Given its Greek roots, Celebrity tends to be staffed by Greek officers, while the Italian officer class on Costa Cruises, MSC and Silversea reflects a different Mediterranean heritage.

Norwegian officers naturally thrive on NCL and Fred Olsen ships, while British officers predominate on P&O vessels and the upmarket Windstar ships, and Holland America favours British and Dutch officers.

Even so, certain cruise lines, such as Royal Caribbean, have a policy of encouraging a

and varied itineraries. Seasonal deployment of cruise ships helps crews see more of the world, as does the option to switch to another ship in the fleet. In order to attract the best staff and crew, some cruise lines compete on pay, while others focus on working conditions and the total benefits package. A hotel director would receive greater rewards for managing a big resort but is prepared to forego financial gain for the excitement and variety of a career at sea.

Crew retention is also helped by the provision of superior amenities, from computer learning centres and staff gyms to shopping discounts, rental bikes and hire boats at various ports of call. Several cruise companies even offer staff a private pool and spa on board. Another motivational factor is staff training for personal development and career prospects. In this, Royal Caribbean leads the way, providing a computer with e-mail access in each staff cabin, and excellent training programmes, as well as rising pay scales, share options and a pension scheme for all employees.

Officers' perks

The entitlement to home leave is one of the clearest indicators of rank and seniority. A captain might be entitled to 13 weeks on duty, 13 weeks off, while a chief purser and other senior officers might receive four months on, followed by two or three months off. However, six months on and six weeks off, or eight months on, two months off is more usual for the lower ranks, including waiting staff and cabin stewards. Flexibility is required on both sides, but normally the constant juggling of home leave means that the management has to cope with a 6–10 percent staff change-over every week.

Apart from enjoying more frequent leave, senior officers benefit from off-duty retreats to the public bars and restaurants. Since all crews work a seven-day week, with only a few hours off a day (depending on the shift), free time is sacred. However, given the space constraints aboard, the issue of access is crucial: to avoid swamping public bars with crew, and to discourage fraternisation with passengers, only privileged staff are allowed to stray into public areas beyond their designated work space.

This policy also acts as a form of control, with access synonymous with the perks and privileges of seniority. The chief purser or hotel director will avoid staff scrutiny by disappearing to the Dog and Duck pub. Some cruise lines inject a more democratic note into proceedings. Carnival champions a single staff menu so that, in theory, the captain and the cleaner eat the same food. RCI, on the other hand, provides the officer class with a separate mess.

Crew facilities

The absence of a crew mess bar is a controversial issue. In the interests of good working relations, some cruise lines favour private bars for the crew. Other, generally smaller, lines take the opposite view, fearing that excessive drinking could encourage rowdiness. On the principle that "sailors will be sailors", management prefers drinking to be confined to port.

Fortunately, the new mega-ships and mid-sized super-liners have impressive purpose-built crew quarters, complete with television rooms, games rooms and sports facilities. Conversely, older or smaller ships provide more cramped crew quarters. Space on board is at a premium, with rank determining the size of staff cabins. On older ships, four low-ranking crew may share an inside cabin. More common is a cabin for two or, on modern mega-ships,

single cabins, even for junior ratings. Naturally, the captain and the hotel director enjoy spacious suites, often at the level of the bridge.

The Master

The captain, respectfully known as the Master, exudes authority and calm, either by courtesy of his role or his character. Many captains, especially the Scandinavians, have a seafaring background, speak good English, and tend to make speedy progress up the ranks. Thomas Wildung, a Royal Caribbean International captain from a Swedish merchant shipping family, is typical of this self-assured breed of Scandinavian seafarers.

The captain, rather like an ambassador sent

LEFT: lunch is served at a trattoria on an NCL ship.
RIGHT: passengers on board can relax.

abroad to lie for his country, has to act diplomatically while always ensuring the safety of his ship. For instance, maritime law dictates that the ship has to accept the services of a local pilot in each port. Although they supposedly bring a wealth of local knowledge to the task, the reality is that the pilots are rarely capable of handling a mega-ship – but the pretence of services rendered and gratefully received is maintained.

The captain is supported by the staff captain, his number two, and the first officer – both senior officers – who host tables on some ships and regale their dinner companions with nautical tales. They all have special radio headsets that can communicate between the bridge, the ship and the lifeboats in the event of an emergency.

Expecting the unexpected

Facing the unexpected is a feature of life at sea. In the Caribbean, the captain is occasionally involved in rescuing boat-loads of refugees, generally fleeing Cubans, who have to be supervised on board and deposited at the next port. Recently, the luxurious *Crystal Harmony* rescued four people who were floating on a life raft off St Thomas, having escaped from a freighter that was engulfed in flames. The captain downplayed his help as a nod to "the brotherhood of sailors, and how we all look out for each other's welfare". More common are the challenges of the high seas, the hurricane season, or the political situation, all of which can force a captain to change course and choose a different port of call from that on the itinerary. This is particularly true where passengers are transported to shore by tender (small boat), for instance in the case of Virgin Gorda or St Barts.

Key personnel

At some point in a cruise, the key personnel are introduced to passengers, often at the Captain's Cocktail Party. The hotel director is in charge of all non-marine affairs; as the person responsible for the largest department, he is usually an excellent administrator, linguist, mediator and troubleshooter. The post is often titled general manager in recognition of the responsibilities of the role: the incumbent is effectively in charge of a floating resort and responsible for the welfare of several thousand passengers and a thousand-strong crew. Joseph Falceto, an ebullient Spaniard, acts as a trouble-shooting hotel

director across the Royal Caribbean fleet. Falceto has been at sea since the age of 16, including several years on a Spanish naval submarine. His passion for on-board education, favouring formal training courses interspersed with self-study, stems from his younger days: he received all his early education at sea, with "lessons" restricted to immersion in the history, culture and geography of various ports of call.

It is invidious to select on-board roles that are more significant than others, but on the level of personality and entertainment value, passengers tend to be intrigued by the cruise director, the gentlemen hosts, the comedians

THE BLUE BOYS

Generally dressed in blue overalls, the "blue boys" are deckhands extraordinaire who can be seen all over the mega-ships performing anything from the most menial tasks to amazing aerial feats. These deckhands, who are usually Filipino, Thai or Indonesian, are chosen for their agility and dexterity in performing tricky tasks.

Passengers looking up from their sun-loungers are often astonished to see a couple of "blue-boys" washing vast wrap-around windows below the bridge; one may be suspended in mid-flight, nonchalantly chatting to an equally carefree colleague who has dispensed with his safety harness.

and the ship's doctor. The cruise director is responsible for the smooth running of social activities and entertainment. Depending on the ship, he can be a holiday-camp figure of fun, a third-rate comedian, or a slick showman with the charm to quell a piratical invasion. As the most high-profile member of staff, he (it is virtually always "he") is a character passengers tend to like or loathe. In his *Passenger's Prayer*, cruising expert Douglas Ward mocks the breed: "Grant us a cruise director who does not overly stress the spoils of bingo or horse racing, or does not stress only those jewellery stores from which he receives an offering."

heavy swells cause the cruise ship to abandon tendering at St Barts in favour of a safe berth at Antigua, the cruise director summons the guest lecturer to give an impromptu talk on the new port of call. In emergencies, every additional talent is exploited in the name of entertainment. The director knows the Brazilian waiter can play the guitar while concocting a Cuba Libre, the Mexican sous-chef can do a mean Elvis impersonation, the Filipino deckhand can turn his hand to ice sculpture, the Thai cabin attendant can improvise a temple dance.

The cruise director can be responsible for several hundred staff, including stage performers,

Blessed with problem-solving and public relations skills, the best cruise directors are adept at fine-tuning the entertainment in response to passenger reactions. If clients are tired, shows are timed to start earlier; if Hispanic guests seem restless, a Latin dance session is swiftly set up. The role also necessitates a fast response to changing events: if a tropical storm confines passengers to the public lounges, the director has to cancel his deck programme and improvise new entertainment. If

sports personnel, social hosts (also known as cruise hosts) and the youth staff.

Social hosts and comedians

The versatile social hosts, who have shipboard experience and a background in the entertainment and hospitality industry, may find themselves accompanying a shore excursion or supervising the men's international belly-flop competition. Tireless youth staff may spend the morning teaching dinosaur survival skills to the under-fives, followed by games involving glow-in-the-dark slime.

On another deck, their colleagues may be supervising basic army training and camouflage

LEFT: on the sports deck of *Radiance of the Seas*.
ABOVE: Captain Martin Scott demonstrates the steering of *Wind Song* from the "flying bridge", in Costa Rica.

Aye, Aye, Captain

I n his crisp white shirt with gold epaulets, Captain Johnny Faevelen commands one of Royal Caribbean International's ships with an air of confidence and calm. He strolls the promenade, checks in with the helmsman, and poses with passengers who want a picture of him to take home. No sweat on his brow, no tension in his face, no weariness in his eyes.

Is it really that easy? Or does the master of this 138,000-ton behemoth just make it look that way?

"Being a cruise ship captain may look like an

easy job, but there is nothing easy about it," says Faevelen. "I have an enormous amount of responsibility and I'm on duty 24 hours a day, seven days a week. It's like running a city with 5,000 people, and it takes a lot of work and administrative details to make it all look like magic."

About 1,200 of those 5,000 people are fellow crew members, and managing them, says Faevelen, is the most challenging part of a captain's job.

"The crew members are the pulse and blood of the ship. I have people on my staff from 64 different countries and I devote a lot of energy to treating them with respect and making sure they are happy because if they're not, it can be a terrible experience for everyone on board".

Along with maintaining harmony among the multicultural crew, Faevelen has to oversee all the day-to-day operations, know exactly where the ship is at all times, implement safety precautions, monitor weather conditions, divert the ship around storms, order and inspect repairs, maintain environmental standards, manoeuvre in and out of small ports, remain in constant contact with the command centre in Miami, and schmooze with the many passengers who want to shake his hand. The one thing he doesn't do is perform wedding ceremonies.

"I don't have the authority to marry people; I can only separate them," he says.

Born in a small town near the Arctic Circle in northern Norway, Faevelen has worked for Royal Caribbean since 1975, and has been a captain with the company since 1994. As a child, his father ran a shrimp trawler, so being at sea comes naturally to him. His standard routine is to work back-to-back Caribbean cruises for 14 weeks straight, and then take off for 14 weeks to spend time with his wife and two children in Norway.

The pressures of the job can be tremendous, and, like most captains, Faevelen makes an effort to allot himself some private time while on board to avoid burnout.

The most annoying part of the job, says Faevelen, is "the one question I hear over and over and over again from the passengers when I'm walking around the ship – 'Hey Captain, who's driving this thing?' Having to answer that while keeping a smile on my face can get very tiring," he says.

And then there are the Captain's Table dinner parties. About three times a week Faevelen sits down with invited guests to share a meal.

"The dinners are only difficult if the people don't talk among themselves and I have to carry the conversation all night," says Faevelen. "But for the most part I enjoy it because I like meeting people from all over the world."

While passengers often think there is some mystery surrounding how people get chosen to join these formal fêtes, it's not that complex. Most are repeat customers who, after a dozen or so sailings, are known by the crew. A few are celebrities or industry VIPs. And some get invited by sheer luck. On Faevelen's ship, however, there is a little secret to being invited to dine with the captain.

"Come on, I have to keep up with the gossip from back home somehow, don't I?" he says. ❏

LEFT: Captain Johnny Faevelen, Master of *Mariner of the Seas*.

face-painting to a bunch of nine-year-olds, or roller-blading with manic 12-year-olds.

Most medium-sized ships employ comedians, entertainers who stroll though the ship, creating havoc in their wake. The cruise comics, professional clowns and stilt walkers are performers who also appear in the spectacular Disney-style evening parades. Royal Caribbean's circus-trained "Kruze Komics" roam certain ships performing banana-skin jokes on anyone foolish enough to encourage them.

One northern English stand-up comedian covers the world every year, beginning in the Caribbean before moving on to the Amazon

male counterparts, and often select a cruise specifically for the ballroom and Latin dancing. The hosts rarely choose to work full time since they have a life outside cruising, conceivably running a dance school, or enjoying early retirement in sunny climes.

Apocryphal tales abound as to the additional services provided by the dance hosts. One recounts how a cruise high-roller paid him several thousand dollars to keep his wife amused all night, in a bid to discourage her from returning to the marital stateroom until dawn. Even so, while the illusion of romance is part of the appeal of a cruise, a dance host

and the Baltic, and is skilled at adapting his patter to suit the differing audiences and routes.

The gentleman host

The "gentleman host", also known as the dance host, is a feature on the more traditional cruises with Cunard, Crystal, Silversea, Holland America and Fred Olsen. Personable single men in their fifties and sixties are employed to act as dancing and dinner hosts to unaccompanied older women, or those whose husbands hate dancing. More single women cruise than their

ABOVE: there is plenty to amuse passengers aboard a large, modern ship.

caught indulging in any improper behaviour can expect to be unceremoniously deposited at the next port of call – the modern equivalent of walking the plank.

Doctor at sea

Given that a typical cruise covers everyone from the newly-wed to the nearly-dead, the ship's medical officers are kept busy. Most medical emergencies are linked to elderly passengers who have pre-existing conditions or who are simply too frail to undertake a long voyage. According to one doctor, a classic response to being diagnosed with a terminal illness is to book a Caribbean cruise. Naturally, doctors are reluctant to reveal that deaths occur on board, but on cruises with a high proportion of vulnerable passengers, one or two deaths are not exceptional. Curiously enough, these deaths often occur on the final or penultimate night, perhaps linked to cumulative exertion, a reluctance to return home, or simply over-indulgence at the Captain's farewell dinner.

Dr Carroll, the *QE2*'s senior medical officer, attributes some heart attacks to the elderly "who decide to discover the treadmill for the first time in their lives", but links other seizures to an over-indulgent lifestyle: "And what a great way to go, in your sleep, having had a wonderful bottle of Chateau Petrus '61 the previous night." He crosses his fingers that no one has ever died of a seizure during his shift.

Helicopter transfers to airlift a passenger off a ship are rare, but the captain, when advised by the doctor, is empowered to do whatever is deemed to be in the best interests of the patient. By and large, ships' doctors have the same record of success in treating illness as their colleagues ashore and, in terms of expertise, they claim that, within the Caribbean, only the island of Barbados can provide similar standards to those which are typically available on board.

MEET THE MAÎTRE D'

The ship's maître d'hôtel, normally a master of diplomacy and tact and an assiduous "meeter and greeter", has usually worked his way up from assistant waiter to wine waiter or captain waiter. He has an unenviable role, particularly at the start of cruises that don't offer open seating, when he is often inundated by requests for changes to seating plans.

The less glamorous side of this challenging job involves daily briefings, in-service training and supervision of the dining staff, from the wine waiter to the fruit-juice maker. If most passengers come back late from an excursion, the dining staff has to allow some leeway for mealtimes, which eats into their limited free time. On some ships, the maître d' liaises with the executive chef and the ship's chandler, who is responsible for provisions, including the selection of fresh seafood and fruit at key ports.

The maître d' is also one of the key figures involved in assuring standards of cleanliness. Hygiene on board needs to be stringent since any virus tends to be transmitted through the air-conditioning system. Every night, the restaurant may be sprayed with cyrocide, a powerful disinfectant which kills all bacteria and insects. The dining staff may even be called upon to stay up all night to give the restaurant a total spring clean – then they make a party of it, with a dawn feast.

Maritime misadventure

A "man overboard" emergency happens occasionally but the passenger is usually rescued safely, unless suicide is the intent. Statistically, neither suicide nor death by misadventure should be regarded with surprise, given that ships are floating resorts of several thousand people. Fortunately, murders aboard ship are as rare as deadly hurricanes. Even so, a recent family cruise off the island of St Maarten provided the setting for a marital murder.

According to the Norwegian captain, an American footballer allegedly murdered his wife and tossed her body onto the pool deck. The FBI was dismayed that the ship's crew had then trampled all over the murder scene in an amateurish attempt to help. Yet budding crime writers would do better to go on a murder mystery cruise (run by Windjammer Barefoot Cruises and Cunard), where the fantasy body count should be far higher.

Personal relations

The best cruise ships are characterised by an easy camaraderie and the mingling of different nationalities, roles and ranks. Some cruise lines encourage married couples to work together while others frown upon such entanglements, fearing that any potential estrangement could jeopardise their work performance and disrupt the smooth running of the ship. The more charitable line is that coupledom promotes happiness and harmony on board, and liberal cruise lines do their utmost to keep couples on the same ship. Relationships with passengers are regarded with suspicion: the crew are allowed to "socialise but not fraternise" – but only blatant transgressions are punished.

Those who cope best with separation and homesickness tend be the young and single, or older staff with grown-up families. Crew members who suffer the most are parents with young children, particularly the Filipino, Thai and Indonesian women, cast in the role of main breadwinner. By entrusting their children to the care of grandmothers or aunts, they sacrifice their own happiness on the altar of economic prosperity, despite the management's blithe dismissal of their sacrifice as "cultural tradition".

LEFT: let them entertain you in a ship's theatre, which compares favourably to those found on dry land.
RIGHT: the lively promenade on *Explorer of the Seas*.

Given the constraints of life aboard, the crew is always delighted to let off steam in port. Cruise lines do their best to encourage camaraderie and strengthen team spirit with watersports, football and basketball, barbecues and beach parties. However, the most poignant sight is of crew members waiting to call home, desperate to hear news of loved ones they may only see six months hence. Once this is done, many set off in search of solitude or solace.

Time to go home

The end-of-cruise crew show is where the upstairs-downstairs worlds come together. The

show reveals the hidden talents of the motley crew, whose range embraces Thai dancing, Spanish flamenco, Filipino acrobatics, and Russian folk songs. However, when the crew let their hair down, and tear up the musical score, passengers are even more delighted.

The official Farewell Message from the Master encapsulates the best of cruising, the coming together of the two worlds, landlubbers and seafarers, passengers and crew. The captain usually pays tribute to all aboard with his farewell from the bridge: "We trust you will have pleasant memories in reflecting on your sailing experiences. We have been friends and shipmates for 1,197 nautical miles. Godspeed." ❑

GLAMOUR, GLITZ AND GAMES

A cruise can take you into a fantasy world quite unrelated to daily life.

What it won't do is give you much time for peaceful contemplation

All the cruise lines are in the business of spinning dreams from scraps of seafaring history and promises of romance at sea. From the sleek mega-yachts to the mammoth cruise liners, the ships slip into their seductive sales pitches. Most cruise companies deliver the glamour and glitz, even if some go overboard on the latter. While subtlety sometimes slips out of the porthole, the sheer scale of the razzmatazz compensates for any churlish quibbles about quality. The Captain's Cocktail Party, the sail-away rituals, the spectacular carnival parades, the surreal themed evenings, the celebratory parties, the gala dinners – all form part of the "showbiz at sea" approach that characterises contemporary cruising.

Fantasy worlds

By definition, a ship is neither a destination nor rooted in any culture, so ship designers have *carte blanche* to transport passengers into a fantasy world. The result is often a knowing parody, an ocean of kitsch redeemed by panache. Designers are committed to themes but these are capacious enough to encompass every whim. With a wave of the wand, a cavernous shopping mall is transformed into the Champs Elysées, or an idealised Main Street USA. Come evening, it is a stage set for a Disney-esque parade of circus clowns, stiltmen, Mickey Mice, or Marilyn Monroe lookalikes in drag.

A more sophisticated version of Americana is available on Celebrity Cruises ships such as the *Mercury*, with the Manhattan restaurant decorated in a lavish tribute to its namesake: amid the glitzy allusions to the metropolitan high life are Art Deco staircases and screens depicting New York's Flatiron Building. Yet even Celebrity can't resist resorting to gleaming chrome, fake zebra skin, futuristic marble, and leather wing-back armchairs that supposedly symbolise the golden age of cruising.

LEFT: dancing the night away on board ship.
RIGHT: the slot machines in *Millennium*'s casino.

On the Contemporary-class mega-ships, run by the likes of Carnival Cruise Line and Royal Caribbean, American heritage becomes a glorious dressing-up box, conjuring up Vegas gambling palaces, Hollywood film sets, Wild West saloons, or halls of fame encrusted with sporting heroes or stars of the silver screen. As

for the restaurants, the re-creation of a 1950s' diner on Royal Caribbean's Voyager Class ships comes complete with singing and dancing staff who deliver French fries with a rendition of *West Side Story*. To dance the night away, there may be a garishly decorated disco inspired by the Expressionist work of Jackson Pollock. An internet café might be incongruously cast as an old-school English gentlemen's club, complete with creaky leather armchairs.

European motifs

When American ship designers want to project an upmarket image, they raid the dressing-up box of European culture, working on the assumption that Europe is synonymous with visions of Venetian gondoliers, French shepherdesses, Roman emperors or Greek gods. Some on-board spas and restaurants have Italianate rococo ceilings inspired by Venetian palaces, scenes which clash with pastoral views of French châteaux and cavorting chatelaines. Elsewhere, a nightclub designed to reflect a Van Gogh painting of a starry night sky is incongruously preceded by a scene of English country-house chic. On deck, a sparkling swimming pool may evoke ancient Rome, with scenes of toga-clad centurions reclining against lascivious-looking consorts.

Carnival Cruise Line's cavernous public rooms twinkle with star motifs, Egyptian sphinxes and classical nudes, including a life-size reproduction of Michelangelo's *David*, while even Royal Caribbean (often more restrained than Carnival) has solaria inspired by Roman temples, Maya villages and African watering holes, the latter – on *Brilliance of the Seas* – complete with giant stone elephants and leaping gazelles. Travellers on big Contemporary-class ships – operated by Star Cruises, Costa Cruises, Disney Cruise Line and NCL, as well as Carnival and Royal Caribbean – can tour the world via the Florentine Lounge, the Strauss Restaurant, the

THE CAPTAIN'S TABLE

Being selected to dine at the captain's table on formal nights is both a privilege and a potential source of friction. Companies such as Costa Cruises dispense with the whole thing, claiming that it is counter-productive, pleasing the dozen chosen passengers but deflating the rest. However, as a high-profile exercise, this event has its place on most traditional cruise ships. In preparation, the maître d' and the captain study the passenger manifest and select favoured VIPs, repeat passengers, high-spenders in the best suites, including a token attractive woman, and a sprinkling of personable officers in full naval dress. The captain may add one or two favourites he has met during the cruise.

The dinner, often preceded by the Captain's Cocktail Party, involves a grand entrance, a commemorative photo and a gala menu signed by the captain.

Over champagne and sometimes decent wines, the captain either regales his guests with his best nautical anecdotes or retreats into shyness, depending on mood and nationality. While Greek, Latin and American captains generally rise to the occasion, Norwegian captains are notoriously tongue-tied, more at home with nautical manoeuvres than making small talk. Over coffee and petits-fours, one taciturn captain confessed that he would rather face a medical emergency at sea than make a speech.

Vivaldi Bar, the Taj Mahal Theatre, the Tosca Tavern, the Pompeii Gym, the Dog and Duck pub, or the Fantasia Plaza. Welcome to the land of fantasy cruising – and to one of the most entertaining aspects of life at sea.

The upmarket version

Premium cruise ships – which offer more space per passenger and (in some cases) better quality food than Contemporary-rated vessels – still offer a version of "Fantasy Cruiseland" but it is more discreet and restrained. Princess Cruises, Holland America Line, Cunard Line and Celebrity Cruises, Windstar Cruises and Star Clippers all have Premium-rated vessels.

On sleek simulations of mega-yachts, the favoured theme is an idealised version of life at sea, complete with paintings of nautical battles and replicas of tall ships. Larger cruise ships may celebrate the glories of the British Empire and colonial living, from Victorian parlours and Edwardian libraries to tropical hot-houses and wood-panelled card rooms. Only Celebrity Cruises eschew such affectionate pastiche in favour of sleekly contemporary design, symbolised by the cutting-edge glass elevators that slice through the decks, revealing stylish artwork and panoramic ocean views.

As a rule of thumb, the more exclusive the cruise line, the more plush its yacht-like atmosphere and the less significant the entertainment: the seriously wealthy wish to spend their days doing as little as possible and prefer their entertainment fairly discreet. SeaDream Yacht Club, for example, offers low-key piano recitals and film shows, while the Yachts of Seabourn provides cabaret-style performers in its show lounges and bars. Silversea Cruises provide rather more substantial performances in its ships' main theatres, supplemented with piano music and the occasional concert. This discreet approach to entertainment is reflected in the restrained, some might say understated, stylish décor of most of the deluxe ships.

On-board entertainment

Entertainment is inextricably linked to the ship's category, size and cruising style. American or international-style cruises are perceived as more fun, offering the glitziest, most upbeat

entertainment, especially on the mega-ships. No cruise company throws a party more enthusiastically than Carnival, with its cheerful vulgarity and irrepressible spirit. Royal Caribbean's Voyager-class mega-ships rival these sea-going theme parks. A multi-deck boulevard runs down the centre, the lowest level lined with boutiques, cafés and bars, which becomes the nightly setting for carnival parades and theatrical set-pieces, including a camp send-up of the captain in a be-sequinned parody of a naval uniform.

As for the family-minded Disney Cruises, the line naturally features the company's most

famous mouse, as well as all the other familiar characters that have endured from the animated films of the 1930s and 1940s.

The entertainment on British-style ships tends to be more restrained and old-fashioned, with bridge, bingo, traditional deck games, trivia quizzes, panel games and lectures on the ports of call *(see page 76)*. The somewhat prim, tea-drinking style of certain British ships could not differ more dramatically from the carefree, cocktail-sipping crowd on the American mega-ships. However, that is changing, due in part to the launch of *Ocean Village* with its younger, predominantly British guests and a drop in the average age of cruise ship passengers worldwide.

LEFT: a romantic evening on board.
RIGHT: an al fresco lunch is served.

Fun for the family

Cruises are perfect for satisfying different generations at the same time. A family can cruise together, amuse themselves separately and share stories over dinner. However, the best cruise companies manage a clever segregation of fun-loving families and privacy-seeking couples. The most child-friendly cruise companies, such as Carnival, Royal Caribbean and Disney Cruise Line, offer fully supervised children's centres, divided according to age group, giving parents freedom from their offspring.

To win children's hearts, minds and stomachs, each cruise company tries to outdo its

rivals with games and gimmicks: biscuits before bedtime delivered to children's cabins, or pizza parties and teenage discos. Separate, age-related activity clubs offer programmes tailored to suit different age groups: young children enjoy bouncy castles and ball games, as well as paddling pools, deck games and treasure hunts, interspersed with arts and crafts, cartoons, fancy dress parties and ice cream on tap; teenagers respond to karaoke, discos, thematic parties and murder mystery games, not to mention crazy golf, basketball and tennis, as well as the chance to chill out in their own pool, Jacuzzi and video arcades. NCL is stronger on sporting pursuits than educational activities,

while Disney Cruises delights in its brand of wholesome, if saccharine, family fun.

The most enlightened cruise lines offer engaging educational activities, from stargazing to hands-on science experiments with computer labs, navigation and water challenges. Princess Cruises are leading the way with an impressive on-board educational programme backed by the California Science Center. On offer are such intriguing activities as astronomy, ocean and coral reef studies, the construction of sailing boats, and even the dubious privilege of learning how to dissect squid.

Catering for everyone

As for couples and singles and first-time passengers, they are certainly well catered for these days. Most cruise lines have special packages for honeymooners or couples celebrating an anniversary; some cruises court romantics by featuring "renewal of vows" ceremonies, while on several Princess and P&O cruises, couples can actually marry at sea (most ships can only marry couples in port).

Several lines run cruises dedicated to "Newcomers" – first-time holiday-makers at sea – while all host a range of cocktail parties aimed at different niche markets, from high-spending VIPs to repeat cruisers and solo passengers in search of companionship. Some lines employ "gentlemen hosts" to keep unaccompanied ladies happy with conversation, card games and dancing *(see Secret Life, page 65)*. Dance classes are also popular for get-togethers: for some people, "beginner's rumba and merengue" represents the highlight of their cruise.

These "gentlemen hosts" are a throwback to a more sedate style of cruising, associated with the heyday of ocean-going liners. Yet, even today, certain British or European-style ships can feel demure and nautical rather than exotic and fun-loving. Typical European-style deck games include shuffleboard, deck quoits, or the bizarre game of dolphin racing, involving betting on wooden dolphins. Carpet boules can be a popular pursuit for elderly passengers, while golf-putting, tennis and basketball appeal to a wider age range.

Sport

At the other end of the scale, international-style ships come into their own with sports, spa and fitness facilities. All the mainstream lines offer a huge range of sporting pursuits and vigorous exercise, from combat aerobics and aqua aerobics to tennis and volleyball tournaments. The sundeck forms an intrinsic part of the cruising experience, ideally complemented by exotically themed pools and whirlpools. As for fitness centres, many vessels have a well-equipped gym with an ocean view, as well as studios equipped for body conditioning, yoga, Pilates and power walking.

Royal Caribbean's new Voyager-class megaships currently set the standards for spectacular sports facilities, from a rock-climbing wall, running up the side of the ship's funnel, to an ice-skating rink cut into the heart of the vessel. Organised activities on offer are advanced ice-skating, mini-golf tournaments or a rock-climbing tournament. Rival cruise lines have to decide whether to compete. Joe Farcus, the design architect for Carnival Cruises, defends his company's decision not to create such facilities, believing that valuable deck space should be dedicated to deckchairs and pools, traditional features passengers expect to find in abundance. Couch potatoes can retreat to the sybaritic spa or a dedicated sports bar, both firm features on the mega-ships.

Spas

Certain large ships contain spas as lavish as any that you might find on shore. Those of Celebrity Cruises and Royal Caribbean are particularly impressive, while at the other end of the size scale, the tiny ships of SeaDream Yacht Club feature Thai spas designed by the Haworth Consultancy, who masterminded the well known Banyan Tree spas in Asia.

The dominant spa brand is Steiner, and although it is facing competition from up-and-coming spa operators such as Harding Bros and Canyon Ranch, it maintains a tight grip on many lines' spa activities. This means that, although spa facilities are impressive, treatments are highly (and in some cases prohibitively) priced. Steiner has also been criticised for training its staff to "hard sell" costly creams and products with scant regard to passengers' desire for peace and quiet, and a brief respite from consumerism.

LEFT: children enjoy an afternoon treat from NCL's Sprinkles ice-cream bar.
RIGHT: the teenager's pool on *Radiance of the Seas*.

Casinos

According to inveterate gamblers, ships' casinos and the Caribbean-style casinos ashore are more laid-back than any heart-attack inducing session in Las Vegas. The games move at a slightly slower pace, the rules may be slightly looser, and games are friendlier and more entertaining. Even so, casinos produce extreme reactions among many cruise passengers: for the Americans gambling is a standard activity while the British tend to have a more ambivalent attitude to it, on the one hand decrying it as vulgar, on the other relishing the fun and excitement generated.

ART AUCTIONS

On-board art auctions are a popular activity, even if "world-class art at a fraction of gallery prices" can be interpreted to cover original Disney cartoons and sports memorabilia. Park West Gallery, the market leader on cruise ships, claims "the finest collection on the seven seas", with lithographs and prints by Dali, Picasso and Chagall. Passengers are tempted by the offer of "free fine-art prints", complimentary champagne and the extension of a credit line. Billed as a "fast-paced rock and roll auction" with bids opening at US$100, the entertaining event can also be accessed on the internet, with silent bids entered from your cabin, if you wish.

Typically, passengers appreciate the chance to lay bets in a safe, welcoming environment. Certainly, gambling is a feature of most of the mega-ships, with American and international-style lines generally outshining their European rivals with dazzling, Las Vegas-style facilities and – in some cases – free drinks for players. Most casinos provide gaming lessons to novices, as well as offering slot machines with "unprecedented state-of-the-art features".

Let them entertain you

Evening entertainment on board generally embraces blockbuster movies, international

theme nights, from an "Ahoy me hearties" extravaganza featuring a pirates' poolside buffet and ice sculptures, to a horror night celebrating "the dance of the vampires, and the election of the infernal couple". Less spectacular cruise lines favour "gypsy flamenco nights", karaoke evenings, singles' parties, love songs on deck, strolling *a cappella* groups, and talent contests. Cruise ship entertainment is rather scorned in the business, yet some of the younger entertainers, particularly the headliner singers and dancers, could hold their own in most capital cities.

Musical offerings

As for music, the cruise lines face the challenge of pleasing impossibly varied tastes. Given the mixed age groups in the discos and nightclubs, the resident DJs have a particularly hard task. Elsewhere on the ship, the cruise director matches specific venues to the right mood music. There is nearly always a discreet piano bar where a handful of musicians play mellow background music, including old-time ballroom tunes and classical favourites.

Old-fashioned but endearing Fred Olsen cruises are typical of the genre in inviting guests to "let the soothing melodies of Ingrid Vanherpe ease you into the early hours". Classical concerts and recitals are a feature of sophisticated ships but are more at home on European itineraries, when, for instance, Grieg can be played in his natural setting, on a Norwegian fjords cruise.

Among the major lines, Princess Cruises has a reputation for playing good country and western music, cool jazz and timeless classics. However, it is arguable that the most successful musical interludes are provided by the cruise lines' specialist bands and musicians, from classical guitar aficionados to country and western bands or Latino groups starring Brazilian and other South American musicians and singers.

While Latin music, in all its diversity, is showcased mostly on southern Caribbean routes, most cruise ships plying the eastern and western Caribbean routes have a resident Caribbean band based on board (the majority are a mixture of steel drums and electric guitars) to provide an authentic flavour of the "what's happenin', man" island culture.

ice shows and theatrical extravaganzas, with guest appearances by ventriloquists, jugglers, magicians and stand-up comics. All the mega-ships and mainstream cruise lines flaunt variants on West End musicals or Broadway-style shows featuring show-stopping soloists and gravity-defying stunts enhanced by special effects of varying quality.

While the emphasis is always on international appeal, cruise ships occasionally dare to bend the winning format. While in the Caribbean, *Adventure of the Seas* offers a Midnight Latin Parade, "a salute to our home port of San Juan".

Carnival and Costa Cruises also favour

An evening in port

Cruises often spend one long evening at a particular port, which can provide a welcome opportunity to explore independently, and an escape from the relentless rhythms of life at sea, with its enforced sociability and self-conscious bonhomie. Most cruises, however, leave the port of call at sunset, providing passengers with the nightly ritual that is sail-away. The official line is that a timely departure allows the ship to reach the next port on schedule, but the reality is related to ship revenues: the hard commercial logic is that the casino and on-board shops can only open once the ship is sets and the staff serve poolside rum punches, there is always an ideal deck from which to view the spectacle of the ship gliding out of port. At its best, the sail-away party is one of the highlights of a cruise: the quayside lined with smiling Caribbean islanders waving good-bye to the ship; a small band of passengers dancing to the steel band on deck, and the rest sipping complimentary rum punches while lapping up the views, the sunset, and the twists and turns of the vessel.

It is a cruising credo that passengers should be royally entertained, whether they wish to be or not. As a result, cruises are rarely restful

at sea. Commercialism aside, if the ship is perceived as the prime destination, the floating resort, then the company is entitled to feel that the more time passengers spend on board, the better: the ship is simply fulfilling its brief.

Sail-away

Each cruise line treats sail-aways rather differently but the spectacle always raises the spirits, reminding one why cruising has the edge over conventional land-bound holidays. As the sun affairs, even on small ships – although old cruising hands manage to create a capsule of quiet self-containment. Since more than half of first-time cruisers are celebrating a special occasion, it behoves the cruise lines to create even more special moments. For those in search of restfulness, the rhythm of a longer cruise and a smaller ship is best. Short mega-ship cruises can create an overwhelming surfeit of choice, especially as many cruisers like to visit all the ports of call, and this pleasurable duty can create its own pressures. Rather like the "death by chocolate" midnight buffet offered on some ships, the pleasures of cruising come double-edged. But what a delicious way to go. ❏

LEFT: at Dazzles disco.
ABOVE: a spectacular interpretation of *Les Misérables* on a Norwegian Cruise Line ship.

TOPICAL TALKS

From haute cuisine to hidden treasure, political gossip to hot shopping tips,
guest speakers aim to entertain passengers and even enlighten them

The selection of the right celebrity guest speaker can help to sell a cruise, set the cultural tone or transform a potentially dull day into an engaging event. Entertaining and informative talks about ports of call have long been a staple of traditional cruises, with Caribbean culture and heritage to the fore.

However, the international mega-ships are increasingly opting for guest speakers who can tap into mass interests, such as the cult of celebrity, or an appreciation of food and wine. For example, Julia Child, America's favourite celebrity chef, took a tour on the *QE2* as the main attraction in a Chef's Palate cruise. Child, who is noted for popularising classic French cuisine in the States, created her signature dishes before an adoring audience. In tribute to the skills of the celebrity chef, Child's floating islands dessert appeared on the ship's dinner menu, and was duly appreciated.

Silversea Cruises, Radisson Seven Seas and Crystal Cruises are among the cruise companies offering themed gastronomic cruises. Crystal even stages a wine and food festival, with celebrity chefs revealing their secret recipes.

On a more humdrum level, in the absence of celebrity speakers, the ship's executive chef is normally cajoled into giving cookery demonstrations: an air of surrealism hangs over passengers' chance discovery that a corner of the casino has been given over to a spaghetti bolognese demonstration, with sizzling pans placed between the slot machines.

Diverse topics

Some of the most intriguing guest lecturers appear on thematic cruises, speaking on topics ranging from calligraphy to comedy, finance to film-making, or maritime history to murder mystery. Cunard's Beyond the Human Limit cruise aboard the *QE2* features celebrity survivors, from Stephen Venables, the first Briton to climb Everest without supplementary oxygen, to Terry Waite, who was taken hostage in Beirut in 1987.

In tapping into human curiosity about natural or man-made disasters, similar talks on the perils of Caribbean volcanoes, hurricanes and shipwrecks also tend to be well attended.

The distinction between European-style and American-style companies is irrelevant to the choice and quality of their guest lecturers. Crystal Cruises, Seabourn and Cunard offer lectures by equally prestigious speakers. Crystal has invited such celebrities as US news anchorman Walter Cronkite, as well as former American Secretaries of State, film critics, biographers, broadcasters and game show hosts.

In its turn, Cunard favours statesmen, writers or comedy actors of the calibre of John Cleese, along with a raft of maritime historians, academics and the occasional royal-watcher or court correspondent. Seabourn also prefers substance over style in its choice of celebrity speakers, ranging from actors to academics. Conductor André Previn, actress Lynn Redgrave and writer Frank McCourt have all spoken about their specialist areas.

Caribbean themes

In keeping with the Caribbean routes, the themes of talks are often nautical, piratical, botanical, or linked to the exotic history and colonial culture of the islands. On Star Clipper cruises, lectures focus on navigation and nautical themes, while Clipper Cruise Lines regularly invite experts to talk on reef fish, rainforests, plant life, or the geology of the islands.

Seabourn often invites a botanist on board to present the splendid botanical gardens in islands as diverse as Barbados and St Lucia. Likewise, Holland America favours low-key talks on history, astronomy and archaeology.

As for the sea itself, several cruises offer lectures on marine archaeology, inspired by tales of bounty hunters, pirate treasure and coves concealing sunken shipwrecks. Sixteenth-century Spanish galleons, which came to grief on the Caribbean's jagged coral reefs, have revealed enough deep-sea treasure trove to encourage shipwreck search teams to persevere.

The coral reefs off Costa Maya, on the Mexican coast, have already proved a rich seam for bounty hunters. The glamour and mystery of the search for sunken treasure is a perennial favourite for cruise talks. Holland America is just one of the upmarket cruise companies operating this Mexican Caribbean itinerary, but this line is exceptional in employing an expert speaker on Maya culture and archaeology.

Finding a niche

Celebrity Cruises, P&O Cruises and Crystal Cruises have been leading the way in serving the diverse interests of the expanding cruising market. While committed to worthy, self-improvement lectures, the company also reflects a trend towards satisfying the vagaries of emerging niche markets. Typical themes for talks range from maritime history, botany and bird-watching to financial investment and pensions, wine-tasting and bar-tending, computing, art appreciation and craft skills.

On many modern ships, it is not uncommon to find guest lecturers covering more esoteric subjects, from gambling to graphology, body language to beauty, and even talks on how to cope with the trauma of divorce or bereavement.

LEFT: learn about Maya ruins and archaeological digs, such as this one at Xuanantunich in Belize.
RIGHT: an exhibit in the Gold Museum, Costa Rica.

The best guest lecturers are not restricted to the most exclusive cruise lines. Curiously enough, although Disney Cruise Line panders to its past and to passenger expectations, with lectures on film studies and the Disney legacy, the fleet also offers talks on weighty maritime themes, such as navigation and ship-building, or even star-gazing at sea.

As a rule, the cruise company's cultural heritage and the nationality of the core clientele also influence the choice of speakers. Given that Fred Olsen's clientele is predominantly British, guest lecturers tend to be opinionated British politicians, from the controversial

Edwina Currie to Bernard Ingham, Margaret Thatcher's former press secretary. By the same token, the Italian heritage of Costa Cruises and Mediterranean Shipping Cruises (MSC) means that both companies are keen to play the Italian card. In practice, this means promoting Italian in language classes, and encouraging an appreciation of art history, wine and cuisine through the skills of the guest lecturers.

Ports of call

The tradition of talks on ports of call is an essential piece in the cruising puzzle, and is greatly appreciated by older British and European passengers. The more European-style cruise companies, such as Cunard, P&O and Fred Olsen, are rightly proud of their specialist lecturers who present the history, culture and attractions of the ports of call.

At its best, as on Fred Olsen ships, this is an informed and objective overview with no attempt to push passengers into booking shore excursions. Aided by slides and maps, the lecturer enthuses about the island's cultural origins, botanical attractions and marine life.

The cultural information is leavened with personal anecdotes and recollections of the island in question, as well as touching upon its politics, economy and social life. In response

to questions about the offshore status of the British Virgin Islands, Barbara Taylor, a seasoned British lecturer on Fred Olsen Caribbean routes, replies in depth, while casually revealing how one of her relatives was instrumental in establishing the BVI as a tax haven.

On culturally orientated cruises, shopping advice is secondary to a full appreciation of each island's charms and attractions, but specific beaches are often recommended, along with suggestions for independent excursions and advice on personal security and taxi hire.

In theory, American or international-style cruise companies provide a similar service but, during on-board talks, the emphasis tends to be on shopping, restaurants and beaches rather than on cultural pursuits. The North American lecturer's exhaustive shopping suggestions are often accompanied by a map and a listing of recommended outlets for jewellery and crafts, as well as advice on beaches and bars.

Passengers benefit from knowing that they have a guarantee as to the quality of their purchases and, in the unlikely event of shoddy goods, have some recourse. The only drawback is that the cruise company or its representative may take commission on passengers' purchases, so shopping advice, although sound, is not necessarily wholly independent.

Where cultural attractions of an island are concerned, some cruise companies encourage their lecturers to tailor presentations towards persuading passengers to book shore excursions. While not dishonest, this approach discourages less independent-minded souls from jumping into a taxi to explore the port of call. At worst, passengers may sign up for the cruise company's over-priced beach excursion without realising that an acceptable beach is within walking distance, or a short taxi ride away.

Covering the options

However, the more scrupulous cruise companies either expect the lecturer to cover the options for independent exploration, or else they employ an on-board adviser to help passengers wishing to explore ports of call on their own. Fred Olsen takes the former approach, but Costa Cruises favours the latter. While the company may lose revenue from failure to book shore excursions, overall customer satisfaction is paramount.

Royal Caribbean opts for a slightly different approach to the issue: the shopping lecturer has a higher profile than the port lecturer, reflecting priorities on board; shore excursions are presented on video, as are shopping options, although the shopping lecturer also gives comprehensive talks and can be consulted for specific advice.

Given the range of talks available at sea, it is only a question of finding the right ship: culture or consumerism, celebrities or cooking, the choice is as wide as the ocean. ❑

LEFT: Caribbean crafts, St John, US Virgin Islands.
RIGHT: an itinerary that includes Grand Cayman is popular with diving enthusiasts.

THE A–Z OF CRUISING

Which islands to visit? What kind of ship to choose? This round-up of
who goes where and what's on offer will help you decide what suits you best

Where changing tastes in holidays are concerned, cruising is the new rock 'n' roll. These days, more than a million Britons choose a cruise as their main holiday – an increase of more than 300 percent on a decade ago. If you compare that to the increase in bookings for foreign holidays as a whole (82 percent) you get an idea of just how far cruising has progressed.

It's a similar, if not quite so spectacular, story in the United States, where nearly 9 million people a year take a cruise – a 105 percent increase on a decade earlier. The Caribbean is second only to the Mediterranean as the favourite cruise region for UK travellers, while for Americans the sunshine islands on their doorstep are the clear first choice. More than 5 million US cruise passengers a year choose the Caribbean as their cruise destination.

The success story has been built upon burgeoning variety. In the early 1980s, the building of a new cruise ship was a rare event; by the end of the decade – and throughout the 1990s – an extravagant investment programme has seen many new vessels, each more innovative than the last, rolling out of shipyards.

Variety is the spice of life

The upshot has been that ships are now as varied as hotels and resorts on land and cater for travellers of every age, taste and budget. Some ships are like floating country houses, with substantial libraries, wood-panelled bars, elegant lounges and intimate restaurants; others are big, glitzy ocean-going resorts, with state of the art spas, sparkly nightclubs, themed restaurants and spectacular show lounges.

You can learn the ropes and sleep beneath the stars on a sailing ship, or pretend you are a millionaire for a week or two on an intimate private vessel. And the good news is that ships of all types spend all or part of the year exploring the Caribbean, which is the true heartland of

LEFT: relaxing by the pool on board ship.
RIGHT: an early morning jog on deck is invigorating.

the cruise business, as you will soon realise if you stroll along the Miami harbour front and see skyscraper-high ships lined up at the piers.

Why choose the Caribbean?

The Caribbean islands are synonymous with sun and fun; even the occasional shower seems

little more than a burst of liquid sunshine. With soft-as-talc beaches, hospitable people, a laid-back lifestyle and wonderful shopping, the calypso islands are the place to chill out, soak up the sun, swim, snorkel and forget the pressures of everyday life.

But they offer far more than that; you'll also find lavish plantations, gorgeous scenery, a rich history, varied local cuisine and plenty of things to do – from undersea exploration in a submarine, to playing with dolphins, enjoying a world-class round of golf, discovering the secrets of a rainforest, learning how rum is made or going deep-sea fishing.

Some people prefer to stay on one particular

island and get under its skin, but many travellers find this restricting, and that is where cruising comes into its own.

A typical seven-night cruise from Miami or Fort Lauderdale will visit four islands – and seven-day itineraries can be combined with island stays or with a different cruise, to create a 14-night "back to back" trip that offers a real insight into the region and a chance to sample the unique personality of many different islands. This makes a good introduction if you're planning a holiday on land at a later date but are unsure which island you would prefer.

Many big-ship lines also own or lease private

bond if the company goes out of business, or if the cruise schedule changes and you cannot alter flights. (To find a local cruise specialist, British holidaymakers can contact Leading Cruise Agents Alliance of the UK (tel: 0870 122 5115; www.thelca.com. US vacationers can get advice from the Cruise Lines International Association, tel: 212-921 0066; www.cruising.org).

Most cruise companies now have flexible pricing systems (like the low-cost airlines), whereby the price of a cruise varies according to availability when you book, so brochure prices are increasingly becoming a moveable feast. Also, many lines offer discounts for early

islands or sections of beach where visitors can play Robinson Crusoe, enjoy a barbecue and take part in a variety of water sports.

Finding a bargain

Because so many new ships have entered service over the past two decades, bargain prices abound as cruise lines strive to ensure their ships are all filled – so, if you hunt around you can save money.

The best way to bag a bargain cruise is to trawl Teletext, newspaper offers and the internet. UK holidaymakers should be aware that booking directly with a cruise line's US office may mean a cheaper deal but doesn't provide cover with a

VALUE FOR MONEY

Cruising is the best-value way to tour the Caribbean. As well as all-inclusive cruises, others have all meals and entertainment (and children's clubs) included in the price. Some lines also offer unlimited soft drinks for a payment of around US$15–$20 per person, per week.

If you haven't chosen an all-inclusive ship, you may only have to pay extra for alcoholic drinks (expect hotel prices), tips (around US$7–$10 per person, per day spent on board, plus 15 percent service charge on bar bills) and optional excursions (around US$15 for a walking tour to $115 for a full day out with lunch). Use of the health spa is an optional extra but it doesn't come cheap.

bookings, so you won't necessarily get the best deal by waiting until the last minute.

Specialist cruise agencies are a good source of bargains, as many cruise lines pass on spare capacity for them to fill – and they are adept at putting together no-hassle (and protected) fly-cruise packages.

Floating resorts

In the 1980s, the cruise lines designed a new generation of big ships as "floating resorts", with a range of facilities from vast casinos to multiple restaurants and health spas, akin to those of the all-inclusive resorts ashore.

Royal Caribbean's next level of gigantic ship, *Freedom of the Seas* (launched in 2006), smashes all records to date at a staggering 160,000 tons.

Life on board

These leviathans are more like miniature cities than traditional cruise ships; with – literally – acres of space on board they offer around-the clock action and plenty of nightlife.

Pulsating discos vie for attention with intimate piano bars. You can prepare for dinner with a visit to a Champagne bar, and round it off with coffee at a cappuccino café and a spec-

Royal Caribbean International set the trend for "mega-ships" with the launch of the 73,192-ton, 2,524-passenger *Sovereign of the Seas* in 1988. At the time, the world's largest cruise ship was NCL's 76,049-ton *Norway*.

To get an idea of how far the big-ship concept has progressed since the 1980s, consider that the current holder of the "world's biggest" ship title – Cunard Line's transatlantic liner *Queen Mary 2* – is more than twice the size of the *Norway*, at a whopping 150,000 tons. And

LEFT: on the beach.
ABOVE: a cruise ship dominates the landscape while in port at Pointe-à-Pitre, Guadeloupe.

tacular show. You can opt for a casual meal in a pizza parlour or enjoy an evening pint at an English-style pub. During the day you can swim, jog, visit the golf driving range, work out in the gym with a personal trainer, or have a game of deck tennis or basketball on a full-scale court. If you prefer sheer indulgence, you can visit a health spa for a massage or wallow in a thalassotherapy bath. If you feel like shopping, the outlets on board sell everything from sunblock to designer gowns.

Best of all – if you're travelling with children – these ships offer extensive facilities for kids, with all-day supervision and activities geared to different age groups. So you can let your hair

Cruising with Children

The cruise ship building boom of the 1980s and 1990s was accompanied by a drive to attract younger people, especially young married couples with kids – and win the hearts of tomorrow's holidaymakers. An intrinsic part of this was the creation of large-scale facilities for children. Teen discos, virtual reality games, indoor and outdoor play centres, children-only swimming pools and supervised activity programmes are now *de*

rigueur on all modern mega-ships, as are kids' menus and dedicated mealtimes for youngsters.

Carnival Cruise Lines attracts around 300,000 youngsters every year – and keeps them happy with their own pools and deck areas, playrooms, video arcades and teen discos, as well as a "Camp Carnival" activity programme that includes face painting, quizzes and treasure hunts, educational computer games, learning about science in a fun way and backstage tours by ships' entertainers.

Royal Caribbean International is Carnival's biggest rival and its ultra-modern ships have indoor and outdoor facilities, plus an age-related Adventure Ocean Youth Programme. The biggest ships, *Voyager, Explorer, Adventurer, Mariner* and *Navigator of*

the Seas, all have huge dedicated areas for young-sters as well as ice rinks, rock climbing walls, roller blading circuits and 1950s' diners with jukeboxes and staff who perform rock 'n' roll dance routines.

Celebrity Cruises also tries to attract families during school vacations; its facilities include American-style Slumber Parties – an unusual variation on the babysitting services offered by other lines.

Disney Cruise Line, of course, offers mind-blowing facilities for the youngsters – and has cartoon characters on board to add to the fun *(see page 88).*

Holland America Line is also worth considering (in school holiday time). It has a children's pro-gramme and, on some cruises, offers youngsters aged six and over shore excursions just for them; options include hikes and treasure hunts for six- to 12-year-olds, and sea kayaking for teenagers.

Norwegian Cruise Line's ships don't have such extensive facilities but they do include a "Circus at Sea", which teaches juggling, clowning and other circus skills as part of a Kids' Crew programme.

Princess Cruises, a division of P&O (which also has excellent kids' facilities), keeps one of its ships, *Royal Princess,* virtually child-free, but its Grand Class ships – the *Sun* and *Dawn Princesses* – offer age-related youth programmes, as do the older *Regal Princess* and *Crown Princess*. Best for kids are the largest ships, *Grand* and *Golden Princess*, with virtual reality rides and games.

Points to consider

● Mega-ships have the best facilities but they do tend to be American-dominated. If you want British-style children's entertainment, choose P&O Cruises or an operator like Ocean Village (a sub-brand of P&O and Princess Cruises).

● Check what's on offer for your child's age group and whether it's available outside school holidays.

● Check the level of supervision; reputable lines will happily tell you the ratio of "child counsellors" to youngsters and outline required qualifications.

● Age limits vary; some ships cater for children as young as two, on others, the minimum age is four.

● Babysitting can cost extra – from US$5 to $15 per child per session.

● One parent may have to be present at all times if the child is very young, and remain on board if the child attends clubs on port days.

● You must bring any medication your child needs and you will probably have to administer it. ❑

LEFT: at the kids' club.

down secure in the knowledge that your children are happy and safely occupied.

The big ships have a wide range of accommodation, from small, inside single cabins to spacious suites with jacuzzis and roomy balconies. Cabins, whatever their size, are furnished to a high standard and each will have an ensuite bathroom (with a shower in the lower grade accommodation, and shower plus bathtub in higher grades), and a colour TV.

Meals, by and large, are three- to four-star restaurant standard rather than haute cuisine but the food is varied and, as a rule, it is nicely presented and plentiful. Those so inclined can eat and drink all day, starting with early bird coffee at 6am and finishing up with the Midnight Buffet – taking in breakfast, lunch, tea and dinner as they go, of course.

The most recently built ships have made room for speciality restaurants where – usually for a surcharge of between US$10 and $30 – passengers can celebrate a special occasion, indulge their gourmet tastes, or simply take a break from the main dining rooms and try something different.

Pros and cons of mega-ships

These huge ships are smart, well-equipped, lively and offer good value for money. Their comfortable cabins and varied facilities can make travelling around the Caribbean islands as interesting and enjoyable as visiting them – particularly if you have children in tow. On the down side, ships that carry more than 2,000 people are bound to feel crowded, especially when embarking and disembarking.

Multiple facilities mean that you will rarely encounter hordes of people in one place at a time, but on days when the ship does not visit a port, sunbathing on deck can be rather a cheek-by-jowl affair, as can the buffet breakfast – so be prepared to queue. And, on some ships, the relentless "fun, fun, fun" atmosphere of pool games, fashion shows and tannoy announcements can be wearing if you're trying to relax.

To win over first-time cruise passengers, the big-ship lines also tend to cram itineraries full of port calls, which does mean you get a lot of variety for your money, but with so many people on board, the process of disembarking and getting passengers off on tours is a major process. Some ships organise it better than others, but if you have picked one that doesn't do it too well, the constant sound of passengers being summoned ashore makes a lazy lie-in out of the question.

As a rule, the bigger the vessel, the longer the wait to disembark, and the sheer size of these vessels means they have to anchor off some ports and ferry passengers to the quayside by tender – something to consider if you feel seasick in small boats or have mobility problems.

Families, young sporty types and sociable,

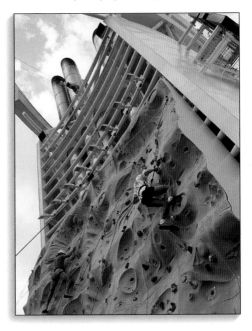

outgoing types will love these ships; they're also good for single travellers and for people who've never cruised before and fear they'll go stir crazy if they don't have enough to do.

Home ports and destinations

Most of the big ships are based at Florida's three main ports. Miami is home to many Royal Caribbean, Carnival, Celebrity and Norwegian Cruise Line ships. Fort Lauderdale/Port Everglades is the base port for several Holland America, Princess, Celebrity and Royal Caribbean vessels and is also a key turn-around port for lines whose ships only cruise the Caribbean occasionally, such as Crystal

RIGHT: *Voyager of the Seas*, one of the biggest ships in the Caribbean, has a rock-climbing wall.

Cruises, Cunard Line, Seabourn, Silversea and Seven Seas Cruises. Port Canaveral is the home port for Disney Cruise Line and for some Carnival, Royal Caribbean and Holland America ships.

Florida-based ships mainly operate regular seven-day runs to the Eastern Caribbean (the Bahamas, St Thomas, St John's, Haiti and Puerto Rico) or the Western Caribbean (Mexico, Belize, Grand Cayman and Jamaica).

But to gain easy access to Southern Caribbean islands, including Dominica, St Kitts and Nevis, Grenada, St Lucia, Aruba, Curaçao and Martinique, some mega-ships have moved

away from the traditional ports. San Juan on Puerto Rico is now home to ships from RCI, Carnival, Celebrity, NCL and Princess fleets, while Barbados attracts NCL, P&O Cruises, Ocean Village and Windstar, among others.

The terrorist attacks of September 11th, 2001 prompted a surge of interest in US "Homeland Cruising" as nervous American travellers sought to avoid flying and to cruise instead from a gateway near their home. This has resulted in a growth of Caribbean cruise business to previously underused ports including Jacksonville in Florida, New Orleans in Louisiana, and the Texan ports of Galveston and Houston. For British fans of Caribbean

cruising, this has increased the options for add-on drive packages allowing them to explore lesser known parts of the US before or after their cruise.

Getting the ratio right

If you are attracted to "floating resort" style cruising, be aware that there are two types of mega-ship: Contemporary and Premium. Contemporary ships are aimed at the mass market (and priced accordingly), while Premium-rated ships are higher priced, carry fewer cruise passengers, and offer a touch more class.

A quick way to discover whether the ship you're considering is Premium or Contemporary is to divide its tonnage by its passenger capacity to get the Passenger Space Ratio (PSR). This gives the clearest indication of how crowded you will find life on board a particular ship. For example, the 101,509-ton/2,758-passenger Contemporary ship *Carnival Victory* has a PSR of 36.8, while the 108,806-ton/2,600-passenger Premium ship *Golden Princess* has a PSR of 41.8. The higher the PSR, the less likely it is that you will feel hemmed in by your fellow passengers.

On nearly all the big ships that sail in the Caribbean, the majority of passengers are North American and the on-board currency is the US dollar. Crew nationalities vary – the average ship will garner its officers from Europe and Scandinavia and the rest of its crew and staff from 25 or more countries, but the on-board language is always English.

The mega-ship operators

Websites are given below; for telephone numbers, see the listing in the Travel Tips section.
● CARNIVAL CRUISE LINES (www.carnival.com). King of the swingers and part of the world's most successful cruise company (Carnival Corporation), Carnival Cruise Lines has 21 Contemporary-rated ships, the majority of which are based in the Caribbean. They range in size from medium (the 47,262-ton/1,486-passenger *Celebration*) to mega (the 110,000-ton/ 3,700-passenger sister ships *Carnival Conquest*, *Carnival Glory*, *Carnival Triumph*, *Carnival Victory* and *Carnival Liberty*).
On-board style: bold, brash and buckets of fun, this is where America's blue-collar workers let their hair down. The décor can be kitsch, but high quality, and children's facilities are excellent.

Perfect for: Party lovers of all ages, young families, singles on the razzle.

Not for: Those in search of a quiet life.

● HOLLAND AMERICA LINE (www.holland america.com) is also owned by Carnival Corporation. It is a Premium operator which currently has 12 ships (plus one on order) ranging from the medium-sized 55,451-ton/1,266-passenger *Maasdam*, *Ryndam*, *Statendam* and *Veendam* to the large 81,769-ton/2,272-passenger *Oosterdam*, *Zuiderdam* and *Westerdam*.

On-board style: smart, elegant and traditional – the on-board décor harks back to the line's Dutch origins and includes some genuine antiques.

wall, themed nightclub, 1950s' diner, roller-blading circuit and full-size ice rink on board. The cruise line's next three ships – headed by *Freedom of the Seas*, first to launch in 2006 – will be by far the world's largest cruise ships to date – at a massive 160,000 tons apiece.

On-board style: attractive décor adds a touch of class to Royal Caribbean's mega-ships, although many public rooms are open plan, so it's difficult to feel really cosy.

Perfect for: families, sporty types, those who enjoy a lively atmosphere but hate kitsch.

Not for: some older people, or the less mobile,

Perfect for: older travellers, traditionalists.

Not for: party people or families outside school holidays – the line's older ships do not have many children's facilities.

● ROYAL CARIBBEAN INTERNATIONAL (www. royalcaribbean.com). Royal Caribbean's 19 ships range from the 48,563-ton/1,600-passenger *Empress of the Seas* to the 137,280-ton/3,114-passenger *Adventurer of the Seas*, *Explorer of the Seas*, *Mariner of the Seas*, *Navigator of the Seas* and *Voyager of the Seas*, each with its own rock-climbing

who may find making their way round the huge ships a challenge.

● CELEBRITY CRUISES (www.celebrity.com) is also owned by Royal Caribbean. It is a Premium line which has 10 ships with a further two on order. Size range is from the 46,811-ton/1,354-passenger *Zenith* to the 90,288-ton/1,950-passenger *Millennium*, *Summit*, *Infinity* and *Constellation*.

On-board style: elegance for big-ship lovers; the giant new ships have lovely top-grade suites and beautiful spas, while the older, smaller ships are less well equipped but more cosy.

Perfect for: young(ish) high achievers who want to let their hair down; health fanatics.

LEFT: relaxing in the hot tub on board *Wind Song*.
ABOVE: on *Royal Odyssey*.

Not for: serious drinkers (high prices); lovers of good entertainment – but, on the whole, the shows are unimaginative.

● **PRINCESS CRUISES** (www.princesscruises. com). Carnival-owned, US-based line which has 14 ships (with two more on order). Its largest is the 116,000-ton/3,800-passenger *Caribbean Princess*.

On-board style: a British flair for organisation combined with American pizzazz puts this Premium-class line a notch above others. Clever buffet restaurant design means that you'll rarely have to queue up for your meal, and disembarkation and shore excursion departures are

handled with military precision, minimising the annoying loudspeaker announcements.

Perfect for: people who love the facilities of big ships but not the hassle that goes with them.

Not for: people who like to be spoon-fed (you'll be given a time and place for embarking on a tour, then it's up to you); families – smaller ships have few family facilities.

● **NORWEGIAN CRUISE LINE** (www.ncl.com). The main NCL brand covers nine Contemporary ships (with two more on order), ranging from the 38,000-ton/1,462-passenger *Norwegian Majesty* to the 90,000-ton/2,240-passenger *Norwegian Dawn*, *Norwegian Star* and *Norwegian Jewel*. A separate Hawaii-based brand,

NCL America, has two ships – the 77,104-ton/2,450-passenger *Pride of Aloha* and 81,000/2,440-passenger *Pride of America* – with *Pride of Hawaii* sailing from 2006. A subsidiary of the Far East-based Star Cruises, NCL has adapted Star's "Freestyle" concept of casual, multi-restaurant cruising, preferred by many Western travellers.

On-board style: relaxed and friendly, with lovely restaurants, attractive deck areas and good entertainment (including full-scale Broadway shows). Late check-out on disembarkation day is a rare – and real – boon to travellers facing transtlantic flights home. As on most of the big-ship lines, tipping levels are hefty (around US$10 per person per day, with a 15 percent service charge added to all drinks bills).

Perfect for: families, young couples, people who like to mix and enjoy big ships with style.

Not for: those who like formality.

● **COSTA CRUISES** (www.costacruises.com). Another Carnival subsidiary, Contemporary-class Costa Cruises has 10 ships (with three more on order). They range from the mid-sized 24,430-ton/820-passenger *Costa Allegra* to the 105,000-ton/3,470-passenger sister ships *Costa Magica* and *Costa Fortuna*. All have a distinctly European feel, since the company was founded by Italians and has a strong following in Italy and other European countries. It has a range of winter Caribbean cruises, spanning eastern and western routes from Fort Lauderdale, and including Panama cruises from Miami covering the Southern Caribbean from La Romana in the Dominican Republic.

On-board style: expect later meal times than on American-dominated ships, as well as livelier bars and cafés, lessons in Latino dances like the *lambada* rather than the usual line dancing, and an international crew who are happy to let linguists practise on them, although English is the main on-board language.

Perfect for: Europhiles who enjoy a lively cosmopolitan atmosphere

Not for: those who like to dine in peace (Italian exuberance en masse can get *very* noisy); lovers of comedy – entertainment is dominated by magicians and singers, thus avoiding language problems with an international audience.

● **DISNEY CRUISE LINE** (www.disney.com/ DisneyCruise). The entertainment giant broke into cruising with the 83,338-ton/1,750-passenger *Disney Magic* in 1998, launching the sister-ship *Disney Wonder* a year later. Both ships spend all year in the Caribbean sailing from Disney's own dedicated terminal at Florida's Port Canaveral. Cruises can be packaged to include stays at Walt Disney World and, as you might imagine, the children's facilities on board these floating theme parks are dazzling (Disney characters mingle with young guests and even tuck them in at night).

But Disney has also gone all-out to attract child-free couples, too, offering them an elegant Italian restaurant, one swimming pool and particular areas of each ship designated for adults only.

On-board style: elegance with a touch of Disney magic; highlight of each ship is the Animator's Palate dining room, which goes from black and white to full-colour as you dine.

Perfect for: families and Disney fans.

Not for: those who are not enamoured of Mickey Mouse.

European lines

Mega-ships may dominate the Caribbean but there are also plenty of options for travellers who prefer a more intimate or unusual holiday. Broadly, these can be broken down into several categories. First, there are European lines with older or smaller ships. These lines include:

● **MSC Cruises** (www.msccruises.com) has become a cruise line to watch in recent years. From small beginnings running older ships like the 600-passenger *Monterey*, the 768-passenger *Rhapsody* and the 1,064-passenger *Melody*, the Italian line forged ahead with a major fleet development programme in the early years of the 21st century, and currently has a seven-strong fleet comprising the older ships, the 2003 and 2004 vessels *Lirica* and *Opera*, and the former Festival Cruises ships *Armonia* and *Sinfonia*. With two more ships on order, MSC has dramatically expanded its presence in the Caribbean during the winter – good news for Europhiles who will enjoy the ships' "Italy at Sea" ambience.

● **Ocean Village Cruises** (www.ocean villageholidays.co.uk). A sub-brand of P&O and Princess Cruises (which is itself a sub-

sidiary of the Carnival Corporation), go-getting, youth-orientated Ocean Village gains a second ship in 2007, when the 70,000-ton, 1,690-passenger *AidaBlu* switches from Carnival's German Aida Cruises to join the 64,000-ton, 1,600-passenger *Ocean Village*.

The operator runs budget-priced cruises around the Mediterranean during the summer months and the Caribbean in winter, using Barbados as its base and offering a range of cruise-and-stay packages at hotels around the island. Ports of call on its seven-night itineraries (which operate alternately so can be combined into a back-to-back 14-day sailing)

CARGO CRUISES

If you feel like something really different, many cargo ship lines have a few cabins for use by passengers, and these are worth considering as an unusual way to sail around the West Indies. You certainly won't be just one of a crowd – in fact, they carry so few passengers, that you could feel like a character in an Agatha Christie thriller. The down side is that they call at freight, not passenger, terminals (so there will be few facilities) and sailing times are based on the rate at which cargo can be loaded and discharged – so there is no fixed schedule. Strand Voyages (tel: 020 7836 6363) and Andrew Weir Shipping (tel: 020 7265 0808) are two of the UK's top agencies.

LEFT: keeping busy in the fitness centre on *Crystal Symphony*.
RIGHT: people-watching at the café promenade on *Explorer of the Seas*.

include Isla Margarita, off the Venezeulan coast, and the Caribbean islands of Dominica, St Lucia, Grenada and St Kitts.

Aimed predominantly at British travellers, Ocean Village appeals to younger holidaymakers with a taste for adventure, offering offbeat, action-packed shore excursions such as cycle tours and rainforest hikes.

Cruises from UK ports

If you are a UK resident and you like a home-from-home environment on your travels, or if you don't want to fly to the embarkation port, there are a number of Caribbean cruises

starting from the UK, run by major operators. For more details, contact **P&O Cruises** (www.pocruises.com), **Cunard Line** (www.cunardline.com) or **Fred Olsen Cruise Lines** (www.fredolsen.co.uk).

These cruises usually last at least three weeks, so they tend to attract a high proportion of retired people who have more time to spare. P&O is generally best for family holidays.

Luxury ships

If you have a taste for luxury and the money to go with it, try a Caribbean cruise aboard a luxury ship. Five-star operators include **Silversea Cruises** (www.silversea.com), **SeaDream**

Yacht Club (www.seadreamyachtclub.com), **Yachts of Seabourn** (www.seabourn.com) and **Radisson Seven Seas Cruises** (www.rssc.com). All these companies have fleets of smallish deluxe vessels offering top-class cuisine and service, all-suite accommodation and, in some cases, all-inclusive prices. Also the ships can usually slip into the region's smaller exclusive ports, like St Barts.

Another five-star-plus operator is **Crystal Cruises** (www.crystalcruises.com), which offers similar service and facilities on somewhat larger ships. Expect spacious, elegant surroundings and a high standard of service.

Oceania Cruises (www.oceaniacruises.com) is a Miami-based luxury operator with a predominantly American clientele. Its three mid-sized ships have open-seating dining options and upmarket accommodation, and itineraries include some overnight stays.

All of these deluxe cruise lines operate worldwide itineraries, including Caribbean sailings.

Sailing ships

Windstar Cruises (www.windstarcruises.com), **Windjammer Barefoot Cruises** (www.windjammer.com) and **Star Clippers** (www.starclippers.com) all have sailing ships in the Caribbean for all or part of the year. They are a popular option for people who want to be on the water but don't want the whole big ship cruise experience *(see The Caribbean Under Sail page 93)*.

Windstar is the poshest (but it's sail assisted, so runs largely on engine power); Windjammer is affordable, with few frills but great fun; while on Star Clippers' tall-masted ships, passengers can learn the ropes by helping the crew hoist sails – but only if they want to.

Repositioning cruises

While some ships spend all year in the Caribbean, others go there only for the winter months, spending the summer in the Mediterranean, the Baltic or Alaska. Joining them for what is called a repositioning sailing to or from the Caribbean (flagged in the spring and autumn sections of brochures) is a good way to tour the region and enjoy a long-ish cruise on the cheap. ❑

ABOVE: taking a night time dip in *Norwegian Dawn*'s floodlit pool.

The Big Time

For entertainers on a cruise ship, every night is show night. Ship-based singers, dancers, comics and musicians are likely to be called on to turn out shows in several different styles, seven days a week. Musicians could be playing calypso and reggae at the poolside during the day, providing smooth jazz at sunset, then dashing to the theatre for the song-and-dance spectacular. Come the midnight hour, they could well be the cool combo maintaining the beat at the disco. A dancer will also be making quick changes – by day a salsa teacher, by night, member of the Jets in *West Side Story*.

Ian Brock, a British musical director employed by Celebrity Cruises, says, "Players have to have a strong musical background and be able to sight-read music, but even more important is the ability to think on your feet. If you're backing a singer, it could be a guest celebrity or even a passenger. You have to adjust your style and tempo, sometimes even the key, to suit." Ian, who got some of his own musical training with the Royal Marines Band, is clearly hooked. He has been a band leader on the seas for five and a half years.

For dancers, the demands are even tougher. As well as turning out two or three shows a day – physically strenuous enough to tax many athletes – there is the small matter of a moving stage. Andreas Rashchke, Dance Captain on the *Galaxy* explains, "Jumps are just a little more adventurous on ship than they are on land. You have to guess where the stage is going to be when you land." At least they get some time to practise. Dancers for a major show often rehearse for four weeks in Las Vegas, then two weeks on board before leaping into the footlights.

Unfortunately, many cruise line executives, who know little or nothing about entertainment, still believe that sophistication consists of plumes and large feather boas paraded by showgirls who *step* but don't *dance*.

Musicians are usually expected to work the day they arrive. If a guest celebrity is joining the ship, the band may get an hour's rehearsal. "That's mainly for the guest's benefit, though," says Brock, wryly.

Contracts for ship-board entertainers are typically for six months. Non-US citizens on American

cruise lines are exempt from US income tax, which is one reason so many entertainers come from Europe or even further away. They are also paid in American dollars, which appeals to people like Rashchke, who, as a South African, enjoys a very good exchange rate when he takes his wages home. There are no bills to pay on board – food and accommodation are included, with a bar, a mess and a gymnasium strictly for the crew.

To keep a freshness to the shows, a cruise line may move headline performers from ship to ship every few weeks or so, meaning that entertainers tend to live out of suitcases. Like so many who work for cruise lines, either they get hooked by life

on the waves, or they quit after as short an engagement as possible.

All show-folk insist that they have been forced to become more flexible than when performing on shore. Weather conditions are checked daily, even hourly, with the captain. If a ship is heading for stormy waters, dancers may have to rethink their steps, and a magician may have to replace the juggling section of his act. In moderate weather, the band may strike up *Singing in the Rain*, but in a hurricane, they may have to play a part in soothing the passengers. As the *Titanic* went down, the band in the ballroom really did continue playing, heroically taking the spirit of "the show must go on" about as far as it's possible to go. ❏

RIGHT: for a ship's dancers, such as those on the *Crown Princess*, the demands are high.

THE CARIBBEAN UNDER SAIL

The choice is vast, from a crewless bareboat to the legendary super-yacht
aboard which Maria Callas supposedly sang along with Frank Sinatra

A sign in a Tortola bar reads: "Yachting – the fine art of feeling sick, getting wet and going nowhere at great expense." Given that the British Virgin Islands promise the finest sailing waters in the Caribbean, any nautical mockery is presumably tongue-in-cheek. Boats and the British Virgin Islands go together like sun and sea. For aspiring sailors, the Caribbean has it all: marinas full of sleek yachts; safe anchorages and classic coves; gentle trade winds and perfect sweeps of sand; waterfront bars and beach-side barbecues; cutlasses and casks of rum; coral reefs and chic regattas.

As the Caribbean epicentre of the yachting world, Antigua has a similar status to Newport or Annapolis in American eyes. The island's picturesque English Harbour comes alive for regattas, when sailing craft manoeuvre around the headlands much as they did centuries ago. Antigua Sailing Week (late April) is the highlight of the Caribbean yachting calendar, held before the sleekest yachts cross the Atlantic to summer in the Mediterranean. Every class of boat competes, from racing sloops and cruising yachts to catamarans and trimarans. The climax, the Antigua Classic Yacht Regatta, sees hulking schooners and ketches pitted against converted oyster boats and fishing smacks, as well as flashy J-class super-yachts.

Island hopping

Regattas aside, island hopping by yacht is the ultimate way to appreciate the Caribbean. Compared with the Mediterranean, the Caribbean offers greater challenges, with the constant trade winds suiting more experienced sailors. A flotilla option makes sense for bareboat novices. To be on the safe side, cautious sailors can usually join a "learning flotilla" at home, which ensures a few coaching sessions and short sailing trips prior to embarking on the adventure. But for aspiring sailors who barely know port from starboard, a fully-crewed charter,

complete with captain and cook, is the soft option, allowing clients to decide the itinerary and the extent of any hands-on sailing.

However, at the stretch-limousine end of the market, super-yachts come complete with the peaked-cap servility of a captain and a multi-talented crew, as well as services befitting a

shipping tycoon. Indeed, the yacht belonging to the late Aristotle Onassis can now be chartered by clients who only feel at home with a deck-side heli-pad or staterooms hung with Old Masters; even the swimming pool converts into a dance-floor where Rudolf Nureyev once pirouetted, and where Maria Callas supposedly sang along with Frank Sinatra. Sailing in such style should guarantee admiring glances from the in-crowd. Ocean-going snobs will be delighted to point out the sleek super-yachts owned by the Italian fashion mafia, from Armani to Prada and Valentino, or by princely sailors such as the Aga Khan, King Juan Carlos of Spain, and the Crown Prince of Denmark.

LEFT: a sailing ship off the coast of St Lucia.
RIGHT: Sandy Bank Bay, St Kitts.

Plain sailing

The yacht charter companies offer all kinds of rental, from crewless bareboats to a skippered vessel for as many days as it takes to get your sea legs. Since a bareboat charter presumes sailing competence and confidence in plotting Caribbean routes unaided, it makes sense to opt for a skippered charter in the first instance. Best booked through a reputable yachting broker or a charter company, the craft range from simple 30-footers to sleek, luxury motor-cruisers. An owner-operated crewed yacht may be more personal, but the spell of the sea will be the same. Even the choice of a fully-crewed charter

should not feel second-best: the creak of canvas and the sound of the rope slapping the mast should still create a magical atmosphere.

Yachting snobs look askance at large flotillas, but it can be a wonderful way of stretching your sailing horizons, and is better than group therapy. It gives sailors the privacy of their own boat combined with support and safety in numbers and a social element. All flotillas have a lead boat with a company-approved skipper, as well as an engineer on call to the fleet. At the start, chart-briefing sessions cover the itineraries, the schedule and social events, including optional kayak and dingy races, picnic lunches, and rum-punch parties.

For a successful bareboat cruise, flotillas are generally limited to 12 boats, with couples chartering 30-footers, and families opting for a boat from 40 to 52 ft (13–17 metres) in length. Before embarking on a bareboat charter, it is essential to consider issues of privacy and luxury as well as such standard sailing concerns as the boat's speed, stability and handling qualities under sail and power. After deciding between chartering a mono-hull and a catamaran, and agreeing on the number of berths and cabins required, sailors need to ponder the size and scope of the facilities: can you cope with cooking in a tiny galley? Is a beautifully varnished teak interior really essential?

Despite the likelihood of clear, sunny skies and light breezes, tranquillity can swiftly give way to the adrenalin rush of challenging the winds and the waves in stormy conditions. In the hurricane season, squalls from a tropical depression can sizzle into full-blown storms with swells and winds gusting at well over 50 knots. Many a crew has been forced to batten down the hatches waiting for a storm to pass. Even heavy fogs and high winds can force the craft to stay tied to its mooring buoy. At worst, in the case of a capsized catamaran, which remains upside-down if rolled, the crew may have to resort to the escape hatch in the floor.

The tall ships tradition

If a commitment to real sailing is a charter too far, a cruise under sail still provides a liberating change from the constraints of a typical cruise ship. Several cruise lines hark back to the era of traditional sailing ships, each with a different ethos and a distinctive spin on the tall ships' theme. Yet what these sailing ships share is the fostering of a sense of camaraderie, a carefree informality and a close connection with the sea. Passengers are encouraged to think of themselves as swashbuckling adventurers, even if most swashbuckling is restricted to a knot-tying session or the telling of salty tales.

The sense of adventure is sustained by the sailing ships' ability to sweep into smaller ports, to moor at picturesque marinas and to drop anchor at deserted beaches, delivering the elusive dream to latter-day Robinson Crusoes.

At the luxury end of the market, Windstar operates contemporary sail-cruise ships, inspired by clippers from the golden age of seafaring (*see Tall Ships, page 39*). These sleek, sexy, mega-yachts have encased cutting-edge engineering in a classic clipper shell but remain compact enough to slip into the smaller Caribbean ports. The illusion of adventure and nautical nostalgia is sustained by tall masts and lashings of teak and brass. In reality, the computer-controlled sailing rig ensures that the sails are unfurled with a touch of a button from the bridge. Although these cruise-sail ships need engine power to sweep them into port, the engines are turned off for spells at sea to display

DRASTIC MEASURES

Seasoned sailors say the only real disaster is having to break open emergency rations: choppy seas are nothing compared with the prospect of yet another tin of tuna.

rigger. Here, novices learn how to distinguish an inner jib from a fore topmast stay-sail, or a mizzen royal topsail from a spanker-gaff topsail. Since sail-trimming is focused on the bow and amidships, the stern is left to those more interested in a tan than in the intricacies of sailing.

The indulgent crew also lets passengers help with deck duties, from raising the sails to climbing the masts (in harness) and trying to keep the deck shipshape. In time, even the least nautically minded find themselves negotiating

the ship under full sail. Moreover, the illusion of sailing is particularly convincing during a dinner on deck, when the grand opera of wind, rope and canvas combines beneath a starry sky.

If Windstar represents sophisticated replicas, Star Clippers are real sailing ships, operated by dedicated seamen with a passion for tall ships. Passengers can watch the crew working on an authentic sailing ship, engrossed in winching, hoisting, trimming or repairing the sails, and can even attend classes on sailing a square-

coils of rope on the teak deck, ducking under booms, climbing up to the crow's nest, hauling in the sails, taking a turn at the wheel, wandering to the open-air bridge to chat with the captain, watching a sunset from the bowsprit, or even snoozing in the bow netting, the giant hammocks suspended over the sea. By the end of a cruise, a whole afternoon can pass in solitude, spent leaning over railings watching the sea crashing against the bows, interrupted only by dolphins prancing in the bow wake.

In essence, Star Clippers provide soft adventure and a swashbuckling atmosphere, evoking the romance of life on a luxury yacht a century or so ago. These are traditional square-riggers,

LEFT: a ship anchored off one of the most beautiful beaches in the Caribbean: Trunk Bay, St John, USVI.
ABOVE: be part of the crew on a small sailing vessel.

The Deep Sea

Whales, dolphins, sharks, hawksbill turtles and stingrays are among the impressive creatures that inhabit Caribbean waters. Most cruise lines organise marine life excursions, from scuba trips and submarine voyages to big game fishing or whale and dolphin safaris.

Stingray City on Grand Cayman is an opportunity for tame, velvety-skinned stingrays to get fed by fish-wielding cruise passengers. For divers, it is also the place for dramatic drop-offs encrusted with colourful corals or sponges, some of which

can be seen from the comfort of a mini-submarine. Smaller ships, especially those under sail, visit such islands as Bequia, where giant turtles can be seen in their natural habitat. Hawksbill and leatherback turtles can also be spotted in Barbados, around Christchurch, where a conservation scheme is in operation. Visitors arriving by yacht need to be careful to avoid stepping on one of the creatures who come ashore here to lay their eggs.

The Caribbean has a number of marine parks, from the Cayman Islands to Bonaire, all swarming with rainbow shoals of wrasse, groupers, snappers, angelfish and barracuda. Sea turtles, stingrays, mantas, reef sharks and even whale-sharks also lurk in these waters. If serious diving appeals, then the Caymans, Grenada, Tobago and Bonaire represent some of the best sites in the Caribbean. Exhilarating dives visit historic shipwrecks or lurch into dramatic drops. The 1977 film *The Deep* was shot around the wreck of the *Rhone* off the British Virgin Islands. Today, the wreck, which sank in 1867, is part of a marine park, home to a kaleidoscope of tropical fish, as well as pods of humpback whales, who bring their calves here between January and March. Several islands offer submarine (or semi-submersible) trips to explore marine life: Aruba, Curaçao, Barbados and Grand Cayman are popular destinations. St Thomas provides a memorable marine experience: delicate corals and rainbow-coloured fish are visible from a submarine and an underwater observatory.

Excursions involving frolics with dolphins are a feature of the Mexican and Costa Maya itineraries, as well as off the coasts of St Lucia and Dominica. Bottle-nosed dolphins surf the seas in search of food, leaping out of the waves like faulty torpedoes. Six dorsal fins may swim into view before the dolphins arch out of the water, dancing backwards on their tails, spinning into the distance. These boisterous, inquisitive creatures love food, games and attention, so greet every new cruiseload of passengers with unabated affection.

Whale-watching excursions are a popular attraction, with a classic whale and dolphin safari offering a 90 percent success rate in spotting both creatures, ideally between November and March. Using sonar tracking devices, expert sailors position their craft in an inviting position so that the whales move alongside, under the bow or the stern. Preceding a sighting is the acrid smell of whale's breath, a faint trace on the wind. But exhilaration swiftly follows: a lumbering whale will flick its vast tail-fin out of the water, or roll over, rocking back and forth to outstare you with a single eye.

As for sharks, they received unequivocal support from Jean-Michel Cousteau, son of the late Jacques Cousteau, during a visit to the British Virgin Islands. In his capacity as trustee of the marine park, Cousteau defended the killers: "Sharks have been around for 360 million years and humans for three million. The sharks' job is to clean up the seas of sick and wounded marine life", and should not be blamed for "mistakenly identifying a flapping white human for food". So there: simply accept your place in the great food chain of life. ❑

LEFT: a snorkeller and dolphin up close and personal in the open sea.

towering, four- or five-masted ships which are tall, fast and soaringly beautiful. The *Star Clipper*, a four-masted barquentine, was the first clipper sailing ship to be built for 140 years, and the first commercial sailing vessel to cross the Atlantic for 90 years.

The flagship *Royal Clipper* was modelled on the great steel *Preussen* which, at its launch in 1902, was the largest and fastest fully-rigged sailing ship of its age. This five-masted barquentine has 42 billowing white sails and masts 195 ft (60 metres) above the waterline. The blue and white hull is painted in the traditional chequer-board pattern of merchant sailing ships, designed to imitate gun-ports and hence deter pirates. Below decks, the antiquarian prints, burnished brass and nautical fittings are reminiscent of the grand age of sail, while the occasional choppy swell sloshing against the porthole acts as a reminder that this is a clipper voyage, not a cruise.

When itineraries permit, *Royal Clipper* and *Star Clipper* race one another off the coast of Dominica, with the start of the race signalled by the sound of a cannon. The ships rely on sail-power for up to 80 per cent of the time, with engine-power used only to ensure that the ships meet their schedules. The ships can do 15 knots under sail, but nine to 14 knots provides a smoother cruising experience.

Barefoot cruising

With its piratical feel, the less upmarket Windjammer Barefoot Cruises promise seafaring soft adventure, with a riotous twist. A rousing rendition of *Amazing Grace* is broadcast every time the ship's sails are hoisted. Since the boat is moored at a new port most days, on-board activities, such as knot-tying skills or a tour of the bridge, take place on sea days.

Evening entertainment is as laid-back as life on the tropical islands: sunset is heralded by complimentary rum punches, with the evening enlivened by a beach barbecue or guest appearances by melodic West Indian steel bands. The fleet includes several significant tall ships, including *Yankee Clipper* and *Legacy*, a French research ship converted into a traditional windjammer. Powered by both sails and engines, this four-masted barquentine slips into such

small islands as St Croix, Virgin Gorda and Jost van Dyke easily.

Itineraries

Both sailing ships and yacht charters benefit from being able to berth at islands slightly off the beaten track. The best sailing is generally to be had around the British Virgin Islands and the Grenadines, although each archipelago has its fans. The Grenadines, strung out between St Vincent and Grenada, are made for island hopping. The picture-postcard perfection of Mustique, Bequia and Tobago Cays has made the archipelago popular with celebrity residents and

sailing devotees, often one and the same. This air of exclusivity is sealed by the islands' relative inaccessibility: the lack of any significant anchorage means that no cruise ships call, apart from small, clipper-style craft.

The British Virgin Islands are the most popular sailing waters, blessed with endless anchorages and the comfort that nowhere is too far from anywhere else. Hundreds of islands face one another across Sir Francis Drake Passage, which separates the American and British Virgin Islands. Successions of secluded coves conceal eccentric beach bars which have acquired a loyal yachtie following.

Enhanced by a reputation as a sophisticated

RIGHT: a yacht mooring at the landing, Christiansted, St Croix, US Virgin Islands.

playground, the BVI have more sailing schools, bareboat yacht charter companies and flotilla sailings than anywhere else in the Caribbean. The range of watersports on offer simply confirms the islands' appeal to visiting sailors, from windsurfing and sea kayaking to swimming in quiet coves, snorkelling in eerie caverns, or diving to explore wrecks.

Not that the Virgin Islands have a monopoly on lovely bays and moorings. The Caribbean abounds in chic marinas and functional boatyards where sailors can service a yacht, take shelter, re-stock provisions, or re-plot routes. Soper's Hole Marina in Tortola on Frenchman's

Cay is a self-consciously quaint marina. With a working boatyard and chic pastel clapboard boutiques and bars, it's a carefree place where crews disappear into rum-drenched watering-holes. Neighbouring Jost van Dyke island is a particular favourite for its waterside bars.

Steep-sided Marigot Bay on St Lucia is one of the most pleasing anchorages in the Caribbean, while Bobby's Marina is where yachties touch base on St Maarten. On St Barts, Gustavia is the sophisticated capital, where a Swedish sense of order is softened by French *joie de vivre*. Antigua's English Harbour is equally chic but more historic, characterised by the Georgian complex of Nelson's Dockyard.

Anguilla is an exclusive haunt in the British Leeward islands, while Ile des Saintes is a delightful French dependency off Guadeloupe. Although off the cruise ship route, the Turks and Caicos are increasingly popular for their burgeoning resorts and secluded coves. In the Yucatán, Maya Caribbean, Calica and Cozumel make atmospheric alternatives to boisterous Cancún.

The call of the sea

Yet for all the pleasures of languishing in port or being pampered on a cruise, many people yearn to pit themselves against the elements. For the most adventurous, the ultimate voyage would be crewing a tall ship, whether a square-rigger, clipper, barque, barquentine, brig or topsail schooner. This is not beyond the reach of most landlubbers.

International sail-training associations encourage novice sailors to make their dreams come true at minimal cost. As a result, would-be buccaneers can board spartan schooners safe in the knowledge that their sailing skills will be developed and truly tested.

The timelessness of life on a sailing ship remains the same, as do the duties of keeping watch, scrubbing down the decks, and forming human chains to heave the endless ropes. In a crisis, recruits could find themselves changing sails on a foredeck submerged under water. There are subtle rewards for keeping everything shipshape. For the endless painting of the ship's hull and the days of polishing brass at dawn, there are shanty songs to learn, new friends to tease and towering masts to climb in perfect sailing weather. A heightened sense of space and smell also ushers in new sensory pleasures, with the briny scent of the sea mixed with the smells of fresh paint and hot tar, of strong coffee and newly baked bread.

The greatest challenge is to re-enter the spirit of the great age of sail. Taking the night watch with a full moon overhead cannot fail to stir the imagination. The crashing of bow on water is mesmerising, as is the wind whistling in the rigging, and the hoisting and trimming of sails. The romance of the legendary sailing ships and the jauntiness of the Caribbean ports make a heady and irresistible combination. ❑

LEFT: the pretty clapboard shop of a spice seller, Road Town, Tortola, BVI.
RIGHT: the marina at Soper's Hole, Tortola, BVI.

PLACES

A guide to the most popular ports of call, with principal sites clearly cross-referenced by number to the maps

The chain of islands that stretches from off the southern coast of Florida to the north coast of Venezuela are diverse and fascinating places to visit. Add a warm climate cooled by trade winds and you have almost perfect cruising conditions. The proximity of the Caribbean islands to each other make them ideal ports of call for cruise ships, many of which attempt to take their passengers to paradise and back in just seven days.

Whether you want to slap on the sun lotion, read a good book and bask in the sun, dive in the sea to discover pristine coral reefs and shipwrecks, hike through a rainforest, or explore Maya ruins, a Caribbean cruise can give you a taste of all of these things and more.

The Places section aims to cover the most popular ports of call, which make up the three most typical Caribbean cruise routes: western, eastern and southern. The following chapters have practical advice about excursions, to help make the most of your time ashore, includes attractions in the Caribbean and ventures to places not considered part of the region, such as Bermuda and the Bahamas, Mexico and Central America, but which are often included on cruise itineraries.

A western cruise route almost always begins in Florida, which is also a convenient choice for a pre- or post cruise stopover. This itinerary is ideal for diving enthusiasts, who can take a trip to some of the best dive sites in the western hemisphere: in Belize, Honduras and the Cayman Islands. Dry land excursions include the Maya ruins of Chichén Itzá in Mexico and Tikal in Guatemala.

An eastern itinerary takes travellers to the Bahamas, with its collection of private islands, and to Spanish-influenced Puerto Rico and Cuba, though the latter is off-limits to most US residents. St Thomas, part of the US Virgin Islands, has more than a little something for the shopaholics in Charlotte Amalie.

The southern cruise route is where you'll find some of the best beaches and picturesque towns in the British Virgin Islands, dense rainforests and the dramatic Trafalgar Falls in Dominica, and the spectacular peaks that are symbols of St Lucia – the Pitons. Only the small cruise and sailing ships can reach the 30 or so islands and cays in the Grenadines, many of which remain unspoilt by tourism. Often the final stop on this route is Aruba or Curaçao, which lie just off the north coast of Venezuela. Curaçao's capital, Willemstad, provides an insight into the Dutch Caribbean with its colonial architecture that is reminiscent of Amsterdam. ❑

● *For more detailed information on a particular destination, note that there are conveniently portable Insight Pocket Guides and Insight Compact Guides to most major Caribbean islands.*

PRECEDING PAGES: the Carenage, St George's, Grenada; snorkelling in the Bahamas; on the beach at La Sagesse Nature Centre, Grenada.
LEFT: crystal clear water, Coco Plum Caye, Belize.

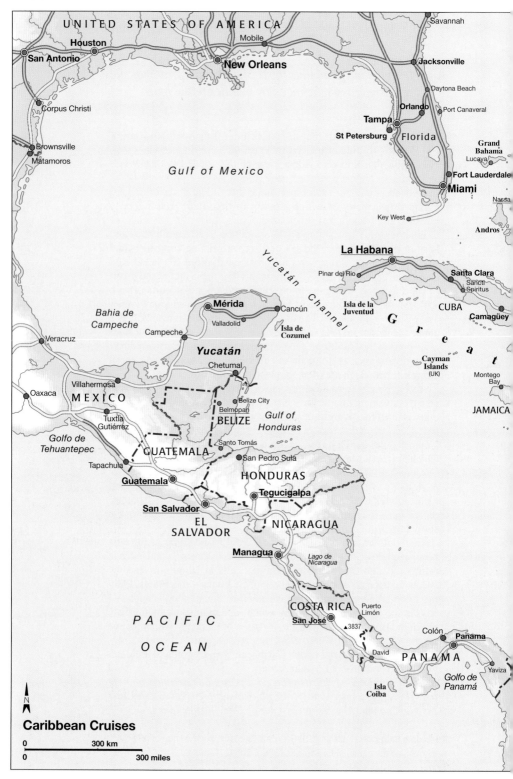

Caribbean Cruises

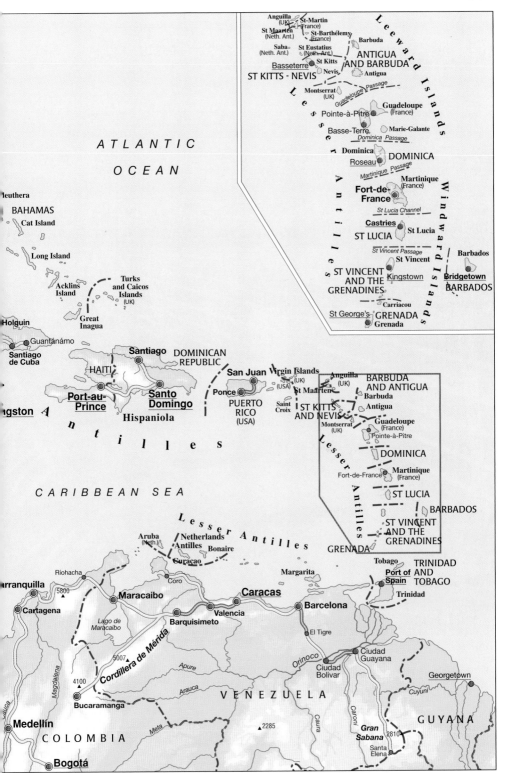

Anguilla (UK)
St-Martin (France)
St Maarten (Neth. Ant.)
St-Barthélemy (France)
Barbuda
Saba (Neth. Ant.)
St Eustatius (Neth. Ant.)
ANTIGUA AND BARBUDA
Basseterre
St Kitts
ST KITTS - NEVIS
Nevis
Antigua
Montserrat (UK)
Guadeloupe Passage
Pointe-à-Pitre
Guadeloupe (France)
Basse-Terre
Marie-Galante
Dominica Passage
Dominica
DOMINICA
Roseau
Martinique Passage
Martinique (France)
Fort-de-France
St Lucia Channel
Castries
St Lucia
ST LUCIA
St Vincent Passage
St Vincent
Barbados
ST VINCENT AND THE GRENADINES
Kingstown
Bridgetown
BARBADOS
Carriacou
St George's
GRENADA
Grenada

Leeward Islands
Lesser
Antilles
Windward Islands

A T L A N T I C

O C E A N

Eleuthera
BAHAMAS
Cat Island
Long Island
Acklins Island
Turks and Caicos Islands (UK)
Great Inagua
Holguin
Guantánamo
Santiago de Cuba
HAITI
Santiago
DOMINICAN REPUBLIC
Port-au-Prince
Santo Domingo
Hispaniola
ngston
San Juan
Ponce
PUERTO RICO (USA)
Saint Croix
Virgin Islands (UK) (USA)
Anguilla (UK)
St Maarten
BARBUDA AND ANTIGUA
Barbuda
Antigua
ST KITTS AND NEVIS
Montserrat (UK)
Guadeloupe (France)
Pointe-à-Pitre
DOMINICA
Fort-de-France
Martinique (France)
ST LUCIA
BARBADOS
ST VINCENT AND THE GRENADINES
GRENADA

A n t i l l e s
Lesser Antilles

C A R I B B E A N   S E A

Lesser Antilles
Aruba (Neth.)
Netherlands Antilles
Bonaire
Curaçao
Coro
Margarita
Tobago
Port of Spain
TRINIDAD AND TOBAGO
Trinidad
Riohacha
rranquilla
5800
Maracaibo
Caracas
Barcelona
Cartagena
Lago de Maracaibo
Valencia
Barquisimeto
El Tigre
Georgetown
Cordillera de Mérida
5007
Magdalena
4100
Apure
Ciudad Guayana
Ciudad Bolívar
Orinoco
Cuyuni
Medellín
Bucaramanga
Arauca
V E N E Z U E L A
2285
Meta
Cauca
Caroni
Gran Sabana
28104
G U Y A N A
C O L O M B I A
duca
Bogotá
Santa Elena

CHOOSING A ROUTE

Map on page 108

The tastes and interests of cruise passengers are diverse and the choice of trips can be confusing. This chapter offers advice on how to identify the cruise that will suit you best

If all you want to do is eat, sleep and indulge in the luxurious amenities found on most cruise ships, it doesn't matter all that much which route you take. But if your goals are more specific, the route you choose can matter a great deal. Have you always dreamed of scuba diving along the Cayman Trench? Would you like to climb an ancient pyramid? Pay homage to Bob Marley's music? Mingle with the Carib Indians? Sprawl out on a deserted beach? See where Nobel Prize-winning authors Derek Walcott or V.S. Naipaul grew up? Swim with dolphins? Explore Dutch architecture? Sip afternoon tea on the veranda of a Great House? Ride jet-skis at full throttle? Attend services at the oldest synagogue in the Caribbean? Savour the exotic blooms of a tropical garden? Take in a cricket match? Wander around Empress Josephine's childhood home? Shop for a diamond-studded Rolex watch?

If any of these are on your list of things you'd like to do while on a Caribbean cruise, it's a good idea to read the glossy cruise brochures very carefully in order to determine which destinations are the most suitable.

Many companies and ships offer the same routes because they have already proved successful with millions of passengers. Logistically, most of these tried-and-tested itineraries make sense when you consider the geographic proximity of the islands involved. But even so, different cruises sailing on the same routes can vary enormously, and aside from specific activities or sites, there are a few important points to consider when choosing a route.

Specifics to consider

In an effort to pack more excursions into a shorter period of time, some cruise lines offer a different port of call every day. While these routes may be good for first-time visitors to the Caribbean who want to see as much of the region as they can, other passengers may find them overwhelming – if it's Tuesday it must be Trinidad, and so on. Although island-hopping like this can be stimulating and fun, it leaves little time to get to know a specific port of call. Memories of such a port-packed cruise can wind up being one big blur. They can also leave you feeling as if you need another week to recover from the trip once you get home.

How much time is spent in each port is an important factor. Does the shore excursion give a full day on the island, or just a few hours? If it's just a few hours and there's something you really want to see, you could wind up spending more time looking at your watch than at the sites in the port. Along with the number of hours allotted for the port, whether the ship actually docks at the pier or has to anchor offshore and ferry passengers to shore will affect the amount of time available for exploring the destination.

LEFT:
relaxing on *Voyager of the Seas.*
BELOW:
Jamaica's natural beauty, as seen at Reach Falls.

Once in the port, does the cruise line offer prearranged excursions that are clearly explained in advance? Or are you left at the pier to handle shore arrangements on your own? Prearranged trips are headache-free and are the most efficient way to explore a port of call but they can be expensive. Also, if you are going to sign up for a land excursion, you need to know if it includes some free time built into the schedule to allow you to wander around on your own.

Another good thing to ask is how many full days at sea the itinerary includes. Most Caribbean cruises have at least one when you see nothing but the sea. A few have two or three full days at sea. For some people, spending a whole day and night at sea with no port diversions is a calm and relaxing experience. For others, it can seem boring, monotonous and a waste of time.

The type of islands the cruise visits is something else to consider. Do you want a route that takes in the smaller countries of the Eastern and Southern Caribbean, the larger ones of the Western Caribbean, or a little bit of both? Do you want a route that takes in the most popular and most visited ports such as Nassau, St Thomas and San Juan? Or do you want one that visits quirky, off-the-beaten-track islands such as Dominica, Bequia and Tobago?

Lastly, there is the most important question to ask yourself when deciding on an itinerary. What do you want to see?

Best beaches

Trying to devise a "best beaches list" often leads to heated debates, but there are a few gems that most people agree upon. On Eastern Shores cruises some of the prettiest stretches of sand include Gold Rock Beach in Freeport, Cable Beach in Nassau, Harbour Island near Eleuthera, Puerto Rico's Luquillo Beach, Trunk

This vivid hibiscus bloom in the Queen Elizabeth II Botanic Garden, Grand Cayman, is typical of the Caribbean's tropical flora.

BELOW: Grand Anse beach, Grenada.

Bay and Francis Bay in St John, Orient Beach and Baie Longue in St Martin, Buck Island in St Croix, and Varadero Beach in Cuba.

Western Shores favourites are Negril Beach and Doctor's Cave in Jamaica, Seven Mile Beach in Grand Cayman, Smathers Beach in Key West, Labadee in Haiti, Ambergris Caye in Belize, Playa San Francisco and Playa del Carmen in Mexico, and Key Biscayne in Miami.

On the southern routes, top spots include Grand Anse in Grenada, the Platinum Coast in western Barbados, Cane Garden Bay in Tortola, St Jean Beach in St Barts, Half Moon Bay in Antigua, Anse Tarare in Guadeloupe, Grand Anse des Salines in Martinique, Palm Beach and Eagle Beach in Aruba, Pink Beach and Sorobon Beach in Bonaire, and almost all the pristine beaches in tiny Tobago.

Tropical gardens

Along with strolling on beaches, smelling the exotic floral scents of a tropical garden is another luscious treat, and several Caribbean islands have world famous botanical treasures. Among the prettiest is Martinique's Jardin de Balata in the hills outside Fort-de-France, where footpaths meander around giant ferns, lotus ponds, and sweet-smelling ylang-ylang trees. In Barbados, Andromeda Gardens is widely known for its variety of orchids, heliconias and cacti. St Vincent's Botanical Garden is said to be the oldest in the western hemisphere, and contains a breadfruit tree supposedly planted by Captain Bligh. Bath Garden in Jamaica dates back to the mid-1700s, when it was established by British colonials. The Bahamas has The Retreat in Nassau and Garden Groves in Freeport. And Puerto Rico's Jardín Botánico, just outside bustling San Juan, holds one of the most extensive collections of tropical plants in the world.

Map on page 108

Captain William Bligh transported breadfruit (artocarpus altilis) trees and plants from Tahiti to Jamaica in 1793. The breadfruit, which is a rich source of carbohydrate and B vitamins, were intended to provide food for the African slaves on the island.

BELOW: a voyager tree (*ravenala madagascariensis*) at Jardin de Balata, Martinique.

Great snorkelling and scuba sites

Although the larger cruise ships offer scuba and snorkelling excursions from many ports of call, the smaller lines such as Star Clippers, Windjammer and Windstar are better equipped to give divers a thrill because they can stop right at the best spots and allow passengers to dive overboard from the deck or from drop-down marinas at the stern of the ship.

Considered by many to be the best snorkelling experience in the world – not just in the Caribbean – Grand Cayman's Stingray City is top of the list for cruise stops because of its easy-to-access shoal, surrounded by friendly rays. Grand Cayman also has hundreds of official scuba diving sites where the steep drop-off of the Cayman Trench, along with dozens of sunken ships, provide some fascinating underwater adventures.

Saba has some of the finest diving in the area with about 40 official dive sites marked by black coral, underwater lava flows, and a vibrant assortment of marine life. Regularly described by *Scuba Diver* magazine as one of the top dive spots in the world, the waters off of St Croix provide dramatic underwater trails full of brilliantly coloured coral canyons. Nearby Trunk Bay on St John is also noted for its calm aquamarine waters and a 225-yd (205-metre) snorkelling trail, where underwater signs explain the resident marine life.

Other locations that regularly make it on to lists of best Caribbean dive sites include Palancar Reef and the Chankanab Lagoon near Cozumel, Blue Hole off Belize, Mary's Place near Roatán in Honduras, Town Pier off of Bonaire, the famed wreck of HMS *Rhone* in Virgin Gorda, the *Bianca C* wreck off of Grenada, Pinnacles off of St Lucia, Mushroom Forest off of Curaçao, and Ambergris Caye off the coast of Belize.

The stingray, a familiar symbol of the Cayman Islands, is featured on the label of a locally brewed beer.

BELOW: a visit to Stingray City is top of the list for many cruise passengers.

Other excellent snorkelling sites include the calm waters that surround Antigua, the shallow waters of Buccoo Reef in Tobago, the entire French side of St Martin, Coki Point Beach in St Thomas, the Curaçao Underwater Park, Shoal Bay East off of Anguilla, and the Baths off Virgin Gorda.

Map on page 108

Retail therapy

If it's shopping opportunities you are after, several Caribbean ports are known for their mega-shopping malls with duty-free stores full of brand-name goods. Typical items on sale in these modern enclaves include fine jewellery, watches, camera equipment, nautical maps and antiques, china, perfume, linen, clothing, leather goods, woodcarvings, local art and crafts, cigars and alcohol.

American shoppers often favour the Virgin Islands because the US government allows its citizens to bring US$1,200-worth of goods home tax free (from other islands the amount is $400). Puerto Rico is also a great place for American shoppers because it levies no taxes on goods brought into the US.

With more stores than any other Caribbean island, St Thomas is shopping heaven. In the capital, Charlotte Amalie, countless boutiques offer brand-name goods at discount prices. It's advisable to know the cost of things at home to ensure you are getting a good deal. And when several ships are in at once the atmosphere can be hectic, and the chances of negotiating lower prices are slim.

Charlotte Amalie is a shoppers paradise: reasonably priced goods on sale include quality local art and crafts. Shops are open on Sunday only when there is a cruise ship in town.

Grand Cayman also has a good shopping district, with hundreds of first-rate stores surrounding the port. Although many of the products sold here are quite expensive, they are usually of excellent quality, and the country has no sales tax. In the Bahamas, Freeport's International Bazaar features over 100 shops with vendors from around the world. Aruba and Curaçao are noted for a wide assort-

BELOW: shopping in Charlotte Amalie, US Virgin Islands.

ment of Dutch products, and the Dutch side of St Martin offers some of the best discounts on European products in the Caribbean. In Martinique and Guadeloupe French wines, food products and perfumes are abundant.

If collecting locally made arts and crafts is one of your holiday goals, there are a few things to look out for. San Juan is noted for its colourful carnival masks that look great on walls and Haiti is good for metal sculptures and primitive paintings. Batik fabrics are plentiful in Jamaica and Martinique. The finest straw baskets and hats, laboriously plaited by hand, can be found in the Bahamas. The best wood sculptures are made in Jamaica. Miniature model boats with minute, detailed work are made in St Vincent and the Grenadines.

The Dominican Republic is the place to buy amber, the honey-coloured gem that is turned into jewellery and trinkets by local artisans, since it is one of the few places in the world with a natural supply. In Saba, an intricate thread-knotting technique produces Saba lace, a trademark souvenir of this tiny Dutch island. The San Blas Islands of Panama, and the Port of Colón near the Panama Canal, are noted for bold and beautiful embroidered *molas*. And in just about any port in Mexico you will find Taxco silver jewellery, clay pottery, hand-painted tiles and dishes, embroidered blouses, wool blankets, and naturally dyed textiles.

Private islands

If the idea of shoulder-to-shoulder crowds makes you cringe, choosing a route that visits a private island is the solution. Most cruise lines now have their own island – or at least a private beach – where they have created a perfectly controlled environment, free of the hassles found in most commercial ports. Naturally, the advantage of a private island is that passengers have it all to themselves, and are made to feel like visiting royalty.

Just about all of the private getaways offer a beautiful beach, lounge chairs, hammocks, swimming, snorkelling, volleyball, hire of sailing boats and jet-skis, children's play areas with supervised activities, ice-cold alcoholic drinks, and a gourmet picnic lunch. Some also provide live calypso or reggae music and the opportunity to buy goods made by local vendors.

Mostly found on routes to the Bahamas and the Eastern Caribbean, private island choices include Disney Cruise Lines' Castaway Cay in the Bahamas, Celebrity/Costa Cruises' Catalina Island off of the Dominican Republic, Royal Caribbean's Coco Cay in the Bahamas and Labadee in Haiti, Princess Cruises' Princess Cay in the southern part of the island of Eleuthera, Premier's Blue Lagoon Island near Nassau, and Great Stirrup Cay in the Bahamas used by both NCL and Holland America.

One note of caution: most private getaways are reached by tender, which means that they are occasionally skipped due to bad weather or choppy seas, so be prepared for this possible disappointment.

History and architecture

Although nature provides most of the best scenery on Caribbean cruises, there are destinations where history and architecture are the main characters in the local story. Some of the oldest and most dramatic can

TIP

Molas make great purchases. They are a kind of intricate patchwork made by the Kuna Amerindians of Panama.

BELOW: a fine example of an embroidered *mola* from Panama.

be found in Mexico, where the ancient Maya cities of Tulum and Chichén Itzá provide a vivid history lesson on pre-Columbian life.

Old San Juan in Puerto Rico and Santo Domingo in the Dominican Republic are the places to go for Spanish colonial architecture and history. Both have great bastions of defence in the form of old brick forts and arsenals, as well as grand Spanish-style mansions, relics from the age of Juan Ponce de León and Christopher Columbus, ancient cathedrals and excellent museums.

On the islands formerly colonised by the British, where sugar plantations once provided wealth for the settlers, many historic Great Houses still stand. Among the more interesting are St Nicholas Abbey and Sunbury Plantation House in Barbados, Rose Hall and Greenwood Great House in Jamaica, Montpelier Great House in Nevis, and Pedro St James in Grand Cayman. The French-colonised islands also have historic Great Houses – two of the most beautiful are Habitation La Grange in Martinique and Maison Zevalos in Guadeloupe.

Other enclaves of great architecture and history include the buildings in the old city of Willemstad in Curaçao, which are reminiscent of Amsterdam, Nelson's Dockyard National Park in Antigua, the ruins of Port Royal in Jamaica, El Morro the imposing fortress in Havana, and the ancient stone carvings – petroglyphs– executed by the Amerindians around AD 300 in Guadeloupe.

Popular shore excursions

Trying to rate shore excursions is difficult as it is often a matter of taste and interests, but there are a few in the Caribbean that are universal favourites.

The Xcaret Ecological Park near Playa del Carmen, Mexico, is a Disneyesque destination in itself, that fills a whole day with swimming, snorkelling, water

Map on page 108

BELOW: the ancient Maya ruins at Chichén Itzá.

TIP

Don't forget to pack sturdy walking shoes and waterproofs if you plan to hike through a rainforest such as Puerto Rico's El Yunque. Take a pair of jeans for a horseback riding excursion, and waterproof boots to protect your feet if you want to climb Dunn's River Falls in Jamaica.

rides, dolphin encounters, and ancient Mayan games. There is so much to do and see that passengers are often exhausted (but happy) when they return to the ship.

Excursions that offer rides on the Atlantis Submarines – in Barbados, Grand Cayman, Aruba and St Thomas – are always thrilling, informative and fun. A tour of the Carib Territory in Dominica gives visitors a chance to interact with the only real "natives" left in the Caribbean. Excursions to Puerto Rico's El Yunque rainforest, one of the most beautiful in the world, allow passengers to experience the lush, cool and extremely wet interior of a tropical island.

An trip to Jamaica's Dunn's River Falls, near the port of Ocho Rios, usually amazes visitors, giving them the best photo opportunity of their entire holiday. A side-trip to the town of Hell, in Grand Cayman, provides a good laugh and is the best place in the Caribbean from which to send postcards home.

Bicycle excursions in Bonaire, where the flat landscape is dotted with wild flowers and pink flamingos, are a delight for athletic nature lovers. Wandering around the Hato Caves in Curaçao, where there's a maze of grottos filled with stalactites, makes a surprisingly offbeat Caribbean tour. In St Lucia, a visit to the world's only "drive-in volcano" near the city of Castries affords passengers close-up views of a lava-filled crater and a thoroughly bizarre experience. Last of all, there are excursions that take passengers horse-riding on a beach – in Jamaica, St Lucia, St Thomas, Barbados, Tortola, St Martin or Aruba – which are often the perfect land-based diversion needed after several days at sea.

Round-up of the routes

The exact routes and ship allocations vary from year to year, but as a broad rule of thumb the main Caribbean cruise itineraries are:

- **Carnival Cruise Lines** offers cruises to the Eastern, Western and Southern Caribbean, and Panama Canal itineraries. Departure ports include Miami, Tampa, Port Canaveral, Baltimore, Houston, Jacksonville, New York and Galveston.
- **Celebrity Cruises** spans the Caribbean region departing from a range of ports that include Miami, Fort Lauderdale, Tampa and Jacksonville in Florida, San Juan in Puerto Rico, New York and Philadelphia in Pennsylvania.
- **Costa Cruises** operates 7-night Eastern and Western routes from ports such as Fort Lauderdale, Guadeloupe and La Romana in the Dominican Republic.
- **Crystal Cruises** offers a variety of Caribbean and Panama Canal cruises; some sail round-trip from Fort Lauderdale, or between Fort Lauderdale and Costa Rica, and a few link Tampa or Miami to Costa Rica.
- **Cunard** offers Caribbean cruises round-trip from Southampton, Fort Lauderdale and New York.
- **Disney Cruise Line** has Bahamas and Eastern Caribbean cruises based at their dedicated terminal at Port Canaveral, Florida.
- **Holland America Line** has Eastern, Western and Southern Caribbean cruises operating from the Florida ports of Fort Lauderdale, Port Canaveral and Tampa. The line also offers Panama Canal cruises linking Fort Lauderdale or Tampa with San Diego in California and Vancouver, Canada.

BELOW: children of all ages have fun at Xcaret in Mexico.

● **MSC Cruises** offers a variety of Caribbean and Panama Canal itineraries out of the Florida port of Fort Lauderdale.

● **Norwegian Cruise Line** offers Eastern, Western and Southern Caribbean itineraries from a wide range of ports including Miami, New York, Charleston in South Carolina and Houston, Texas.

● **Ocean Village** offers 7-day Eastern and Western Caribbean sailings out of Barbados in the Eastern Caribbean.

● **Princess Cruises** has Eastern, Western and Southern itineraries from Fort Lauderdale, Barbados and San Juan, and Panama Canal cruises from San Juan.

● **Radisson Seven Seas Cruises** spans the Eastern Caribbean from San Juan and the Western islands from Fort Lauderdale.

● **Royal Caribbean International** operates a wide range of itineraries spanning the Eastern, Western and Southern Caribbean and sailing from Miami, Fort Lauderdale, New York, Houston, San Juan, Boston and Baltimore.

● **SeaDream Yacht Club** visits offbeat ports along the Maya Riviera from Puerto Morelos (Cancun), as well as offering itineraries between St Thomas and St Martin via off-track islands such as Jost Van Dyke and Virgin Gorda.

● **Silversea Cruises** has arguably the most extensive spread of ports and itineraries, with sailings from Willemstad in Curacao and St John's in Antigua as well as more usual base ports like Fort Lauderdale and Bridgetown, Barbados.

● **Yachts of Seabourn** offers sailings from St Thomas, with other cruises based at Fort Lauderdale and Bridgetown, Barbados.

UK-based passengers who want to sail rather than fly to the Caribbean should try Cunard Line, P&O Cruises and Fred Olsen Cruises, all of whom offer some Caribbean itineraries on a return trip from the UK. ❑

Map on page 108

After Hurricane Katrina severely damaged the Port of New Orleans in 2005, Carnival, Crystal and NCL, temporarily relocated ships to ports in Mobile, Tampa and Galveston.

BELOW: boating in the mangrove swamps of Belize is a good choice.

Shore Excursions

Booking shore excursions is a guaranteed way of bumping up the cost of your holiday. One in each port of call on a seven-day cruise could add more than US$500 to the overall cost. So it is important to understand the benefits and limitations of these brief snapshots of island culture.

Shore excursions have improved dramatically as passengers become better travelled and more demanding. As the average age of the typical cruiser comes down, excursions revolve more around activities – kayaking, hiking, mountain biking, horse riding and scuba diving. This type of "soft adventure" is accessible to passengers of virtually all ages and fitness levels.

Caribbean cruising typically involves big ships and big numbers, so it is inevitable that you will feel regimented when 2,000 passengers pour down the gangway to a waiting fleet of coaches. If you want to travel at your own pace, mingle with the local people, sample street food and soak up the atmosphere, then you should do your own thing.

Pros and cons

Shore excursions are planned to give an overview of a destination or a taste of an activity, rather than a deep insight. You will travel by bus, usually (but not always) with an English-speaking group and guide, although some trips are by self-drive Jeeps, so remember to take your driving licence.

Having to pre-book shore excursions as soon as you board the ship takes away the spontaneity of visiting new places. Sadly, this is a fact of life; for the sake of logistics, numbers have to be finalised some days in advance. It is also a way of getting you to

part with your money upfront. The daily on-board talks on shore excursions can be a heavy sell, but they do present an opportunity to ask questions.

Many excursions do sell out, so it is worth researching the itinerary thoroughly before boarding. Some cruise lines, such as Royal Caribbean, Ocean Village and NCL, detail shore excursions on their websites and you can book even before joining the cruise.

Sometimes, it is difficult to better a cruise line's excursion. Scuba diving is a case in point. NCL's Dive In programme, for example, includes all equipment and instruction and some dives in resorts, all pre-arranged by diving experts. Seabourn, an upscale line, offers tailor-made excursions, including a chance to crew an America's Cup yacht in Philipsburg, St Maarten, in a mini-regatta.

Some excursions, though, seem pointless. At Nassau in the Bahamas, all the shops, most of the decent colonial architecture and the Straw Market are within easy walking distance of the port, yet cruise lines charge upwards of US$40 for a harbour cruise and tour of the grounds of the opulent Atlantis hotel.

Dolphin "encounters" are invariably disappointing. Typically, visitors stand waist deep in water while a solitary dolphin meanders around an enclosed area. A lot of beach excursions, too, are a waste of time, at up to US$50 for a morning on a beach; all you are paying for is the coach transfer.

Some of the better shore excursions in the Caribbean are the adventurous ones. Kayaking through the mangroves in Antigua, looking out for sea turtles and frigate birds; riding a horse across the highlands of Barbados; or hiking through the El Yunque rainforest in Puerto Rico. Perhaps the ultimate (and most expensive) trip is a descent to 800 ft (240 metres) down the Cayman Wall in a research submarine, to spot deep-water corals and deep sea life. The excursion, offered by most of the big lines or bookable privately, costs several hundred dollars a head and must be arranged in advance since the sub only takes two people, five times a day.

Planning your own excursion

When it comes to planning where to go, the shore excursion staff will be able to help, although they cannot be expected to have in-depth knowledge of every port. They will get their ground operator to arrange car rental, or

LEFT: water sports such as kayaking are popular.
ABOVE RIGHT: meet a dolphin, Roatán, Honduras.
RIGHT: at the butterfly farm, Aruba.

a taxi or minibus with guide, and assist with itinerary planning. Give as much notice as possible and don't expect it to be cheap. If your heart is set on something like tickets to a cricket match in Barbados, arrange it before you leave through a specialist operator. Book golf tee times well in advance, too. Don't be over-ambitious; you will have only a few hours and, if the ship is anchored outside the port, passengers on official excursions get priority for the tenders.

A taxi can make life easier; always agree the fare before you depart and pay only when you are back at the ship. Don't misjudge the journey time back to the port. A ship will wait for a delayed tour bus but not for a lost individual, and it is your responsibility (and expense) to rejoin the cruise at the next port.

Several Caribbean ports are perfect for self-guided tours. Take your own map as cruise lines often provide only rudimentary photocopies. In Bridgetown, Barbados, there are shops, galleries, markets and historic buildings a 15-minute walk from Deep Water Harbour, where ships moor up. The island is safe and easy to get around by car or minimoke – but allow time for getting lost in the country lanes, and the slow pace of traffic.

In busy, commercial St Thomas, hop on a ferry to the beautiful beaches of St John. Grand Cayman is regarded as a model island in terms of safety, cleanliness and a hassle-free attitude. Curaçao's capital, Willemstad, with bright buildings and pavement cafés, is easy to explore on foot. Chic, celebrity-studded St Barts can be explored in a day by hire car; the best beach is Colombier, a 30-minute hike from where the road ends. In St Vincent, hike up Mount St Andrew, near Kingstown, for incredible bird life and views.

Sometimes, though, DIY exploration is impractical. Car hire in Jamaica and St Lucia is expensive; distances are long and you may be hassled. If you don't want a coach trip, join forces with other passengers to book a minibus and enjoy the scenery rather than worrying about getting lost. ❑

SAILING THE WESTERN SHORES

Map on page 108

Western Shores cruises offer a fascinating first taste of the region, so they are a good idea for people who want to see if they will enjoy cruising, or those who have time only for a short break

Sailing through the Caribbean and the Gulf of Mexico, Western Shores cruises don't take in a great many countries, but the ones they do visit offer a condensed and varied introduction to the diverse cultures, histories and landscapes of the region. Occasionally, they also offer the added bonus of stopping at Central American ports of call, which can be a distinctly different experience from those found in traditional West Indian destinations of the Eastern or Southern Caribbean.

With departures from Miami, Fort Lauderdale, Tampa, Port Canaveral, New Orleans, which is being rebuilt after Hurricane Katrina hit, Houston and Galveston, Western Caribbean cruises don't travel as far as the Eastern or Southern Caribbean ones, and they tend to last for a week or less. This makes them perfect for first-time cruisers who want to test the waters but don't have much time to spare. Another advantage of Western Shore cruises is that they remain closer to the US coast, so it is much easier for a passenger to fly home in hurry, should an emergency arise. A further asset for American passengers of being closer to the US is that big and bulky souvenirs can be shipped home on a cargo vessel without it costing the earth. Last of all, the waters in this area are almost always placid and clear.

The Western Caribbean itinerary tends to appeal more (although not exclusively) to American holidaymakers, because it takes in ports that are more developed, more commercial, and have far more modern amenities than many of the smaller Caribbean islands. However, more developed and more commercial also means more *Americanised*, so Western Shores cruises may not appeal to people wanting to get away from areas of mass tourism.

Another thing to take into account when choosing a Western Shores route is that it does not offer the French West Indian flavour found in places such as Martinique, Guadeloupe, St Barts or St Martin. Nor does it have any Dutch Caribbean components. A few of the cruise lines – Royal Caribbean in particular – call into the Haitian port of Labadee, a private little beach usually described in brochures as being in Hispaniola (which contains both Haiti and the Dominican Republic). But Labadee is a protected and exclusive enclave, and doesn't offer much opportunity for interacting with the Haitian people or culture.

PRECEDING PAGES: passengers celebrate the ship's departure. **LEFT:** in South Beach's Art Deco district, Florida. **BELOW:** diving at Key Largo.

Western delights

The Western Caribbean still has plenty to offer, however – awesome Mayan Indian ruins, a stunning barrier reef, breathtaking waterfalls, sugary sand beaches, towering mountains, lush and exotic gardens, colonial history, designer goods at duty-free prices, championship golf courses, funky tropical architecture, colourful arts and crafts, pulsating reggae music, smooth Caribbean rum, potent Mexican tequila, and a chance to mail a postcard from a tiny town called Hell.

Ports of call

The specific routes described here are determined by which ports the ships depart from, but most Western Shores cruises take in very similar ports of call. Starting off in the US, at the southern tip of the Florida Keys chain, is Key West. Although it is not, of course, a Caribbean island, Key West has a definite Caribbean mentality and atmosphere. In fact, the city once jokingly tried to secede from the US, and declare itself the Conch Republic of Key West. It provides a gentle introduction to the more foreign destinations soon to come.

With a modern port near the historic Old Town area, Key West is easy to explore and is full of offbeat museums, gingerbread architecture, literary history, and eccentric characters. Aside from wandering around on foot, organised shore excursions of the city usually include a narrated trolley tour that stops at the Ernest Hemingway House, Key West Aquarium, the Mel Fisher Maritime Heritage Museum – a brick fort dating back to the American Civil War – and the Key West City Cemetery, where several tombstones are proof that the local people have a sense of humour – one reads: "I told you I was sick!"

As long as Cuba remains off limits to US-based cruises, a stop in Key West may be the closest many Americans will ever get to the island. Key West has a great deal of Cuban history of its own, and a wealth of art, antiques, maps and artefacts relating to the island are on display at the city's San Carlos Institute.

Key West is only 90 miles (145 km) from Cuba.

BELOW: Key West, Florida, has a Caribbean atmosphere.

Heading south

About 500 miles (800 km) southwest of Key West is the jewel in the crown of most Western Shores cruises – Mexico. The country's Yucatán Peninsula has several world-famous ports – Cozumel, Playa del Carmen, Costa Maya – that are extremely popular on this route. Along with the ancient Maya cities of Tulum and Chichén Itzá, where stone pyramids stand as sombre reminders of this once great culture, ports of call in the Yucatán have excellent beaches, great shopping, several water sports theme parks, internet cafés, and a lazy, laid-back lifestyle that quickly puts people at ease. Mexican ports also offer horse-riding trails, scuba diving and snorkelling excursions, botanical gardens, colonial architecture, museums full of pre-Columbian artefacts, and a chance to see crocodiles and jaguars in the wild.

Directly south of Mexico are the tiny, English-speaking Central American country of Belize and the larger, Spanish-speaking Honduras. Both these destinations are included on a few Western Shores cruises, and the main attraction is the barrier reef just offshore. Considered to be one of the best dive sites in the western hemisphere – if not *the* best – the reef is a natural wonder marked by brilliantly coloured coral. It also has several sunken ships and an assortment of exotic marine life. To access the reef in Belize, ships call into Belize City and offer passengers excursions by motor boat. In Honduras, they sail right into the Bay Island of Roatán where the reef is within swimming distance of the port.

Another major highlight on this itinerary is Grand Cayman, an English-speaking British colony known as a shoppers' paradise. Ships here sail into the capital city of George Town, where an endless assortment of duty-free stores lures passengers with fine quality jewellery, clothing, leather goods, camera

Map on page 108

New Orleans is the birthplace of Louis Armstrong.

BELOW:
Mardi Gras time in New Orleans.

TEXAS AND LOUISIANA

Several companies, including Carnival, Royal Caribbean, Celebrity and Princess, offer cruises from the Port of Galveston (tel: 409-765 9321) on the Gulf of Mexico. Itineraries usually include Mexico, Belize, Honduras, the Cayman Islands and Jamaica. Galveston is popular with American passengers who prefer not to fly to Florida to start their trip. Within walking distance from the port is the historic Strand District, with architecture listed on the National Register, and plenty of shops, restaurants and bars too. The Galveston Island Trolley is a good way to see the town, stops include the cruise terminal and the Silk Stocking Historic District. About 50 miles (80 km) north, the Port of Houston (tel: 713-670 2400) operates cruises to similar destinations, but as it is inland and requires a canal journey to the sea, it is less desirable than Galveston.

The Port of New Orleans (tel: 504-522 2551) was one of the busiest in the US, catering to luxury cruise liners and rusty old cargo freighters, but that was before Hurricane Katrina struck. The facilities are being rebuilt and should open again soon. The Julia Street Cruise Ship Terminal is conveniently located within walking distance of the French Quarter. Most cruises from here head for the Western Shores, especially Mexico's Yucatán Peninsula.

Map on page 108

equipment, crystal, china and silver. British, American and Canadian currencies are all accepted, which makes saying no to bargains even more difficult.

Easily arranged, excursions from George Town include snorkelling tours of Stingray City *(see page 114)*, and visits to the Cayman Turtle Farm, Cayman Islands National Museum, Queen Elizabeth II Botanical Park and Pedro St James – a classic West Indian Great House with an important colonial history. One excursion that most cruise passengers take in Grand Cayman is to the little town of Hell, where the urge to mail a postcard is almost impossible to resist.

Last on the list of Western Shores ports are Ocho Rios and Montego Bay, both on the English-speaking island of Jamaica. Much larger than Grand Cayman, Jamaica is a mountainous country with a clearly defined national identity that is apparent as soon as passengers come ashore.

As the most-visited port on the island, Ocho Rios often has several ships in port at once and at times can feel as congested as a big northern city. Excursions here are usually to Dunn's River Falls, where passengers climb barefoot near the 600-ft (200-metre) cascading waters. There are also horse-riding trips to Chukka Cove, rafting down the peaceful Martha Brae River, and bus tours to the grand plantation houses in the nearby countryside. If ships sail into Montego Bay, excursion options include the Rose Hall Great House, the Greenwood Great House, and the Old Fort Craft Park, where vendors sell woodcarvings, trinkets, straw baskets, and the locally made Appleton rum.

Departures and duration

While the specific routes and the number of nights that various cruise lines offer for Western Shores journeys change on a yearly basis, there are a few things to consider before booking a trip. The first thing to decide is which departure city – Miami, Fort Lauderdale, Tampa, Port Canaveral, Jacksonville, Tampa, Galveston or Houston – better suits your air or road travel plans. Also, since most cruises leave in the late afternoon, a tour of the departure city itself can be incorporated into your vacation, so it's worth thinking about which of them you might like to see.

Another variable is how many and which ports the ships sail into. Some cruises make stops at all the above-mentioned ports; others stop only at two or three. A few – especially those departing from Miami and New Orleans – make a circular loop around the island of Cuba and on these a typical itinerary might be: Miami, Key West, Playa del Carmen, Grand Cayman, Ocho Rios, Miami. Others zigzag between destinations: Tampa, Grand Cayman, Belize City, Cozumel, Tampa. Naturally, the choice of the cruise line itself will influence the atmosphere of the trip.

Three- to five-night cruises on the Western route make for great long-weekend mini-escapes. The longer, seven- to 11-night cruises feel more like a real vacation. Available at all times of the year, the companies that offer Western Shores cruises include Carnival (3, 4, 5 and 7 nights), Celebrity (7 nights), Costa (7 nights), MSC Cruises (11 nights), Norwegian Cruise Line (7 nights), Princess (7 nights), and Radisson Seven Seas Cruises (7 nights). ❑

BELOW: only small turtles can be handled at Cayman Turtle Farm, Grand Cayman.
RIGHT: the busy cruise terminal at the Port of Miami.

FLORIDA PORTS OF CALL

Art Deco architecture, old cigar factories, rockets blasting into space, and Ernest Hemingway's favourite bar are just a few of the things to be found in Florida's five cruise ship ports

Maps:
Miami
134
Area 137

With the largest cruise port in the world, handling over 3 million passengers a year, **Miami ❶** is the main gateway for all types of Caribbean cruises. Only 8 miles (14 km) from Miami International Airport, and easily reached from the I-95 highway, the **Port of Miami** (tel: 305-371 7678) is a state-of-the-art facility with plenty of parking, a large staff of ground personnel, excellent security, luggage conveyer belts, and convenient airline check-in counters capable of issuing boarding passes for flights home. Along with an ample supply of taxis, a fleet of shuttle buses designated specifically for cruise passengers is permanently stationed at the airport.

Many of the passengers who embark from here can't resist Miami's exotic, multi-ethnic atmosphere, and wind up taking advantage of the special "cruise layover" packages offered by most major hotels in the city.

South Beach Art Deco

A sprawling and intense metropolis of over 2 million people, Miami offers a vast and varied list of diversions to choose from. The one thing most tourists make a point of seeing, especially if they are only in town for a few hours, is **South Beach's Art Deco National Historic District ❷**. At the southern end of Miami Beach, just a few miles east of the Port of Miami, this dense little enclave contains over 800 Art Deco buildings and is one of the liveliest and most flamboyant neighbourhoods in the US. The **Art Deco Welcome Center** (daily 10am–6pm; tel: 305-672 2014), on Ocean Drive, holds a wealth of information on the area and offers free maps and walking tours. Along with the pastel architectural masterpieces that line the streets, South Beach is full of colourful characters – New York fashion models, Hasidic jews, trendy locals, European tourists, Cuban salsa singers, Haitian drummers, and gay couples who proudly kiss in public.

In addition to Ocean Drive and Collins Avenue, the **Lincoln Road Mall ❸** on South Beach is always bustling with locals and visitors. A pedestrian-only avenue jam-packed with outdoor cafés, boutiques, and restaurants, Lincoln Road is home to the **South Florida Art Center** (Mon–Wed 11am–10pm, Thurs–Sun until 11pm), a collective of more than 100 artists. Just a few blocks away is **Española Way ❹**, a stunning group of flamingo pink Mediterranean Revival buildings that houses more art galleries, cafés and shops.

Downtown Miami

Closer to the Port, **Downtown Miami** has several interesting spots all within walking distance from each other. **Bayside Marketplace ❺** (daily 10am–11pm), a 16-acre (6.5-hectare) waterfront entertainment complex, is

PRECEDING PAGES: a lifeguard station on South Beach.
LEFT: on Ocean Drive, South Beach.
BELOW: roller bladers are a familiar sight in trendy South Beach.

full of unusual shops and restaurants, and usually has free live music. Directly across the street is the peach-coloured **Freedom Tower**, the Spanish-style 1925 building that once served as a processing centre for immigrants. A few blocks inland from the Port is the **Miami-Dade Cultural Center** (daily 9am–5pm; entrance fee; tel: 305-375 3000), a sprawling modern complex containing the excellent **Historical Museum of Southern Florida** and the **Miami Art Museum**.

From dolphins to dominoes

A few miles to the south is the **Miami Seaquarium** (daily 9.30am–6pm; entrance fee; tel: 305-361-5705), a popular attraction with dozens of marine exhibits and water shows starring playful bottle-nose dolphins and Lolita the Killer Whale. Nearby is **Coconut Grove**, a one-time art colony turned upmarket neighbourhood and home of **Vizcaya Museum and Gardens** (daily 9.30am–5.30pm; entrance fee; tel: 305-250 9133), a 70-room Italian Renaissance-style palace full of European antiques. A short distance west is **Coral Gables**, an enchanting district with glorious old houses, the historic **Biltmore Hotel**, and the lush lagoons of the **Venetian Pool** (call for opening hours; tel: 305-460 5356).

For a taste of the Cuban flavour that makes Miami such a rich experience, a trip into the neighbourhood of **Little Havana** is in order. Along with the main commercial artery of **SW 8th Street** (Calle Ocho), where the scent of Cuban coffee permeates the air, other places of note include: the **Bay of Pigs Monument**, which pays tribute to those who lost their lives in the foiled 1961 invasion of Cuba; **Domino Park**, where elderly Cubans gather to play dominoes and talk about the lives they left behind; and **Woodlawn Park Cemetery**, where three former presidents of Cuba are buried.

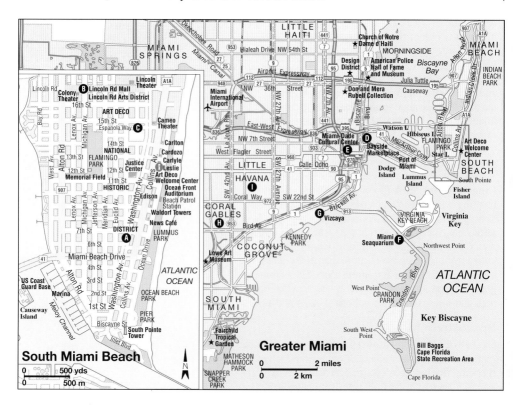

Fort Lauderdale

About 35 miles (56 km) north of Miami, the ultra-modern **Port Everglades** (tel: 954-523 3404) ranks after Miami as the second busiest cruise port in the world, but is far less congested than its neighbour to the south. Equipped with plenty of parking spaces, taxis, kerbside baggage handlers and comfortable waiting areas, Port Everglades is 2 miles (3 km) from **Fort Lauderdale/Hollywood International Airport** and just a few minutes' drive from Fort Lauderdale's popular attractions. World famous for its silky 2-mile (3-km) beach, 300 miles (480 km) of navigable waterways, and wealthy yachting community, **Fort Lauderdale ❷** is one of the most cosmopolitan cities in Florida.

Dedicated to the good life, the city's persona is most evident along **Las Olas Boulevard**, a red brick street with old-fashioned gaslights, horse-drawn carriage rides, outdoor cafés, antique shops and art galleries. Towards the western end of Las Olas, a series of footpaths known as the **Riverwalk** leads past several historic sites on the banks of the **New River**. The new kid on the block is **Las Olas Riverfront** (daily 10am–11pm), a modern and meandering outdoor complex filled with restaurants, art galleries, boutiques and bars.

Not far from Las Olas Boulevard are several attractions. Housed in a rustic 1905 inn, the **Old Fort Lauderdale Village and Museum** (Tues–Fri 11am–5pm, Sat–Sun noon–5pm; entrance fee) contains exhibits on the area's history, including Indian artefacts, historic photos and fine antiques. The plantation-style winter home of the late art collector Frederick Bartlett, **Bonnet House** (Wed–Sun 10am–2pm; entrance fee; tel: 954-563 5393), is a grand estate filled with unusual art and artefacts from around the world. The **Museum of Discovery and Science** (daily 10am–5pm, Sun pm only; entrance fee; tel: 954-467 6637)

Maps:
Miami
134
Area 137

BELOW:
a poser in Little
Havana, Miami.

offers educational hands-on exhibits for children. Finally, the small **Museum of Art** (daily 11am–7pm, Thurs until 9pm, closed Tues Feb–Dec 2005; entrance fee; tel: 954-525 5500) offers displays of European and American art.

Port Canaveral

Catering mostly to the three- and four-day Caribbean cruise market, **Port Canaveral ❸** (tel: 321-783 7831) may not be as busy as Miami's or Fort Lauderdale's ports, but it is a first-rate facility none the less. And because of the location, about 50 miles (80 km) east of Orlando, cruises departing from here often offer special pre- or post-cruise packages to Walt Disney World and other central Florida attractions.

What is also desirable about Port Canaveral is its proximity to Kennedy Space Center and the Merritt Island National Wildlife Refuge. Sprawling over 140,000 acres (57,000 hectares), the **Merritt Island National Wildlife Refuge** (open daily, closed prior to shuttle launch; tel: 321-861 0667) is peaceful with hundreds of species of water birds, alligators, manatees and loggerhead turtles living on its salt marshes – all oblivious to the rockets taking off nearby. At the northern boundary is NASA's **Kennedy Space Center** (daily 9am–5.30pm, closed some launch days; entrance fee; tel: 321-449 4444). A theme park-style attraction that is great for adults as well as children. It features an authentic space ship control room, an IMAX theatre, and regular bus tours that explore the launch pads, launch control centre and training facilities.

A little to the north of the Space Center is the **Canaveral National Seashore** (open daily 6am–6pm, extended summer hours), a protected barrier island sandy beach strewn with sea grapes, sea oats and cabbage palms. Marked canoe trails

Information Central at the Kennedy Space Center has a roundup of schedules for films, live events and tours.

BELOW: a snake charmer delights her young audience at Busch Gardens.

inside the park meander through a lagoon that is almost always bustling with egrets, ibis, cranes, terns and herons.

Map
on page
137

Tampa

On Florida's Gulf Coast, the **Port of Tampa** and its 30-acre (12-hectare) **Garrison Seaport Cruise Terminal** (tel: 813-905 5131) specialises in cruises to Mexico and other destinations in the Western Caribbean. Thoroughly updated in 1998, the terminal contains the enormous **Channelside**, an entertainment complex with dozens of shops, bars, cinemas and an aquarium.

A fast-growing and very modern city, **Tampa ❹** has several interesting attractions for those who want to add a few days on to their cruise holiday. **Busch Gardens** (daily 10am–6pm, extended hours in summer and holidays; entrance fee; tel: 813-987 5000), one of the more popular theme parks in the state, is world famous for its thrilling rides and excellent wildlife exhibits.

More formal attractions include the **Henry B. Plant Museum** (Tues–Sat 10am–4pm, Sun noon–4pm; entrance fee; tel: 813-254 1891), a former luxury hotel built by a Florida railroad magnate in the 1890s, and the **Tampa Museum of Art** (Tues–Sat 10am–5pm, Sun 11am–5pm; entrance fee; tel: 813-274 8130), housing ancient Greek and Roman artefacts and 20th-century American art.

Established in 1886 by a Cuban cigar factory owner, **Ybor City** is an historic neighbourhood of old buildings, colourful Spanish-style tiles and wrought-iron gates. Many of the old cigar shops and factories have been transformed into up-market restaurants, bars, antique shops and boutiques. The **Ybor City State Museum** (daily 9am–5pm; tel: 813-247 6323) does a good job of explaining the history of the cigar-manufacturing community.

One of Tampa's loveliest historic neighbourhoods is Old Hyde Park, where Gothic Revival homes, antique shops and art galleries line the streets.

BELOW: Orca, the Killer Whale show, at the Miami Seaquarium.

Enjoy a slice of key lime pie, a Key West speciality, at 424 Greene Street, which has seating outside.

BELOW: views of yachts from the pier at Key West. **RIGHT:** sunset on the waterfront, Florida Keys.

Key West

The southernmost city in the continental US, **Key West** ❺ (pop. 28,000) has a flamboyant, anything-goes atmosphere that has made it a tropical refuge for many offbeat characters. Barely 4 miles (6 km) long by 2 miles (3 km) wide, it is truly a great port of call and welcomes about 700,000 cruise passengers each year. It's a small city, easily explored on foot, and full of gingerbread architecture, literary legacies and interesting nooks and crannies.

Passengers disembarking in the **Port of Key West** (tel: 305-293 8309) do so at the main pier near **Mallory Square**. Right in the heart of **Old Town**, the square is by the bustling marina that hosts the **Sunset Celebration** every evening. Jugglers, mime artists, musicians, dancers and animal tamers put on a free show with the orange setting sun as their backdrop.

Departing from Mallory Square, the venerable **Conch Tour Train** (daily 9am–4.30pm; entrance fee) has been taking visitors on narrated treks through the city since 1958 and provides lots of juicy history along with the fun, open-air ride. A tribute to the late treasure diver, after whom it is named, the **Mel Fisher Maritime Heritage Society Museum** (daily 9.30am–5.30pm; entrance fee; tel: 305-294 2633) displays a bounty of treasures – coins, jewels, silver bars – that have been salvaged from sunken ancient Spanish galleons found in the waters offshore. Occupying the oldest house in Key West, the **Wreckers Museum** (daily 10am–4pm; entrance fee; tel: 305-294 9502) contains antiques and artefacts that tell the story of the notorious pirates who raided ships off this coast during the 1700s. The **Little White House** (daily 9am–5pm; entrance fee; tel: 305-294 9911), which chronicles the many holidays that US President Harry S. Truman took here during the 1940s, is another popular attraction.

Hemingway House

While there are many historic homes in Key West, the one that draws the crowds is **Hemingway House** (daily 9am–5pm; entrance fee; tel: 305-294 1136) on the corner of Whitehead and Olivia Streets. It was here, in this beautiful Spanish colonial mansion, that the Nobel Prize-winning author spent his winters during the 1930s. Perfectly preserved, the house is filled with Hemingway's antique furniture, art, old books and hunting trophies. Down the road is **Sloppy Joe's**, a boisterous old saloon with peanut shells covering the floors and said to be Hemingway's favourite bar. Other famous watering holes in the city include the **Hard Rock Café**, **Captain Tony's Saloon** and the **Margaritaville Café**, owned by singer Jimmy Buffet.

Adding more oddness to this already delightfully odd place is **Ripley's Believe It Or Not! Museum** (daily 9.30am–11pm; entrance fee; tel: 305-293 9939), a bizarre repository of antique diving gear, authentic shrunken heads and a hurricane tunnel complete with gusts of gale force winds. Dating back to the 1800s, the **East Martello Tower** (daily 9.30am–5pm; entrance fee) is an old red brick fort containing a history museum that houses objects from the Spanish-American war as well exhibits on Florida's Native Indians and the many writers who have called Key West home. ❑

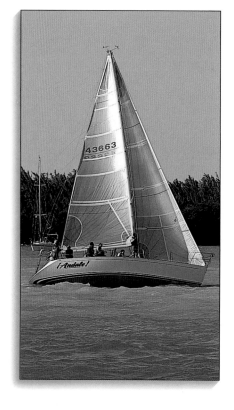

MEXICO AND CENTRAL AMERICA

Maya ruins, a wealth of wildlife, colonial cities, and islands where the traditional Kuna culture remains unchanged, all present a great contrast to the engineering marvel of the Panama Canal

Maps on pages 144/146

F
ull of ancient Maya ruins and ripe with strong national identities, ports of call in Mexico and Central America offer a rich experience not found in most small Caribbean islands. Routes in this area vary greatly and are often determined by the size of the cruise ship. While some companies feature three- or four-day itineraries, more often than not cruises here last for 10–14 days, and some include a transit through the Panama Canal.

The Yucatán Peninsula

Jutting out into the Gulf of Mexico and the Caribbean Sea, Mexico's **Yucatán Peninsula** was destined to become a major cruise destination. Just 500 miles (800 km) from the Florida Coast, it is blessed with white sand beaches, calm turquoise waters, a vibrant arts and crafts tradition, and pyramids left behind by the Maya Indians who lived here long before colonial times. It is also an efficient and well-managed place with every modern amenity imaginable.

Topping the list of most loved and most visited ports is the small island of **Cozumel ❶**. In the 1980s, only a handful of ships a week docked here, but it now draws so many that some have to anchor offshore and ferry passengers to land, usually right into **San Miguel ❷**. Those lucky enough to dock do so at the **International Pier** or the newer **Puerto Maya Pier**. Just a few miles from town, both piers are modern facilities with information booths, international phone access and plenty of taxis (tel: 987-872 0236) and rental cars (tel: 987-872 0903). And as it is only 12 miles (20 km) long, Cozumel is easy to explore on foot.

Exploring San Miguel

Across from the pier is the **Plaza del Sol**, the main town square where locals and tourists gather. The nearby seaside promenade, the **Malecón**, is jammed with craft and souvenir shops, as is the busy **Rafael Melgar Avenue**. Also on Melgar is the **Museo de la Isla de Cozumel** (Cozumel Island Museum; daily 10am–5pm; small entrance fee; tel: 987-872 1434), a former luxury hotel that now contains exhibits on pre-Columbian and colonial history, maritime artefacts and displays on indigenous endangered animals. Tours of the museum are in English and Spanish.

About 2 miles (3 km) south of San Miguel, at the Casa del Mar Hotel, is the home-base for **Atlantis Submarine Tours** (tel: 987-872 5671). Ideal for non-swimmers who want to see the world below the water's surface, the 48-passenger Atlantis Submarine offers a delightful tour of the offshore reefs.

PRECEDING PAGES: *El Castillo* temple, Chichén Itzá. **LEFT:** at the top of the main pyramid, Tikál, Guatemala. **BELOW:** the ruins at Chichén Itzá.

Ruins and beaches

A few miles inland from San Miguel is **El Cedral**, a small collection of Maya ruins; close to the central area of Cozumel is **San Gervasio**, another Maya site. Both sites are well preserved but seem almost insignificant when compared to the size, scope and historic value of other Maya cities on the mainland.

At the southwestern end of the island is **Playa San Francisco**, a 3-mile (5-km) beach dotted with restaurants and water sports operators. Other good beaches are **Playa del Sol**, **Playa Plancar** and **Playa Bonita** – the latter is one of the most secluded beaches on the island. But the pride and joy of Cozumel is the beach at **Parque Nacional Chankanaab** (Chankanaab National Park; daily 8am–5pm; tel: 987-872 0914; small entrance fee). Along with a beautiful soft sand beach, the park contains a land-locked natural pool connected to the sea by an underground tunnel. It also features a botanical garden with 800 species of plants, a small natural history museum, and a swim-with-dolphins programme.

In Cozumel, as in other ports of call in the Mexican Caribbean, the most popular shore excursions are to the Maya ruins of **Tulum** ❸ (daily 7am–6pm). Costing about US$75 per person, this day-long trek is worth the time, money and effort. Perched on a cliff, the walled city of Tulum is the only Maya site that fronts the sea. Most of it is flat and easy to explore, but for those who have difficulties with walking there are jitneys (small buses) running from the main entrance to the centre of the site. Beautiful beaches complete with cafés and restaurants just below the ruins offer a pleasant way to wind up the tour.

Other excursions from Cozumel include horse-riding tours, jeep trips through the jungle-like mangroves of the island, and shopping tours that take in some of the best shops on the island.

It is said that in ancient times, Maya women travelled from the mainland to Cozumel at least once in their lifetimes to pay homage to Ixchel, the Goddess of Fertility. Ixchel was the wife of Itzamná, the revered Maya Sun God, so it is no wonder that over 40 shrines devoted to her are scattered throughout the island.

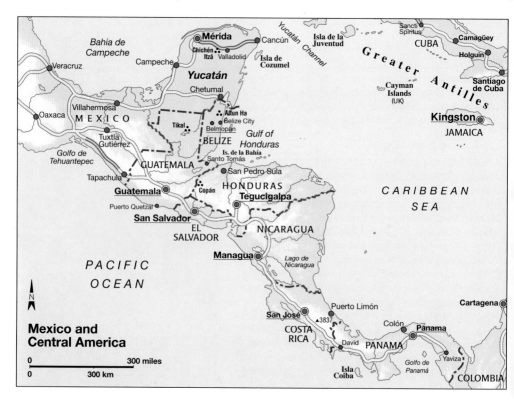

Mexico and Central America

Playa del Carmen

On the mainland a few miles west of Cozumel is **Playa del Carmen ❹**, one of the busiest cruise ship ports in Mexico. Cruises with Playa del Carmen on their itinerary have several options; they can anchor off the coast and ferry passengers to shore here; they can dock at Cozumel and ferry passengers from there to Playa; or they can dock at the **Puerto Calica Cruise Ship Pier**, about 8 miles (13 km) south of Playa del Carmen, and bus passengers to Playa. Many local operators and taxi services offer customised tours of the area, but be warned: passengers booked on ship organised excursions sometimes take priority on tenders ferrying people to land, so you should check this out in advance.

Twenty years ago, Playa del Carmen was a sleepy fishing village with no electricity, but today, it's a pulsating port of entry for American cruise passengers, and a favourite getaway for young European travellers who get here by land. Full of old clapboard houses, Playa hasn't lost its counter-culture, rustic atmosphere despite its popularity. At the heart of town is **Avenida Cinco** (Fifth Avenue), a busy street full of inexpensive restaurants, bars with potent margaritas, internet cafés, and shops selling silver jewellery and crafts.

Xcaret

One of the more popular excursions from Playa is to **Xcaret ❺** (daily 9am–9pm winter, 10pm summer; entrance fee; tel: 988-883 3144), a uniquely designed ecological and archaeological theme park. The Yucatán's answer to Disney World, Xcaret (pronounced *ish-car-et*) is a stunningly beautiful and thoroughly modern attraction with myriad diversions including palm-lined beaches, a snorkelling lagoon, botanical garden, sea turtle nursery, replicas of Maya ruins,

Map on page 144/146

IF YOU CAN READ THIS IT'S BECAUSE WE ARE ON THE BEACH.

BELOW: swim with the dolphins at Chankanaab.

water rides, horse riding and a Dolphinarium where visitors can swim with them for a hefty fee (about US$80). While it is very commercialised, Xcaret can provide an entire day's worth of activities and is great fun for children.

Offering similar experiences to Xcaret, are two other theme parks **Xel-Há** (daily 8am–6pm; entrance fee; tel: 984-875 6000), pronounced *shell-hah*; and **Xpu-Há** (daily 8.30am–5.30pm; entrance fee), pronounced *ish-poo-hah*. Both have snorkelling, scuba and other water sports.

Chichén Itzá

The most spectacular excursion in this area, however, is a full-day trip to the Maya ruins of **Chichén Itzá** (daily 8am–10pm), about 150 miles (240 km) inland from the coast. While it is costly (more than US$200), time consuming and tiring, a trip to Chichén Itzá is the highlight of any Yucatán holiday. Among the best known ruins in Latin America, the fabled ancient city provides a fascinating picture of Maya life in the 10th century. Covering 4 sq miles (10 sq km), the site contains the towering **Pyramid of Kukulkán**, several temples, an observatory, ball courts, steam baths, a sacrificial well and a council house. Local guides offer excellent tours in English, and there's an on-site restaurant for refreshments. In the evening, Chichén Itzá puts on an impressive **sound-and-light show**.

Costa Maya

The newest Mexican Caribbean port of call, **Costa Maya**, is located about 75 miles (120 km) south of Playa del Carmen, near the border with Belize. Ships coming ashore here stop at the **Port of Majahual ❻**. Opened in 2001, this small but efficient terminal known as the **Costa Maya Cruise Ship Pier** has plans to expand and become a major cruise destination.

A small coastal settlement with a pretty beach and a few shops and restaurants, this area is known more for its natural beauty than for modern,

Cozumel and Costa Maya

Map on page 146

man-made attractions. The best excursion here is a snorkelling or scuba trip to the impressive **Parque Nacional de Chinchorro Submarino ❼** (Chinchorro Underwater National Park). About 30 miles (48 km) long and 9 miles (14 km) wide, this atoll is one of the last virgin reefs in the region and has areas that drop to depths of 3,000 ft (900 metres). Surrounded by an intricate maze of coral heads, it is nearly always teaming with exotic tropical fish, and has over 30 sunken ships to explore. Enormous leatherback turtles are often spotted by snorkellers here, as are numerous dolphins, which love to mingle with visitors.

Another favourite tour from Costa Maya is to the **Reserva de la Biósfera Sian Ka'An ❽** (Sian Ka'an Biosphere Reserve; tel: 984-871-2499), a 1.3-million acre (526,000-hectare) nature preserve about 50 miles (80 km) north of the Costa Maya port. Divided into three distinct coastal zones, the Sian Ka'An contains broad savannas, dense mangroves, lush tropical forests and many different types of marine habitats. It is also home to pumas, jaguars, spider and howler monkeys, ocelots, white-tailed deer, tapirs, crocodiles, loggerhead turtles and manatees. Along with numerous flamingos and brightly coloured parrots, it contains and protects over 300 species of birds. Be warned: the mosquitoes can be fierce – hence the name Mosquito Coast – so cover up well and wear repellent.

A small museum at Lamanai displays artefacts discovered at the ancient Maya ceremonial site in Belize.

Belize

A tiny, English-speaking country with a stunning Caribbean coastline, **Belize** is noted for its breathtaking barrier reef – the second largest in the world. While small cruises tend to anchor at Belize's offshore islands, most large cruise ships call at Belize City, anchor offshore and use tenders to transport passengers to the **Radisson Fort George Dock**, where tour buses await. Currently under construction, a new full-service cruise ship terminal is expected to open sometime in 2007.

BELOW: Ambergris Caye, Belize.

Although it has a weathered, run-down, Caribbean atmosphere, Belize City (pop. 70,000) contains a few points of interest that can be explored by taking a city tour excursion or hiring a local taxi. Towering over the harbour is the **Baron Bliss Lighthouse and Park**. One of Belize's greatest benefactors, Baron Bliss was a wealthy Portuguese yachtsman who took ill and died while in port. At his request, his body was entombed in front of the lighthouse, and his money used to build local schools and hospitals.

Not far from the harbour is **St John's Cathedral** (daily 7am–3pm), the oldest Anglican Church in Central America, built in 1812. Across the street is **Government House**, a beautifully preserved colonial mansion; and a block away is the **Yarborough Cemetery** with gravestones dating back to the 1700s. On North Front Street, the **National Handicraft Centre** (Mon–Sat 9am–5pm) is a market place that sells Belizian crafts, pottery and woodcarvings. The **Great House Hotel** on Cork Street houses the **Smokey Mermaid** (daily 11am–10pm), an outdoor restaurant that serves wonderful local seafood dishes.

Rather than spending time in Belize City, many cruise passengers prefer to take day-long excursions to the **Crooked Tree Wildlife Sanctuary**, **Cockscomb Basin and Jaguar Preserve**, the **Belize Zoo**, or the

Maya archaeological sites of **Xuanantunich** and **Altun Ha**. There are also excursions that take passengers for **inner tube river rides** through a series of caves; on snorkelling trips to the strikingly beautiful coral reef at the **Hol Chan Marine Reserve** on Ambergris Caye; and to **Lamanai**, an ancient Maya ceremonial centre amid a lush jungle landscape on the New River. Local **water taxis** (Andrea Ferry Boat, tel: 501-226 2656) are also available for those who want to make independent day-trips to **Ambergris Caye** and **San Pedro Island**.

The grandest public holiday in Guatemala is Semana Santa, held the week before Easter, when the entire country – including cruise ship ports – take part in festivities that include religious processions and street parties galore.

Guatemala

Located just to the south of Mexico, **Guatemala** shares a border as well as a rich Maya history with its neighbour. Almost 60 percent of the local population here are indigenous, with roots traceable to the ancient Mayas, and this cultural link is evident in the colourful designs of their textiles as well as in their music, folklore and religious ceremonies. Guatemala is also rich in nature, in the countryside there are more than 600 species of orchids and 300 species of birds.

Although it doesn't have pretty beaches and it is not a major destination for Caribbean cruises, two Guatemalan ports are often included in Panama Canal itineraries – **Puerto Quetzal** on the Pacific Coast and, on the Caribbean Coast, **Santo Tomás**. Built a century ago as a company town for the United Fruit Corporation, Santo Tomás serves as the headquarters of the Guatemalan Navy, and is the more interesting of the two towns.

Both ports, however, are used as jumping-off points for day-long excursions to the Spanish colonial city of **Antigua**, the capital of **Guatemala City**, **Lake Atitlán**, and especially the Maya ruins of **Tikál** (daily 6am–5pm). The largest and most impressive of all the classic Maya sites, Tikál contains over 500 excavated structures including the **Temple of the Giant Jaguar** and the **Lost World Complex**, a recently discovered group of pyramids. There are two on-site museums and well-trained guides who offer excellent historical tours explaining the architecture, customs and lifestyle of the Maya people. Excursions to Tikal, however, usually cost several hundred dollars per person, and involve both a plane and a bus ride.

BELOW: Tikál – the most impressive classic Maya site.

Honduras

Like Guatemala, **Honduras** is known for the spectacular Maya ruins in the interior, but it also has a cluster of offshore islands, the **Islas de la Bahía** (Bay Islands), which attract Caribbean and Panama Canal cruises. The main islands are **Utila**, **Roatán** and **Guanaja.** The largest and most-visited of these is Roatán (pop. 26,000), a lush, 25-mile (40-km) long strip of land that is world famous as a dive destination and has a long history as one of the best boat-building enclaves in Latin America. Most of the people here speak English rather than Spanish, and the island has several small hotels, restaurants and dive operators who take passengers out to the coral reef. There are also bikes for hire and taxi services available near the cruise ship pier.

Anthony's Key Resort in the **Sandy Bay** area of Roatán serves as the home for the **Roatán Institute for Marine Sciences** (Mon–Sat 8am–5pm; entrance fee), a conservation group that conducts environmental

Map on page 144

tours of the island. Visitors to the Institute can also see dolphin encounter shows (daily, 10.30am–4.30pm; entrance fee).

Along with Roatán, cruise ships also call in at **Puerto Cortés**, a palm-fringed bay on the Caribbean Coast that bustles with commerce. Excursions here (by plane and bus) are to the famous Maya ruins of **Copán** (daily 8am–4pm; entrance fee). The most important archaeological site in Honduras, the ruins of Copán consist of a sprawling collection of pyramids, ceremonial courts, temples and altars said to date back to AD 464. Adjacent to the ruins is the colonial town of Copán. Full of cobblestone streets and red-tiled roofs, the town contains the **Copán Museum** (Mon–Sat 8am–noon, 1–4pm; entrance fee), a fairly impressive repository of Maya art, jewels and artefacts.

Costa Rica

A peaceful and dramatically beautiful country, Costa Rica is often called the Switzerland of Central America. With its tropical rainforests, gushing rivers and glorious beaches, it does not disappoint visitors. While a few ships stop at the Pacific port of **Caldera**, which is an ideal jumping-off point for excursions to national parks in the Middle Pacific area, the majority of Caribbean cruises stop at **Puerto Limón**. Formerly an ancient Indian village where Columbus landed on his final voyage, Limón is a palm-fringed city with a mountain backdrop and an atmosphere that is more Afro-Caribbean than Latin American – many residents here speak English. Far less congested than the capital, San José, it is a lively but slightly run-down city full of old wooden houses painted in bright pastel colours.

Not far from the port is the Chinese Cemetery, where many Chinese immigrants, who worked on the local railroad, are buried. At the centre of town,

Artefact on display at the Jade Museum in San José, Costa Rica.

BELOW: a river trip through Cahuita National Park, Costa Rica.

next to the old harbour is **Parque Vargas**, a bustling promenade dense with tropical trees and plants.

The best time to be in Cahuita is from February to April, and in the second week of October for Carnival.

Ferried ashore by tender, passengers have several excursions to choose from. Popular choices are whitewater rafting trips to nearby rivers and visits to **Parque Nacional Cahuita** (Cahuita National Park; daily 8am–5pm), where glass-bottomed boats offer views of the coral reef and hiking trails wind through a lush rainforest. Local tour operators also offer specially designed bird-watching, turtle-watching and eco-tours.

For passengers with a whole day to spend, bus tours can be taken to **San José**, about 70 miles (112 km) inland. In the heart of the country, San José is home to almost 1 million people and visiting it can be an intense experience. Founded in 1737, it is dotted with Spanish colonial architecture and is full of splendid museums. Among the best are the **Museo Nacional** (National Museum) (Tues–Sun 8.30am–4.30pm; entrance fee), where the history of the country from pre-Columbian days to the present is explained; the **Museo del Jade** (Jade Museum; Mon–Sat 12pm–8pm, Sun 12pm–6pm; entrance fee), which displays the world's largest collection of pre-Columbian jade jewellery and artefacts; and the **Museo del Oro** (Gold Museum; Tues–Sun 10am–4.30pm; entrance fee), which contains the most comprehensive collection of pre-Columbian gold artefacts in Central America.

Other stops often included on San José tours are the **Serpentarium** (daily 10am–5pm), the **Simón Bolívar Zoo** (daily 9am–4.30pm) and **El Pueblo Shopping Centre** (daily 24 hours), where a number of cobblestone streets and adobe buildings contain dozens of shops selling Costa Rican arts, crafts, coffee, rum, cigars, embroidered blouses and woodcarvings.

BELOW: a young Kuna fisherman.

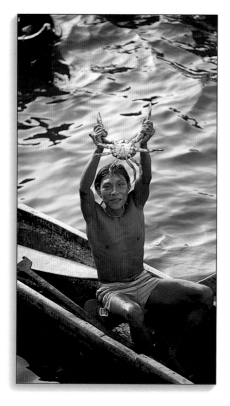

If you don't have enough time for a drive to San José, a smaller and funkier town is **Puerto Viejo de Limón**, about 15 miles (24 km) from Limón. An eclectic mix of surfers, Rastafarians, expats and world-weary travellers gathers here and the party atmosphere is contagious.

Panama

Although traversing the canal *(see page 152)* is the main tourist attraction of this small Central American country, Panama has worked hard in recent years at wooing Caribbean cruises to its city of **Colón**. Located near the Panama Canal's Atlantic entrance, the **Port of Colón** underwent a US$45 million expansion in 2000, and now the modern facility is capable of catering to mega-cruise ships and their passengers.

A sprawling glass and marble complex known as **Colón 2000**, the port includes a duty-free shopping mall, cultural centre, information booth, several restaurants and an internet café. Adjacent to the port is the **Radisson Hotel**, complete with an on-site casino (daily 24 hours). Although the port itself is very pleasant, there's not much else to see in Colón, and most passengers take excursions to nearby sites.

The most popular excursion (for those whose cruise doesn't include a canal crossing) is a ferry trip organised by **Aventuras 2000**, the port's on-site tour company, that sails through portions of the Panama Canal and then continues with an eco-tour of the area.

There are also half-day bus tours to the Canal's **Gatún Locks**, as well as excursions to **San Lorenzo Fort**, the **Barro Colorado Nature Preserve**, and a **Native Indian village** on the banks of the Changres River. A few tour operators allow passengers to go for a swim in the Panama Canal from the shores of the **Gatún Yacht Club**, and helicopter tours of the canal are available.

Map on page 144

San Blas Islands

Just off the northeast coast of Panama are the **San Blas Islands**. Here it is not engineering wonders that draw visitors, but a simple Indian lifestyle that has managed to hold tight to centuries-old traditions. The autonomous home of the **Kuna Amerindians**, the San Blas are beautiful Caribbean islands without the razzle dazzle of development. Spread out over 60 islands, there are about 50,000 Kunas still living here.

As cruise ships sail into the waters, the Kunas paddle out in their dugout canoes to greet passengers and hawk their wares; after that, tenders bring passengers ashore. Once they have arrived on land, visitors are often dumbstruck by the simplicity of it all. Most of the Kuna speak only their native language, rather than Spanish, and live in bamboo huts without electricity or running water. Fishing, farming and making *molas* are their means of survival. An intricate, patchwork-type embroidery done on black fabric, *molas* make an irresistible souvenir. Boldly beautiful, the embroidered pieces are sometimes sewn onto blouses and shirts, and are also used for place mats and as cushion covers.

In late February, the Kuna commemorate the anniversary of the **Kuna Revolution**, when these bucolic little islands come alive with celebrations and ceremonies conducted by local chiefs. ❑

BELOW: the Kuna have preserved their traditional way of life.

The Panama Canal

I t's not a pretty sight, but one that boggles the mind with the colossal magnitude of its engineering ingenuity. One of the Seven Wonders of the Modern World, the Panama Canal has received over 725,000 ships since it first opened in 1914, and is now one of the more interesting destinations for many Caribbean cruises.

A 50-mile (80-km) long slice of land and water that connects the Atlantic and Pacific Oceans, the canal affords ships direct passage through Central America (rather than the 8,000-mile/12,800-km journey around South America) and now services about 35 to 40 vessels per day.

Political wrangles

Although it was marred by political undertones, the building of the Panama Canal is considered one of the greatest human accomplishments of the 20th century. After a failed attempt by the French in the late

1800s, construction was turned over to the US government in 1903. At the time, the Republic of Panama was struggling to gain its independence from Colombia, and the deal it cut with the US government – US$10 million up front and $250,000 per year afterwards – was its ticket to freedom. Desperate for economic development, Panama also granted the United States the administration rights to the canal in perpetuity. By 1906, more than 25,000 people were employed in the massive undertaking. And when it finally opened, seven years later, it did indeed bring a boom to the area.

In 1977, US President Jimmy Carter agreed to revoke the original treaty, and worked out an arrangement that would grant Panama control of the canal by 1999. Today, the canal is managed entirely by Panama and represents 10 percent of its GNP, bringing in about US$500 million per year.

ABOVE: a steam shovel works on the canal, *circa* 1913. **BELOW:** transiting the Panama Canal.

Fees for crossing are calculated using a formula based on water displacement, with large cruise ships usually paying (48 hours in advance) about US$100,000 for a one-way passage. Smaller, cargo vessels pay about $40,000 for the crossing, and ships registered in Panama get a discount.

The lowest fee ever charged was 36 cents, when adventurer Richard Halliburton swam across the canal in 1928. Some might feel that the canal authorities should have paid him instead.

For the majority of cruise passengers, a trek through the canal stands out as an amazing experience. While it is always being upgraded, the majority of the canal is still in its original condition. It usually takes about 24 hours to sail through, with more than half of that time spent waiting in a queue with dozens of other ships.

Engineering experts, as well as Central American history specialists, accompany the cruise ships and offer a blow-by-blow account of the transit. Surrounding the canal and visible from the ships is the Panama Canal Zone, a small city full of schools, homes and churches that cater to canal employees.

Complicated process

While being towed through the canal entrance, ships enter a series of three locks – the Miraflores, Pedro Miguel and Gatún – which are connected by artificial lakes and canals. The locks are like giant aquatic elevators that raise the ships up over the land and then gently lower them down to sea level. Once the ships pass through, the locks empty their water and fill back up again ready for the next ship.

Each time, millions of gallons of fresh water from nearby lakes is used (salt water would damage the machinery). For safety reasons, cruise ships always pass through the canal during daylight hours, while cargo and private vessels pass at night with bright lights guiding the way.

Whether sailing from the Caribbean to the Pacific or vice versa, most Panama Canal cruises are one-way trips. For most passengers, although it's a fascinating experience, once is quite enough. ❏

BELOW: ships make a daylight passage through the canal.

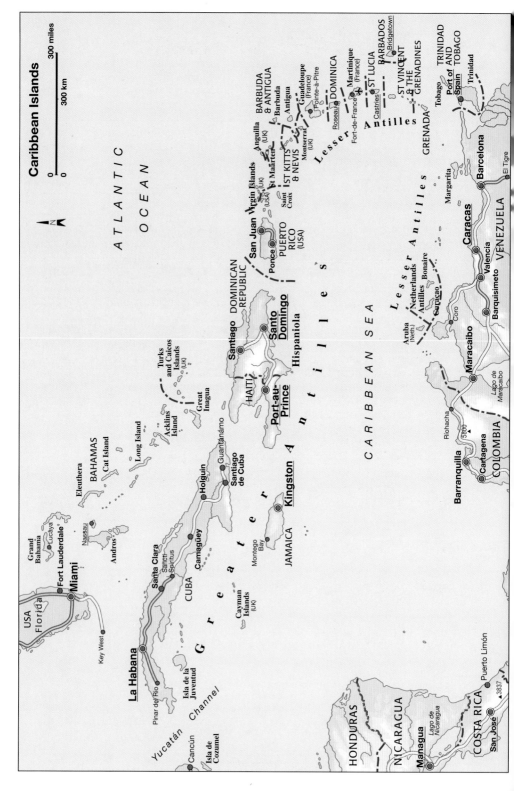

Caribbean Islands

0 300 miles

0 300 km

ATLANTIC OCEAN

USA
Florida

Key West

Grand Bahama
Lucaya

Fort Lauderdale
Miami

Nassau
Andros

Eleuthera

BAHAMAS

Cat Island

Long Island

Acklins Island

Great Inagua

Turks and Caicos Islands (UK)

Pinar del Río

La Habana

Isla de la Juventud

CUBA

Santa Clara
Sancti Spíritus

Camagüey

Holguín

Santiago de Cuba

Guantánamo

Yucatán Channel

Cayman Islands (UK)

Montego Bay

Kingston

JAMAICA

Cancún
Isla de Cozumel

HONDURAS

NICARAGUA

Lago de Nicaragua

Managua

COSTA RICA

San José

▲3837

Puerto Limón

CARIBBEAN SEA

HAITI

Port-au-Prince

Hispaniola

Santiago

DOMINICAN REPUBLIC

Santo Domingo

PUERTO RICO (USA)

Ponce

San Juan

Virgin Islands (USA)

Saint Croix

Anguilla (UK)

St Maarten (UK)

ST KITTS & NEVIS

Montserrat (UK)

BARBUDA & ANTIGUA

Barbuda

Antigua

Guadeloupe (France)

Pointe-à-Pitre

DOMINICA

Roseau

Martinique (France)

Fort-de-France

ST LUCIA

Castries

BARBADOS

Bridgetown

ST VINCENT & THE GRENADINES

GRENADA

Lesser Antilles

G r e a t e r   A n t i l l e s

L e s s e r   A n t i l l e s

Netherlands Antilles

Bonaire

Curaçao

Aruba (Neth.)

Margarita

Coro

VENEZUELA

Caracas

Barcelona

El Tigre

Valencia

Barquisimeto

Lago de Maracaibo

Maracaibo

COLOMBIA

Riohacha

▲5800

Barranquilla

Cartagena

TRINIDAD AND TOBAGO

Tobago

Trinidad

Port of Spain

THE CARIBBEAN ARC

Like a necklace of precious stones, these diverse islands stretch almost from the Gulf of Mexico to South America

The islands of the Caribbean are physically and culturally places of distinct difference. From the Greater to the Lesser Antilles, each country has its own character, atmosphere and flavour, shaped by its history and its people. The region has more depth than the stereotypical images of sunkissed beaches and friendly people would have us believe.

Here the topography reveals nature at work, from the lush rainforests of Dominica to the limestone caves and thorny scrubland on the northeast coast of Aruba, the majestic Blue Mountains in Jamaica to the rocky outcrops at Bathsheba that are pounded by Atlantic waves on Barbados' wild east coast.

The people who populate the islands are as diverse as the languages they speak. During a shore excursion you are likely to hear French, Dutch, Spanish and English, as well as infinite combinations of creole and patois.

A Latin flavour awaits visitors to Puerto Rico and Cuba, while on St Maarten you can experience two cultures in one trip: the island is Dutch on one side and French on the other. French-African culture prevails in Martinique and Guadeloupe, while the British influence is unavoidable throughout Barbados.

Further south you can explore Grenada, the Spice Island, known for it's aromatic nutmeg and lush vegetation, which is making a rapid recovery from 2004's Hurricane Ivan, and, almost at the tip of the Caribbean arc, is Trinidad, a land famous for its special brand of bacchanalia – Carnival. This island combines a big city attitude with a serene pastoral landscape, abundant wildlife and, as elsewhere in the tropical region, a seamless mix of diverse cultures. ❏

PRECEDING PAGES: Maho Bay, St John, US Virgin Islands.

THE CAYMAN ISLANDS

A tiny island with a sweet mixture of Caribbean heritage, British sensibility and American modernism, Grand Cayman is a major port of call that attracts more than 1 million visitors a year

Map on page 160

Breathtaking dive sites are what usually come to mind when thinking of **Grand Cayman**. But this peaceful little paradise is also an affluent and sophisticated place with the highest standard of living in the Caribbean.

Similar in many ways to Bermuda, Grand Cayman (population 35,000) is a British Overseas Department with a modern and well-managed infrastructure that gracefully coincides with an old-fashioned sense of values. The island has no inner-city slums, no poverty in the countryside, and no street vendors harassing tourists to buy their wares. Nor are there any casinos – conservative Christian churches hold a great deal of sway here.

Only 28 miles long and 7 miles wide (45 by 11 km), Grand Cayman is the largest and most developed of the Cayman Islands chain, which includes **Cayman Brac** and **Little Cayman**. With a population of 1,600, Cayman Brac is a rugged limestone island with about a dozen hotels that cater mostly to scuba divers. Also for divers, Little Cayman is even tinier, with a resident population of about 150 and just a handful of rooms offering accommodation. Both are accessible by commercial planes from George Town and by private yacht.

Just 480 miles (770 km) south of Miami, Grand Cayman is the only one of the three islands that accepts major cruise ships. In an effort to maintain its quiet atmosphere, it allows no more than four ships in port at any one time and requires them to anchor offshore and ferry passengers to the dock via tenders.

Debarkation takes place in the capital city of **George Town ❶**, at either the **North Terminal** or the **South Terminal**. Located just a few hundred yards apart, both are modern, well maintained facilities and within walking distance of several interesting spots in the city. Small and compact, George Town is dense with commerce and classic Caribbean architecture and is easy to explore on foot. For other points of interest outside the city, large air-conditioned buses offer excursions and taxis are readily available.

Hurricane Ivan passed Grand Cayman in September 2004, causing damage to more than 80 percent of the island's buildings. And although recovery has been swift some attractions listed here may be unavailable.

Touring George Town

Right on the waterfront alongside the terminals, **Fort George Ⓐ** is the first thing most passengers notice. Built in 1790 as defence against the Spanish, the original fort was made of solid coral rock with walls 5 ft (1.5 metres) thick. While not as large as many other Caribbean forts, it was strategically positioned and has warded off many attacks.

During World War II it was used as a watchtower to spot the German submarines that often patrolled the

LEFT: sailing in Grand Cayman.
BELOW: footprints in the sand on Seven Mile Beach.

Bold stained-glass windows adorn Elmslie United Memorial Church known locally as Grand Cayman's "cathedral".

coast. To make way for new construction, most of the fort was demolished in 1972, and all that remains are three small portions of the wall, two long cannons, and a look-out hut.

Across the street from Fort George on Harbour Drive is the **Elmslie United Memorial Church ⓑ** (Mon–Fri 9am–5pm, Sun 9am–noon). Named after a Presbyterian minister who served here from 1846 to 1863, the church is an impressive structure with a timber roof shaped like an upturned schooner hull, brightly coloured stained-glass windows and sleek mahogany pews. The grounds surrounding it contain several memorial plaques and old stone grave markers that look like little houses.

National treasure

Further along Harbour Drive stands a sprawling white building with green hurricane shutters and a bright red roof. This is the **Cayman Islands National Museum ⓒ** (Mon–Fri 9am–5pm, Sat 10am–2pm; entrance fee; tel: 345-949 8368), a treasure trove of artefacts that serves as the country's collective memory. One of the finest in the Caribbean, the museum opened in 1990 in the city's Old Courthouse, which dates back to the 1830s. It is the second oldest surviving building in Grand Cayman and a fine example of classic Caymanian architecture. The first floor is constructed of wattle and daub, and the second floor – complete with veranda – is of framed timber. Along with a 10-minute film in an air-conditioned theatre, the museum's many exhibits include a three-dimensional depiction of the undersea mountains and canyons that make up the Cayman Trench, scientific displays of the island's natural habitats, and a collection of locally made furniture, tools, nautical antiques and artwork.

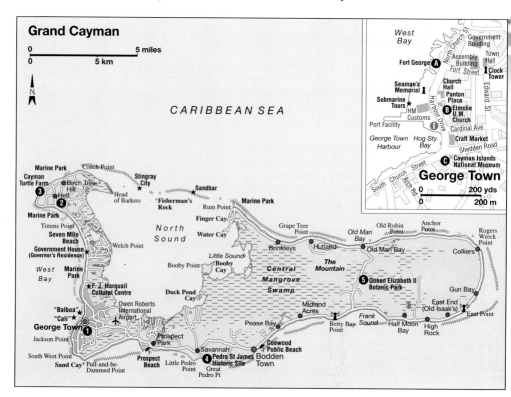

Pleasures above and below water

Across the street from the museum, the **Atlantis Seaworld Explorer** (daily, with departures on the hour from 9am–5pm; fee; tel: 345-949 7700) offers submarine tours that drop 100 ft (30 metres) below the surface of the sea and are ideal for those who don't have time for a dive. Views from the portholes of the comfortable, air-tight ship are stunning – intricate coral formations, lush sponge gardens and exotic marine creatures in a rainbow of tropical colours.

Other points of interest nearby are the **Cayman Islands National Archives**, the **Farmers' Market** and the **Craft Market** – a favourite stop for visitors shopping for island-made souvenirs. And at the intersection of Fort and Edward streets is the **Clock Tower**. Built in 1937 in honour of King George V, it is just one of many monuments on the island representative of the Caymanian allegiance to Britain. Also on Edward Street is the **Public Library**, well stocked with books on island history and culture. Scattered throughout the town are duty-free shops selling jewellery, clothing, perfume, gold coins, china, crystal, Irish linen, leather goods, cameras and the locally produced Tortuga Rum.

Postcards from Hell

Just a few miles from George Town, Grand Cayman becomes more tranquil. Tropical cottages painted in bold Caribbean colours dot the landscape, and the pace of life is slow and sleepy. After passing the high-rise hotels that line **Seven Mile Beach**, north of town, a tiny sign points the way to **Hell ❷**. The entire town consists of a petrol station, a post office and a few quirky gift shops. A touristy but fun place, it got its name from the surrounding acres of pockmarked limestone rocks that look like the charred remains of an inferno. A wooden platform leads

Map on page 160

TIP

One thing to look out for while shopping in Grand Cayman is caymanite. A semi-precious stone found only in these islands, caymanite ranges in colour from beige to pink to brown, and makes beautiful jewellery.

BELOW: the rock formation known as ironshore distinguishes Hell.

Map
on page
160

*Turtles at the
Cayman Islands
Turtle Farm are
usually fed in the
early morning and
late afternoon.*

BELOW: a face-to-
face encounter
with a stingray.
RIGHT: West Bay and
Seven Mile Beach.

to an observation deck above the eerie landscape. A statue of the devil stands guard, and several signs warn: The Removal of Hell Rocks is Prohibited.

One shop worth seeking out is the **Devil's Hangout** (daily 7am–5pm). Dressed in a devil costume complete with red cape, owner Ivan Ferrington greets visitors here with his standard repertoire: "How the hell are you? What the hell do you want?" As in the other gift shops, the shelves are stocked with Hot-as-Hell pepper sauce and T-shirts proclaiming "Been to Hell and Back". Next door is the **Hell Post Office** (Mon–Fri 8.30am–5pm, Sat 8.30am–noon), it is from here that most visitors mail a postcard home from Hell.

Stingrays and sea turtles

Just a few miles from Hell is the **Turtle Farm ❸** (daily 8.30am–5pm; entrance fee; tel: 345-949 3894). Founded in 1968, it has successfully implemented a breed and release programme that has returned over 30,000 tagged turtles to the wild. Once a staple of the local diet and a major part of the local economy, the green sea turtle is now an endangered species. A walkway takes visitors to salt water tanks and within a few feet of the lively creatures that range in size from 6-lb (3-kg) babies to fully mature ones weighing about 600lbs (272 kg). In 2006 the farm will become part of a multimillion dollar theme park, where guests will be able to swim in a salt water lagoon with turtles, fish and other marine life.

Another favourite attraction is **Stingray City**, often called the best 12-ft (3.5-metre) dive spot in the world. Off the northern end of the island and accessible only by tour boats (which can be arranged at the port), this is a shallow, sheltered bay consisting of a barrier reef, a sandbar, calm water and hundreds of curious stingrays. Equipped with handfuls of raw squid, visitors are dropped into the waters and, within seconds, a feeding frenzy begins with the stingrays eating right out of their hands.

Colonial homes and gardens

To the east of George Town, in **Savannah**, is one of the most important historic sites on the island. **Pedro St James Historic Site ❹** (daily 9.30am–5pm; entrance fee; tel: 345-947 3329) is a magnificently restored manor house with formal English gardens, perched on a limestone cliff. It was here, in 1835, that the Declaration of Emancipation was read, freeing local slaves from bondage. Built in 1780 by slave labour, the house is the oldest stone structure on the island and offers a realistic view of Caribbean colonial life. With a glistening gabled roof, exterior staircase and wrap-around veranda, it is furnished with antiques including four-poster beds, mahogany tables, wrought-iron candelabras and lace curtains.

A few miles inland from Pedro St James is **Queen Elizabeth II Botanic Park ❺** (daily 9am–6.30pm; entrance fee; tel: 345-947 9462), a 65-acre (26-hectare) nature preserve and one of the finest botanical gardens in the Caribbean. Amid lush foliage dotted with wild orchids and other exotic flowers, this oasis in the island's interior is equipped with marked trails that guide visitors past 600 species of indigenous plants, interpretive exhibits, a freshwater pond and dozens of rare, endemic Cayman blue iguanas. ❑

JAMAICA

You can go to Jamaica for the reggae and Red Stripe, but other attractions include river rafting, bird-watching, exotic botanical gardens and colonial Great Houses

Maps on pages 166/68

Jungly hills and ravines, the misty Blue Mountains, powdery beaches and vibrant coral reefs are reason enough to visit Jamaica, named Xaymaca, or the "land of wood and water" by the Taíno indians who first settled here. The island's irrepressible spirit is another: scruffy towns resounding with the deep bass tones of the ever-present reggae music; a rusting Red Stripe sign swinging in the breeze, promising deliciously strong, ice-cold beer; or a road-side shack selling spicy patties and jerk pork.

It is true that Jamaica has had highly publicised security problems, and there have been instances of tourists being robbed at gunpoint and even kidnapped, but these incidents should be kept in proportion. A more commonplace problem is the relentless hassle from street traders pouncing on cruise passengers as they emerge from their ship, making shopping, or simply walking around town, an exhausting experience. There has been a government clamp-down on these traders but many visitors choose to shop in the air-conditioned malls, or the artificial environment of a craft market in the grounds of their hotels.

In spite of this, a trip to Jamaica can be a rewarding experience and warrants in-depth and independent exploration. Don't hire a car – the roads are potholed and the local driving haphazard, at best. Distances between the main north coast resorts are large, so it is advisable to get around by taxi and stay within the vicinity of the port, be it Ocho Rios, which attracts the majority of ships, or the main tourism centre of Montego Bay.

LEFT: on the beach near Half Moon Bay.
BELOW: views of Firefly, once Noël Coward's home.

Ocho Rios

In the northern county of Middlesex lies the parish of St Ann, and at its heart is **Ocho Rios ❶**, known locally as Ochi. The coastal town, which depends almost entirely on tourism, is backed by scenic hills of coconut palms and fruit plantations, while its soft, sandy beaches are protected by coral reefs inhabited by colourful varieties of sea life. Contrary to popular opinion, the name Ocho Rios does not come from the Spanish for eight rivers, but is a corruption of the original name *Las Chorreras*, "the waterfalls", of which there are several, creating a perfect environment for some of the island's most spectacular vegetation.

The cruise ship terminal, on the edge of town, has telephones, toilets, an information desk and a taxi rank. The main shore excursions on offer are to Dunn's River Falls, to various botanical gardens, to Prospect Estate, and to Noël Coward's former home, Firefly. If you want to venture out on your own, getting around independently is relatively easy since taxis can be picked up at the terminal. Be sure to use only the licensed JUTA taxis, which publish fixed fares and agree on a price in advance.

The Ocho Rios Jazz Festival began in 1991 and has become a hugely popular event. Held for eight days each June, it provides a showcase for the best of Jamaican jazz musicians, as well as top-notch international players. Free concerts are held every day and associated events take place all over the island.

BELOW: Fern Gully.

It is easy to walk around town from the terminal, but on a hot, humid day, the temptation to take an inexpensive taxi ride is hard to resist. Shopping is good, if you have the stamina. In the town centre, a big shopping mall, the **Taj Mahal**, is a good bet for gemstones, jewellery, designer watches, Blue Mountain coffee and cigars. Craft markets are better places to find wood carvings, batik, fashion jewellery, toys, hats and T-shirts; on Main Street, try Dunn's River and the **Olde Craft Market ⒶＡ**. All the prices are inflated, particularly in the markets, and haggling is expected – be bold but polite and enjoy it. Jamaicans generally have a great sense of humour, but good manners are considered very important and politeness will usually pay off.

Highlights of the Jamaican calendar include pre-Lent Carnival, with parades and bands in all the main towns; the Ocho Rios Jazz Festival in June; and Independence Day on 6 August, a public holiday with street parades and concerts.

Forest and gardens

On a journey around the town, ask the taxi driver to head inland for a trip through **Fern Gully**, a lush, hardwood rainforest where the road is overhung with giant ferns and lianas. In the past more than 60 species were recorded here, but the fern population has dwindled slightly as a result of hurricane damage and possibly pollution, including increased car fumes. However, the winding road bordered on all sides by the trees and vegetation is still worth seeing.

Ocho Rios is one of the best areas on the island for plant life and has two excellent botanical gardens. **Shaw Park Botanical Gardens ⒷＢ** (daily; entrance fee; tel: 876-974 2723) comprises 25 acres (10 hectares) of tropical trees and shrubs set around a natural waterfall and is within walking distance of the cruise

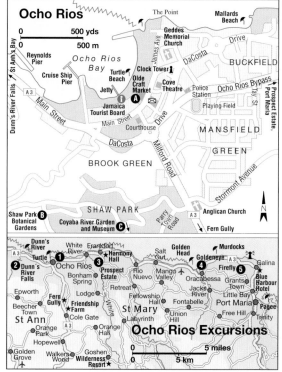

terminal. Nearby, **Coyaba River Garden and Museum** (daily 8am–5pm; entrance fee) is a beautifully serene water garden that surrounds a small building containing rare Taíno artefacts.

River falls and riding

On a hot day, **Dunn's River Falls** ❷ (daily 7am–5pm; entrance fee), five minutes' drive from the port and 2 miles (3 km) from the west of the town centre, is irresistible. Dunn's River cascades for 600 ft (180 metres) down a series of limestone shelves through the dappled shade of the rainforest. Official guides lead chains of visitors up the slippery rocks, stopping for photos in the freshwater pools; get there early to avoid the crowds, especially if more than one cruise ship is in port (it can take three at a time). The guide he will expect a tip. It is possible to climb independently, but be careful because the rocks are slippery and the water is powerful enough in places to make you lose your footing. Wear rubber-soled shoes or hire shoes at the falls, and prepare to get soaked.

Seven miles (11 km) west of Ocho Rios is **Chukka Cove** (daily; tel: 876-972 2506), which organises horse-riding excursions. The three-hour beach ride meanders through two of the island's oldest sugar estates before stopping at Chukka Cove's private beach for a swim. Chukka Cove is also known for its polo, and international tournaments that take place here during March and April.

A taste of plantation life

A short drive east of Ocho Rios is **Prospect Estate** ❸ (daily, closed 2–3pm; entrance fee), one of the best examples of a working plantation, where you will find bananas, sugar cane, cocoa, coconuts, pineapples and cassava cultivated

Blue Mountain Bicycle Tours organises guided cycling trips down the 1,500 ft (460 metres) from Murphy Hill to Dunn's River Falls (Tues–Sat; tel: 974 7075 for details).

BELOW: at the market in Ocho Rios.

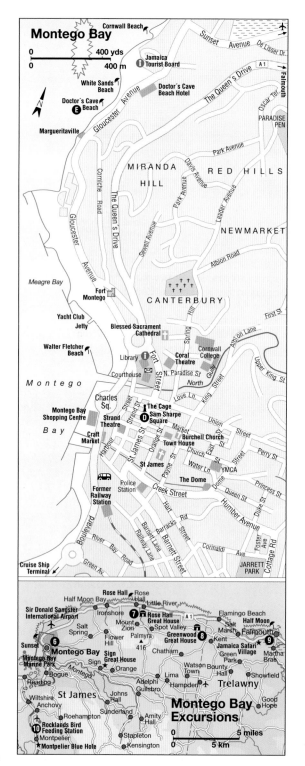

Montego Bay

over 2,000 acres (800 hectares). There are tours of the plantation, the **White River** gorge, **Sir Harold's Viewpoint** overlooking the coast, and a grove of memorial trees.

You could combine a visit to the plantation with a stop at the pretty, gingerbread-house Harmony Hall (Tues–Sun 10am–6pm; free), nearby. Formerly a Methodist Manse built in the mid-1800s, it is now an art gallery showing the work of established and upcoming Caribbean artists. Alongside the paintings and sculpture on display there is an interesting gallery shop, and an elegant restaurant on the ground floor of the property.

Sophisticated places

Ocho Rios has several decent beaches ideal for a day of sun-worshipping and splashing about in the sea. **Mallards Beach**, at the eastern end of town, will be busy, but a 20-minute taxi ride further east, out of Ochi and past Rio Nuevo, lies **Oracabessa Bay**.

This is the location of **Goldeneye ❹**, which was once the home of novelist and former British Naval Intelligence officer, Ian Fleming (1908–64). The building is now a hotel and leads to the predictably named **James Bond Beach Club** (Tues–Sun; entrance fee). The club has three beaches, a Jamaican restaurant and water sports equipment for hire. The snorkelling from here is good, too.

Just down the coast from Oracabessa you will find a fine place for a few moments of quiet contemplation, if you can time your visit for late afternoon without missing the ship. **Firefly ❺** (daily; entrance fee) is the former home of Noël Coward (1899–1973), now managed by the Jamaican National Trust. The house has breathtaking views of the north coast and offers a fascinating insight into the colourful past of the multi-gifted and popular actor, composer and playwright, who entertained the likes of Errol Flynn, Sean Connery and Elizabeth Taylor, among many others.

Montego Bay

The island's second largest town (after Kingston) and the main centre for tourism, **Montego Bay ❻** sprawls around a jagged, semi-circular bay towards the western end of the north coast. The area is divided into distinct sections, with the part of most interest to visitors, containing the shops, bars and restaurants, located east of Sam Sharpe Square and along the waterfront. Cruise ships dock at the multi-million-dollar Freeport complex, on a spit of reclaimed land to the west of the bay, 1 mile (2 km) or so from the centre.

There is little of real interest here apart from the **Montego Bay Freeport Shopping Centre**, a good source for gemstones, watches, cigars, rum and designer labels. Most ships run a shuttle service covering the 10- to 15-minute journey into town; failing this, there will be a long line of willing taxi drivers waiting outside the modern terminal.

Historians claim that "montego" comes from *manteca*, a Spanish word meaning lard, which was made from the fat of the wild boars that inhabited the area before the Spanish colonised it in the 16th century. The Spanish used the bay to ship the fat abroad. Today, local people simply refer to the town as MoBay.

A poignant reminder of the misery of slavery is the stone **Cage**, once used to contain drunks or errant slaves, on display in **Sam Sharpe Square ❼**, named after Sam "Daddy" Sharpe who led slave revolts during the winter of 1831–32. The British authorities responded harshly, hanging Sharpe in The Parade in 1832 and also killing 500 of his associates. The square has a memorial sculpture to Sharpe. Otherwise, apart from a smattering of Georgian buildings in the streets around the square, there is little else of historic interest in Montego Bay, a place given more to shopping and partying than to heritage.

Map on page 168

Several of the large hotels run shuttles for guests, to and from the beach.

BELOW: busy Doctor's Cave Beach.

Map on page 168

The White Witch, an 18-hole championship golf course, is part of the luxurious Ritz-Carlton Rose Hall Hotel in Montego Bay (tel: 953 2800). Two other local courses are the Half Moon (tel: 876 953 2560) and Tryall (tel: 876 956 5681).

BELOW: the Martha Brae River.
RIGHT: a garden view of Rose Hall Great House.

Hip Strip

The Montego Bay Shopping Centre, the Craft Market and a long line of bars are all located along the beach on Gloucester Avenue, otherwise known as the "Hip Strip", ending at **Doctor's Cave Beach** Ⓔ (daily; entrance fee). The beach was made famous in the early 1900s by Dr Alexander McCatty, whose claim that the water here had curative powers brought rich Americans flocking in their hundreds. The strip of fine sand, with good beach facilities, still attracts visitors today. There are coral gardens close to the shore, a lively bar, a food court and a cyber café where you can check your e-mail at rates far cheaper than those on the cruise ships.

If you stroll along Gloucester Avenue you can enjoy some harmless, if mindless, fun at **Margaritaville**, a noisy, action-packed beach bar serving Jamaican food and *fajitas*. There is a choice of 52 varieties of margarita with which to wash the food down, or you can be entertained in the bar's hot tubs and on water trampolines and a monster water slide. This is also a good place to watch stunning sunsets. Alternatively, try the outdoor **Pork Pit**, a local institution, which sells sizzling, peppery jerk pork and chicken accompanied by ice-cold Red Stripe beer.

Montego Bay also hosts the Reggae Sumfest in a variety of venues around town. This is a massive annual music festival held in August, with bands playing round the clock for five days. The event attracts thousands of visitors from all over the world, drawn by the island's musical culture.

Great Houses, river rafting and bird-watching

Behind the mass commercialism, Montego Bay has, nevertheless, a colourful history and several Great Houses still bask amid massive plantations. **Rose Hall Great House** Ⓖ (daily; entrance fee), the 18th-century home of alleged "white witch", Annie Palmer and now a resort and golf course, is the best known. It lies on a ridge east of the city past Ironshore and Half Moon Bay.

Nearby, heading eastwards, is **Greenwood Great House** Ⓗ (daily 9am–6pm; entrance fee), which was built by the ancestors of the poet Elizabeth Barrett Browning between 1780 and 1800. Greenwood contains a great many antiques and the largest collection of rare musical instruments in the western hemisphere.

Further east along the coast, about 22 miles (35 km) from Montego Bay, is **Falmouth** Ⓘ, a quiet, laid-back little town with pretty Georgian architecture and access to river rafting trips (daily; tel: 809-952 0889) along the **Martha Brae** river. One of the most popular excursions on the island, the trip takes one hour from Martha Brae village to the coast, as you are punted gently down the river on a bamboo raft for two. Rafting is offered by all the cruise lines as a shore excursion but is usually less expensive if you arrange it independently.

Bird lovers can head inland, south west of Montego Bay, taking a taxi to Anchovy and the **Rocklands Bird Feeding Station** Ⓙ (daily 2–5pm; entrance fee). This is a bird reserve, established in 1958, where visitors can experience excellent sightings of various attractive indigenous species, including the wonderful, tiny, colourful hummingbirds. ❏

BERMUDA

Maps on pages 176/79

In Bermuda, the ports of Hamilton and St George provide a wealth of things to see and do and eccentric characters to discover, even if you don't have time to visit the historic Royal Naval Dockyard

The semi-tropical island of Bermuda is not, of course, in the Caribbean at all, but some cruise lines include it on their Caribbean itineraries so it would be a pity to ignore it. Lying 774 miles (1,245 km) southeast of New York in the Atlantic Ocean, Bermuda consists of seven islands, linked by bridges. However, cruise ships usually call only at Hamilton, the capital, St George in the East End, and sometimes at the historic Naval Dockyard in the West End.

Exploring Hamilton

Hamilton has two distinct characters – one for day and another for night. By day, it is the nearest Bermuda achieves to a bustling metropolis. The narrow streets beyond the harbour teem with shoppers and office workers, and there is a busy, urban ambience. As dusk falls, the streets echo to the clip-clop of horses' hooves, and the scent of night blossoms from nearby Par-la-Ville Park fills the air. Later, the only sound will be the whistling tune created by tiny tree frogs, those invisible residents who provide the night-time chorus for Bermuda.

The town covers an area of 177 acres (70 hectares), with a resident population of only 2,000. Because the town blends seamlessly into its parish, Pembroke, it seems larger than it is. The cruise ship terminal disgorges passengers onto **Front Street Ⓐ**, from where all the main points of interest are within easy reach. During high season, Wednesday nights are given over to "harbour nights", when sleek cruise ships, such as the *Nordic Empress* and *Zenith*, dock alongside Front Street. Few shops are open late (most close by 6pm), but restaurant and pub balconies come alive at night. When not in use by cruise ships, the terminal buildings serve as entertainment centres, for lively events such as Gombey dance displays.

The tourist information office, the **Visitors' Service Bureau**, lies about 500 yds/metres from the terminal, where Front Street, the premier shopping thoroughfare, becomes Pitt's Bay Road. At the junction, where Queen Street, site of several historic buildings, leads inland, stands one of Bermuda's most famous sights, the **Birdcage Ⓑ**, where a shorts-clad police officer directs traffic during the summer months.

Next door to the Visitors' Service Bureau is the **ferry terminal**, a pink building with candy-striped awnings. Bermuda's ferries are clean, efficient and run to schedule. It is from here, too, that glass-bottomed boats depart for short sightseeing cruises.

A few steps away, down the lane separating the Visitors' Service Bureau from the Bank of Bermuda (where a dozen cubicles allow travellers' cheques to be cashed with ease), is a small promontory jutting out to sea. This is **Albuoy's Point Ⓒ**, a grassy park popular with office workers at lunchtime. At dusk,

PRECEDING PAGES: Beating Retreat at the harbour, Front Street, Hamilton. **LEFT:** a penny farthing outside a quaint St George shop. **BELOW:** the Town Crier, St George.

The tradition of the Gombey dancing is passed down from father to son. Dance troupes perform in Hamilton and at events all over the world.

this peninsula is probably the best place in the centre of Hamilton to watch the sun as it sets prettily over the water. It is also one of the main tourist stops for the shiny black-and-red sightseeing locomotive operated by the **Bermuda Train Company** (tel: 441-236 5972). In 1999, more than half a century after the closure and sale of the Bermuda Railway, which ran from East End to West End and right down Front Street, the 60-seat locomotive began transporting passengers around the capital – a great way to see the town in a short space of time.

Turning left from the Visitors' Bureau, along Pitt's Bay Road, past the **Royal Bermuda Yacht Club** and pretty **Barr's Bay Park**, you soon reach the capital's finest small hotel, called **Waterloo House ⓓ**. Built on a series of undulating terraces that end up by the sea, it is one of the few places in Hamilton where outdoor tables are arranged so people can enjoy the view of the harbour while they eat. For this reason – plus its excellent kitchens – Waterloo House is a popular lunchtime spot for both Bermudians and visitors.

Back to the past

Back at the birdcage, turn left up Queen Street. On your left is **Par-la-Ville Park ⓔ**, Hamilton's largest, most central public garden. There are palm trees, bird baths and flower beds containing plants with exotic-sounding names. The gardens were laid out in around 1850 as part of the estate of William B. Perot, Bermuda's first postmaster, who created a famous postage stamp, for which collectors will now pay a fabulous sum – only 12 are known to exist. (Spick-and-span public toilets can be found by the garden's Queen Street entrance.)

The room in which the postmaster worked has been restored and is now called **Perot's Post Office ⓕ**. An authentic feel prevails, from the brass candlesticks to

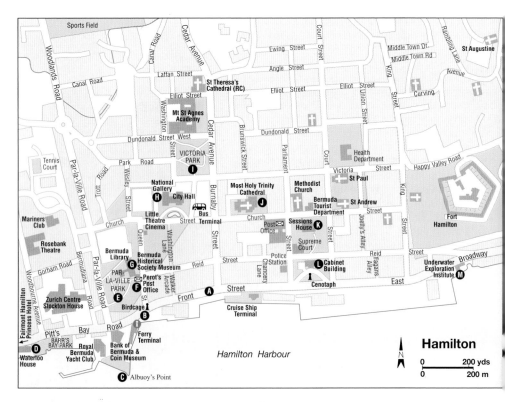

the wooden counter, where simple postal business is still carried out. It's fun to sit on one of the tall wooden stools and write a letter at the old-fashioned desks.

William Perot lived next door in what is now the **Bermuda Library and Historical Society Museum G** (Mon–Sat 9am–3pm; tel: 441-295 2487). The postmaster's passion for collecting exotic plants from all over the world led him to import from Demerara a rubber tree seed, and to plant it in front of the house. The seed grew to the massive tree under which local residents now take refuge from the heat. The museum consists of a series of small rooms decorated in original style with hurricane lamps, cedar furniture and English china.

To the right, along Church Street, is the **City Hall**, a grand building with a profusion of wind-divining instruments on top. Its East Exhibition Room is the site of the **National Gallery H** (open Mon–Sat 10am–4pm; entrance fee; tours). This climate-controlled room houses a collection of Bermuda's best works of art, as well as presenting a variety of exhibits from around the world.

Victoria Park I, directly behind, has a sunken garden. Open-air concerts are held in the ornate bandstand, which was built to commemorate Queen Victoria's Golden Jubilee in 1887. East along Victoria Street is the **Cathedral of the Most Holy Trinity J**, a mix of Gothic and Middle English architecture.

Law and order

The nearby **Sessions House K** was built on the highest hill in Hamilton. It is a conspicuous, dignified edifice, with a handsome clock-tower that was also erected to commemorate the Golden Jubilee. The large chamber in the house's upper storey is reserved for the use of the House of Assembly. In the chamber immediately below it, the Supreme Court holds its sessions. Near the Session

Map on page 176

Near the corner of Reid Street is the Phoenix Drugstore, where the arrival of daily papers from the US (at 3pm) and the UK (at 5.30pm), causes a flurry of activity.

BELOW: a busy shopping day in Hamilton.

In 1999, a statue of a local man, the Spirit of Bermuda, *was sculpted by Desmond Fountain and stands near the roundabout where Johnnie Barnes, a retired bus driver waves to commuters on their way to work each day. Barnes is a notable Bermudian figure, whose radiant eccentricity and loyal presence at the roundabout, rain or shine, says a great deal about the island and its people.*

BELOW: take a leisurely ride through Hamilton.

House stands the two-storey **Cabinet Building** (open Mon–Fri 9am–5pm) and, at the tip of its pleasant (public) lawns, is the stately **Cenotaph**. Based on the one in Whitehall, London, it commemorates those who died in both world wars.

A shopper's delight

You have now emerged once more onto **Front Street**, which follows the line of the harbour all the way to the docks. Turning right (back towards the cruise ship terminal) you will come to a series of two-tiered pastel-coloured buildings. This area signals a fine collection of shops. Many of the family-owned businesses date from the 19th century. Stores where the keynote is quality and service include **Bluck's** (1844; china and crystal) and Bermuda's oldest wine and spirits merchants, **Gosling's** (1806). The **Irish Linen Shop** can be recommended, too. Sadly, **Trimingham's** department store (established in 1844; general goods) and **Smith's** (1889; Burberry raincoats) have closed.

Further along Front Street is **Walker Arcade**, one of Hamilton's prettiest enclosed shopping areas. Lined with shops and offices, it widens into a courtyard, complete with Spanish-style birdbath and terracotta tiles – a pleasant place to pause.

Turning left from the Cenotaph will take you to the docks, where Front Street turns into East Broadway. Before you get to the *Spirit of Bermuda* statue of the official greeter, Johnny Barnes *(see left),* you reach the state-of-the-art **Bermuda Underwater Exploration Institute** (Mon–Fri 9am–5pm, Sat–Sun 10am–5pm; entrance fee; tel: 441–292 7219), a large white structure on the harbour. The institute contains a plethora of hands-on interactive exhibits, including a simulated dive 12,000 ft (3,600 metres) to the ocean floor – plus a fine French restaurant called La Coquille, where you can enjoy a meal along with splendid views of the busy harbour.

Out of town

It is possible to travel to almost anywhere on the island on the efficient pink public buses, all of which originate and terminate at the **bus terminal** next to City Hall. The fare structure is slightly complicated, however, as the island is divided into different "zones". You must have the exact fare in order to board a Bermuda bus, and it is helpful, and cheaper, to buy a booklet of prepaid tickets or a transport pass from the terminal office. You can also rent mopeds or scooters (but *not* cars), by the hour or day; or take a taxi tour of the island. All taxis are metered and the fares are fixed by law. However, most first-time visitors find there is more than enough in Hamilton to keep them busy during their time in port.

St George

A number of cruise ships dock not in Hamilton but in **St George**, which was the capital of Bermuda until it was replaced by Hamilton in 1815. The corporation of St George has recently embarked on an ambitious programme to develop the 17th-century town, but assurances have been given that this will not result in a Disneyland-style replica. Such is the town's historical importance that it has been designated a UNESCO

Map on page 179

World Heritage Site, and restoration plans include burying unsightly modern cables underground, providing street lighting reminiscent of days past and development of the waterfront area. It remains a wonderful place to explore on foot, as benign neglect has left it virtually unchanged. The alleys, with names like **One Gun Alley**, **Shinbone Alley** and **Featherbed Alley**, have not expanded beyond the width needed to roll a barrel. St George is practically as old as Jamestown, the first European settlement in America, and it feels as unaffectedly pristine as any town in the New World.

A walking tour

Most cruise ships dock at **Ordnance Island ⑩**, a former British army arsenal, although a few go to Penno's Wharf a short distance away. The island is a good place to begin a walking tour, starting with the replica of *Deliverance* (Apr–Nov, daily 9am–5pm; entrance fee). The original vessel was improvised out of salvage from another ship, *Sea Venture*, which struck a reef and brought the first, accidental settlers to shore, while en route to Virginia in the 17th century. The interior of the ship is tiny, with little headroom and even less space for sleeping.

The crest of St George, Bermuda.

As you cross to the mainland, you will see the **ducking stool ⑩**, which was notorious as a summary punishment for nagging wives. The stool is still wheeled over to the water's edge for practical demonstrations, although the wet seat now tends to be filled by a volunteer, possibly a selflessly dedicated employee of the Department of Tourism.

The **Visitors' Service Bureau** (tel: 441-297 8138) on the water's edge is well-stocked with information about St George and organises fascinating walking tours of the town. Walking or horse-and-carriage tours will also be organised by your cruise ship, or you can just take off by yourself. The congenial Town Crier, appropriately garbed in period attire, shows visitors around, and the Mayor puts down his pen at about 11 o'clock some mornings, bedecks himself with the chain of office, and emerges into old **King's Square**, to meet and chat to visitors.

The **Town Hall ⑩** (Mon–Sat 10am–4pm; free), the focal point of the square, was built of stone in the early 19th century. Furnished with beautiful Bermuda cedar, the small building is still used for council meetings today.

Another building of interest on the edge of the square is the **Bermuda National Trust Museum ⑩** (Mon–Sat 10am–4pm; entrance fee; tel: 441-297 1423), formerly the Globe Hotel and, for the duration of the American Civil War, the headquarters of the Confederate agent, Major Norman Walker. The museum's exhibit entitled "Rogues and Runners: Bermuda and the American Civil War" examines the period when the island made a small fortune from the blockade-running trade.

The beautifully preserved **St Peter's Church ⑩**, said to be "the oldest Anglican church in continuous use in the western hemisphere", stands above King's Square. The basis of the existing building dates from 1713, but the cedar wood altar is from an earlier structure.

Turning left down Duke of York Street from the

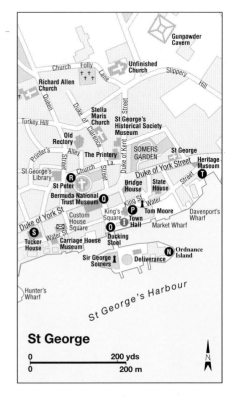

St George

0 ——— 200 yds
0 ——— 200 m

N

Remnants of British influence, such as this red telephone box, are evident throughout Bermuda.

square you will come to the **Tucker House** ❺ (Mon–Sat 10am–4pm; entrance fee; tel: 441-297 0545), which has important architectural features and is now a National Trust property housing a museum with handsome cedar wood furnishings, antique silver and other valuable artefacts. The wealthy Tuckers were descendants of the 17th-century governor, Dan Tucker.

To the east side of the square your walking tour will take you to the State House, to Somers Garden, a favourite spot for local artists, and to the **Heritage Museum** ❼ (Tues–Sat 10am–3pm; entrance fee; tel: 441-297 4126). Housed in the Samaritans Lodge, this traces the history of black people in Bermuda. Back along Duke of York Street is **Bridge House**, once home to several governors. The house is now an office and guest house. In the small, walled garden is the **bust of Tom Moore** (1779–1852), a visiting Irish poet who, it is claimed, fell in love with Nea, wife of one of the indomitable Tucker clan.

The Royal Naval Dockyard

At the beginning of the 19th century the Royal Navy needed a safe haven in the Atlantic. The Crown wanted to keep an eye not only on French privateers in the waters but also on the Americans who, after their successful revolution in 1776, closed all ports to the British. Bermuda was the obvious site and, in 1809, the Royal Naval Dockyard, the most ambitious building scheme in which the island ever engaged, was commenced. Today, there are blue-and-white terminals for cruise ships and modern tenders which transport passengers into Hamilton.

The site on Ireland Island North has now been turned into a vast, upmarket recreational complex, consisting of shops, fine restaurants, a well-appointed marina, a number of workshops and craft centres and a sightseeing train. A tour

of the dockyard begins in the large building opposite the Keep, which is now the premises of the **Craft Market** (daily 9.30am–5pm; tel: 441-234 3208). The fullest collection of island crafts in Bermuda can be found here, from stained-glass figures of indigenous birds to Gombey dolls.

Across the breezeway was the **Smithy**, with its huge stone fireplace. Another fireplace is located in the lobby of the **Cooperage Theatre**, home of the **Neptune Cinema**. The grassy expanse in the middle of the complex was the **Victualling Yard**, where supplies for the base were stored. It's a stately spot, surrounded by imposing two-storey Georgian buildings. From the centre you can see the impressive stone **Commissioner's House**, which has undergone a multi-million dollar restoration and is now part of the Maritime Museum.

One of the later buildings to be constructed at Dockyard was the handsome **Great Eastern Storehouse**, a building with twin clock-towers. Below the towers, the storehouse is now a smart shopping mall with chic boutiques, galleries and reasonably priced souvenir shops ideal for cruise ship passengers in a hurry.

Huge warehouses are now the premises of the **Island Pottery**, the **Bermuda Clayworks** and other workshops, where visitors can watch potters at their craft. The **Bermuda Arts Center** (daily 10am–5pm; free; tel: 441-234 2809) is a non-profit organisation run by volunteers, the arts centre holds changing exhibitions.

The **Bermuda Maritime Museum** (Apr–Oct daily 9.30am–5pm, last admission 4pm; Nov–Mar, 10am–5pm; entrance fee; tel: 441-234 1418) should not be missed. Fascinating displays include the Tucker Treasure and exhibits on diving, navigation, shipping and whaling, plus an interesting walk around the Keep's towering ramparts. The museum will give you a better understanding of Bermuda's links with the sea and send you back to your ship with a lot to think about. ❏

Map on page 179

TIP

If you're hungry, try the Freeport Seafood Restaurant and Bar near the entrance gates, or the Frog & Onion pub, near the cinema. Both serve tasty fresh fish and seafood.

BELOW: the Victualling Yard was built by over 9,000 convicts.

SAILING IN THE EAST

The Eastern Caribbean is ideal for seven-day cruises that take in a culturally diverse range of islands, including a few tiny spots that are exclusive to the cruise lines

Map on page 156

F irst, one needs to define what the Eastern Caribbean consists of – in cruising terms, at least. The main islands covered by the cruise lines on their Eastern Caribbean tours are the Bahamas, Puerto Rico, the US Virgin Islands, St Maarten and Cuba. Although a quick look at a map might suggest that the British Virgin Islands should be included in this list, they are, in fact, usually part of the cruise lines' southern itineraries.

The majority of the major lines cover these eastern ports of call – with the exception of Cuba which, because of the US embargo on trade and travel, is in a category of its own. Because the region is fairly close to the United States, most of the cruises begin in Florida – at Miami, Fort Lauderdale or Port Canaveral – from where they can comfortably cover quite a lot of nautical miles in seven days – the usual length of a trip.

One of the joys of these itineraries is that they visit islands that are culturally so different. The Bahamas has strong British influences combined with all the colour of the Caribbean; Puerto Rico may be part of the USA, but the port of San Juan is an archetypal Spanish colonial town; St Thomas combines excellent duty-free shopping with fantastic beaches, while St Maarten is a pleasing mixture of Dutch and French cultures.

PRECEDING PAGES: cruise ships line up in Nassau, the Bahamas. **LEFT:** lounging by *Fantasy*'s pool. **BELOW:** time to relax in the Bahamas.

Cruising options

The available options range across the spectrum, from Princess Cruises' premium class mega-ship, *Golden Princess* – one of the largest, with a capacity for 2,600 passengers; Norwegian Cruise Line's *Norwegian Dawn*, a premium class ship (and one of the few that includes a stop at Tortola on the British Virgin Islands); through the mid-price, big ships, such as Royal Caribbean's *Explorer of the Seas*; to the small, sail-assisted *Wind Spirit*, Windstar Cruises' luxury vessel, which carries a maximum of 150 passengers (and 88 crew – a great ratio if you want personal service). Most of the cruises include two or three full days at sea to give passengers a chance to enjoy the wide range of facilities they offer on board.

A typical itinerary is one run by Royal Caribbean from Miami to San Juan (Puerto Rico) to Philipsburg, St Maarten, to Charlotte Amalie on St Thomas, then to Nassau, with between six and 10 hours in each port and two full days at sea. Princess Cruises runs another typical cruise, from Fort Lauderdale to St Thomas, St Martin and Nassau, and also Princess Cays, a company-owned island in the Bahamas. Carnival and Holland America run similar itineraries. Disney Cruise Line runs a shorter, four-day tour, which calls only at Nassau and Disney's own private island, Castaway Cay, but allows a long day in each place.

Map on page 156

Several of the cruise lines' "private islands" are in this region. All have wonderful beaches and, after being welcomed ashore with a chilled rum punch and the rhythms of a steel band, passengers spend their time swimming, sailing, water-skiing, soaking up the sun and enjoying a sizzling barbecue. Princess Cruises owns Princess Cays in the Bahamas, while Royal Caribbean owns an island, Coco Cay, not far from Nassau in the Bahamas, and Labadee, a peninsula on the secluded north coast of Haiti (sometimes included on eastern itineraries). Disney's Castaway Cay is one of the best, with a long slither of white sandy beach, and good facilities, including bars and bicycles. It is also reached direct from the ship, rather than by tendering, which can take a very long time on some private isles. Opinions about these islands are mixed. The private islands sound idyllic, but they are totally lacking in Caribbean culture and you will be sharing your "private" spot with the rest of your cruise passengers.

The Bahamas

Even though the Bahamas is actually in the Atlantic, it is invariably included in Caribbean tours, and for that reason we have covered it in this book. In fact, a visit to **Nassau**, capital of the Bahamas, is among the highlights of an Eastern Caribbean cruise. Prince George Wharf can accommodate a dozen cruise ships at a time and the cruise terminal, Festival Place, right on the wharf, has all the facilities a visitor could want. Passengers disembark right in the heart of Nassau, and schedules allow plenty of time for an informative guided walk around the historic capital of this ex-British colony. Alternatively, there is time for a ferry trip to the nearby resort island, Paradise Island. If your ship docks in **Freeport** on Grand Bahama Island, a range of outdoor activities are on offer, from a visit to the Lucaya National Park to a chance to swim with dolphins.

BELOW:
carnival time in
Old San Juan.

San Juan, St Thomas and St John

San Juan, in Puerto Rico (which also acts as a home port for ships venturing further south, *see page 209*), offers a different kind of experience. Most cruise ships dock at Calle Marina, just to the south of the lovely old Spanish colonial town, and the majority of people are content to spend their day soaking up the atmosphere. El Yunque rainforest is not far away. Most ships organise tours but it is easy to reach independently.

The US Virgin Islands are something else again. Ships dock at **Charlotte Amalie**, in St Thomas, which has a lovely harbour and is known as the duty-free shopping centre of the Caribbean. The nearby island of **St John**, two-thirds of which is an unspoilt national park, is reached by a short, inexpensive, ferry ride.

Cruise ships calling at St Maarten usually dock at the main port, **Philipsburg**, and allow passengers time to visit **Marigot** in St Martin, thus giving a flavour of both Dutch and French sides of the island in one brief visit.

Cuba is off-limits to US passengers, but some cruise lines have it on their itineraries for people of other nationalities. Fred Olsen Cruise Lines has several itineraries that include a stop in Havana, Cuba. There is a 14-night cruise which takes in Jamaica, Cuba, Costa Maya and Belize, and a 28-night cruise that stops in Cuba before transiting the Panama Canal. ❑

Private Hideaways

Balmy breezes, sun-drenched beaches, aquamarine seas, lavender-coloured marinas full of luxurious yachts – the rich are richly rewarded in the Caribbean. "You go to heaven if you want, I'd rather stay here," said Voltaire of the Caribbean. Owning a private island is the ultimate fantasy, best embodied by Necker Island, a millionaire's playground in the British Virgin Islands. Richard Branson, founder of Virgin, bought it in 1979 for personal use, but now accepts paying guests, such as Stephen Spielberg or George Michael. The island, a smooth green lump ringed with sand, is designed as an exclusive Balinese-style estate. A constant supply of bands, butlers and speedboats ensures that guests are happy.

Cruise passengers are tempted to think that they, too, can enjoy a private island for a day, but it is shared with thousands of others.

Celebrity hideaways couldn't be further removed from the cheerful inclusiveness of the cruise lines' private ports of call. Each island has its own fashionable following, with Mustique, St Barts and Barbados among the most select. Mustique, put on the map by the late Princess Margaret in the 1960s, has been offering sanctuary to the stars ever since. From David Bowie and Mick Jagger to David Beckham and Tommy Hilfiger, celebrities appreciate the privacy symbolised by a secluded pastel-pink villa and manicured lawns.

St Barts is where the rich like to play poor, but vintage Veuve Cliquot may well accompany the baguette on the beach. The pared-down chic of St Barts has much to do with the cheek of the French in daring to transform this arid rock into St Tropez. As a haunt of Rockefellers and Rothschilds, European royalty and international celebrities, St Barts feels more Côte d'Azur than Caribbean.

Barbados, as anglicised as St Barts is Gallic, represents an equally exclusive haunt for celebrities, who relish the re-creation of a colonial grandeur that never quite existed, typified by the luxurious Sandy Lane Hotel. Not that these islands have a monopoly.

Antigua is home to Eric Clapton, while tiny Barbuda is virtually a fiefdom of Krizia, the Italian fashion designer, who has created the exclusive K-Club for publicity-shy celebrities. Parrot Cay in the Turks and Caicos is the most over-hyped hideaway, a colonial-style resort framed by coral reefs and cactus groves. Bruce Willis, Barbra Streisand, and Britney Spears are all fans. There have been reports that the actor, Leonardo DiCaprio, has bought part of the tiny island, Blackadore Caye. The island, which is a short boat ride from the Belize Barrier Reef, is slated for development as an exclusive eco-resort.

Jamaica has its fans, too. After being "discovered" by Noël Coward, Jamaica appealed to Ivor Novello and Charlie Chaplin, Clark Gable and Errol Flynn. Ian Fleming, creator of James Bond, built Goldeneye, his winter retreat, here. Now owned by Chris Blackwell, the founder of Island Records, it remains a bolt-hole for stars such as Michael Caine and Harrison Ford, Pierce Brosnan and Sting, who penned *Every Breath You Take* while ensconced on the bamboo sofa. ❏

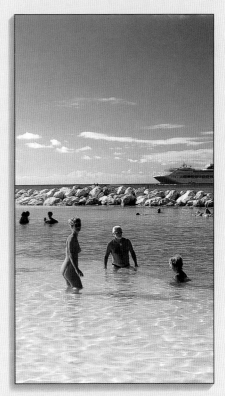

RIGHT: the *Sun Princess*, anchored off Princess Cays, in the Bahamas.

THE BAHAMAS

Learn about Bahamian history in Nassau, see how the rich have fun on Paradise Island, and use Freeport as a starting point for visiting botanic gardens and swimming with dolphins

Maps on pages 192/94

When it comes to cruising the Bahamas, all eyes are on the two main ports: Nassau, the national capital, on New Providence Island, and Freeport, on Grand Bahama. The two islands are truly a study in contrasts, but both offer something for short- and long-stay visitors, from colonial architecture to glitzy casinos, from white, sandy beaches to opportunities to encounter dolphins. The islands received a battering from all three hurricanes that swept through the region in 2004, Grand Bahama suffered the most with a repair bill of around $200 million. As a result, some of the attractions described here may not be open to the public.

New Providence, roughly 20 miles (32 km) in circumference, and 8 miles (13 km) wide, is home to almost a quarter of a million residents. Nassau is situated on the North Shore of the island, approximately 180 nautical miles southeast of Miami, and, for many people, this commercial hub, *is* the Bahamas. It is certainly a more atmospheric town than Freeport, the nation's second city, which was created in the 1955, but the latter is a jumping-off point for an island that has much to offer, from limestone caves to lush exotic gardens.

The Port of Nassau's **Prince George Wharf** underwent an extensive, US$55 million renovation in 1990 and was given a Welcome Centre and all the facilities that cruise ship passengers need, including a Ministry of Tourism office. Most recently, Festival Place has been constructed on the wharf and will include a communications centre, from where local and international calls can be made, an internet café, authentic Bahamian arts and crafts, a banking centre, and the **Junkanoo Expo**, which displays the vivid costumes worn for the Junkanoo celebrations of music, noise and colour on Boxing Day and New Year's Day – a great first taste of Bahamian culture.

PRECEDING PAGES: on the beach at Princess Cays. **LEFT:** a straw market vendor in Nassau. **BELOW:** shopping in Bay Street, Nassau.

The port can accommodate 12 cruise ships at a time and they all berth directly by the pier, so tenders are not needed. Passengers literally walk off the ship and onto Bay Street, in the heart of the city and central shopping area, a few hundred yards away.

Getting to know Nassau

There are dozens of ways to enjoy Nassau if you have only a day in port. Among them are professionally guided walking tours of the city centre, when a Bahamahost, a Ministry of Tourism-trained tour guide, takes groups of up to 10 people on one-hour walking tours of two different areas of historic Nassau. The guides are well informed on everything from local history to archaeology, from flora and fauna to the monuments you will encounter along the route – and these tours only cost about US$5 per person.

As you pass the 19th-century **Public Buildings** **B**,

just off Bay Street, you will probably learn a little about the islands' history. They became English colonies in 1629, briefly fell under Spanish rule in 1782 and, after years as a dependency, became the independent Commonwealth of the Bahamas in 1973. Immediately south of these government offices are the Supreme Court building, and the quaint **Nassau Public Library** which contains, among other things, a small collection of Amerindian artefacts.

The library stands on the corner of Parliament Street, where you will see some lovely historic buildings, mostly dating from the mid-19th century. Prominent among them are **Jacaranda**, with wide, latticed verandas, and **Green Shutters**, now a lively restaurant. Not far away stands **St Andrew's Presbyterian Church** , known as The Kirk, a pleasant, welcoming building; the Trinity Methodist Church; and Christ Church Cathedral, with a beautiful stained-glass window above the altar. From The Kirk you go over George Arch (also known as the Gregory Arch) to **Government House** , a pink and white neo-colonial building that is the official residence of the Governor-General.

If you prefer, you can just wander around by yourself. Or you can take a horse-drawn surrey (with a fringe on top) from **Woodes Rogers Walk**, at the port entrance, for a 20-minute clip-clop along Bay Street and around Old Nassau. Rates are negotiable, and the guides are Bahamahost-trained.

Pirate pleasure dome

A shuttle bus transports cruise ship passengers from the dock to the **Pirates of Nassau Museum** (open Mon–Sat 9am–6pm, Sun 9am–12pm; entrance fee; tel: 242-356 3759; www.pirates-of-nassau.com), just a few blocks away, opposite the cathedral. At this intriguing interactive museum, visitors board a full-size

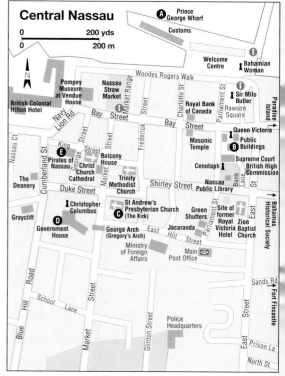

replica of the pirate ship *Revenge* and enter the world of cutlass-wielding, blood-thirsty pirates. You are encouraged to "walk among them as they eat, drink, sleep, gamble, plot and pillage" and, in the process, learn about Bahamian history, and some of the world's notorious buccaneering characters.

A pirate pub serves lunch and dinner, and next door to it "Plunder!", a pirate-themed gift shop, tempts you to buy. On the 10-minute walk back to the ship you could stop at the **Straw Market** to buy souvenirs – baskets, dolls, table mats, hats – made from plaited thatch palm. The market burned down in a fire in 2001, but temporary stalls have been erected close to the cruise terminal; the original market site will no doubt be redeveloped into the bustling place it was before.

Map on page 192

Paradise Island

At Prince George Wharf, ferry boats wait to take passengers to **Paradise Island**, across Nassau Harbour. This resort island (formerly and less glamorously known as Hog Island) is a very swish place indeed. Among its expensive pleasures are the Atlantis Resort; the Hurricane Hole, a haven for luxury yachts; the Yoga Retreat; a 14th-century Gothic Cloister, brought from France and reconstructed stone by stone; the Versailles Gardens surrounding the exclusive Ocean Club Hotel; and the 18-hole championship Ocean Club Golf Course. There is also a slender crescent of white sand called Paradise Beach. There are organised tours to Paradise, or you can just get on a ferry and go independently.

A number of other excursions can be booked on board, or on shore. To go it alone, taxi rates are reasonable and public buses are cheap. Since 2001's September 11 terrorist attacks, the dock has been designated a non-motorised zone, so taxis, buses and tours are available outside the checkpoint.

A seat at Atlantis. The large resort can be seen from almost any point on the northeast coast of New Providence.

BELOW: relaxing by the pool at Atlantis.

Junkanoo masks are bright and colourful. Junkanoo festivities, including street parades, take place the day after Christmas and again on New Year's Day.

BELOW: visitors can explore Grand Bahama by bicycle.

Grand Bahama

Grand Bahama, which is three times the size of New Providence, sits at the northern end of the Bahamas chain, and has just over 50,000 residents. The emphasis here is on the outdoors – from nature walks to fully-fledged eco-adventures, all available on organised tours.

The **Lucayan Harbour Cruise Facility** (formerly the Freeport Harbour Cruise Facility) lies 65 miles (105 km) east of West Palm Beach and 80 miles (128 km) northeast of Miami. Covering 1,630 acres (668 hectares), it can accommodate the largest cruise ships in the world. The total berth length of over 6,000 ft (1,800 metres) accommodates both cruise ship and day ferry berths.

A US$10-million dollar upgrade to the facility was completed in 2001 and the massive terminals now have everything cruise passengers could wish for. The area has a tropical landscape design and encloses a huge, Bahamian-style retail and entertainment village centre and market place, where most of the standard excursions organised by the cruise lines begin. The harbour lies to the west of central Freeport. If you are going to explore alone, the taxi fare to the International Bazaar, costs about US$5–7 per person; to Port Lucaya, about $10.

Things to do in Freeport

Most of the attractions of Grand Bahama lie a little way outside town, but there are some things to see and do in Freeport. The **International Bazaar** ⬤, in the centre of town, has a lot of cheap merchandise but is a good place for cameras and photographic equipment, and the Colombian Emeralds outlet has a huge selection of jewellery. To the east of the bazaar, the **Straw Market** offers some local colour; while on the other side the **Royal Oasis Resort and Casino** ⬤ has

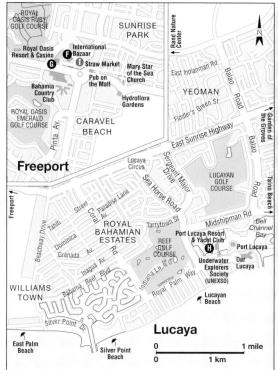

a spectacular 1 million-gallon fresh-water pool (open to the public; US$20 fee), a man-made white sandy beach and two golf courses.

Two more golf courses are part of **Our Lucaya** beach-front resort complex to the east of Freeport, close to the stunning white Lucayan Beach. The **Port Lucaya Resort and Yacht Club ⓗ**, an extensive series of man-made canals, includes a huge yacht basin. The most fun is to be had at **Port Lucaya** itself, which buzzes with activity around the central market place, with shops selling local crafts, trendy boutiques, restaurants and live entertainment.

Nature trails

There is a fascinating excursion to be made to the **Rand Nature Center** (open Mon–Fri 9am–4pm, Sat 9am–1pm; entrance fee; tel: 242-352 5438), to the north of Freeport. Run by the Bahamas National Trust, this 100-acre (40-hectare) national park has some interesting nature trails, a flock of West Indian flamingos and well-informed guides to talk you through it all.

To the east of Freeport and Lucaya lies the **Garden of the Groves** (open daily 9am–4pm; entrance fee; www.gardenofthegroves.com), spectacular, landscaped botanical gardens with waterfalls and a lush fern gully (a popular spot for wedding parties). Children will enjoy the petting zoo, and visitors of all ages should love the African pygmy goats, Vietnamese pot-bellied pigs, colourful peacocks, macaws and cockatoos. Alligator feeding time is always popular, too.

There is also a Bahamian arts and crafts market on the property, a café and a children's party area, as well as the **Grand Bahama Museum**, with reconstructed caves, audio-visual presentations, Lucayan Amerindian artefacts from

Map on page 194

Jazz fans will be pleased to find Count Basie Square in Port Lucaya, complete with bandstand. Born in New Jersey, Basie made Freeport his adoptive home.

BELOW: a dolphin encounter with UNEXSO, at Sanctuary Bay.

Map
on page
194

BELOW: water
sports such as
windsurfing are
popular in Grand
Bahama.
RIGHT: Port Lucaya
is a favourite of
yachties.

the National Park caves and pirate paraphernalia. The garden gets its name, incidentally, not from any natural feature, but from Georgette and Wallace Groves, who created this lovely spot. Groves did much more than that, however – he was the Virginian financier who founded the Grand Bahama Port authority and Freeport itself in the 1960s.

There is also a guided nature tour through the **Lucayan National Park** (open daily 9am–4pm; entrance fee), about 13 miles (21 km) east of the Garden of the Groves. Led by knowledgeable local guides, you can explore the caves that form one of the largest charted underwater cave systems in the world. The park has an extensive figure of eight system of paths that take you into two caves, in one of which were discovered artifacts and bones relating to the island's first inhabitants, the Lucayan Amerindians. Above ground, the 40-acre (16-hectare) park has trails through forests rich in tropical vegetation – cedar and mahogany trees, and mangrove lagoons that support a wealth of birdlife.

All these places can be visited independently, but cruise ships include them on their excursions and that is probably the easiest way to go.

The Dolphin Experience

Among out-of-town excursions, a perennially popular one is to the **Dolphin Experience** at Sanctuary Bay, a 9-acre (4-hectare) lagoon a short ferry ride from the UNEXSO (Underwater Explorers' Society) dock at Port Lucaya. The tour takes approximately 2½ hours and includes informative talks about these intelligent mammals (did you know their gestation period was 12 months?). You can have various kinds of in-the-water encounters with the dolphins, including swimming or even snorkeling with them: rates vary, depending what you want to do – the more interaction, the more it costs. Some of the resident dolphins are international celebrities, having appeared in Hollywood films, but they don't seem to mind mixing with ordinary mortals.

Other alternatives

If you have only a short time in port and don't want to go too far from town, other cruise ship excursions include snorkelling and kayaking trips and beach parties on the lovely Lucayan Beach and Taino Beach (the latter about 2 miles/4 km) from Port Lucaya).

The **Sea Safari Snorkel Adventure** is also popular, and organised cruise ship tours are run twice daily. It's a two-hour foray among Grand Bahamas' tropical fish and living corals, at Rainbow Reef and the surrounding area. It's only minutes away from the dock, and also has a rock-climbing wall and two water slides. All gear is provided and there is professional instruction and supervision.

Transport

Unless you are booked on a cruise ship excursion, the only means of transport from the port is by taxi. Buses take the pre-paid shore excursion passengers on their tours, but otherwise the nearest public bus route begins about 1 mile (2 km) from the port, towards the centre of Freeport. There are also buses from Port Lucaya back to the centre. ❑

CUBA: HAVANA

After years of isolation, Havana has once more become a tourist hot-spot. This vibrant city offers culture, colonial architecture and ever-present irresistible music, all within a compact area

Map on page 202

T he largest of all the Caribbean islands (with a population of 11 million), Cuba was the most-visited country in the Caribbean during the 1950s. But when Fidel Castro came to power in 1959, the tourism boom ended. Thirty-two years later, following the break-up of the Soviet Union and the loss of revenue it represented as a trading partner, Cuba again turned to tourism for its economic salvation. Today, the island is a popular destination once again, catered to by a newly developed infrastructure.

Sultry, exotic, romantic and rich with Latin music and colonial history, the island has a gorgeous landscape of lush mountains, powdery beaches and tropical greenery. A shore excursion offers an eye-opening glimpse of the complex realities of the embattled economy of this socialist island. Cuba is a remarkably safe country, especially considering the poverty of many of its inhabitants, and it puts a great deal of effort into making visitors feel welcome.

Although the island has eight ports of entry, the majority of cruises come ashore in the capital city of **Havana** at the **Terminal Sierra Maestra** (tel: 7-33-6607). Upgraded in the late 1990s, the terminal is an odd blend of old colonial-style architecture, modern chrome-and-glass and, hardwood floors, and has an antique Dodge car propped up on display. Located on **Avenida San Pedro**, it is packed with modern amenities, including a snack bar and gift shop, and disembarks its passengers onto **Plaza de San Francisco**, a small square centred around a lion fountain, right in the heart of Old Havana where tour buses and taxis await.

The first thing passengers spot when sailing into the harbour is the impressive fortress, **El Morro** on one side of the entrance and the **Castillo de San Salvador de la Punta ❶** on the other. Built in the 1500s, both structures provided Cuba with a defence against French and British invaders during colonial times. At the tip of El Morro is a lighthouse that has guided thousands of ships into port with its sweeping beam of light since it opened in 1845.

Habana Vieja

A typical day-long excursion in Havana usually includes a city tour in an air-conditioned bus, a stop for lunch, and a walk though **Habana Vieja** (Old Havana) – a UNESCO World Heritage Site packed with beautiful Spanish colonial buildings, many with brightly tiled, plant-filled courtyards. English-speaking guides usually accompany groups at all times. While some cruise companies insist that their passengers take an organised tour, others allow them to explore on their own. If you opt to do this, you will find there is plenty to see within walking distance of the terminal.

PRECEDING PAGES: a sentry box at Castillo de San Salvador de la Punta.
LEFT: vintage American cars line the Prado.
BELOW: the cigar is a symbol of Cuba.

La Bodeguita del Medio, Hemingway's old watering hole, started life as a grocery store in 1942.

A few blocks away is the **Plaza de Armas** ❸, the city's oldest square, dating back to around 1520. One of the busiest public places in Havana, the plaza is a meeting place for local people by day and night. In the centre stands a statue to Carlos Manuel de Céspedes (1819–74), a Cuban hero who fought unsuccessfully against Spanish rule; and a mass of stalls selling fascinating second-hand books and prints lines two sides of the square.

Several historic buildings sit around the plaza, including the **Palacio de los Capitanes Generales** ❹, a massive baroque structure with thick mahogany doors that served as the headquarters of the Cuban government in the late 1790s. Today, it houses the **Museo de la Ciudad** (City Museum; daily 9am–6.30pm; entrance fee), a repository of paintings, sculptures, artefacts, military uniforms and documents pertaining to the city's history, with a special collection devoted to the Cuban wars of independence.

A few doors down is the **Castillo de la Real Fuerza** ❹, the first fortress constructed by the Spanish in Cuba. Surrounded by a muddy water moat, it was

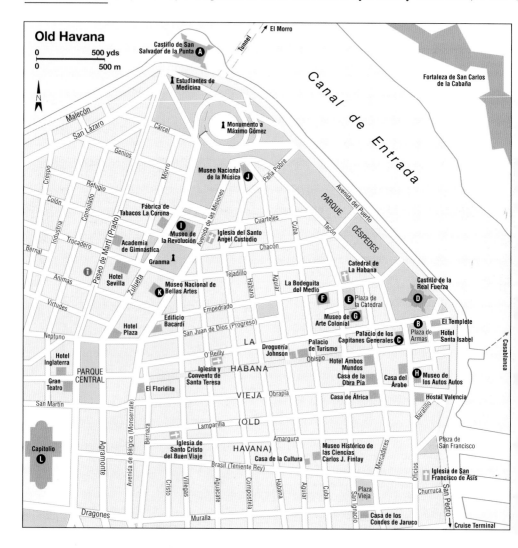

built by the explorer Hernando de Soto in 1538, destroyed by the French a few years later, and then reconstructed in 1558. These days it contains a small arms museum, the **Museo de Armas** (Thur–Mon 9.15am–4.45pm; entrance fee).

Map on page 202

Leaving the square

To the north lies the beautiful **Plaza de la Catedral ⒺⒺ**, dominated by the baroque, 18th-century **cathedral**. Among the Spanish colonial buildings around the square, the **Palacio de los Marqueses de Aguas Claras** is perhaps the most splendid. It now houses El Patio restaurant; this is quite expensive, but the tables set outside make a great place for a rest and a drink, and there's usually a band playing.

More than two blocks away from the plaza, on Calle Baratillo, is **Casa della Comedia**. One of the oldest buildings in Havana, it served as the city's main playhouse during the 18th century, and now contains the offices of several local theatre companies.

One of the most-visited spots in Old Havana is **La Bodeguita del Medio Ⓕ** (daily 10am–11pm; tel: 7-62 4498) on Calle Empedrado. This "little store in the middle of the block" is packed with pre-Revolutionary history and full of Ernest Hemingway memorabilia. A classic Cuban tavern, the Bodeguita's walls are covered with messages written by satisfied customers from around the world. Along with Hemingway, who downed numerous *mojitos* (a rum and lime juice cocktail) at the wooden bar, other notables who have imbibed here include Graham Greene, Errol Flynn, Gabriel García Márquez, Salvador Allende and Fidel Castro himself. With live Latin music most nights and some lunchtimes, the bar is always busy, and the traditional Cuban food – while a bit pricey, because this place is on most tourists' agenda – is hearty and good.

Another place redolent with Hemingway lore is the Hotel Ambos Mundos on the corner of Mercaderes and Obispo streets. The room where he stayed – where his typewriter still sits – can be visited for a small fee.

BELOW: the baroque cathedral in Plaza de la Catedral.

Another world-famous bar, and a lunch stop on most Old Havana tours, is **El Floridita** (daily noon–1am; tel: 537-867 1300/ 1301) on Calle Obispo. Also a Hemingway hangout, the Floridita is where the Nobel Prize-winning author came to drink daiquiris, which were supposedly invented here. Modernised in recent years to accommodate tourists, the Floridita has lost some of its old Bohemian charm, but still serves excellent food.

A few museums

A few museums of note that are worth checking out include two in Old Havana. Most of the city's museums are housed in beautiful old buildings and, unless you go as part of, or at the same time as, a tour group, they usually seem to have more attendants than visitors. The **Museo de Arte Colonial ⑤** (Museum of Colonial Art; Wed–Sun 9.30am–7pm; it has been closed for repairs so check before visiting; entrance fee), on the corner of Calle San Ignacio, overlooking the Plaza de la Catedral, displays a significant collection of 18th- and 19th-century colonial art and furnishings. Not far away, just off Plaza de Armas on Calle Oficios, is the **Museo de los Autos ⑪** (Car Museum; daily 9am–7pm; entrance fee), which contains a collection of beautifully preserved old cars, one of which belonged to the revolutionary hero, Che Guevara.

Towards central Havana, and set between the two main thoroughfares, Avenida de los Misiones and the Paseo de Martí (a broad, tree-lined promenade known as El Prado), you cannot miss the **Museo de la Revolución ⑪** (Museum of the Revolution; daily 10am–5pm; entrance fee). It holds a wealth of material on the Cuban revolution – including some wonderful photographs and torn and blood-stained garments – the years of struggle that preceded it and its accomplishments.

The huge Plaza de la Revolución is the site of all Fidel's major speeches. In the centre of the square is a monument dedicated to national hero, José Martí (1853–95) – you can take a lift to the top; and there's a large, illuminated mural of Che Guevara on the side of a modern government building.

BELOW: Che Guevara looks on.

THE CUBA QUESTION

Although travellers from Europe, Canada and Latin America are flocking to the island in droves, for most Americans, Cuba is forbidden fruit. Due to the US embargo – in place since 1961 – it is illegal for US citizens to "spend money" in Cuba. Yes, the US is still fighting the Cold War when it comes to the socialist government of Cuba, and most cruise companies are not happy about it.

Technically, the embargo means that commerce, rather than travel, is what is forbidden. But loopholes abound, and the US Treasury Department estimates that almost 100,000 American tourists visit the island illegally each year, usually via Mexico or the Bahamas. Hundreds have been threatened or fined (US$5,000) since the department started cracking down on violators in the 1990s.

No cruise companies that do business in the US sail into Cuba, but Italian, French and British companies that depart from Jamaica, Mexico or the Cayman Islands welcome US citizens. Some companies claim that Americans are paying the cruise line, and not spending any money in Cuba. But Americans wishing to travel with these companies do so at their own risk. For more information, visit a few of the following websites: www.treas.gov, www.cruisehavana.com, or www.4cubacruises.com.

Map on page 202

Attached to the museum is the **Memorial Granma**, where the *Granma,* a motor boat that brought Fidel Castro from Mexico to Cuba at the start of the revolution, is displayed in a glass case, Outside, a bullet-pocked delivery van, used for an attack on the Presidential Palace, and remnants of a U2 spy plane shot down over Cuba in 1962, stand under the watchful eyes of military guards. Close by, going towards the sea, and housed in a colonial mansion, is the **Museo Nacional de la Música ❿** (Museum of Music; Tues–Sat 9am–5pm, Sun 8am–noon; entrance fee; tel: 537-861 9846), which pays tribute to the island's contribution to world music, with a large collection of drums and stringed instruments.

Heading back towards the palm-fringed Parque Central, you will find the huge and airy **Museo Nacional de Bellas Artes ⓚ** (National Museum of Fine Arts; Tues–Sat 10am–6pm, Sun 10am–2pm; entrance fee), which holds an extraordinary international collection of paintings, by artists ranging from Velásquez to Canaletto, as well as the works of Cuban painters, and Greek and Roman statuary. The grandiose, domed building at the far side of Parque Central is the **Capitolio ⓛ**, built in the 1920s as the presidential palace and modelled on the Capitol in Washington. It now houses the Academy of Sciences. Next to it stands the flamboyant **Gran Teatro**, where national ballet and opera companies perform.

The Tropicana has glamorous, sexy floor shows that are popular with tourists.

Nightlife

If a cruise ship is in port during the evening, excursions usually include a pre-arranged trip to the famous **Tropicana Nightclub** (Tues–Sun 8.30pm–3am). Known for its live salsa bands and sexy floor shows, the Tropicana delivers a once-in-a-lifetime treat. Beneath an open-air canopy of palm trees, the high-energy, ostentatious Tropicana ballroom features over 200 performers in each cabaret show. The food is fairly good, the potent rum is generously poured, and the shows are fantastic, but the cost of an evening here can be steep, with the entrance fee alone being more than US$60.

BELOW: a street musician entertains in Havana.

The Tropicana, however, is not the only hot nightspot in town. In a city where music seems to seep out of every nook and cranny, there are numerous clubs, bars, cafés, and dance halls where the local acts are first rate – and far less expensive than at the Tropicana. In fact, you can chance upon excellent bands and singers in some small and unprepossessing places, where you can listen for hours for the price of a couple of drinks or a light meal

Festivals

Annual events worth planning a cruise around include the **Havana Film Festival** in December, when film producers, directors and actors from across the globe gather for a series of screenings, discussions and parties; and **May Day**, when the workers are honoured and President Castro gives one of his typical – long – speeches to the massive crowds that fill the Plaza de la Revolución *(see box, opposite).*

The most vibrant event in the Cuban capital is the **Havana Carnival** in July, a flamboyant musical and cultural extravaganza, with a parade of colourful floats, Afro-Cuban drummers, dancers, ballet performances, and salsa, salsa and more salsa. ❑

PUERTO RICO: SAN JUAN

*Concentrate on the lovely Spanish-colonial old town if you have
a one-day stop in San Juan, or take a trip to El Yunque rainforest.
For extended stays, hire a car and go exploring*

Map
on page
210

San Juan is ideally placed as a home port for cruise ships heading into the Southern Caribbean, and it is also superbly sited for passengers coming ashore when ships are paying a visit to Puerto Rico. The port acts as the unofficial gateway to El Viejo San Juan (Old San Juan). Dating back to 1521, this is the most attractive part of the city and one of the most fascinating historic areas in the Caribbean.

The vast majority of ships dock at Calle Marina, just to the south of the old town. New berths for mega-ships have been added and the cruise terminal upgraded with more facilities (shops, ATMs, telephones, etc). San Juan is, however, the busiest cruise port outside the US mainland, especially at weekends, so there are times when ships have to use berths in other parts of the city – usually at the Pan American Dock. These are some distance from Old San Juan (certainly not walkable), but ships usually provide a free shuttle service to the old town to make up for this inconvenience.

Exploring the old quarter

If you are one of the majority who disembarks at Calle Marina, turn left past the tourist and post offices in Plaza Marina into Paseo de la Princesa and start up the gentle incline that is Calle San Justo. You are now in **Old San Juan** (El Viejo San Juan) – and it shows. Puerto Rico may have been a US territory for over a century but little here appears to have changed since the days of Spanish rule. The narrow, cobblestone streets are lined with 16th- and 17th-century Spanish colonial houses, with plants hanging from the balconies.

San Juan is one of the hottest places in the Caribbean but don't let the heat deter you from walking – there is plenty of shade in the old town's streets – and the traffic is pretty terrible, especially later in the day. You will find you overtake the tourist coaches if you walk, and you see a lot more. There are frequent, free, open-air trolley buses, too, which you can hop on and off if you get tired. Their rattling progress over the cobbles and loud guided commentaries ensure you can always hear them coming.

The best way to organise your tour of the old town is to make an early start from the ship and head straight for the 16th-century fortress, El Morro, the town's focal point, and then meander back through the streets, taking in the other sights. It is an easy 30-minute stroll to the fortress, which stands in glorious isolation facing out to the Atlantic on the far northwest corner of Old San Juan.

The most scenic route is to follow Paseo de la Princesa along the old city walls, stopping off at the impressive **La Fortaleza Ⓐ**, a 16th-century fortress

PRECEDING PAGES:
surfers ride
the waves.
LEFT:
Antigua Casino
de Puerto Rico.
BELOW:
the modern La
Rogativa sculpture.

which became a lavish mansion for the governor of San Juan. It still serves that function today, but part of it is open to the public for guided tours.

Alternatively, you can take Calle San Justo or any of the streets leading up from Paseo de la Princesa where it meets Plaza Marina, then turn left at the top from where **El Morro ❸** (daily 9am–5pm; entrance fee) and Calle del Morro, the access road through its extensive grounds, are clearly visible. There are official US National Park guided tours of the fortress every hour but it is more fun to take off on your own. It is a hugely atmospheric place – the walls are 20 ft (6 metres) thick in places and inside them is a maze of medieval nooks and crannies, dungeons, lookouts, courtyards, ramps, hidden staircases and gun turrets. There is a small museum which gives some information on the fort's history, but don't waste too much time on it as the whole site is a living museum.

Famous connections

Leaving El Morro, turn left at the end of Calle del Morro along Norzagaray, and a 15-minute walk will take you to 17th-century **Castillo de San Cristóbal ❻**, which is larger than El Morro but not as impressive. Alternatively, take a right turn from Norzagaray into Plaza San José, one of several attractive, Spanish-style squares. In the centre, there is a huge statue of Juan Ponce de León, the founder of the first settlement in 1508 and the first governor of Puerto Rico.

The most interesting site, however, is the **Museo de Pablo Casals ❶** (Tues–Sat 9.30am–5.30pm; small entrance fee), which illustrates the life and some of the works of the Catalan cellist who lived in San Juan for more than 20 years.

Head south from the plaza and you come to the heart of the Old Town shopping district, which lies along Calles Fortaleza, San Francisco and Cristo. San

Juan Ponce de León (1460–1521) was a member of Columbus's second expedition to the Americas in 1493. He later discovered and settled Puerto Rico but was less successful with Trinidad. He occupied the island for a while but was unable to conquer the indigenous Carib Indians.

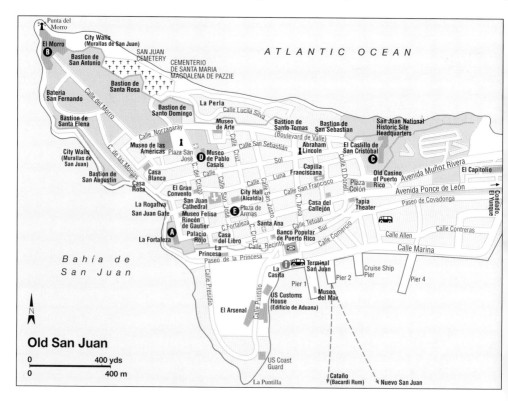

Old San Juan

Map on page 210

Juan used to have a reputation as a cheap, duty-free shopping port, especially for gold jewellery. There are still plenty of fancy jewellers, but if your cruise is going to St Thomas it's better to wait, as prices are generally better there. On Calle Cristo, there is a bargain-packed Ralph Lauren Polo Factory shop, conveniently close to a favourite Old San Juan watering hole – El Gran Convento Hotel. It was originally a 17th-century Carmelite convent and much of its architecture remains intact, but it has long been operating as a classy hotel. You could have lunch at its Café de Nispero or a drink in the delightful courtyard.

If you prefer something less touristy, though, the old town is full of small, unpretentious cafés serving authentic Puerto Rican cuisine – a variation on traditional Spanish food, with rice and beans the staple dish.

El Convento is right opposite the city's **cathedral** (daily 8.30am–4pm) – the final resting place of Ponce de León. From here, the attractive main square, **Plaza de Armas ❸**, is just a short walk south, and it's on the way back to the ship. If you are running out of time, you can hop on a trolley, as they stop right by the cruise piers.

A detail of the Raices (Roots) *bronze sculpture, which stands on the Paseo de la Princesa.*

Excursions outside San Juan

The most popular shore excursion outside San Juan is to **El Yunque** (free; small charge for El Portala visitor centre). This 27,000-acre (11,000-hectare) area of rainforest (a designated national forest) is home to about 250 species of trees and plant life, plus hundreds of frogs and tropical birds, including colourful Puerto Rican parrots. This makes a half-day organised tour, including a photo-stop at **El Luquillo Beach**, the most attractive on the island. However, it is a relatively easy place to reach independently by taxi or even by bus (there is a bus station

BELOW: aerial view of El Morro and modern San Juan.

**Map
on page
210**

*New San Juan is less
interesting. The main
shopping area is a
45-minute walk, or a
15-minute taxi ride
from port, although
cruise lines may pro-
vide a free shuttle.
Most shops shut on
Sunday, so ships try
to avoid that day but
sometimes schedules
make it unavoidable.*

BELOW: horseback
riding on the beach.
RIGHT: La Mina
Falls, El Yunque.

on Calle Marina near the dock), and is easy to explore since there are many
marked trails.

Another popular tour is to the **Bacardi Rum Distillery** at Cataño, across the
bay south of the old town. If you want to go alone, a ferry leaves every 30 minutes from a berth next to the cruise ships (the fare is less than US$1). Entrance
to the distillery is free – they hope you are going to buy what you taste there.

El Condado

The main tourist area of **El Condado**, where there is a line of four- and five-star
high-rise hotels on a sandy beachfront, is a long hot walk from town and the
beaches can be pretty crowded in the high season (winter). There is usually the
option of organised ship's excursions that include lunch at one of the hotels
and time on the beach but you can easily take a taxi or a bus

There is a 24-hour casino in the Condado Plaza hotel and others in several
hotels in the centre. The nearest to the ship will probably be the one at the Wyndham Old San Juan Hotel, which is almost directly opposite the cruise ship berths
on the other side of Calle Marina. Note that no alcohol is served in the casinos.

If your ship is in overnight or at least until late in the evening, there will be
excursions to the Las Vegas-style shows at one of the largest hotels. It is better
to take the tour than to book independently; the cruise lines have been good customers over many years so their passengers are given the best seats in the house.

San Juan, linked by causeways and bridges to the rest of Puerto Rico, is the
main jumping-off point for Southern Caribbean cruises, which means that passengers have an overnight stay before joining the ship or may choose to stay longer.
If you only have one night, try to book a room at El Convento, one of very few
hotels in Old San Juan. Longer stays usually include a
week at one of the hotels along El Condado beach strip.

Beyond San Juan

On a first visit to San Juan, there is no real need to
venture far out of town. But on a return visit, or if you
are staying on, it is worth hiring a car and exploring
further afield. At 100 miles (160 km) long and 40
miles (64 km) wide, Puerto Rico is one of the larger
islands in the Caribbean and has one of the largest
populations – nearly 4 million.

Your first stop could be **Ponce**, a Spanish colonial
town towards the south coast. There is a good direct
(toll) road so it only takes about 90 minutes. Further
southwest, near La Parguera, is **Phosphorescent Bay**,
so-called because its microscopic marine life lights
up at night when disturbed by larger fish or boats.
There is a similar phenomenon on **Vieques**, one of
three tiny islands off the east coast. But to see that, or
the sea turtle nests on the island of **Culebra**, you need
to book a tour locally.

If you enjoy snorkelling, head for a beach east of El
Condado along the Atlantic coast – Ocean Park, Isle
Verde and the palm-fringed and coral reef-protected
Luquillo (*see page 211*). For golfers, the best courses
are about an hour from San Juan. Advance notice is
necessary, so book an organised trip from the ship or
contact one of the clubs direct to book a round. ❑

US VIRGIN ISLANDS

Map on pages 218/19

St Thomas is known for its retail therapy, but there is also an interesting port to explore. A ferry ride away lies St John's, which is mostly a national park, while St Croix hides its secrets underwater

US Virgin Islands

Caribbean Sea

St Thomas is the duty-free shopping hub of the Caribbean, a fact you'll notice the moment you step ashore. Although a few ships anchor in the bay and tender passengers into the heart of the capital, Charlotte Amalie, most come alongside at Havensight Dock, just over 1 mile (2 km) east of town.

But this wasn't close enough for the local shopkeepers, so they created Havensight Mall. Every major duty-free retailer has an outlet here and in the capital's shopping centre, and boxes of the duty-free drink and cigarettes that the (mainly American) passengers buy are delivered to the ships in huge quantities all day. Cruise staff aren't joking when they say that ships leave lower in the water after a day in St Thomas. The mall development does mean that it's hard to see the port for the shops, but it also means you can fit your shopping in quickly and conveniently before you go off exploring the rest of the island.

More ships are starting to use Crown Bay, on the other side of the harbour, about twice as far from the capital as Havensight. There are few passenger facilities, but there are plans to develop a multi-million dollar terminal in the future.

Charlotte Amalie

The first-time visitor will, however, want to see **Charlotte Amalie ❶**. It is the capital, after all, and also has one of the most attractive harbours in the region, especially when the sun sets behind the sails of the yachts that usually fill the bay.

There are always scores of taxis waiting by the dockside – not all official but all operating on a shared basis, and most of them of the large "people mover" variety. There is a fixed rate into Charlotte Amalie, but you will just join a slow-moving line of traffic that could take more than 20 minutes. It really is better to walk into town and use a taxi to come back. To do this, go through the mall, turn left out of the dock gates and follow the road; it takes 15–20 minutes and, although it is along that taxi-clogged road, there is a good view out to sea for most of the way.

Fort Christian, which is now a museum (open 8.30am–4.30pm; free), marks the start of the town centre. There is a small market next door selling souvenirs, cheap T-shirts and sunhats. Right behind is Emancipation Garden, overlooked by the local tourist office, the Grand Hotel and the Post Office.

This is the start of Main Street, the main shopping area, which runs parallel with the waterfront with endless alleyways connecting the two, each with their own mini-shopping mall. At the entrance to each shop will be some out-of-work actor or comedian using magic tricks and jokes to sweet-talk people inside. There are also outdoor bars and cafés, which sell snacks and exotic cocktails at high prices.

PRECEDING PAGES: a day sail to Buck Island, St Croix. **LEFT:** view over Charlotte Amalie from the tramway. **BELOW:** sport fishing, St Thomas.

Historical surprises

Although it is richer in shops than it is in conventional sights, Charlotte Amalie does have a few places of historical interest that are worth a detour. Turn right by the tourist office instead of left, and walk in the other direction along Main Street, which becomes Norre Gade. Almost immediately there is a flight of steps cut into the hillside which lead up to Kongens Gade. Turn right to **The 99 Steps** (although, if you count them, you'll find there are actually 103). Near the top is what's left of **Blackbeard's Castle**, built by the Danish government but used (allegedly) by Blackbeard – the pirate, Edward Teach – as a lookout. And who could blame him, as there is such a splendid view over the harbour.

Further on from Blackbeard's Castle is the **Seven Arches Museum** (open Tues–Sat; entrance fee) on Government Hill. This was a 19th-century Danish artisan's house, now a private museum housing artefacts from that era.

Near the foot of the 99 Steps is the Hotel 1829, built for a French sea captain and now a hotel with a top-class restaurant. Turn right and go down the next flight of steps, continue along Crystal Gade and you find **St Thomas Synagogue**. Constructed in 1796, but rebuilt three times since, it remains the second oldest synagogue in the Caribbean (the oldest is in Curaçao)

Back on Norre Garde stands the impressively large 18th-century **Frederick Lutheran Church** and, nearby, Government House, which is a more recent building (1867) of less interest but with a spectacular view of the harbour.

Perhaps the most surprising find is in the middle of the shopping frenzy in Main Street: on the right as you come from the dock, at No. 14, is the place where artist Camille Pisarro was born in 1830, which is now an **art gallery** (open Mon–Sat; free). It's hard to know why he swopped the balmy climate and Caribbean lifestyle of the Virgin Islands for the doubtful pleasures of South London, but artists are rarely conventional.

Further afield

If you have only one day in St Thomas (which is probably the case), you should allocate at least half of it to exploring beyond the capital, on an organised

Genuine bargains can be found in the shops (particularly drinks and cigarettes in Sparky's or A H Riise, and jewellery in Cardow), and there are guarantees that the goods (and the discounts) are bona fide. The retailers know that if they rip-off passengers, the cruise lines will stop recommending them – and that would spell disaster for their sales figures.

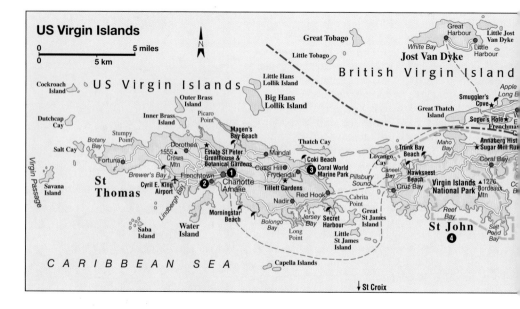

excursion or on your own. The majority of the excursions are water-based – trips on sailboats, catamarans or kayaks for swimming, snorkelling and scuba-diving. The offshore waters are remarkably clear and, as well as umpteen coral reefs, several old shipwrecks (including a mailboat which went down in 1967) have become popular dive sites since they are home to some colourful marine life.

The cost of half-day trips ranges between US$50 and $100, depending on what's on offer. There is also an Atlantis submarine that takes you down about 90 ft (20 metres) on a 45-minute trip. Other tours include seaplane and helicopter trips that offer spectacular views of the island but they are fairly brief (from 25 to 40 minutes) and quite expensive. You could try a cheaper alternative, the Paradise Point Tramway – a seven-minute cable car ride that takes you up 700 ft (210 metres) to a viewing platform from where the views are just as good. The tramway station is just across the road from Havensight Mall.

Getting around

Taxis trips around the island or to particular beaches can be arranged through your ship or independently (which is cheaper). Renting cars and bikes is easy and the roads are good, but, although this is not a huge island (12 miles long by 3 miles wide/20 km by 7 km), there's a surprising amount of traffic congestion, especially in and out of town, so allow plenty of time to return to the ship. Taxis are probably the best bet as the drivers know how long journeys are going to take. There are so many of them and competition is so fierce that they all stick to official fixed rates so you don't need to haggle.

Places to avoid include Bluebeard's Castle – not to be confused with Blackbeard's. Taxi drivers will suggest it, but it's just a hotel beside a stone watchtower around which developed a dubious legend about the pirate, Bluebeard. Equally dubious is the claim made for Magen's Bay (on the north coast) as one of the world's top 10 most beautiful beaches. The evaluation was true once but the beach has fallen from grace, partly because it gets so overcrowded. There is also a small charge to use it. There are far better beaches on the east coast – Sapphire and Secret Harbour – and on the south coast – Brewer's and Morningstar.

The stairway known as the 99 Steps was built by the Danes in the 1700s. There are similar steps cut into almost every hillside in St Thomas.

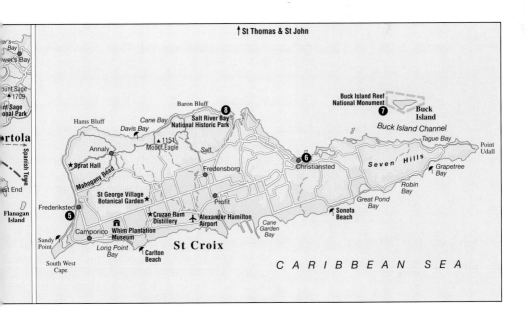

The Emancipation Garden, between Tolbod Gade and Fort Christian, has a bronze bust of a slave blowing a conch shell. It marked the 150th anniversary of emancipation celebrations.

BELOW: snorkelling at Lenister Bay, St John.

Apart from those excellent beaches, where should you head for? There's **Frenchtown ❷** for a start, just the other side of Charlotte Amalie from Havensight (head out along Veterans' Drive). The original community was set up by French émigrés from St Barts and this fishing village still has some French style, especially in the cafés and restaurants.

Almost due north (although to drive there you must head back into Charlotte Amalie then follow a winding route towards the north coast) is the **Estate St Peter Greathouse and Botanical Gardens** (Wed–Mon 8.30am–4pm, last entry 3.30pm; entrance fee; tel: 340-774 4999). If you take a taxi, you can spend as much time as you like walking through the 11 acres (4 hectares) of landscaped gardens. It is about 1,000 ft (305 metres) above sea level and, from an observation deck, it is possible to see not just one but four and twenty Virgins.

Coral World Marine Park ❸ (open daily 9am–5.30pm; entrance fee), by Coki Point on the island's north east coast, is easy to reach independently as it is only a 15-minute drive from Havensight. The centrepiece is a three-level underwater observatory from which to view an enormous range of marine life. But the highlight is watching the divers from the observatory when they come to feed the sharks, moray eels and stingrays in the predator tank. There is also a semi-submersible – a sort of mini-Atlantis trip. Small groups can follow a trail along the sea floor, which requires the wearing of a specially designed helmet.

St John

It may seem strange to land on one island then take a trip to another, but a visit to the neighbouring island of **St John ❹** is one of the most popular excursions, either organised or done independently. Two-thirds of St John is an unspoilt national park (gifted to the US by the Rockefellers) with 110 different types of tree affording a habitat for hordes of birds and butterflies. It also has more than 40 beaches and coves. Caneel Bay is the most popular, but Trunk Bay, with its underwater snorkelling trail, is probably the best.

There are regular (and cheap) ferries across from Charlotte Amalie (a 45-minute journey) and from Red Hook, which is about 25 minutes from Havensight on the east coast, from where they are cheaper, more frequent, and the journey takes only 20 minutes. Do leave enough time to get back to the ship, though.

St Croix

Large cruise ships arrive at **St Croix** in the port of **Frederiksted ❺**, which offers little for the visitor beyond a handful of shops by the pier entrance. The island's other port, Christiansted, is the capital and has far more in the way of welcoming shops, bars and restaurants, but only the smaller ships can get in there.

However, there is much more to the island than immediately meets the eye. At 82 sq miles (212 sq km), St Croix is larger than St Thomas, but it is generally much less developed, and far less crowded with people and traffic. Some of the most popular places to visit are only a short coach or taxi ride from Frederiksted (agree the taxi fare in advance, there are no meters). Interesting sites include the Cruzan Rum

Distillery, the St George Village Botanical Garden and the Estate Whim (sugar) Plantation Museum. Some of the best beaches – and St Croix is rightly known for its beaches – are equally close: Sandy Point, Cane Bay and Davis Bay.

Some ships organise shuttle buses from Frederiksted to **Christiansted ❻**, about 30 minutes away. If yours doesn't, take a taxi-van (about US$20) or a bus (about $1). Although the architecture still shows clear signs of Christiansted's 18th- and 19th-century Danish heritage (visit the Steeple Building, a local history museum), there has been some rebuilding following serious hurricane damage in the past. The most striking is the King's Alley Complex of shops and boutiques, but shopping here is nowhere near the scale of that on St Thomas.

Underwater treasures

Christiansted is the embarkation point for boats to 850-acre (344-hectare) **Buck Island Reef National Monument ❼**. This underwater National Park has its own marked underwater trails 12 ft (3 metres) down among the coral reefs, which teem with exotic fish and other marine life. There will be organised excursions from your ship, but dive shops all along the waterfront at Christiansted sell scuba-diving and snorkelling trips to the island, so it's easy to go off on your own. If you leave the ship straight after breakfast, there's time to reach Buck Island independently, enjoy two or three hours of scuba diving there and get back for departure time.

Salt River Bay National Historic Park ❽, on the north coast, is of particular interest to US visitors. The site of a Columbus landing – the only one on US territory – and a battle between his men and the Carib Indians, it has a huge mangrove forest and an underwater canyon which is ideal for scuba diving. ❑

Map on pages 218/19

TIP

St Croix has two 18-hole golf courses, one of which (Carambola on the North East Coast) was designed by Robert Trent Jones and is particularly attractive, as well as challenging enough for players visiting St Thomas to fly across just to play.

BELOW: Danish Customs House, Christiansted.

Map on page 226

ST MAARTEN

You can experience three different cultures in one day – remnants of Dutch colonialism in Philipsburg and French chic in Marigot, both infused with Caribbean flair

St Maarten's main port, Philipsburg, may be familiar to some cinema enthusiasts – it was here that the climactic scene of *Speed 2: Cruise Control* was filmed – the bit where the ship (*Seabourn Legend* in real life) crashes dramatically into the harbour front, demolishing the entire pier as it goes. Had you been a passenger on board, you might well have been catapulted through the air to land outside one of the cafés that line Philipsburg's Old Street – handy, at least, for quick access to a restorative drink.

Although cruise ship passengers, fortunately, do not arrive in quite such a dramatic manner, convenience is the key to Philipsburg's appeal as a cruise stop. Tendering into this port from a big ship is an advantage, as tenders will take you to the Little Pier in the main town; if you berth, you will be out at Pointe Blanche's cruise terminal which – although it has shops and other facilities – lies 1 mile (2 km) away from the centre of town. Taxis proliferate, however, and a multi-passenger minibus (a better option, as taxis are expensive) will get you into the centre for about US$3 a head.

Around town

Once in **Philipsburg ❶**, the going is easy, although you should be prepared for crowds. This compact little port can be explored easily in less than an hour and, since the main shopping streets are called Front Street (Voorstraat) and, running parallel, Back Street (Achterstraat), it's not hard to find your way around.

Old Street lies at the end of Front Street and here you will find pretty, al fresco restaurants and the Old Street Shopping Centre, a small mall with more than 20 shops as well as grill and pizza restaurants. Good places for lunch are Antoine's on Front Street or The Greenhouse, nearby, for catch-of-the-day specials.

First, though, you should head for **Wathey Square**, which has a late 18th-century courthouse and some beautiful old buildings decorated with traditional West Indian "gingerbread" fretwork. A lively market, a selection of restaurants and plenty of shops make this a magnet for visitors, but it's also worth wandering around the *steegjes* (the little lanes connecting the main streets), which conceal some lushly planted courtyards lined with more boutiques and cafés.

Among the best buys is jewellery, which is reasonably priced (as it is throughout the Caribbean); Colombian Emeralds, a chain with a good reputation among cruise passengers, is represented in Philipsburg. There are also posh shops selling Gucci and other designer goods as well as alcohol and leather products at duty-free prices – although not as low as they are in St Thomas.

PRECEDING PAGES: view over French St Martin from Pic du Paradis. **LEFT:** Marigot's busy waterfront. **BELOW:** the Old Street shopping arcade, Philipsburg.

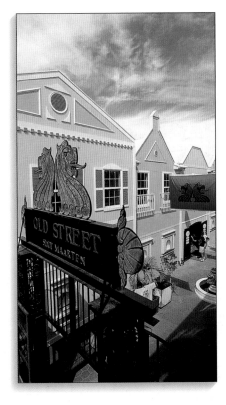

But for a real taste of the West Indies, call in at one of the small local stores crammed with spices, cane sugar, batik clothing, handwoven hammocks, local craftwares and guava berry liqueur, the local rum-based firewater which, although an acquired taste when drunk neat, gives a cocktail considerable kick.

The French side of the island

TIP

If you visit the island on a small- to medium-sized ship (such as one of the Star Clippers vessels), you could well call at Marigot – the French capital – instead of Philipsburg.

Unless your time here is very short, try to get over to **St Martin**, the French side of the island since it was divided between Holland and France in 1648. This is the prettier part, and the big cruise ships will usually offer tours to Marigot, the French capital, from Philipsburg – a three-hour excursion will take you past the Great Salt Pond at the rear of town to Mount William's Hill, where there is a good view of the port. From there you'll travel to the Dutch-French border and drive through the district of Orleans to visit **La Ferme aux Papillons**, a butterfly farm featuring species from around the world. Then it's on to Marigot, via some traditional French villages, for some free time.

Other excursion options include catamaran trips from Philipsburg, lasting about 3½ hours, with opportunities to swim or snorkel, with lunch and drinks included in the price; or a drive to the lovely Baie Orientale for a swim, a sunbathe (chairs provided) and lunch, which is also included.

Marigot

BELOW:
beach vendor,
Friars Bay Beach,
Marigot.

Most island tours allow some time in **Marigot ❷**, which is less commercialised than Philipsburg and has retained the atmosphere of a French seaside resort. It has colourful markets and a broad, beautiful harbour overlooked by restaurants and cafés featuring the best of Caribbean and French cuisine – so make time for

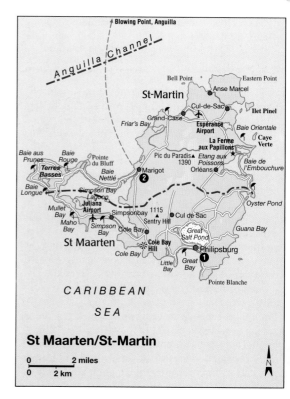

Map
on page
226

lunch if you can. Try Petit Club on Front de Mer, which serves Creole and French dishes in a colourful setting, and La Vie en Rose on rue de La République, for a good set menu French-Caribbean lunch.

If you are more keen to shop, head for rue de la République, rue de la Liberté or the Marina Port La Royale, a haven of stylish shops and smart cafés. Or walk off your lunch with a 15-minute stroll up to the ruins of Fort St Louis – you will be rewarded by fantastic views.

Obviously, time will be limited on a ship's tour to Marigot. A better option, if you have a full day ashore, would be to take a taxi tour of the island or a cab from Philipsburg to Marigot. Negotiate the fare in advance (from US$30 for two hours is average; US dollars are accepted) and ask the driver to build in waiting time, or come back at a specified hour if you fancy a swim or a lazy lunch.

The best beaches

The most convenient beaches are **Great Bay** – just along from Philipsburg's Front Street – and **Little Bay**, slightly further west, but they may both be crowded. For more privacy, take a taxi further afield to Simpson Bay Beach (good for water sports and for gambling, as the nearby Pelican Resort has a big casino); Dawn Beach (great for snorkelling); or Maho Bay Beach, where you can sunbathe in style or play the tables at the Maho Bay Hotel and Casino.

On the French side, **Baie Orientale** is gorgeous, with good beachside cafés and a classic French Riviera atmosphere. Baie Rouge is best for snorkellers, while Baie Longue is uncrowded – but be careful when swimming since the 1995 hurricane which devastated the island altered the below-water topography. Clothing is optional on most beaches on the French side. ❏

A statue of Christ crucified on the cross stands at the foot of the ruins of Fort St Louis.

BELOW: there are good beaches near Philipsburg.

SOUTHERN SAILING

Map on page 108

It was when the cruise lines started basing some of their ships in Caribbean ports that they were able to respond to demand and make more of the southern region available to passengers

When modern Caribbean cruising began in earnest in the late 1960s, most ships started in Miami and went no further than the Bahamas, the US Virgin Islands and maybe San Juan, on itineraries that lasted a week – the favourite duration for most passengers, then as now. But, once hooked, cruise passengers tend to come back for more, and the lines realised that they needed to come up with new ports and new islands on their itineraries.

First, they sent their ships west to Mexico's Yucatán Peninsula, to Cozumel and Playa del Carmen (in reach of the Maya ruins), and then they turned south. But to get down south and see more than just one or two islands would take longer than a week if a ship started in Miami or another Florida port, so the cruise lines started to base some of their ships deep in the Caribbean.

From San Juan, Puerto Rico and Barbados, ships can reach a lot of the Southern Caribbean ports in a week. Ships sail east then due south from San Juan; from Barbados, they cruise north, west and south and most of the Southern Caribbean islands lie between the two.

Southern variety

Southern Caribbean cruises now encompass an ever-expanding range of port and island combinations. There is also quite a variation in the number of ports featured on the different itineraries. Some passengers – usually first-time cruisers – prefer to visit a port a day; others enjoy having days at sea. For a variety of reasons (slower speed, more restricted access to smaller islands and greater facilities to entertain passengers on board), the largest ships tend to include fewer ports per cruise.

The lines with the biggest ships and largest fleets are in the Caribbean year-round and their ships tend to follow each other around to the best-known islands. Lines with smaller ships, which are more luxurious and more expensive, including sail-assisted or even authentic sailing ships, are able to offer more innovative itineraries. They go where the real yachties go, to the smaller islands – or the smaller ports of the larger ones – in the Windwards, Leewards and Grenadines.

One of the bonuses of starting and ending a cruise in a Caribbean port is that a holiday can be extended by staying an extra week on the island. It is also possible to combine one cruise with another (on the same ship or two different ones) for two weeks' cruising.

If passengers find it more convenient to cruise from Florida, it is still possible to reach the southern islands in a single week, although these cruises inevitably feature calls in other parts of the Caribbean and include fewer ports than those which start and finish in the Caribbean itself.

PRECEDING PAGES: cruise ships in the harbour at dusk, Fort-de-France, Martinique. **LEFT:** a detail from the banana bus, Aruba. **BELOW:** a friendly Martinican sports a traditional bacoua hat.

European preferences

In recent years, more Europeans have been converted to cruising, and this has led to European-based lines designing cruises to appeal specifically to their tastes and travel habits. There are now ships based in the French Caribbean (Guadeloupe) for the winter months, with passengers from Europe flying directly to the island to join them. European lines and passengers also have the advantage of being able to cruise to Cuba – off-limits to Americans because of the US embargo on trade with Castro's regime. But, so far, cruises from Cuba have tended to go west rather than south.

Whichever combination of ports and islands makes up your Southern Caribbean itinerary, there will always be a cosmopolitan flavour to the cruise. A visit to a number of different islands in this region delivers a heady cultural mix of European and indigenous influences.

New experiences

To this mix has been added new South and Central American experiences. Venezuela's La Guaira is a fairly nondescript port but it is only 40 minutes from Caracas, the archetypal bustling South American city. Cruise lines have been adding it to their itineraries for some years now, but periodic problems (it is a favourite conduit for drug smuggling) has seen it fall from grace, and off the cruise routes, from time to time.

Panama's problem was different. Cruises into and through the canal became increasingly popular but none of the ships actually stopped in Panama itself. There were no cruise ports and no tourist infrastructure. Since Panama regained control of the Canal from the USA at the end of 1999, this has all changed.

If you want a longer cruise, there are 12-day and two-week itineraries to the Southern Caribbean from Tampa or Fort Lauderdale. There are also some that start and end mid-week, thus avoiding weekend crowds at air- and sea ports.

BELOW: sailboats crowd English Harbour in Antigua during the annual Sailing Week.

Billions of dollars have been spent on developing cruise ports at Colón (and Balboa) on the Pacific side, and cruise lines have been given financial incentives to call there. Frequent Caribbean cruise passengers needed no incentive to pay Panama a first visit, especially since, from Colón, a historic railway link to Panama City has been reactivated.

The investment has not been as large, but the Central American countries of Belize, Costa Rica, Honduras and Guatemala *(see pages 147–50)* have also been sprucing themselves up to encourage cruise calls. Usually found on Western Caribbean cruise itineraries, the attractions here include the rainforests and the Maya ruins, and – like Panama and Venezuela – they provide a fascinating contrast in lifestyles to the Caribbean islands.

Map on page 108

RAFTING
COSTA RICA

Contrasting islands

There is also a contrast within the Southern Caribbean itself, between the larger, more developed islands, which have become major tourist destinations in their own right, and the smaller islands, which are still largely off the main tourist track and have a pleasantly undiscovered feel.

The larger islands include the almost genteel Barbados, with its English-style parishes; cosmopolitan Trinidad and Tobago; the volcanic island of St Lucia, with its dramatic Pitons and lush interior contrasting with the well-developed resort areas; the sophisticated French islands of Martinique and Guadeloupe; the distinctly Dutch-flavoured ABC islands of Aruba, Bonaire and Curaçao just off the South American coast; and the double-value St Maarten/St Martin *(see pages 225–7)*, which is half Dutch and half French, divided by the least secure and most nondescript border crossing in the world.

LEFT: Cascade du Saut de Gendarme, Martinique.
BELOW: De Olde Molen Windmill, Aruba.

Map on page 108

Magical beaches

It is also down in the south that the classic Caribbean islands of everybody's dreams are to be found. The white sandy beaches, the fishing boats in hidden coves, the safe and scenic harbours sought out by the private yachts of the rich and famous, all combine with each other and with the larger islands to ensure cruises with genuinely romantic appeal. Whichever you visit, there are superb beaches and great underwater sites for snorkelling and scuba-diving.

Nowhere in the world – including the South Pacific – is there such a wide collection of exotic islands to which ships, even some of the largest ones, can cruise. For a real escape from the 21st century, it's hard to beat the British Virgin Islands. These are 40 tiny islands, few large enough for the smallest cruise ships. Tortola and Virgin Gorda are the largest and even these are minuscule. And now it's possible to cruise to even smaller islands, like Jost Van Dyke and Norman Island.

The US Virgin Islands, St Thomas and St John, with wonderful beaches and some of the cheapest and best duty-free goods, usually appear on Eastern Caribbean itineraries *(see page 217)*, but there is some cross-over. Best of all, it is a short boat ride from St Thomas to St John – a delightful island which, courtesy of the Rockefellers, is almost entirely a national park. Some ships call at St John instead of St Thomas, but regular cruise visitors to the latter know that they should do their shopping in the morning in Charlotte Amalie, then take a short water-taxi ride to St John for an afternoon on one of its glorious beaches.

BELOW: Le Morne Rouge Bay, Grenada.
RIGHT: an aerial view of Tobago Cays, The Grenadines.

The Leewards and the Grenadines

The gems in the next cluster of islands (the Leewards) include St Barts (or St Barthélemy, to give its full name), which is a smaller version of Martinique or Guadeloupe: very French, with glitzy boutiques and fine – if expensive – restaurants and glamorous people eating in them; St Kitts and its smaller sister island, Nevis, both lush and verdant islands which prospered through their sugar plantations. Nevis, with its exclusive plantation house hotels, is particularly tranquil; and beautiful, unspoilt Dominica, which is right on the whale migration route, making for some exciting boat trips.

Further south, it is mainly the smaller cruise and sailing ships that call at the 30-odd coral islands known collectively as the Grenadines. This is the most popular part of the Caribbean for private and chartered yacht sailing since there are scores of beautiful bays, beaches and good sites for swimming, snorkelling and diving. Also, at the handful of islands in the Grenadines which are inhabited, such as St Vincent and Bequia, an infrastructure has been built up to serve the visiting yachties' needs – stores, boat-taxis, restaurants, etc – useful for cruise passengers, too.

Finally, cruising further south, lies Grenada, one of the larger islands in the region and one of the most beautiful before Hurricane Ivan struck in 2004. However, this Spice Island, has rapidly put itself back together and due to the clement climate new vegetation has been shooting up everywhere. St George's, although temporarily dishevelled, can still claim to have the most beautiful harbour as its capital. ❏

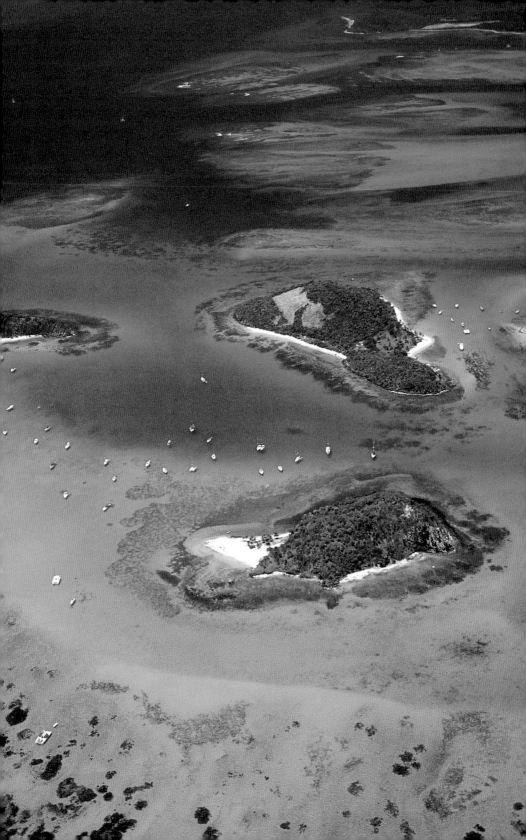

THE BRITISH VIRGIN ISLANDS: TORTOLA

Map on page 240

Tortola and Virgin Gorda are lazy, laid-back islands where some gentle swimming, snorkelling and shopping will be quite enough activity to fill a day ashore

British Virgin Islands

Caribbean Sea

More than 50 volcanic rocky outcrops set in the Caribbean Sea, a stone's throw from the much snazzier US Virgin Islands, the British Virgin Islands might – at first sight – seem less than impressive. Indeed, Christopher Columbus found them so when he first clapped eyes on them in 1493. Two centuries later, however, the British took a different view; they took possession of them in 1664 and have hung on to them ever since, although nowadays they are a British Overseas Territory, in which the islanders govern themselves.

The majority of the British Virgin Islands are uninhabited, the 18,000-strong population being concentrated on the three biggest – **Tortola**, **Virgin Gorda** and **Jost Van Dyke**. The topography of Tortola and Virgin Gorda – both of which rise sharply from the sea to volcanic heights – is rugged: Tortola's Mount Sage is 1,709 ft (536 metres) and VG's Gorda Peak 1,369 ft (414 metres). This has made the islands hard to get around and difficult to develop, but it has also been the key to the islands' success as a tourist destination.

These islands are the place to visit if you prefer people unaffected by tourism, quiet beaches and a calm, frozen-in-time atmosphere to skyscraper hotels, casinos and glitzy shopping malls. Their main visitors are "yachties" who know more than most about the pleasures of the simple life. The islands are more likely to feature on the itineraries of small-ship cruise companies such as Windstar, Seabourn, Star Clippers and Windjammer than on the big-ship schedules.

Trips to the best beaches

Visiting ships usually anchor in the harbour and tender passengers ashore at Tortola's pretty capital, **Road Town ❶**. This lies on the island's south coast, while the best beaches – Robinson Crusoe-style havens rich in banana trees, palms and mangoes – are on the north coast, overlooked by dramatic mountain peaks. Fortunately, a road around the island was completed in the early 1980s and, with taxis lined up to greet every visiting cruise ship, it's relatively easy to get about.

As on many Caribbean islands, round-trip taxi tours are available; both fares and pick-up times for the return journey should be negotiated in advance. (As a rough guide, expect to pay around US$15 each way for a 25-minute trip to a beach.)

The best beach for an all-round good time is **Cane Garden Bay**, where Rhymers' restaurant serves tasty seafood, makes great barbecues and provides showers, towels and some water sports (for a fee). Snorkellers, on the other hand, will find the most vivid sea life at **Lower Belmont Bay**.

PRECEDING PAGES: Road Town, Tortola's capital. **LEFT:** The Caves, Norman Island. **BELOW:** Cane Garden Bay.

TIP

Although these are the
British Virgin Islands,
remember that the
local currency is the
US dollar, so don't go
ashore laden with
sterling.

To the capital

Road Town has very little to offer in its own right, so you should spend your time ashore exploring the rest of the island, but devote a little time to the capital first. Main Street – five minutes' walk from the tender pier at Wickhams Cay – is worth a stroll. Many of its traditional, Caribbean wooden houses are being restored, a variety of shops are starting to open up and there is a lively crafts market to explore.

Local ceramics, glassware from Mexico, Cuban cigars and, strangely, English chinaware, are the best buys in the shops – alongside the ubiquitous spices. In the crafts market, look out for brightly coloured mobiles, driftwood napkin rings and other whacky-but-fun items.

For lunch, try Pusser's Pub on the waterfront if you want good, basic English food. Otherwise, there are pizza parlours, or plenty of places selling local dishes if you are feeling more adventurous.

Checking the possibilities

Some ships offer excursions on open-air safari buses (around US$30 for a three-hour trip), including a stop for a swim at Cane Garden Bay. There are also companies that organise boat and snorkelling tours from the pier (where you'll arrive by tender), so, before you leave Road Town, take stock of what local tours are available. You can get a two- or three-hour island tour for about $50 (per taxi) and – if you've time and confidence – local buses will get you round the island very cheaply. Just hail them and they'll stop – in theory, at least.

If you fancy a good walk, the best bet is to head by taxi to the **Mount Sage National Park ❷**, where you can hike along a rainforest trail and enjoy a picnic.

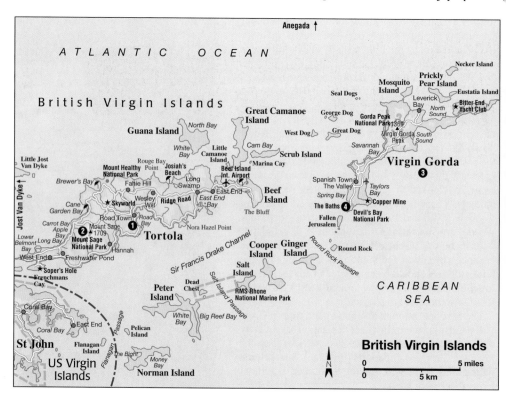

If you feel like some good music and a great local atmosphere, jump in a taxi and ask for Bomba's Surfside Shack at Cappoon's Bay – the driver will know where it is. It is a bit of a dive but it's fun.

Virgin Gorda

Most ships will offer tenders to **Virgin Gorda ❸**, 12 miles (20 km) from Tortola (if yours doesn't you can easily find a boat to ferry you out from the pier). Try to visit this little place if you can – it's a real fantasy island with silvery beaches and the most enticing turquoise waters you'll see outside the South Pacific.

Many cruise ships run shore excursions to **The Baths ❹**, a beautiful beach where gigantic boulders have toppled together to form myriad cave-like structures and salt-water pools, but these trips are about the same price as an island tour. Alternatively, you could negotiate a round-trip fare to the Baths or the island's best beach, **Spring Bay** (excellent for snorkelling), with one of the taxi drivers plying for trade at **Spanish Town**, where the small boats to Virgin Gorda disgorge their passengers.

If you go to the Baths, leave time to make the 15-minute walk through the boulder-strewn coastal scenery to **Devil's Bay National Park**.

Spanish Town itself offers limited shopping at a waterfront plaza. Walk past this to the Virgin Gorda Yacht Harbour and you'll find a pretty view and a great place to eat, **The Bath and Turtle Pub**, which serves everything from freshly caught seafood to pizzas, nachos and chilli.

However you choose to spend your day ashore in the British Virgin Islands, don't rush about and try to do too much. The secret here is to relax and let the islands' laid-back atmosphere wash your cares away. ❑

Map on page 240

Don't miss local specialities.

LEFT: getting around Tortola by mountain bike.
BELOW: snorkelling at Spring Bay, Virgin Gorda.

ANTIGUA

A stroll around St John's will give you a flavour of a small Caribbean town, while excursions further afield take you to a renovated 18th-century dockyard and some stunning beaches

Map on page 244

Caribbean Sea

Numerous gleaming, multi-decked vessels have glided into port since the intrepid Lady Liston penned her travel journal in 1800: "The bay of St John's is extremely pretty, and though a bar prevents the entrance to large ships, it is filled with smaller ones." Today, St John's, the capital of Antigua, still gently tumbles to the sea along narrow, trenched streets and canopied terraces, while the wooden jetties continue to harbour fishing boats and small craft. The sand bar, however, has long since been dredged, allowing modern nautical colossi to muscle into the sheltered waters. Once dependent on slave and merchant vessels to fill its wharves, the present economy relies on cruise ships. In addition to the busy itineraries that can be pre-booked before landing, Antigua offers much for the visitor beyond beach, boat or boutique trips.

On the quayside

In **St John's ❶**, **Redcliffe** and **Heritage** quays, are the first points of call. The former is the more picturesque, offering a range of shops and restaurants in a pleasantly shaded setting of restored wooden buildings, with lattice-work balconies. The latter is a breezy, pastel-coloured mall, with an air-conditioned casino, and duty-free shops to lure visitors out of the sun. Between them, local traders selling bright sarongs, sunhats and T-shirts are gathered under the roof of the Vendors' Mall. Three centuries ago, the scene was very different. The "passengers" tripping off the gangplanks were enslaved labourers from West Africa, lined up for sale to plantation owners.

A third quay, **Nevis Street Pier**, has opened up the waters to even larger ships and their holiday cargoes. With full moorings, up to 10,000 visitors may arrive in the otherwise unruffled capital of Antigua. The centre of town can get crowded at peak hours, but a quieter, calmer Caribbean lies just a five-minute roam up the sloping streets. A short walk north along Popeshead Street, east up St Mary's Street or south via Market Street reveals the full range of city life.

Urban walkabout

The port side area provides the entire selection of shopping, eating, banking and telecommunication facilities. The last two are located on High and Long Streets, while the rest are sandwiched between the sea and Thames Street. Island cash tills readily swallow US dollars, although paying with local currency normally means slightly lower prices, once the exchange rates have been calculated.

Depending on consumer or culinary diversions, a half-hour stroll allows a good glimpse of life around the quay. Before long, a serene side street will greet

LEFT: the beach at Ffryes Bay.
BELOW: the restored waterfront of Redcliffe Quay.

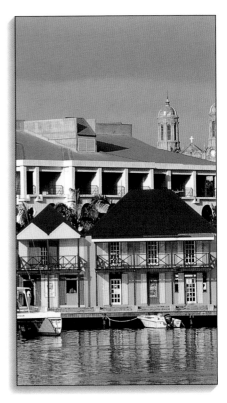

the independent wanderer. Only a rear-view glance at the cruise ship towering over the muted hues of the single-storey wooden-houses that flank the capital's grid of narrow lanes, will shatter the illusion of having left the ballroom worlds away. A walk through town might not be the usual agenda for a cruise holiday, but St John's offers the perfect chance to see something of the urban Caribbean.

Island history

An early morning start, grabbing a coffee and cake from one of the excellent local bakeries or cafés in lower St Mary's Street or Redcliffe Quay, accompanied by a copy of the *Outlet* or *Daily Observer* newspaper, will catch the cool of the day and give an insight into the often intriguing events of a small Caribbean island. A few minutes from the quayside, the former courthouse on Long Street, solidly built in 1747 from local stone, is now the **Museum of Antigua and Barbuda** (Mon–Fri, 8.30am–4pm, Sat 10am–2pm; donation). The renovated building is packed with local heritage. A bright and airy main hall highlights island life and history, while next door houses a database of monument inscriptions from around Antigua and the associated isle of Barbuda.

The Anglican **Cathedral of St John the Divine**, a few minutes further up Long Street, originally dates from 1683 but, like so many buildings, it was damaged and restored after a severe earthquake in 1834. The landmark towers of this striking baroque edifice have long proclaimed St John's presence to new arrivals. The impressive interior is clad in dark pine, offering a cool respite, with marble reliefs and plaques commemorating former church-goers.

Across the road, the **Antigua Recreation Ground** is the hallowed home of Antiguan cricket, and the spot where local hero Sir Vivian Richards, the "Master

One of the beautiful stained-glass windows in the Cathedral of St John the Divine.

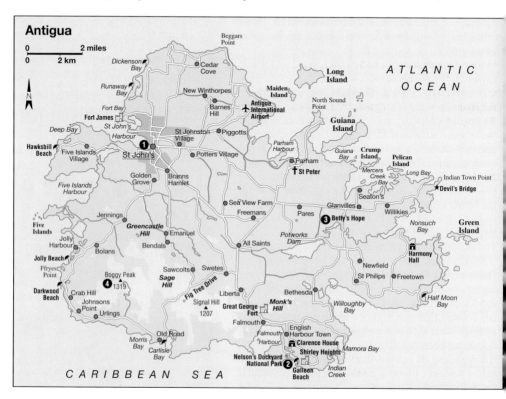

Blaster", knocked off the fastest century in cricket. Returning down Redcliffe and St Mary's streets, the Ebenezer Methodist Church was completed in 1839, but twice restored after earthquakes rattled its foundations. A solid external structure houses a beautifully simple white plaster and wood-panelled interior.

On Market Street, opposite the West Bus Station, you can buy tropical fruits in the covered **Heritage Market**, and craftwork in the building next door.

The sites beyond the town

No where is far away in Antigua, but the full range of stunning beaches and historic sites lies out of walking distance. Cycling will get you a bit further under your own steam, and the best biking destination is **Fort Bay**, a leisurely 20-minute ride northeast of the town centre. Continue along Popeshead Street and turn left at the sign for Miller's-by-the-Sea to reach this popular locals' beach. At the southern end of the promontory, **Fort James** dates from 1739 and guards perfect views out to sea. At weekends, impromptu merengue and salsa fiestas boom on the beachfront while bars offer daily sustenance.

Further afield, on English Harbour to the southeast, lies one of Antigua's most popular attractions, **Nelson's Dockyard ❷** (daily 9am–5pm; entrance fee). It's about 30 minutes away by regular bus service from the West Bus Station or by taxi (check the fixed rates). A series of beautifully restored mid-18th-century buildings bring this harbour to life. Described as "a queerly moving place, heavy with melancholy and the allusions of ancient fame", it was once a key command post for the British Navy, and home to Admiral Horatio Nelson while he commanded HMS *Boreas*. The stunning bay is overlooked by the impressive fortifications of **Shirley Heights** (daily; combined ticket with the dockyard), which comes alive with reggae and steel bands and barbecues on Sunday afternoon and evening.

Taxi drivers offer a tour of the whole island, but if time is limited, it's worth slowing down to savour one or two sites. **Betty's Hope ❸** (Tues–Sat 10am–4pm; entrance fee), on the loop back from English Harbour, was built in the 1650s as the first sugar plantation on the island. An interesting little museum tells the story. The husks of former sugar mills are scattered across the island, but here an active survivor can be visited and occasionally grinds in full sail.

To the east, the natural limestone arch of **Devil's Bridge** and art gallery of **Harmony Hall**, a former plantation house, offer relaxing excursions, en route to the sands of **Half Moon Bay**. Every Antiguan promotes a favourite beach, and competition is tough. Darkwood Beach, Hawksbill Bay, Dickenson Bay and Ffryes Bay on the west coast are all strong contenders.

If you have the time and feel energetic enough, **Boggy Peak ❹** (1,319 ft/402 metres), at Antigua's highest point, is a rewarding two-hour hike in the southwest of the island. Ask the taxi or bus driver to drop you off at the start of the track just beyond Urlings. After the quietly engaging town of Old Road, the return route to St John's climbs **Fig Tree Drive**, lined with wild bananas, lianas and remnants of rainforest that once covered the isle and much of which is now protected as the Wallings Forest Reserve. ❏

Map on page 244

TIP

For a taste of good, local food, try the Commissioner Grill on Redcliffe Street, tel: 462 1883, a stone's thrown from the quay. Set in an old tamarind warehouse, its local specialities include foongee (cornmeal and okra) and grilled red snapper.

BELOW: view of English Harbour from Shirley Heights.

ST KITTS AND NEVIS

St Kitts is less tourist-orientated than other islands – which is why many people like it so much. If you get your timing right, you can also sample the charms of nearby Nevis

Map on page 248

St Kitts
Caribbean
Sea

Travellers in search of the "real" West Indies will get a feel for it on this plangent island, which crams an astonishing range of terrain – from cane fields to rainforest and mountains – into its 65 sq miles (170 sq km). Fanatical shoppers, on the other hand, will be disappointed in St Kitts, as it lacks the glitzy stores that line the streets in other parts of the Caribbean.

Arriving at the capital, **Basseterre ❶**, you can start exploring almost immediately since the Port Zante cruise terminal lies only a few minutes' walk from the heart of town. Hurricanes in the late 1990s took their toll but the terminal – designed to provide duty-free shops, restaurants and a casino – is finished, and a programme of intelligent restoration has returned many of Basseterre's gingerbread-trimmed public buildings and homes to their former glory.

Palm-filled Basseterre has old world charm by the bucket-load and, although the island still depends on sugar cane rather than tourism for its living, the restoration has made it a big hit with cruise passengers. **Independence Square**, a former slave market and now an attractive park surrounded by 18th-century houses, is particularly worth a look; as is The Circus traffic intersection on Fort Street, with a clock-tower of elaborately worked cast iron. One of Basseterre's liveliest restaurants, Ballahoo, famed for its spare ribs, is situated here.

For local colour, wander through the back streets off Bay Road, where you'll find goats and chickens wandering free and roadside stalls selling fish, fruit and flowers. The town has a few galleries stocked with good-quality art, crafts and antiques. The best local buys are leather and cotton goods, spices, pottery and sea opal jewellery. Fort Street and Liverpool Row are good sources of unusual stuff; those who prefer brand name shopping will find a few stores to suit them in the Pelican Shopping Mall.

Exploring further afield

If you plan to explore further afield by taxi, check the rates listed in the cruise terminal, as they are not displayed in cabs. You should also establish the fare before boarding – although the Eastern Caribbean Dollar is the local currency, US dollars are widely accepted, so make sure you know which currency the quoted price is in.

Up to four people in a taxi will be charged about US$35 each way for a trip to **Brimstone Hill Fortress National Park ❷** (9.30am–5.30pm; entrance fee), a huge fortress set atop an 800-ft (245-metre) volcanic mound. The British called this "the Gibraltar of the West Indies" until, embarrassingly, it was captured by the French in 1782 (although they were thrown out a few months later). Don't miss it if you are interested in the island's history and culture.

LEFT: cannon at Brimstone Hill overlooks Basseterre.
BELOW: The Circus clock-tower landmark.

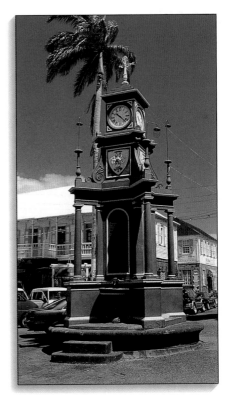

Even if you're not, Brimstone Hill is worth a visit as it's set in a national park where you can follow nature trails and spot green vervet monkeys larking about – a good way to stretch your legs after being on a ship. Take your credit card since the gift shop sells some very tempting prints of old Caribbean maps.

Another option, which is perfect for horiculturalists, is a visit to **Romney Manor** ❸, 6 acres (2.4 hectares) of glorious gardens containing the ruins of an old sugar plantation, an ancient bell tower and a tree believed to be more than 350 years old. It's a good place for a picnic and has a batik factory where you can watch the creation of these traditional hand-printed fabrics.

If you'd prefer to play at "real" plantation life, head off for lunch at Rawlins Plantation Inn, which also has wonderful gardens; or Ottley's Plantation Inn which has a spring-fed pool and rainforest trails.

A day at the beach

If a day at the beach is more to your liking, the best one to head for is **Frigate Bay** ❹, a long stretch of soft white sand a few miles to the southeast of Basseterre. Beyond it is **Friar's Bay**, a narrow strip of land where you can have the wonderful experience of swimming in the Atlantic Ocean from one beach and the Caribbean from the other.

Still further along is **Turtle Beach**, which is heaven for bird-watchers, nature lovers and water sports enthusiasts. Here, you can snorkel, feed monkeys, spot rare birds, hire a kayak or windsurf, or even zap over to Nevis, St Kitts' sister island, in 15 minutes (it costs about US$25 each way to hire a motorboat).

You may decide that the easiest way to get around when time is limited is to book a shore excursion from your ship. You can visit both Brimstone Hill and

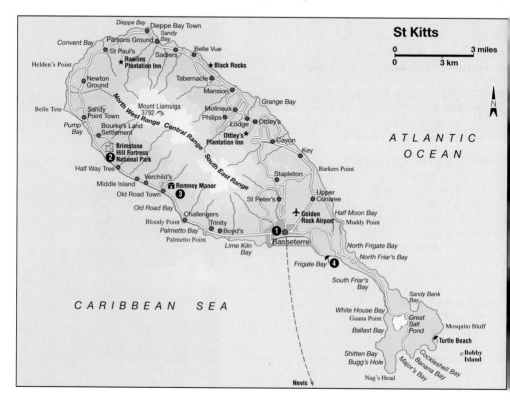

Romney Manor on a three-hour tour, or go for one of the more active options, which include a four-hour tour to Romney Manor, including a rainforest hike; kayaking at Frigate Bay (three hours); a power-boat trip along the coast to a good snorkelling site (another three-hour excursion); or a horseback ride along Frigate Bay Beach, which usually lasts two hours.

Map on page 248

Visiting Nevis

If you have enough time, you could cross the 12 miles (20 km) to **Nevis** in 30 to 45 minutes by ferry, which is an experience in itself, you can either travel in style or choose the cargo boat and find yourself sharing the ride with livestock and sacks of vegetables. The round-trip (which costs from US$8–$15) will take you to the capital, **Charlestown**, an attractive place of leafy gardens and pastel-tinted, gingerbread-trimmed houses.

Here, street vendors will ply you with fruit wines made from gooseberry, sorrel and pawpaw (papaya) – and you may need them if you sample the island's speciality hot pepper sauce. You can also buy colourful batik and unusual hand-icrafts from local artisans at the Cotton Ginnery on the waterfront. For a lovely beach and a good lunch, grab a cab to **Pinney's Beach**, which is just a short hop from Charlestown.

Some cruise lines offer excursions from St Kitts to Nevis, which may include a visit Charlestown and the Botanical Gardens, or a tour to Nevis Peak and a rainforest hike. They are quite expensive, but at least everything is organised for you in advance and saves you time. If you decide to go it alone, *do* check ferry schedules and allow plenty of time. St Kitts and Nevis are lovely, but you don't want to miss your ship as it won't wait unless you're on a ship's excursion. ❑

Giant philodendrons in the island rainforest.

LEFT: at the market in Basseterre.
BELOW: Charlestown, Nevis.

DOMINICA

Untamed and beautiful, this lush volcanic island has jungle trails, sulphurous pools and coral reefs. It is also the whale-watching capital of the Caribbean

Map on page 253

Dominica
Caribbean Sea

A s the most lushly mountainous island in the Eastern Caribbean, Dominica is a place of lofty peaks and precipices, tropical forests and steep-sided valleys, white-water rivers and sulphurous springs. Yet Dominica is defined as much by what it is not as by what it is. It is not a Caribbean Eden of palm-fringed white sandy beaches and boisterous rum punch parties. It has no casinos, no celebrity residents, no golf courses, no notable beaches, no marinas lined with sleek yachts, no all-inclusive resorts, no over-hyped attractions, nor significant shopping opportunities. Instead, Dominica offers nature in the raw, on an island where the locals outnumber the tourists. The jungle-clad land appears to shoot straight out of the sea, yet conceals majestic underwater seascapes, from submerged pinnacles to corals camouflaged by reef fish.

The heart of the volcanic island is a cloud-covered spine of forested peaks, narrow ridges and bubbling waterfalls. Unsurprisingly, Dominica is a popular choice for film-makers in search of doom-laden, apocalyptic settings. The island has dramatic weather to match: on the same day that torrid sun bakes the Caribbean side, storms break on the Atlantic coast, and the interior dissolves into rolling clouds, mists and rainbows. Wild and untamed, Dominica is conceivably the only island that Christopher Columbus would recognise some 500 years later.

LEFT:
Trafalgar Falls.
BELOW:
Carib basket
weaver at work.

Colonial past

Set in the Windward Islands, between French Guadeloupe and Martinique, Dominica bears the imprint of both Britain and France. English is the official language, but a French-influenced Creole patois is equally prevalent. In the 1750s, the French settled the island, virtually wiping out the Carib race, before the territory was first declared British in 1763 and colonised as a plantation economy. Yet, despite persecution, Dominica remains the last outpost of the Carib Indians, Amerindians who have called the Caribbean home since the days of Columbus.

Cocoa and coffee-growing under the French gave way to the cultivation of sugar and limes under the British. Dominica was the world's foremost lime-producer before bananas became the byword for economic success in the 1930s. Since the failure of the Caribbean to compete with cheaper South American bananas, Dominica has turned to eco-tourism as its salvation. This laudable but challenging strategy should pay dividends in the long run but there have been setbacks.

In 1978, the island's delight at gaining independence was dashed by the devastation of Hurricane David, which ravaged the island a year later, and flattened the capital, Roseau. The toil of subsistence farming and the reality of unemployment drive a lot of Dominicans to start a new life in Antigua, St Thomas or Guadeloupe.

Classic shore excursions

As far as excursions are concerned, eco-tourism is the buzz-word, a term which embraces everything from soft adventure to an appreciation of the island's natural wonders. Since Dominica has two cruise ship terminals, certain excursions are more convenient from one or the other. **Portsmouth ❶**, the northern port, is the perfect starting point for a canoe ride along Indian River, for scenic wanderings in the Cabrits National Park, or for a foray into Carib territory, home to the only remaining Carib Indians in the region. **Roseau ❷**, the capital in the south, offers an even wider range of options, from a Jeep safari into the tropical interior to a trek to the Valley of Desolation and Boiling Lake. Most cruise lines focus on trips (by minibus or Jeep) to the Emerald Pool, Titou Gorge or Trafalgar Falls, but these are also accessible by taxi. There are also kayak, snorkelling and scuba-diving trips, as well as whale-watching safaris on the west coast.

Whale-watching trips

As the whale-watching capital of the Caribbean, Dominica is the ideal place to spot pilot whales, false-killer whales, mixed pods of sperm whales and spotted whales, as well as bottle-nosed dolphins. Between November and March, a classic whale and dolphin safari offers a 90 per cent success rate in spotting both creatures. The catamaran skippers have boats equipped with sonar, backed up by a look-out scanning the surface for tell-tale signs, including the distinctive musky, oily scent of a sperm whale. The boats head along the west coast, stopping regularly to take soundings and listen for each creature's signature tune, from the singing of humpbacks and the clicking of sperm whales to the pinging of pilot whales and the whistling of dolphins. The humpback whale is

Jean Rhys, the Dominica-born writer, evoked her childhood holidays in a purple patch in her novel, Wide Sargasso Sea*: "Too much purple, too much green. The flowers too red, the mountains too high, the hills too near."*

BELOW: deep waters provide perfect feeding and breeding grounds for the planet's largest mammal.

more often heard than seen, but the flipping of any great black fin tail creates a frisson of excitement, particularly as a whale can dive as deep as 6,000 ft (2,000 metres). The pilot whale prefers to travel in pods of 60 while the sperm whale might be accompanied by 20-ft (6-metre) calves. As for dolphins, apart from the bottle-nosed variety, acrobatic spotted and spinner dolphins love to surf the wake of the boat and provide ample consolation for any missed whale sightings.

Map on page 253

Beneath the waves

Most shore excursions include the option of exploring the volcanic, coral-encrusted reefs or snorkelling in the shallows. Scuba-diving is centred on Soufrière Bay and Scotts Head, where hot and cold water springs bubble under the surface, but diving is also feasible in the north, around the Cabrits peninsula. Part of Dominica's appeal is the sharpness with which the ocean floor drops off from the shore, reaching depths of several hundred metres just a stone's throw from the coast. Divers also appreciate the way the sediment swiftly falls away, leaving the water crystal-clear for sightings of sea-horses and secret caverns, shipwrecks and marine life. At night, octopuses, turtles, stingrays and black-tipped reef sharks come out to play. Kayaking and snorkelling are also best in the calm waters on the leeward side, including around Scotts Head, where leaping dolphins or frigate birds diving for fish draw your eyes upwards.

The highly symbolic Dominican flag features green for the forest, white for the river, yellow for the sun and black for the soil, but also red for bloodshed, with the 10 stars representing the island's 10 parishes.

Jeep safari to the interior

For those who want soft adventure, the best land-based excursion is a half-day Jeep safari into the jungle. The drive leaves the ramshackle capital, Roseau, with its tin roofs and faintly sombre air, for the rugged interior. Old French

BELOW: rowing down Indian River, Portsmouth.

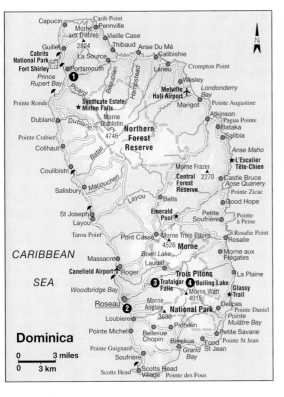

Ken's Hinterland Adventure Tours (tel: 767-448 4850), based at the Fort Young Hotel in Roseau, can organise virtually any kind of excursion, from whale-watching to extreme sports. Trips to rivers, falls and pools are available at relatively short notice. For diving and snorkelling, call Dive Dominica (tel: 767-448 2188).

BELOW: colours of Cabrits National Park and Prince Rupert Bay.

colonial houses with hanging verandas give way to a striking church, the **Lady of Fair Heaven**, built out of volcanic rock. From the heights of **Morne Bruce**, one's gaze is drawn down to the botanical gardens, port and cruise ship. The **Botanical Gardens** (daily 9am–4pm), set in a bowl bordered by mountains, are divided into an ornamental and a nursery section, where cherries and avocados are grown for profit. Poor Dominica cannot afford the luxury of gardens purely for pleasure. In 1979, Hurricane David devastated the vegetation, leaving uprooted trees still visible, including an African baobab tree. In better condition are the carib tree, banyan, pine cactus and century palm, as well as the vivid red African tulip, crawling with huge caterpillars, proof that everything in Dominica grows on a gigantic scale. Other highlights are the ackee tree, which produces the Jamaican national dish, as well as the West Indian palm, the balsam tree, a precious mahogany tree with hanging pods, and the bizarre cannon-ball tree.

The tour then sets off into rainforest towards **Trafalgar Falls ❸** (daily; entrance fee), crossing a wild valley that was once a productive lime and cocoa plantation. All around are kalabash trees, bananas, avocados and mangoes. Beyond are orchids and heliconia, orange and green African tulips and red-flowering ginger lily, as well as the cinnamon tree. Close to the trail entrance to Trafalgar Falls stands an elephant's ears tree, whose roots are used to make basket handles. The short trail to the waterfalls is signalled by a handy bar and restaurant, and a view of sulphur springs. An invigorating but comfortable climb through dense vegetation ends in a viewing platform overlooking two waterfalls. Keen swimmers can clamber over slippery rocks to bathe in the pool, but swimming is better at the **Titou Gorge**, where hot and cold streams intermingle in a natural plunge pool. The gorge looks distinctly unprepossessing but it is an outlet of the Freshwater Lake, one of the most significant mountain crater lakes in the Caribbean. After clambering into the invigorating waters of the pool, the group swims in Indian file towards a luminous cavern. The tour closes with rum punch and coconut cakes before the short drive back to the ship.

Boiling Lake Trail

The Boiling Lake trail is a spectacular trek, one of the toughest in the Caribbean, used as a fitness test by the Dominican army, and offered only by cruise lines with a fair proportion of active passengers. This full-day hike from the Titou Gorge takes up to four hours in each direction. Rewards include the pleasures of passing under canopies of greenery formed by giant tree ferns, of fording mineral-rich streams, relishing rare vistas of Martinique and Guadeloupe, and climbing knife-edged ridges into a primeval landscape. The **Valley of Desolation** is a long, jagged volcanic fissure with fumaroles venting stinking clouds of sulphurous gases. The rocks are cast in metallic colours and bisected by a scalding river rich in mineral deposits.

Beyond lies the **Boiling Lake ❹**, often concealed behind clouds of steam: when the seething mists clear, the magma-heated cauldron reveals a surface ruffled by bubbles. As the second largest cauldron of boiling water in the world, this flooded fumerole is the highlight of the exhilarating trek.

Map on page 253

Carib culture

Dominica is home to the last surviving pocket of the Carib Indian people. The island's 3,000 Caribs are descendants of the Amerindian people who once dominated the region. Waves of colonial persecution forced the Caribs to retreat to Dominica, the last island to be settled by the European powers. The most popular shore excursion from Portsmouth sets off in search of their culture, skirting their lands in the northeast. As well as growing coconuts and bananas, the Caribs survive on fishing, carving, weaving and basket-making. At one settlement, a tribal chief generally presents Carib history, story-telling and crafts before a singing and dancing folklore troupe bids visitors a traditional farewell.

Independent excursions

Official taxis are generally reliable and an independent journey from Roseau to Trafalgar Falls, similar to the excursion described above, could be covered in three hours. For all independent trips, bear in mind that Dominica's changeable micro-climate means that water-laden winds can sweep the interior unpredictably, so come equipped (most tour operators provide waterproofs).

In Portsmouth, one of the best independent excursions is to be paddled in a wooden dug-out canoe along the **Indian River**, which is festooned with foliage – the boatman will point out herons in the reeds. It does not need to be booked: enterprising boatmen will be keen to strike a bargain for around US$20.

If you wish to restrict your visit to Roseau, consider a visit to the **Dominica Museum** (open Mon-Fri 9am-4pm, Sat 9am–noon), followed by a meal in La Rose Creole restaurant. Facing Bayfront, the engaging museum covers everything from island geology and economy to the history of the slave trade. ❑

South American Indians from the Orinoco River region are believed to be the forbears of Dominica's Caribs.

BELOW:
the Emerald Pool.

MARTINIQUE

This far-flung département *of France has some stunning and original buildings as well as fascinating botanical gardens, rum distilleries and the poignant ruins of a volcanic eruption*

Map on page 260

Martinique
Caribbean
Sea

Welcome to France! Strange as it may seem, setting foot on the island of Martinique means that you are entering the French Republic and visiting a far-flung corner of the European Union, where the local currency is the euro. It may not look much like it, but this Caribbean island is politically and constitutionally a part of France. Since 1946, when its people voted to become an overseas *département*, Martinique, like Guadeloupe, has been a little, tropical piece of Europe. Its people are French citizens, enjoying the same rights as any other *citoyens*, and in many ways act just like their European compatriots, but with one major exception – they are also Caribbean.

Although all Martinicans speak Creole, the local French-based dialect, the official language is French. Many people don't speak English and they appreciate a visitor's attempt to communicate, however clumsily; so have a go, if you speak any French at all. However, most people you'll come into contact with as a tourist, such as taxi-drivers and guides, will do their best to speak English.

Fort-de-France

Cruise ships arrive in **Fort-de-France ❶**, the island's main port and capital, a city of more than 170,000 inhabitants. Some dock at the commercial port, to the east of the city, an unlovely expanse of wharves, cranes and modern buildings. From here it is a US$10-taxi ride into the centre of Fort-de-France, or a long, hot walk. If you are luckier, your ship will berth at the purpose-built Pointe Simon terminal, close to the heart of the city. In a matter of minutes you are in the bustling and unmistakably French-flavoured shopping streets of the centre of Fort-de-France. There is little to keep you at the cruise terminal and it is better to head straight out onto the Boulevard Alfassa, the road running parallel to the waterfront. Take any of the major streets to your left and you will quickly find yourself in the middle of things.

Like most Caribbean ports, Fort-de-France has had its fair share of fires, earthquakes and other natural disasters, so there are many modern structures among the more interesting 19th-century (and earlier) buildings. What hasn't changed, however, is the grid of narrow streets, which makes driving a nightmare and walking a pleasure. In these busy thoroughfares are countless small boutiques selling the latest Paris fashions as well as local crafts and clothes. Heading away from the sea up rue de la République or rue Victor Schoelcher (named after an anti-slavery campaigner), you reach rue Victor Hugo, where a couple of small shopping malls offer an impressive array of designer perfumes and clothing. Elsewhere, you will find good-quality jewellery, glassware and paintings.

PRECEDING PAGES:
ships at anchor in Fort-de-France.
LEFT: a cruise ship dominates a city street.
BELOW:
in traditional Martinican dress.

French impressions

Occasional buildings stand out as a reminder of Martinique's long French history. Some houses have ornate gingerbread fretwork, a style imported from Louisiana in the 19th century, intricate wrought-ironwork and pretty pastel colours. Most eye-catching, perhaps, are two buildings credited to the architect Henri Pick, a contemporary of Gustave Eiffel and, some claim, the true designer of the Eiffel Tower. The Romanesque-style **St Louis Cathedral**, on rue Schoelcher, hints at the architect's love affair with metal girders and joists, its steel-reinforced spire rising 200 ft (60 metres) into the sky. Built in 1895 to withstand any earthquake, this strange blend of tradition and innovation, known as the "iron cathedral", has a cool interior and fine stained-glass windows.

A few streets away stands Pick's other lasting contribution to Fort-de-France's exotic architectural heritage. The imposing library, the **Bibliothèque Schoelcher** (Mon–Thurs 8.30am–5.30, Fri–Sat 8.30am–noon; free), is a spectacular blend of Romanesque, Byzantine and Egyptian influences, again dominated by pre-fabricated cast-iron and steel features. With ornate gables, a large glass dome and coloured metal panels, this is a truly unique building, illuminated at night, and decorated with clusters of French flags and exotic tropical trees. The library contains the abolitionist Schoelcher's private collection of books, and often stages exhibitions.

This eccentric structure looks over Fort-de-France's "green lung", the large expanse of grass, palms and tamarind trees known as **La Savane**. Traditionally the place for sitting, gossiping and whiling the hours away, the park retains its relaxed atmosphere, even though a craft market has invaded the section nearest the waterfront. You can either browse through the collections of T-shirts and

The stained-glass windows in St Louis Cathedral give colour to the church's interior.

BELOW: a vendor at the city market.

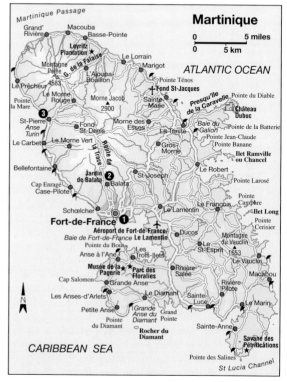

Map on page 260

mass-produced Haitian-style paintings or just sit on one of the benches and watch the coming and going of local ferries that set off from the nearby pier. Alternatively, have a drink or meal at one of the hotels or restaurants that line the rue de la Liberté, next to La Savane.

Two statues on La Savane recall Martinique's Frenchness. A bronze image of Pierre Belain d'Esnambuc, the Norman nobleman who led the first French settlers in 1635, gazes out over the tranquil bay. Further inland stands a statue to the Empress Josephine, Napoleon Bonaparte's first wife, who was born in Martinique. Modern-day Martinicans do not remember Josephine with much affection as she is reputed to have told her husband to reintroduce slavery after it was first abolished in 1791. As a result, the white marble statue has lost its head in a symbolic local version of the guillotine.

Across the bay is the impressive bulk of **Fort St Louis** (Mon–Sat 9.30am–3.30pm; guided tours every half hour; check at the helpful English-speaking tourist information point on Boulevard Alfassa near La Savane). The citadel has been *occupied by the French military since the mid-17th century. One interesting feature is its unusually low ceilings, reputedly designed to deter attacks from taller British troops in the era of inter-European rivalry.

Napoleon was Joséphine's second husband; her first, the Viscount Alexandre de Beauharnais, was beheaded in Paris in 1794 during the reign of terror.

Restaurants and markets

The centre of Fort-de-France can be explored comfortably on foot in three or four hours, and there will still be time for a leisurely meal at one of the city's many excellent restaurants (try the delicious *accras*, deep-fried fritters stuffed with prawns or salted cod). More adventurous visitors might like to round off the tour by taking a look at the busy *markets, which operate all day every day

BELOW: the Pitons du Carbet behind the Sacré Coeur de Balata.

Map
on page
260

Martinicans are proud of their local rum.

BELOW: *Amorpha phallus* flourishes in Jardin de Balata.
RIGHT: St Pierre sits at the foot of Montagne Pelée.

but are most colourful on Friday and Saturday. The fish market takes place from early in the morning until dusk on the banks of the Rivière Madame, a 15-minute walk north of the Pointe Simon terminal. There, and in the adjacent fruit and flower market, you will be dazzled by the sounds, smells and colours, all of which testify to Martinique's exalted culinary reputation. Amid the high-decibel Creole conversations and piles of exotic vegetables, you will realise that this is no ordinary *département* of France.

Outside Fort-de-France

Martinique is not a large island, but it is clearly impossible to see everything in the space of a few hours. Most cruise ships organise excursions to one or more of the chief attractions, and these normally involve a trip to a rum distillery, to the beautiful Balata Botanical Gardens or to the historic town of St Pierre, victim of the 20th-century's worst volcanic disaster. All these are definitely worth doing, although the expedition to St Pierre takes the longest (you should allow an hour each way).

Martinique is dotted with sugar plantations and rum distilleries, producing the world-famous *rhum agricole*, a white rum made from sugar cane juice rather than molasses. Most are open for free visits, but you will be encouraged to taste (and buy) some of the potent rum at the inevitable gift shop. One of the most interesting tours is on offer at the Depaz plantation, north of St Pierre, where a signposted trail leads visitors through the various stages of rum manufacturing.

Those more interested in tropical flora than rum cocktails should take a tour to the **Jardin de Balata** ❷ (Balata Botanical Garden; daily 9am–5pm; entrance fee), just north of Fort-de-France. At their best after the rainy season at the end of the year, these gardens have a stunning collection of anthuriums, as well as an array of exotic trees and shrubs. Jewel-like hummingbirds flit among the flowers, while lizards scuttle along the paths. Nearby, the Sacré Coeur church, a smaller but almost exact replica of the Parisian original, stands among tropical foliage and spectacular mountain views.

Perhaps the most evocative place in Martinique is the town of **St Pierre** ❸, situated on the northwest coast under the brooding Montagne Pelée volcano. In May 1902 this volcano erupted, killing all but one of the town's 30,000 inhabitants and devastating what was known as the "Paris of the Antilles". Many of the ruins of this sophisticated and fun-loving place, such as its grand theatre and main church, lie just as they have for more than a century.

A new town has grown among the rubble of the old, and there are cafés and restaurants to refresh the curious visitor. While the memory of the eruption is poignant, St Pierre is not a gloomy place, and the local tourist office organises fascinating tours of the historic ruins. The **Musée Vulcanologique** (Volcanological Museum) (daily 9am–5pm; entrance fee) has graphic images and artefacts from both before and after the cataclysm, showing the ferocity of Montagne Pelée's eruption and explaining how modern science has made a repetition of the disaster impossible. ❑

GUADELOUPE

The cuisine and the designer goods might be reminiscent of France, but the lush tropical vegetation, white beaches and an active volcano will remind you that Europe is far away

Guadeloupe is shaped like a butterfly, but that's not the only beautiful thing about this volcanic island in the French West Indies. Its terrain is varied and stunning. The eastern region, called Grande-Terre, is a lush land rich in banana plantations, cane fields and gentle hills but with a stormy, wind-hewn Atlantic coastline. It is also reasonably well developed as a tourist playground, with hotels and beach resorts.

Basse-Terre to the west, divided from Grande-Terre by the slender Rivière Salée Strait, has more attractions for hikers and nature lovers. A dramatically mountainous region, it has a live volcano, La Soufrière, and dense forests, but the seas are calm and the beaches are white and glorious. You get from one region to the other via a drawbridge across the strait.

None of these gorgeous attributes will be apparent, however, when you first emerge from the cruise terminal in the capital, **Pointe-à-Pitre ❶**. Although you'll find some nice facilities at the port – including landscaped gardens and duty-free shops, with more shops and small markets close by, you will need to negotiate heavy traffic to explore the main town. Opinions vary as to whether it's worth the effort. If you like your towns neat and pretty, you won't want to waste much time here. But if you enjoy seedy grandeur and a down-to-earth, hard-working atmosphere, you should tarry for a while and let the town work its charm.

Pointe-à-Pitre

A short stroll along the waterfront to **Place de la Victoire Ⓐ** will show you some wonderfully elaborate French colonial houses, complete with balconies and shutters, and the pretty harbour of **La Darse**, which lies off the square. Here you will find the main tourist information office, which is worth popping into since Guadeloupe is not the easiest island to explore on your own. There is also a small but helpful information bureau in the cruise terminal, where you can pick up local maps, hook up with a scrupulous taxi guide, perhaps, and get useful advice on getting about. For example, you can hop on a cheap bus to the beaches of Gosier, if you know where to look.

If your ship gets in early, go to the rue St-John Perse to find the town's covered market, **Le Marché Couvert Ⓑ**, which is bordered by rues St-John Perse, Schoelcher, Frébault and Peynier. It is at its bustling, colourful best in the morning. Here you can pick up stylish cotton clothing, straw bags and local crafts and feast your senses at stalls piled high with fragrant spices and exotic fruits and vegetables, then head off for a decent coffee, a pastry and a chance to watch the world go by from a pavement café.

For more serious shopping, the rues Schoelcher,

PRECEDING PAGES: the striking cemetery at Morne à l'Eau. **LEFT:** spice vendor, Grande Terre. **BELOW:** cruise ship docks at Pointe-à-Pitre.

TIP

You can hire a car in Guadeloupe – companies like Hertz, Avis and Budget are represented – but it's a time-consuming process, and you'll have to negotiate steep mountain roads and drive on the right-hand side.

Nozières and Frébault have the best boutiques, while the Distillerie Bellevue on rue Bellevue Damoiseau is the best place to sample and buy Rhum Agricole, the island's distinctive falling-down water, which locals claim will not give you a hangover because it's made from pure cane sugar juice – but don't take that too seriously. As a French territory, Guadeloupe offers the best bargains for perfume, crystal-ware, cosmetics and fashion accessories from French designer houses; prepare to stock up on Lalique, Hermès, Dior, Chanel, and sexy French lingerie.

Food and culture

With its French Creole heritage, Guadeloupe is a great place to eat; you can sample crayfish, swordfish, stuffed crab and even sea oyster omelettes, and the local speciality goat curry and blood sausage, or *boudin*. The best places to eat food with a view, are Grande Anse, north Basse-Terre, and La Marina, near Pointe-à-Pitre.

If you're interested in history, there are two local museums worth a visit; the **Musée de St-John Perse ☉** (rue Achille Rene-Boisneuf; Mon–Fri 9am–5pm,

Sat 8.30pm–12.30pm; entrance fee) is a beautifully restored colonial building commemorating the work of the island's Nobel Prize-winning poet; while the **Musée Schoelcher** (rue Peynier; Mon–Tues, Thur–Fri 8.30am–5.30pm, closed for lunch and Wed and Sat pm; entrance fee) celebrates the life and anti-slavery campaigns of Victor Schoelcher, a leading 19th-century abolitionist.

Afterwards, head northeast to the Place de l'Eglise to see the exquisite stained-glass (and apparently hurricane-proof) windows of the **Cathédrale de St-Pierre et St-Paul ⓓ**, which has a fragrant flower market near its entrance.

Unlike the inhabitants of most Caribbean islands, the Guadeloupeans are sniffy about accepting the US dollar and insist on the local currency, euros, so take a good supply with you. Also be prepared to trawl your memory for basic French; the local people can be chilly about speaking English, but will be more co-operative if you smile a lot and make a bit of an effort.

You'll also have to negotiate hard over taxi fares if you want to explore further afield. Though fares are theoretically regulated by the government and should be listed at taxi stands, some local drivers will give a Gallic shrug and get more out of you if they can. Always agree a firm price before you start or, ideally, ask the tourist bureau at the port to find you a co-operative driver.

Grande-Terre

The advantage of landing at Pointe-à-Pitre is that it lies on the "body" of the butterfly-shaped island near the bridge over the Rivière Salée, and so is well-placed for exploring both Grande-Terre and Basse-Terre. But if you didn't find the main port to your taste, you may be better pleased by **La Marina** at **Bas-du-Fort**, a 10-minute taxi ride from the cruise terminal. Here, you'll find an attractive, boat-filled

Map on page 268

The racoon is a rare sight in Guadeloupe and is the emblem of Basse-Terre's massive Parc Naturel.

LEFT: Cathédrale de St-Pierre et St-Paul.
BELOW: Musée de St-John Perse.

Map on page 268

TIP

Hikes in the Parc National are graded by levels of difficulty, but it's advisable to hire a guide if you are planning anything really adventurous.

BELOW:
Parc National de la Guadeloupe.
RIGHT:
Chutes du Carbet.

marina surrounded by shops, restaurants and cafés. You can hire a motorboat or join an excursion vessel to tour Guadeloupe's mangrove swamps, or visit a giant aquarium which houses more than 900 Caribbean sea species.

Further east from Pointe-à-Pitre, on Grande-Terre's south coast, lies **Le Gosier**, which has 5 miles (8 km) of beach bordered by some of the region's best resorts. A spectacular 18th-century fortress, **Fort Fleur-d'Epée** ❷, is also situated here and commands fine views. Head even further along, to the east coast of Grande-Terre, and you'll discover breathtaking maritime scenery, somewhat reminiscent of Ireland's west coast. This coast borders the Atlantic, and the ferocity of its waves has carved elaborate patterns into the cliffs – a sight worth seeing if you enjoy high drama and natural beauty.

Basse-Terre

Nature lovers will also be enthralled by Basse-Terre's huge **Parc National de la Guadeloupe** ❸, a latter-day Eden where you can freely enjoy a picnic, a hike and a swim beneath a clear-as-crystal waterfall. Just driving along the coast road which borders the park is a delight – the road winds up through lavish vegetation, passing lovely little bays and picturesque waterfront villages*.

The best beach in Basse-Terre – and, indeed, on the whole island – is **Grande Anse** on the northwest coast, though **Deshaies** (slightly to the south) is more popular with snorkellers.

The biggest attraction on Basse-Terre has to be **La Soufrière** ❹ volcano, which soars 4,812 ft (1,467 metres) above sea level. To reach its peak (if you dare) you'll have to drive up twisting roads past banana trees and tropical vegetation, stopping en route to view the lovely tropical gardens 1,900 ft (580 metres) up at St-Claude. The road ends at 3,300 ft (1,000 metres), but hikers can walk the rest and have the rather scary experience of feeling the ground beneath their feet grow hotter, and the rotten-egg reek of sulphur grow more intense, as they ascend.

The scenery on Basse-Terre's eastern coast, is, by contrast, less dramatic; on your way back to the port from Soufrière, ask your driver to show you the **Parc Archéologique des Roches Gravées** – ancient rocks etched with images of men and animals, which were carved by the Amerindians who originally inhabited Guadeloupe – at Trois Rivières on the southeast coast.

If going it alone sounds like too much hassle on an island where English is not widely spoken and the cab drivers might overcharge, you will find that cruise ship excursions cover most of the main sights outside Pointe-à-Pitre. Most cruise lines offer three- to four-hour tours around one or both parts of the island, and to Soufrière; the price sometimes includes lunch.

Also available are trips to the beach and tours to plantations. For the more adventurous, jungle hikes through the rainforests of Basse-Terre are available from some cruise companies. They include transport to Basse-Terre and a guided 30-minute walk through groves of banana trees and dense tropical vegetation, followed by a refreshing swim beneath the sparkling waters of **Chutes du Carbet**. ❑

ST LUCIA

Map on page 274

*Volcanic peaks, tropical vegetation, whale-watching opportunities
and a vibrant local culture make this delightful island a
popular port of call on cruise itineraries*

Caribbean
Sea

St Lucia

St Lucia is a favourite port of call for all the right reasons: the island is among the loveliest in the Caribbean, and the people are arguably the friendliest. Sandwiched between Martinique and St Vincent, St Lucia is the largest of the Windward Islands, with its calm Caribbean coast acting as a counterpoint to the wind-buffeted Atlantic shore. The mango-shaped island is seductively lush and has preserved its green heart, with banana plantations giving way to botanical gardens and vibrant forests. The south is dominated by the Pitons, the jungle-clad twin peaks that symbolise St Lucia.

Yet these sailors' landmarks are only part of the island's sensory overload. The interior is a Gauguin-esque palette of tropical scenery: primary colours and parrots; hummingbirds and hibiscus; bougainvillaea and bananas; volcanic waterfalls and sulphurous springs; Creole cuisine, calypso and secluded coves; coral reefs, and the best botanical gardens in the West Indies. St Lucia is both the quintessential Caribbean island and an elusive patch of paradise.

LEFT: the magnificent Pitons and Soufrière.
BELOW: stripping coconuts for copra production.

A delightful mix

Culturally, the island is an engaging mix of cultures, with Caribbean flair, Creole artlessness and French finesse underscored by traditional British values. The island has changed hands 14 times, with the French flag and the Union Jack alternating from 1650, when French settlers first landed. From the 1760s, the island operated a plantation economy, based on African slave labour. St Lucia became British for good in 1814; it gained independence in 1979 but remains part of the Commonwealth. English is the official language but Creole patois – known as kwéyòl – is commonplace. French vocabulary imposed on African grammar, with a smattering of Spanish thrown in. St Lucia feels safe but wild, forthright yet not as in-your-face as Jamaica, as friendly as Barbados but less primly British.

Until recently, agriculture, chiefly bananas, was the mainstay of the economy, so tourism has not erased cultural values. The island is currently suffering from the crisis in its cash crops and has yet to make a successful transition to tourism. Even so, St Lucia has its share of luxurious hotels and low-key inns for those who wish to extend their stay. As a port of call, **Castries ❶** is perfectly suited to the largest cruise ships and offers an unparalleled variety of excursions. The only problem is mustering the determination to return to the cruise ship.

Excursion to paradise

While St Lucia is safe for independent visitors following well-trodden tracks to the beaches, or to the peaks and the volcano, first-time visitors would do

well to book the classic one-day excursion through their cruise ship. Generally known as "Land and Sea to Soufrière", this full-day trip is arguably the best excursion in the Caribbean – a voyage through the island's history, culture, geology and geography. The day begins with a visit to the panoramic heights above Castries, followed by a leisurely drive through the lush interior to Soufrière, a walk round a quaint fishing village, and a visit to the "drive-in" volcano cowering under cone-shaped peaks. The volcano acquired its name because cars were allowed to park between two sets of bubbling, belching springs before tourism made this unfeasible. After a stroll around impressive botanical gardens, it is on to a lively Creole lunch on a former plantation estate. From the tiny port nearby, a catamaran sweeps visitors back to Castries, making stops for swimming, generally just before the chic marina of Marigot Bay.

There is usually time for an independent stroll around the cruise terminal, which is packed with jewellery and craft shops. While elements of this trip could easily be done independently, this tried and tested formula is best left to professional guides, who handle it with humour and panache, as well as ensuring a return to the cruise ship in good time. And as the cruise lines generally use comfortable minibuses, rather than coaches, it will not feel blandly impersonal.

Lucky for some

From the cruise terminal, the trip ascends the slopes of **Castries** to **Morne Fortune**, the "hill of luck", yet equally unlucky to French and British forces. The main square in Castries was renamed Derek Walcott Square in 1993, in honour of the St Lucian poet who won the Nobel Prize for literature. The square is shaded by a huge, 400-year-old Saman tree known locally as a *massair*; the

TIP

When deciding whether to take an organised excursion or go it alone, bear in mind that while the ships always wait for delayed official excursions, independent travellers have much less leeway.

BELOW:
a typical West Indian cottage.

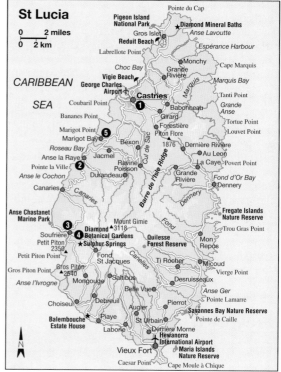

Map on page 274

story runs that a foreigner once asked the name of the tree and was told *massair*, which simply means "I don't know" in Creole, but the "I-don't-know" tree it has been ever since. The undistinguished look of the town is the result of the devastating fire of 1948. Even so, the hill is redeemed by panoramic views of the bay and by pink, weather-boarded colonial-style houses on the hill, which survived the fire. The classic photo opportunity is the view over the bay, usually dominated by sleek cruise ships and a tiny but scenic island where Walcott lives when not lecturing in Boston. After would-be photographers have run the gauntlet of hair-braiders and T-shirt sellers, it is back to the bus for a glimpse of the stately Government House, hidden beyond a series of hairpin bends.

Bags of bananas

The tour continues into the lush interior, beginning with the banana plantations of **Cul de Sac Valley**. Until lack of international competitiveness led to the collapse of the local cash crop, bananas were the backbone of the St Lucian economy, but now the few surviving plantations depend entirely on exports to the British market. Visitors are often surprised to see that the unripe fruit is tied with blue plastic bags to retain its moisture and protect the hands of bananas against the ravages of sun and insects. High in potassium and oil, the precious fruit finds its way into countless local recipes, from sweet banana ketchup and banana bread to banana wine, daiquiri and fruit punch. St Lucians claim that the volcanic soil makes these the sweetest, juiciest bananas on earth.

A foray to the coast reveals the lovely fishing village of **Anse la Raye ❷**, where trinket-sellers and fishermen cluster around the beach front; beyond lie jaunty canoes bobbing beside a battered jetty. Traditionally, the fishermen used

St Lucian bananas are shipped to the UK.

BELOW:
Soufrière nestles in a pretty bay.

to make boats out of gum trees, and sails from sacks. From here, the excursion skirts the lush rainforest, with sightings of the dramatic **Pitons**, the twin cones which tower over the trees. **Gros Piton** rises over 2,540 ft (774 metres) above the sea, while **Petit Piton** stands 2,350 ft (716 metres) high. Thought to be the sides of an eroded volcanic crater, the peaks have always had a certain mystique: the Amerindians left sacred carvings on the rock, believing that the Petit Piton, the "small" peak that dwarfs Soufrière, was giving birth to a baby.

The rainforest has mahogany and red cedars, as well as the gomer trees that spell home to the island parrots. The forests are also home to deadly lance-de-fer snakes, introduced by European colonists who wanted to deter their slaves from escaping. But since the snakes were unable to distinguish between the masters and slaves, the colonials received a taste of their own medicine, especially since the local people rarely revealed which were the secret remedies that might save them.

Diamond Botanical Gardens are filled with colourful, fragrant flora.

Soufrière

The quaintly ramshackle town of **Soufrière** ❸ nestles under the twin peaks and marks the gateway to a 7-acre (3-hectare) volcanic crater. The volcano's fans stress the rejuvenating properties of the sulphurous vapours, the positive effect on the sinuses and the therapeutic value of the volcanic springs. However, most visitors are overwhelmed by the familiar, sickly-sweet rotten eggs smell of the sulphur springs, the result of a volcanic eruption. The collapsed crater has bubbling pools of lava which steam away like an inferno. The seething mass slowly reveals its mineral-rich colours: greenish-yellow spells sulphur deposits; dark-green means copper oxide; white is lime and chalk; and purple is magnesium.

BELOW:
Diamond Falls.

Since a vaporous explosion occurred in 1766, little of significance has disturbed the scene of these hissing grey fumaroles and local people believe the dormant volcano is safe. Even so, one guide nearly died trying to show German cruise ship visitors how unstable the volcanic crust was – it proved his point by collapsing and taking him down to the depths.

Lush vegetation

Nearby are the beautifully maintained **Diamond Botanical Gardens** ❹ (Mon–Sat 10am–5pm, Sun 10am–3pm; entrance fee) and **Diamond Falls**, complete with a waterfall and the remains of a 3-mile (5-km) 18th-century aqueduct linked to the Soufrière Estate. The gardens were created in 1785, just before the French Revolution, with funds provided by Louis XVI. While it is considered unsafe to swim in the volcanic falls, bathing in the rejuvenating mineral baths, fed by hot springs, is permissible. Given time constraints, however, visitors often have to choose between a dip in the baths or a stroll around the grounds, including the Japanese water gardens.

The exotic plants usually win, even if the lack of botanical labelling makes a good guide invaluable. Among the foliage and primary colours are bold red and yellow crab's claw, ginger lily, rare orchids, trailing red heliconia, mimosa, poinsettia, and over 140 types of ferns. Beyond are coconut palms, Honduras mahogany, red cedars, sandalwood and the gri-gri palm, distinguished by its hairy trunk.

Also on display is an array of local crops, from coconuts to cassava and cinnamon, from pawpaw (papaya) to pumpkin and plantain, and yams to breadfruit and dasheen, a root vegetable that the government is hoping will take the place of bananas. Every crop has its own place in Caribbean history: slaves were fed on breadfruit by their colonial masters; coconut trees are known as the trees of life because every part of the palm and nut serves a useful purpose, from food to medicine, baskets to toothpicks; one variant, the graft nut tree, produces medicinal milk, which is still used as a diuretic.

Lunching and swimming

Lunch is on the neighbouring **Soufrière Estate**, which incorporates a former sugar mill and a restored water wheel, first used to crush limes and later to generate power. The property represents the remainder of a 2,000-acre (810-hectare) estate that Louis XIV presented to his loyal subjects, the Devaux family, in 1713. Savouring the Creole buffet offers a chance to taste some of the crops presented in the botanical gardens.

Afterwards, the excursion meets a catamaran at **Anse Chastanet**, the best place on the island for snorkelling and sailing. The catamaran cruise back to Castries conjures up a carnival atmosphere, with Caribbean music, tropical fruit, and unlimited rum punch on board. Views of the Pitons peaks give way to a series of sheltered coves, of which **Anse Le Cochon** is the most beguiling. This is a regular swimming and snorkelling stop, marred only by the myriad conchshell vendors, banana- and bead-sellers, whose frantically paddled canoes

Map on page 274

Anse Chastanet has a sought-after honeymoon hotel, set on a sheltered bay in the lee of the conical Piton peaks. Honeymooners can expect tea-light candles and a bed scattered with hibiscus petals.

BELOW: hike through the lush rainforest.

INDEPENDENT EXCURSIONS

Castries, St Lucia's capital, does not justify much precious time spent in exploration, especially since the island as a whole has so much to offer. If you want to see the island independently rather than on a cruise-ship tour, to visit the beaches on the north coast or to go snorkelling, a taxi from Castries is the obvious option. An official "minder" at the head of the taxi rank establishes routes, states prices, and helps form small groups to visit places together. Prices are standardised for set routes but to double-check, call in at the tourist office booth close by.

The most popular beach is Reduit Beach on Rodney Bay, which has plenty of facilities, from sun-beds and parasols to water sports and restaurants. Official cabs are generally reliable in respecting the agreed pick-up time, but given the proximity of several large hotels, it is easy to call a taxi should the original one fail to turn up.

The *Brig Unicorn*, a distinctive sailing ship, goes from Castries to Soufrière, and was the vessel featured in *Roots*, the epic book and film about slavery, as well as the 2003 film *Pirates of the Caribbean*. Call the company: 758-452 8644, ideally before setting out on your cruise. Costs are around US$85 for adults, $25 for children, but a sunset cruise around Castries is less expensive.

Map on page 274

surround the catamaran. Stray swimmers are rounded up and the catamaran sails north to **Marigot Bay** ❺, a magnificent steep-sided cove which is used as an exclusive marina for glitzy yachts. This upmarket tropical retreat is billed as an artists' colony but has more in common with a chic resort. The excursion ends with happy, rum-sozzled passengers deposited at the cruise terminal, delighted to be addressed by their guide as *dou-dou*, Creole for "darling" or "sweetie".

Dolphins, whales and deep-sea fishing

Dolphin- and whale-watching day trips are always popular, so book early.

While the above trip is probably the best way to spend your day ashore, there are other activities on offer, and for reasons of cost, numbers, reliable timing and tight organisation, certain of them are best organised through the ship's cruise excursion manager. These include whale- and dolphin-watching, deep-sea fishing, helicopter sightseeing, adventure hiking, and riding through the dramatic countryside on the Atlantic coast.

Bear in mind that, on the mega-ships, tours get booked up quickly, whereas, on smaller ships, the more unusual tours might not attract enough people to justify going ahead. It is therefore worth having several options in mind, and knowing whether an organised or an independent excursion appeals to you more *(see panel on page 277 for details of independent excursions).*

The whale and dolphin-watching trips off the west coast offer a 75 per cent chance of seeing humpback whales and dolphins. A hydrophone-equipped boat enables the skipper to trace passing whale pods while on-board sonar equipment allows everyone to tune in to the strange sounds made by these extraordinary and exciting mammals.

BELOW: you can take a sunset sail on the *Brig Unicorn*.

If you are more interested in catching marine life, the deep-sea fishing trip sets out in search of blue marlin and big game fish, from barracuda to tuna and dorado. Depending on the participants' wishes, the fish can be given to the captain or put back in the sea on a conservation-minded "tag and release" basis. Alternatively, for a memorable island overview, a short but dramatic helicopter trip sweeps along the Caribbean coast south towards Soufrière and the Pitons, revealing the majesty of the peaks, rainforest and volcanic springs.

Energetic excursions

Cruises aimed at a more energetic clientele offer kayaking around Pigeon Island national park in the north of the island, scuba-diving near Marigot Bay, or hiking in the rainforest around Soufrière, culminating in a swim in the hot volcanic springs. For reasonably proficient horse riders, there is the Atlantic coast route, which follows the same course as a meandering river and passes old sugar and banana plantations close to the shore, before ending with a canter on the beach.

Jungle bicycle rides can be booked through cruise lines, and generally offer cycling through the rainforest, with a less adventurous alternative following a similar off-road itinerary in a Jeep. One of the best routes heads south to the waterfall close to the fishing village of Anse la Raye and visits the restored 18th-century **Sikwi sugar mill**. ❏

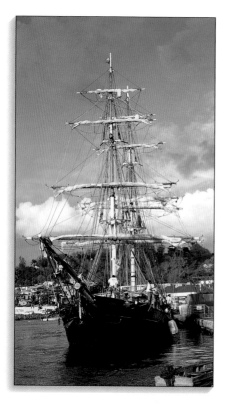

The Tourism Dollar

With some glowing exceptions, such as Barbados, St Barts, the Cayman Islands and the US Virgin Islands, the Caribbean islands have yet to reach a happy accommodation with tourism. While Antigua and the British Virgin Islands have carved out a niche for themselves, other islands with equal appeal are failing to make tourism work for the population as a whole.

In the case of islands such as Dominica and Grenada, it is because of a laudable decision not to opt for the "sun, sea and sand" formula prevalent elsewhere. However, for other islands, equally blessed with natural riches, the situation is more complex. St Lucia is a case in point. Despite its enviable reputation as the honeymoon capital of the West Indies, there is an ambivalent attitude towards tourism.

Even if tourism has replaced cash crops as the island's main revenue earner in recent years, the "tourism dollar" has yet to filter down to most of the local people, who barely benefit at all from the procession of passing cruise ships and honeymooners. If this friendly foreign invasion is still regarded with suspicion in some quarters, the issue is exacerbated by the proliferation of all-inclusive resorts which put little money back into the island economy.

To foster a more inclusive relationship, and a necessary filtering down of wealth, local inns are being promoted as an alternative to isolated luxury hotels, and visiting cruise ship passengers are urged to be supportive of the local economy by buying more handicrafts, eating out whenever possible, and booking guides independently.

In turn, the St Lucian government is putting pressure on the inhabitants to beautify the island, but, as yet, local people fail to make the connection between natural beauty and revenue from tourism.

The problem is clear in the attractive fishing village of Anse la Raye, where disgruntled sellers of giant conch shells, flimsy straw baskets and unwieldy maracas fail to drum up much foreign interest. Instead, most cruise-ship passengers take a few pictures of fishermen with jaunty canoes bobbing beside a battered jetty before returning to their minibuses.

It is hard to apportion blame: understandably, few tourists wish to purchase pointless souvenirs, but local people are failing to make money from either tourism or fishing, thus creating tensions which, in time, foster a culture conducive to petty crime and drug-dealing. As a precaution, cruise passengers are warned not to wander down back-streets, although Anse la Raye is hardly downtown Kingston, Jamaica.

It would be more helpful for the-powers-that-be to foster the development of services and goods that benefit both parties. At Anse la Raye, a fish beach barbecue or "jump-up", the classic Caribbean explosion of fun, is hardly a solution to the island economy but it would be a gesture in the right direction. At least cruise passengers would realise that the locals are friendly – and would be prepared to pay for the privilege. ❑

RIGHT: the luxurious Hilton Jalousie sits on a pristine strip of white sand.

BARBADOS

One of the most popular Caribbean cruise stops, this island has a colourful heritage, an interesting capital, some great hiking trails and an excellent reputation for nightlife and cuisine

Map on page 284

Caribbean Sea

Barbados

The most easterly of the Windward Islands, Barbados is not blessed with dramatic mountains and lush rainforest like some of its neighbours. Instead, it has open, rolling countryside with fields of sugar cane rippling in the breezes coming in off the Atlantic, which crashes in huge rollers along the sweeping beaches of the exposed east coast.

Outside Bridgetown, the bustling capital, the island is dotted with sleepy villages and some beautiful botanical gardens and plantation houses. The pretty chattel houses, wooden shacks that were once home to plantation workers, have become an architectural feature. Painted in primary colours and pastel shades, with intricate fretwork around the windows, they often double as craft shops.

The sheltered west coast is lined with some of the Caribbean's most glamorous and expensive hotels, whose patrons return year after year. The island has gained a reputation as a millionaire's playground, particularly thanks to US$1,500-a-night establishments like Sandy Lane, and several very smart restaurants, as fashionable London venues spread to the tropics.

Barbados has a distinctly British feel, with village cricket and red post boxes. The island was settled by the British in the 17th century and is still a member of the Commonwealth. It is clean, friendly and regarded as safe, although the usual issues of extreme wealth flaunted in the face of relative poverty exist. Despite years of colonialism, Barbados has its own colourful heritage; its annual Cropover festival in July, celebrating the sugar cane harvest, is rated as one of the best events in the Caribbean. The jazz festival in January attracts big names like Patti LaBelle and Ray Charles, while Holders' Season, a wonderful series of outdoor classical music performances on a former plantation estate, draws performers such as Pavarotti and the London Symphony Orchestra.

PRECEDING PAGES: sunset at Carlisle Bay. **LEFT:** the Parliament building overlooks the Careenage. **BELOW:** a Caribbean *trompe l'oeil* in Paynes Bay.

A popular choice

Barbados is one of the Caribbean islands most visited by cruise passengers, with a ship a day calling during the high-season winter months. Apart from an added gleam in the eyes of the shopkeepers, a cruise ship in town does not make a vast difference to daily life, as the island has a well-developed infrastructure and the visitor attractions are spread out.

A lot of cruises start and finish here, particularly those carrying a high proportion of passengers from Europe, as the island is well served by non-stop flights. It is one of the easiest destinations in which to extend a cruise, which is well worth doing, if only to sample the nightlife, which varies from fine cuisine under the stars at Sandy Lane to scruffy rum shops in Bridgetown's Baxters Road.

These colourful batik cushions are a good example of the quality crafts and souvenirs that are available at the Pelican Craft Centre and elsewhere in Bridgetown.

The cruise terminal is about 1 mile (2 km) from the centre of town, at Deep Water Harbour. There's a duty-free shopping centre for jewellery, cameras and electrical goods (which are still more expensive than in the US or Europe), as well as souvenir stands selling T-shirts, and pretty chattel houses displaying local crafts. You need a passport, airline ticket or cruise line ID to qualify for duty-free prices. You can hire bikes, arrange tours and book horse riding here.

Other facilities include an internet café, a sports bar and restaurant. Brighton Beach is right in front of the Deep Water Harbour and perfectly fine for an afternoon if you don't want to travel; there's a popular bar here, Weisers, where you can watch or join in a game of beach volleyball.

The island is sports mad. From January to March and again in October and November, there is high-class cricket to watch. Golf is popular and, if you want to play on a prestigious course like Sandy Lane or Royal Westmoreland, advance booking is recommended. The best horseback riding is across the central highlands and, as you would expect, there's a wide array of water sports to enjoy.

Finding your way around

Barbados is a relatively easy island to explore independently and is only 21 miles (34 km) long, although twisting country roads make distances seem further, especially when the sugar cane is high and views are obscured; they are not always clearly marked, either. Shore excursions involve many permutations of the island tour and are usually comprehensive, but the fun of exploring is lost if you travel by coach. An open-sided mini-moke is a better way to get around, and in a day trip from Bridgetown you should be able to reach the northernmost point and return via the wild coastal scenery of the east coast around Bathsheba.

Driving is on the left, and all visitors must have a visitor's driving permit, which will be arranged by the car hire company. Rush hour starts at 4pm and, while all roads lead to Bridgetown, progress may be painfully slow around this time (nobody is in much of a hurry on Barbados anyway), so do allow for this.

Taxis are plentiful and are lined up outside the cruise terminal. Drivers are more than willing to do day trips. Fares are fixed but there is no meter system, so always agree a price in advance. The island has a comprehensive bus network and the single flat fare is a bargain, but buses are crowded and journeys take time. They are, however, a good way to meet local people.

Bridgetown

If you have only a few hours, there is plenty to see and do without leaving **Bridgetown ❶**. It is perfectly pleasant just to wander along the Careenage, lined with yachts and fishing boats, with a lazy lunch at the famous **Waterfront Café** and a browse around the shops. Broad Street is the main shopping area. Cave Shepherd and Harrison's are the principal Bajan department stores; if you

Map on page 284

LEFT: riding through Bridgetown.
BELOW: Government House.

St Michael's Cathedral was built from coral limestone in Greek classical style. It is believed to have the oldest manual organ in the Caribbean.

BELOW:
Alleynes Bay on the west coast.

don't have time to leave town, look out for the beautifully crafted pottery from Earthworks, made in the parish of St Thomas, which is on sale in Cave Shepherd.

Watch local artisans working at the Pelican Craft Centre, located on the Princess Alice Highway (you will pass it en route from the cruise terminal), where there is also a working cigar producer. There are several art galleries in town – the **Verandah** (Mon–Sat, closed Sat pm; free; tel: 246-426 2605) has good exhibitions of Caribbean art. The Best of Barbados gift shops are a good bet for locally made souvenirs – everything on sale is produced on the island.

History and rum

Bridgetown has several interesting sights. **National Heroes Square Ⓐ** (formerly Trafalgar Square) is dedicated to 10 national heroes – but no longer to Lord Nelson, whose statue is to be relocated. The Gothic-style Parliament building dates back to 1872, while nearby **St Michael's Cathedral Ⓑ** stands on the grounds of the first church in Barbados, built in 1665.

Sugar cane means rum, and close to the port, on Spring Garden Highway, is the **Mount Gay ❷** rum blending and bottling plant (Mon–Fri, tours every half hour from 9.30am–3.30pm; entrance fee; tel: 246-425 8757), which does comprehensive 45-minute tours, including a tasting.

A short taxi ride around Carlisle Bay is the **Garrison Savannah ❸**, dating from the mid-17th century and once the most important military location on the island . The area is packed with historic interest, with forts, monuments, military buildings and the world's largest collection of 17th-century cannons. The **Barbados Museum** (Mon–Sat and Sun pm; entrance fee) is also here, covering everything from historic maps to colonial furniture.

Out of town

The west coast, dubbed the Platinum Coast, is lined with smart hotels and exclusive villas. Narrow side roads lead to emerald polo fields and the undulating fairways of the Sandy Lane golf course on the right opposite white soft sand beaches on the left. The first settlers landed at **Holetown ❹** in 1627, an event which is commemorated every February with street fairs and a music festival.

Lone Star is unquestionably the place to hang out here – an ultra-trendy restaurant, bar and motel, in a beautiful location on the beach, selling everything from Sevruga caviar to Jamaican jerk chicken. Nearby **Folkestone Park and Marine Reserve** (Mon–Fri 9am–5pm; entrance fee) has an underwater snorkel trail over a coral reef, as well as a small aquarium and changing facilities.

Continuing up the coast, stop at the John Moore bar on the beach at Weston. This is the place for flying fish and chips and a cold Banks (the excellent local beer), or the more adventurous pudding and souse, a local speciality containing the ears and snout of a pig.

If you're anxious to feel terra firma after days at sea, take a guided hike along the **Arbib Nature and Heritage Trail** (guided walks take place on Wed, Thur, Sat 9am–2.30pm; tel: 246-426 2421), which starts at St Peter's Church in **Speightstown ❺**, the main shopping town on the west coast. There are two routes, 3½ miles (5.5km) and 4½ miles (7.5km), one leading through the town and one along the coast and through limestone gullies.

Cutting through the parish of St Lucy, you'll come to **North Point**, at the tip of the island, with sheltered but remote beaches, sheer cliffs and pounding waves crashing onto jagged rocks. A lot of the cruise excursions don't get this far. The **Animal Flower Cave** (open daily unless the sea is rough; entrance

A tour of Mount Gay distillery ends with a taste of liquid gold.

BELOW: a guide like Robert Quintyne will lead you through the Arbib Nature Trail.

Map on page 284

Vibrant red flora at Andromeda Gardens.

BELOW: Morgan Lewis windmill.
RIGHT: a fishing boat off Brandon's Beach.

fee) is a network of slippery caves supposedly inhabited by sea anemones. It's not worth the trip in itself, only if you are in the area. A rather more interesting detour is to **Morgan Lewis Mill** (Mon–Sat; entrance fee) in St Andrew. This is the island's only functioning windmill and you can climb to the top. Call at neighbouring Cherry Tree Hill, too, for yet more spectacular views.

Bathsheba and the Andromeda Gardens

The real reason to come here, though, is the beautifully desolate coastal scenery; you can see miles of Atlantic rollers and dazzling white cliffs all the way to **Bathsheba ❻**, and there is little building or development of any kind – just the occasional craft stall by the road. Although you'll see surfers on the beaches, it is not safe to swim, but on a hot and humid day there will always be a cooling breeze and it's a nice place for a picnic.

At Bathsheba itself, the **Andromeda Botanic Gardens** (daily 9am–5pm; entrance fee) are a wonderful place for a rest from driving. Calming waterfalls splash gently through the gardens, dazzling with tropical blooms from all over the Caribbean, including a wide variety of orchids. A couple of miles inland from here, off Highway 3, is **Villa Nova**, an exquisite plantation house, once owned by British prime minister Sir Anthony Eden and now a luxury hotel, containing much of the original rich mahogany furniture. Afternoon tea or lunch here is extremely civilised (book ahead, tel: 246-433 1524).

Forests, caves and pottery

From here, there are three fascinating examples of natural Barbados just inland. The **Flower Forest** in St Joseph (open daily; entrance fee) is a pretty walking trail through lush tropical gardens. **Welchman Hall Gully ❼** (daily 9am–5pm; entrance fee) is a deep ravine just off the main road, Highway 2, maintained by the National Trust, with a ¾-mile (1.2-km) trail leading through rainforest, bamboo, palms, giant overhanging ferns, mango trees and mahogany forest. Look out for monkeys and colourful birds in the trees.

Just south of here is **Harrison's Cave** (open daily; tel: 246-438 6640; entrance fee), a limestone cave complete with underground lakes, cascading water, stalactites and stalagmites, all of which can be experienced by means of a small electric train.

A little further south on Highway 2 is the **Earthworks Pottery** (Mon–Fri 9am–5pm, Sat 9am–1pm; free), which produces unique ceramics decorated in bright Caribbean colours. Next door, the Potter's House Gallery, located in a blue and white chattel house, is a showcase for Caribbean art and crafts.

If you have the luxury of an evening departure, wait until "magic hour", late in the afternoon, to end up at **Gun Hill ❽** (Mon–Sat; entrance fee), a restored signal tower in St George parish, a few miles outside Bridgetown. The signal station served a dual purpose: to watch for approaching ships and to survey the island for slave uprisings after a rebellion in 1816. The views over the south of the island are breathtaking, especially at this time of day, just before sunset, when the light is soft and luminous. ❑

ST VINCENT AND THE GRENADINES

Map
on page
294

Volcanic and lush, St Vincent is a nature lover's paradise. Strong walkers climb Soufrière volcano, others take gentle walks. Bequia and Mayreau are for those who just want to chill out

St Vincent, at 18 by 11 miles (30 by 18 km), is the largest and most developed of the cluster of the 32 islands collectively known as the Grenadines, between St Lucia and Grenada. At **Kingstown ❶**, the island port and capital, there are now berths for two ships, linked to a terminal, so it is rare that ships have to anchor offshore and tender passengers to land as they do at the other Grenadine islands on cruise itineraries, such as Bequia and Mayreau.

Caribbean
Sea

St Vincent and
The Grenadines

This terminal, built in 2001, has telephones, a tourist information desk, exchange facilities (EC dollars is the local currency although US dollars, as ever in the Caribbean, serve just as well), a selection of duty-free and souvenir shops and a number of cafés, bars and fast food outlets. All of this is a lot more than there is in downtown Kingstown, where the shops and street hawkers exist mainly to serve local needs. There is little of the usual Caribbean bargaining here, although the relatively recent additions of a new indoor fruit and vegetable market in the centre (Upper Bay) and a new indoor fish market, known as Little Tokyo, by the dock, has added some colour and interest.

PRECEDING PAGES:
Port Elizabeth and
Admiralty Bay.
LEFT: harbour view
of Bequia.
BELOW: downtown
Grenadine style.

Kingstown has a Catholic **Cathedral of the Assumption**, a bizarre mixture of Moorish, Romanesque, Byzantine, Venetian and Flemish architectural styles, despite being built in the 1930s. And there is an 18th-century fortress, **Fort Charlotte**, above the town, overlooking both Kingstown and the Caribbean.

Making the most of the day

Most visitors head out of town fairly quickly. There are plenty of taxis waiting outside the terminal, all keen to offer guided tours around the island. Alternatively, minibuses heading to specific places leave regularly from the fish market.

Outside Kingstown, St Vincent is a lush, forested island, and this is reflected in one of its main points of interest, the **Botanic Gardens ❷** in Montrose, a five- or 10-minute drive from the port. Dating back to 1765, these gardens are reputedly the oldest in the western hemisphere and have a breadfruit tree that dates back to the original plant brought to the island by Captain Bligh of *Mutiny on the Bounty* fame (or infamy).

The gardens are always included on the basic island tours (lasting between two and four hours) offered on the ships' excursion programmes – as are Kingstown's fort and cathedral – but if there are two or more of you travelling together, all these places can be visited more cheaply on an independent guided taxi tour.

The other popular excursion is by boat (usually a catamaran) from Kingstown along the Leeward

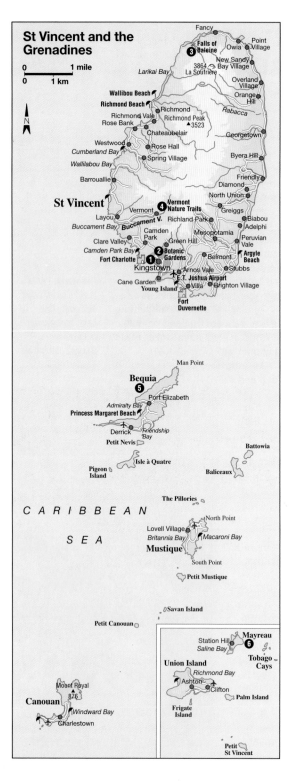

(Caribbean) coast, past sugar and banana plantations, a former whaling village – Barrouallie – rocky coves, black sand beaches and mountains, including the Soufrière volcano which erupted as recently as 1979.

This tour, lasting four to five hours, will include a beach stop for swimming and snorkelling, and possibly a visit to the **Falls of Baleine ❸**, where you can swim in the rocky pool below the 60-ft (18-metre) waterfall.

Walking tours

There is potential for independent diving, snorkelling and fishing trips on St Vincent, but there is less range than on the other Grenadines. The great advantage of visiting St Vincent is the scope for walking tours – from gentle nature hikes right up to a strenuous ascent of the 3,864-ft (1,178-metre) **La Soufrière**.

The latter, however, will take a full day, including getting from Kingstown in the southwest to the volcano's location in the northeast corner; and it will depend on your fitness and walking experience, the weather and the departure time of your ship whether this is a feasible option. Check with the tourist office in the terminal, where it is also possible to hire a guide for the hike.

There are some gentle rainforest hikes along the **Vermont Nature Trails ❹**, in the Buccament Valley, about a 20-minute drive from Kingstown. Just beyond these is the **Mesapotamia Valley** near the east (Atlantic) coast, which offers more challenging walking through forests and plantations.

Beyond Kingstown, St Vincent is largely unspoilt, mostly cultivated for farming. The only major tourist resort is self-contained on **Young Island**, just off the south coast, where at least one cruise line (Star Clippers) now calls.

Bequia and Mayreau

While St Vincent remains a real haven for nature-lovers, more cruise ships are choosing to call at **Bequia ❺** and Mayreau. **Port Elizabeth** is the entry point for Bequia but, although only the

Map on page 294

smallest cruise ships – often sailing vessels – call here, they all have to anchor in Admiralty Bay. Once on the jetty (where the ferries from St Vincent also disembark), it is only a short walk to a group of smart shops and restaurants, with a tourist information office in the middle. There are more places to shop and eat along the front (Belmont Walkway), or you could head inland for a few minutes along Front Street, where you will find an open-air market.

There is not much more to Port Elizabeth but Bequia is really about the water. Swimming, snorkelling and scuba-diving are the reasons people come here – more come by air than by sea – and you can move around parts of the island as easily by water-taxi as by more conventional road taxis.

It costs only a few dollars to go by boat from the main jetty to the nearest beach. And – unlike on volcanic St Vincent – the beaches are all white sand, not black. Slightly further out are the best diving sites within the 7-mile (12-km) coral reef, which has been designated a national marine park. Your cruise ship will organise dive trips on its own or local boats, and this is a better option than wasting precious time trying to sort out something independently.

Mayreau ❻ is treated as a Grenadine version of the private islands that cruise lines own or lease (mainly in the Bahamas), but it is for ships carrying just a few hundred, rather than several thousand, passengers. You will probably be taken directly to **Saline Bay Beach** for a relaxing day just chilling out.

Other Grenadine islands at which some ships call (apart from Carriacou which is part of Grenada; *see page 300*) include Tobago Cays, Palm Island, Canouan, Union Island and Mustique. On the latter there is only limited access for cruise ship passengers because so many celebrities have homes or take holidays on the island and they guard their privacy very fiercely. ❑

TIP

If your cruise calls at St Vincent but not Bequia, you can get a ferry across, but the journey takes an hour each way.

BELOW:

passengers from a clipper snorkel at Saline Bay.

GRENADA AND CARRIACOU

Map on page 298

With a pretty harbour, expanses of rainforest, waterfalls, a bird sanctuary and white beaches protected from development, the Spice Island of Grenada is worth exploring

Caribbean Sea

Grenada

Grenada was the island you could smell before you could see it – in the nicest possible way, of course. Known as the Spice Island, it is not only the world's second largest exporter of nutmeg but also grows more spices per square mile than anywhere else on the planet. However, Hurricane Ivan put paid to this in September 2004 when it ripped through the island felling most of the nutmeg trees and destroying 90 percent of the buildings. But undeterred, with £200 million of overseas aid, Grenada is making a rapid recovery and plans to be fully operational soon. Around 100,000 nutmeg trees are being planted and the sweet smell of spices will soon fill the air again.

Sailors down the centuries have rated **St George's ❶**, the island capital, one of the world's prettiest harbours, and it's hard to disagree. Horseshoe-shaped and set in a long-dormant volcanic crater, it is a natural harbour flanked by two forts (Fort George and Fort Frederick) and has colourful French colonial-style buildings ranged along the front. Some ships still dock alongside, but the larger ones have to anchor out in the harbour. Their tenders come ashore at the same place as the ships dock, right by a small visitors' welcome centre (with telephones, maps and other tourist information) and, of course, the spice market.

The Carenage and Baytown

The inner harbour is known as the **Carenage**, and this name is also used locally for the promenade around the harbour front. Having walked through the busy market – and few people manage this without buying nutmeg or some collection of aromatic spices – just follow the Carenage round past the jetties, the old warehouses, small shops and offices to the opposite side of the harbour, where there is a selection of bars and restaurants. Many of these are on the first floor above shops, where the open windows look out over the harbour and let in the cooling sea breezes.

You will see plenty of seafood – including conch – on the menus and some traditional Grenadian dishes. From the forests comes *tatu* (armadillo), *manicou* (opposum) and iguana. Turtles are protected but there is controlled culling, so they sometimes appear, especially in soup, while the dolphin steaks offered are actually a Caribbean fish called dorado or mahi-mahi.

The food and the cheek-by-jowl seating in the Carenage cafés are – like the rest of St George's – refreshingly unpretentious and very enjoyable. So is a visit to the ice cream parlour on the harbour front which predated Ben and Jerry's with its eclectic range of flavours. Most of them are spice-based, of course, but avocado and Guinness-flavoured cones are also sold – but rarely twice to the same person.

While the Carenage is brash and bustling almost

LEFT: getting away from it all on Grand Anse.
BELOW: market day in St George's.

round the clock, walk only a few yards back and the rest of St George's seems a tranquil, sleepy town. Young Street, off the Carenage near the cafés, leads to the **Baytown** area, so called because it faces St George's Bay. Along the way there is a small museum, where exhibits include a bathtub used by Empress Josephine Bonaparte; and Market Square, which has a lively Saturday market. There is an even more interesting walk if you take the second right from Young into Church Street, where, at the junction with Halifax Street, you will find the atmospheric St Andrew's Church and the cathedral, constructed in 1830.

Grenada's strong local rums are River Antoine and Jack Iron. Trivia fans will be interested to learn that it was the initials on the Grenadian rum stamp centuries ago – Georgius Rex Old Grenada – that prompted the nickname, GROG.

Grand Anse Beach

The first unmissable place out of town is **Grand Anse ②**, just around the bay to the south of the harbour, which is Grenada's main resort area. The 2-mile (3-km) stretch of white sand is one of the Caribbean's finest, and worth a visit even if you do not usually spend time on the beach. There are three ways to get there – by taxi, shared mini-van, or water-taxi. Of these, the water-taxi is easily the best option and – even though the cost has doubled over the years to US$8 for the round trip – it's still cheaper than land taxis and much more fun. It's a short, breezy journey and the boats depart almost non-stop from beside the welcome centre on the pier.

There are strict rules about any kind of development on Grenada, which applies particularly to beaches. Effectively, this comes down to nothing taller than a palm tree and nothing close to the water's edge being allowed. This is one reason why there are still more beaches (about 50) than there are hotels (about 40) on Grenada, although the hurricane took its toll on both. There is one hotel, Spice Island Inn, in Grand Anse but it is set well back and made up entirely of low rise cottages, which were refurbished following storm damage.

BELOW: St George's busy harbour.

Map
on page
298

Finding your way around

Grenada is just 12 miles (20 km) wide by 21 miles (32 km) long, but it seems larger because the interior is so densely forested in parts and journey times are longer than they might appear from the map. A drive through the interior takes in some dramatic sights – waterfalls, mountain valleys, rainforests, lakes and volcanic craters. Driving can be hot and tiring on roads that are sometimes barely adequate, so don't be too ambitious.

Driving is on the left, and you need a special local licence (about EC$30/US$10) that can be acquired either from one of the car rental firms along or near the Carenage or from the Traffic Department offices at the fire station building by the cruise ship pier. But, as you only have a day, you may prefer to take a tour, hire a taxi for a guided tour (negotiate the price before setting off) or, possibly, self-drive but hire a guide. There are old-fashioned and over crowded buses which run (slowly) to most parts of the island from St George's Market Square. Mini-vans are more comfortable, although they operate on a shared basis and only on short routes with flat fares.

Grenada's best

The following are the best places to visit in Grenada. All have nominal entrance charges and there's no need to pre-book. But you will have to choose which you want to see as it is not possible to visit them all in a single day. Grenada's national parks all took a terrible battering by Hurricane Ivan and many hiking trails have disappeared under fallen trees. It will be years before the natural landscape heals completely. Some attractions may not yet be open.

Grand Etang National Park and Forest Reserve ❸ is a rainforest with a

BELOW: hiking in Grand Etang National Park.

Map
on page
298

Nutmeg gives Grenada it's nickname: the "spice island".

BELOW:
Annandale Falls.
RIGHT: Sandy Island, Carriacou.

volcanic crater-turned-lake at its centre. There are hiking and nature trails, and fishing and boating in the shadow of **Mount Qua Qua**, a 2,300-ft (700-metre) peak. The reserve is in the centre of the island, northeast of St George's.

River Antoine Rum Distillery ❹ is further along the same road on the northeast coast. There are guided tours of this working distillery, which uses exactly the same methods as it did in the 18th century.

Levera National Park and Bird Sanctuary ❺ was designated a national park in 1994. It is about 5 miles (8 km) further north, the furthest point on the northeast coast. The park stretches inland from coral-reef protected white sandy beaches to a lake and mangrove swamp full of exotic plants and birdlife.

Gouyave Nutmeg Processing Cooperative is northwest of Grand Etang. The cooperative offers a chance to see how the island's most famous export is handled. It's fascinating, but the heat inside the factory is almost unbearable. Be thankful you are only visiting and don't have to work there. There is an even larger nutmeg plant in Grenville, the second largest town on the island, on the coast roughly due east from Grand Etang. Within a couple of miles of Gouyave, there is the chance to tour a working spice plantation, **Dougaldston Estate**.

Ships' excursions

All these attractions appear on most ships' excursion lists. There is a three- to four-hour island coach tour that takes in Grand Etang, the Grenville Nutmeg plant, the 50-ft (15-metre) Annandale waterfall and some picturesque east coast villages. Similar tours by Jeep are also offered. They are more expensive, but you do have the advantage of travelling in a much smaller group.

Other tours include the Rhum Runner beach party cruise; whale- and dolphin-watching trips – they reckon there is a 90 percent chance of seeing dolphins and a 70 percent chance of seeing pilot or humpback whales; as well as snorkelling and scuba-diving trips.

Sailing and diving are highly recommended for enthusiasts. Most of the dive sites – around coral reefs and shipwrecks – are within easy reach of the shore and were untouched by the hurricane. Snorkellers can reach them from the beach or, occasionally, by a short boat trip. The dive site considered the best – Kick 'em Jenny – is further offshore. Sports fishing is also a popular option; and there is a nine-hole golf course and tennis centre near Grand Anse.

Carriacou

If you admire the way Grenada has remained largely unspoilt, the neighbouring island of **Carriacou** ❻ (23 miles/38 km away) will appeal even more, as it has just a handful of hotels to go with some great beaches and sites for snorkelling and diving. **Sandy Island**, off the west coast and reached by a local motorboat, is the best. There is even a decent museum in the main town, Hillsborough. However, Carriacou is a three-hour boat trip or a 20-minute flight, so cruise ship passengers only have time to reach it by air, and ships rarely include it among their excursions. There are a few small cruise ships that anchor off Carriacou, as part of their itinerary, but the majority don't. ❑

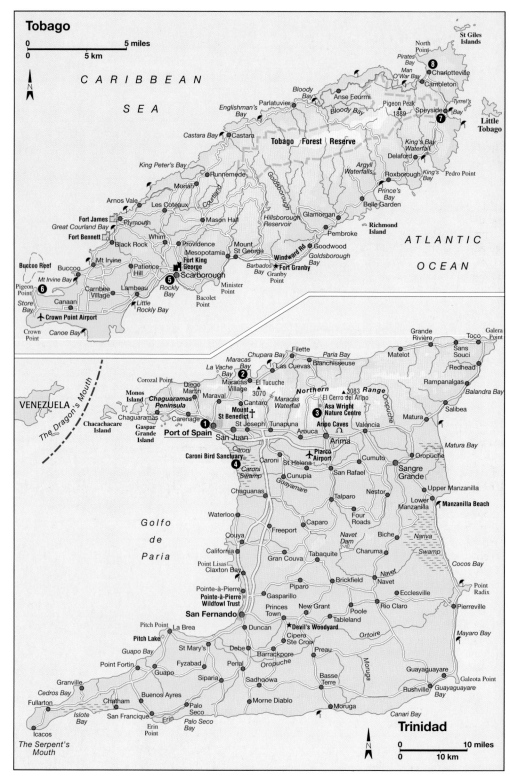

TRINIDAD AND TOBAGO

*Trinidad is famous for its annual Carnival in Port of Spain,
but the colour, music and rich cultural diversity of these
two islands are entrancing throughout the year*

Map on page 304

Caribbean Sea

Tobago
Trinidad

Across the road from the buzzing centre of Port of Spain, lies the modern cruise ship complex, so it is very easy to get to the heart of the cosmopolitan capital of Trinidad, the British Caribbean's most vibrant city and the southernmost port of call in the island chain.

In complete contrast to the sleepy charm of Windward Island capitals or that of its own sister isle, Tobago, fast-paced **Port of Spain ❶** is unique for its ethnic diversity and cultural richness, and mixes styles with a Latin flair born from its proximity to Venezuela. Elegant French-Creole townhouses with distinctive gingerbread fretwork and ornate wrought-iron balconies nestle beneath 21st-century smoked-glass corporate blocks. Rasta craftsmen display their leatherwork on the streets next to country women selling fresh herbs, while air-conditioned malls offer local designer clothes and the latest in Miami consumer retail therapy.

Port of Spain is also home base for the mother of all carnivals, the pre-Lenten festival which climaxes on the two days before Ash Wednesday, when the streets explode with the colours of thousands of local and visiting masqueraders driven by turbo-charged soca music or sweet steelpan.

Getting to know the city

Port of Spain and its suburbs sprawl across a plain that slopes gently from the foothills of the Northern Range down to the Gulf of Paria. On the waterfront, the cruise ship complex, where passengers disembark directly, is located between the container ship docks to the west and Queen's Wharf, the mooring for inter-island traders and the Tobago ferry, to the east.

The complex has the usual facilities, including gift shops. For those who prefer not to stray far from the ship, there are craft stalls outside; and, to the left, on Wrightson Road, is the Breakfast Shed, famous for cheap and authentic Creole and East Indian cuisine: fresh fish, fried, stewed or served in a peppery-hot broth laced with ground provisions such as dasheen, eddoes, cassava or green figs and heavy with dumplings.

Across the road stretches the Brian Lara promenade (named after the record breaking Trinidad cricketer) on **Independence Square**, centrepiece of the modern city centre. Here chess-players congregate round concrete tables with built-in boards, Trinis practise the national pastime of liming (doing nothing in particular, but with style) and free soca, steelpan, jazz or gospel concerts are held. Besides the fast-food outlets, there are vendors selling coconuts full of milk for drinking, and doubles – the cheapest East Indian snack: curried chick peas in batter, garnished with mango or coconut chutney and fiery pepper sauce.

PRECEDING PAGES:
"jump up" with a band at Carnival time.
BELOW: colourful costume.

Although most cruise lines offer guided taxi tours of the city and half- or whole-day excursions outside, it is far more exciting (and quite safe) to cover the city centre on foot – it takes a couple of hours. For moving further afield there are fixed-rate taxis at the rank opposite Frederick Street on Independence Square and much cheaper shared-route taxis at Woodford Square.

Founded by the Spanish in 1757, PoS (as it is known) began to take shape only after the British seized the island in 1797. The square grid plan is the legacy of Governor Sir Ralph Woodford. Many colonial buildings disappeared after independence in 1962 and during the oil boom of the 1970s to early 1980s, but both the Roman Catholic Cathedral on Independence Square and the Anglican Cathedral on Woodford Square are 19th-century survivors. The modern skyline, however, is dominated by the Twin Towers financial complex and the national library currently under construction on Queen Street.

Culture, sport and music

The old Spanish **Fort San Andres** on South Quay is now a museum (Mon–Fri; free) hosting exhibitions by young local artists. British-built **Fort George** in the hills above the western suburb of St James offers both a breathtaking panorama of the city and views of the islands off the Chaguaramas peninsula.

Frederick Street is the main artery, leading north to **Queen's Park Savannah**, via Woodford Square where the imposing Red House parliament building is situated. At the top of Frederick Street, opposite Memorial Park is the **National Museum and Art Gallery** (Tues–Sat 10am–6pm, Sun 2pm–6pm; free; tel: 623 5941). The Savannah plays an integral part in Trinidadian sporting and cultural life. The grandstand is the major venue for Carnival competitions and cultural

The Hosay Festival, celebrated during Muharram, the first month of the Islamic lunar calendar (and therefore a moveable feast), began as a religious festival but has turned into a three-day event with lively processions accompanied by dancing, singing and the sound of tassa drums.

BELOW: view from Fort George above the Gulf of Paria.

shows. On Maraval Road, on the western flank of the Savannah, are the **Magnificent Seven**, a row of early 20th-century colonial mansions, superb examples of idiosyncratic Trini-Creole architecture. To the north are the **Emperor Valley Zoo** (daily 9.30am–6pm; entrance fee), the **Botanic Gardens** (daily 6am–6.30pm; free) and the President's House.

A good introduction to the national instrument, the steelpan, is a visit to a **panyard**, where steel bands rehearse: Amoco Renegades at the top of Charlotte Street, Witco Desperadoes up Laventille Hill or Phase II on Hamilton Street, in the western suburb of Woodbrook, where there are excellent restaurants on Ariapita Avenue. Also in Woodbrook is the Oval cricket ground, where international matches are played. West of Woodbrook is St James, lively with bars and clubs.

Map on page 304

Around the island

There is a wide variety of half- and whole-day excursions available outside PoS. West of town are the **Blue Basin Waterfall**, north of Diego Martin; Maqueripe beach at the end of the beautiful **Tucker Valley**; the **Chaguaramas Military History and Aviation Museum** (daily 9am–5pm; entrance fee), and the **Gasparee Caves** (tel: 868-634 4364/4227) on Gaspar Grande island, a 20-minute round-trip boat ride from the Crews Inn marina (call the Chaguaramas Development Authority, tel: 634 4364, to book tours).

Maracas Bay ❷, Trinidad's most popular beach, is a 40-minute drive north of the capital, while to the east there is the **Maracas Waterfall**, up the valley from the original Spanish capital, St Joseph; **El Tucuche**, the second highest peak (a whole-day strenuous hike); **Mount St Benedict** monastery, with panoramic views of the central plain; and the **Asa Wright Nature Centre ❸** (daily 9am–5pm;

Hummingbird feeding.

LEFT: Queen's Royal College.
BELOW: a Hindu woman prays at a temple.

Map on page 304

Tobago's coral reef is a treasure to scuba divers and snorkellers.

BELOW: Parlatuvier Bay. **RIGHT:** snorkelling at Buccoo Reef.

tel: 868-667 4655; entrance fee), internationally famous for bird-watching. Southeast of PoS is the **Caroni Bird Sanctuary** ❹ (tel: 868-645 1305; entrance fee), where the national bird, the Scarlet Ibis, roosts at dusk; the boom town of Chaguanas; and a Hindu temple in the sea at Waterloo.

Scarborough, Tobago's capital

While PoS is very much a city, **Scarborough** ❺, the capital of Trinidad's sister isle, **Tobago**, has both the look and feel of a small provincial town, and most of it can be covered on foot (with a few steep climbs) in a morning. After the multi-cultural mix of Trinidad, Tobago's predominantly Afro-Creole culture and lifestyle is immediately noticeable, as is the much slower pace.

Cruise passengers disembark at the modern terminal opposite a busy market, a good spot for sampling hearty Tobagonian cooking, especially curried crab and dumplings. The terminal has basic amenities, and taxis for around-town or out-of-town tours can be hired outside, or from SunFun Tours (tel: 868-639 7461).

In town, the main attractions are the Botanic Gardens, the House of Assembly on James Park and the Fort King George complex, which houses the excellent **Tobago Museum** (Mon–Fri 9am–5pm; entrance fee) and which also has fantastic views over the town and up the coast.

As the island is only 26 miles (40 km) long and 9 miles (15 km) wide, it is possible to reach virtually anywhere within a couple of hours by car and sample Tobago's treasures: idyllic white sand beaches and coral reefs; superb scuba diving, snorkelling and water sports; waterfalls, volcanic hills and the western hemisphere's oldest protected rainforest; abundant bird and wildlife and authentic Afro-Creole culture. The latter can be found at its vibrant best in the hilltop villages of Les Coteaux, Whim and Moriah, which are major venues for July's lively Heritage Festival.

The developed southwest

Close to Scarborough is the developed southwest end of the island, where most tourist activity is centred round the luxury resorts and hotels at Crown Point and Store Bay. Glass-bottomed boats can be hired at Store Bay for trips out to Buccoo Reef and the Nylon Pool, while the beach at **Pigeon Point** ❻ has become a familiar Caribbean icon.

On the Windward (southern) coast the First Historical Café and Bar at Studley Park provides an excellent introduction to Tobago's Afro-Creole culture. Inland from here is the Hillsborough Reservoir, a favourite bird-watching spot. Further down the coast, the Argyll waterfalls are a 10-minute walk from the road.

Divers and nature lovers head for **Speyside** ❼ and **Charlotteville** ❽, at the eastern tip. These two fishing villages are spectacularly located at the foot of plunging forested hills and are the jumping-off points for some of the best diving in the Eastern Caribbean, where the rare underwater-life includes giant manta rays. Little Tobago, off Speyside, is a bird sanctuary.

The best beaches (both for bathing and for turtle watching) are on the Leeward (northern) coast: Castara, Englishman's Bay, Parlatuvier, Bloody Bay and Man O'War Bay are all excellent. ❑

ARUBA AND CURAÇAO

These two small islands in the Dutch Antilles make interesting cruise stops. Desert landscapes, international cuisine and protected architecture are among the discoveries to be made

Map on page 314

T he move by cruise lines to base some of their ships in ports beyond Florida for easy access to the "deep Caribbean" has brought a boom in prosperity to the islands of Aruba and Curaçao. Both can be visited as part of a week-long cruise from San Juan, Puerto Rico, although they are also included on some longer trips from Fort Lauderdale, Florida. These small islands in the Lesser Antilles, off the coast of Venezuela, have a lot to offer cruise ship passengers on short stop-overs.

One reason for the success of **Aruba** is that it crams a lot into a little; excellent beaches, world-class shopping, giant casinos, stunning sea views and wild tracts of desert landscape scattered with giant boulders and exotic cacti are all yours to enjoy, without travelling very far.

Oranjestad

The only down side of this success is that you have to share the pleasures of the capital, **Oranjestad ❶**, with thousands of other visitors, particularly when a number of big ships are in at the Aruba Port Authority Terminal. Since the end of 2002, cruise ships have no longer had to share this space with cargo vessels, which have been re-routed to a port elsewhere on the island.

Well-developed Oranjestad has enough facilities to absorb the throng of visitors, however. Turn right outside the cruise terminal and within a few minutes' walk you will find the shop-lined L.G. Smith Boulevard, home to Seaport Market – which has hundreds of shops, many restaurants and two casinos – and the equally extensive, Royal Plaza, which is crammed with posh shops.

If, instead of turning right, you cross the road straight ahead of you, you can explore Oranjestad's prime shopping area, Caya G. F. Betico Coes, where pretty Dutch- and Spanish-style buildings house stores selling top-quality cameras, jewellery and alcohol.

If you are stopping for lunch, it's worth knowing that Aruba's diverse population, whose inhabitants are of Portuguese, Spanish, Venezuelan, Indian, Pakistani and African as well as Dutch descent, makes it a wonderful place to sample international cooking. Options range from Dutch Indonesian dishes at The Paddock (on the waterfront) to classic French cuisine at the expensive, but very pretty, Chez Mathilde on Havenstraat.

The cultural mix also makes Oranjestad a great place to shop. You can pick up Delft china, Dutch cheese, Danish silverware and embroidery from Madeira at low levels of duty and without a sales tax.

US dollars are accepted in Aruba (as they are throughout most of the Caribbean), although the local

PRECEDING PAGES: at the Natural Bridge. **LEFT:** a cruise ship dwarfs a boat in port at Aruba. **BELOW:** a traditional Aruban cottage.

currency is the Aruba Florin. Dutch is the official language but you will hear quite a lot of Spanish, and almost everybody speaks some English, too.

For local colour, head along the waterfront to **Paardenbaai** (Schooner Harbour), which is crammed with brightly painted little boats and craft stalls selling the boat-owners' wares. This is a great setting for a photo, and you will also be entertained by flamboyant exchanges in Papiamento, the local patois.

There is more than a touch of Old Europe to be found here. Oranjestad has some magnificent examples of 16th- and 17th-century Dutch architecture. You should head for Wilheminastraad, a few streets up from the harbour, to see the best examples. Also worth a visit is **Wilhemina Park**, a lovely tropical garden set on the waterfront.

Make a break for the beach

If you are more keen to get to a beach than to admire architecture and gardens, you will find some of the world's best on Aruba. **Eagle Beach ❷** or **Palm Beach**

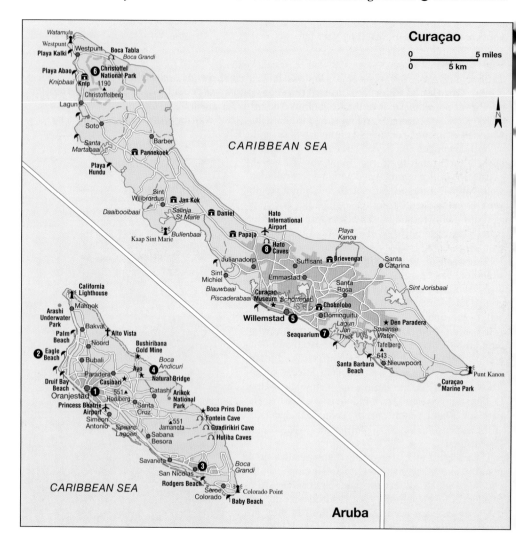

are long stretches of snowy-white sand bordered by casinos and hotels, which will (for a fee) provide all the facilities you need to swim, sunbathe and lunch in style. Use of the beaches is free, however, if you don't want any of the extras. Up to four people can share a one-way cab to these beaches for around US$8–$15.

If you have a young family, the aptly-named **Baby Beach** to the southeast of Oranjestad is the best one to head for since it is shallow-watered, sheltered and very safe. En route to Baby Beach lies Aruba's oldest village, **San Nicolas ❸**, a former oil refinery and port which is now a tourist haven of unusual shops and al fresco cafés. Also to the east – but not as far from the port – is Spaan Lagoen (Spanish Lagoon), which was once the haunt of pirates and is now a scenic spot popular for picnics and country walks.

Excursions

With plenty of taxis serving the cruise terminal and good tourist information available, it's easy to explore Aruba under your own steam (a one-hour taxi tour for up to four people costs from US$30), but some of the cruise line excursions are worth considering. You can spend two hours diving 100 ft (30 metres) beneath the waves in the *Atlantis* submarine, which is a great introduction to the sealife of the **Barcadera Reef**. When fish peer in at the windows you get the surreal sensation of having taken their place in the fishbowl.

Cheaper, and more appropriate for anyone who is claustrophobic, are trips in a glass-bottomed boat; you won't get quite so close to the fish but you can feed them over the side. Among other organised tour options are trips to the beach, with snorkel gear provided, and trimaran trips, which also have snorkelling included in the price.

Map on page 314

Diving excursions are popular.

BELOW: Dutch-influenced architecture in the tropics.

If you feel you see enough of the sea while you are on a cruise, a three-hour coach tour of the island will show you the dramatic landscape of the north, which includes the famous **Natural Bridge ❹** (hewn by nature from limestone), fantastical boulder formations, gigantic cacti and caves full of weirdly-shaped stalactites and stalagmites.

Some cruise lines also offer self-drive safari tours in four-wheel-drive vehicles, where you travel in convoy. This is a good compromise for travellers who are concerned about getting lost on their own but hate to be treated like sheep. Tours last from five to six hours, with a swimming stop, and lunch is included in the price.

The Queen Emma
Bridge is probably
Curaçao's most
photographed sight.
The pontoon bridge,
which is illuminated
at night, has been in
use since 1888.

A tropical Amsterdam

Curaçao, 38 miles long by just over 7 miles wide (60 by 11 km), is the largest island in the Dutch Antilles and home to more than 50 nationalities, who give it a liberal, cosmopolitan and welcoming atmosphere.

If you love the architecture and waterways of Amsterdam but find the weather too dreary, pick a cruise which has Curaçao's capital, **Willemstad ❺**, on the itinerary. Sadly, if you travel on a mega-ship, you might miss the best way of arriving in this pretty port, which is through the swing-aside **Queen Emma pontoon bridge** and up **Santa Anna Bay**, to the old terminal. The bay, which divides the town in two, is a narrow channel flanked by pastel-tinted, traditionally gabled Dutch houses. Instead, mega-ship passengers will disembark at the port's US$9-million big-ship terminal on the coast just outside the bay, which opened in 1999. But at least the newer terminal has good shops and even a nearby golf course, and lies only a short walk from town.

BELOW:
Fort Amsterdam.

ISLA DE MARGARITA

Just 25 miles (40 km) off Venezuela's Caribbean coast, Margarita Island was famous first as a base for pearl diving, but it has been a favourite holiday destination for Venezuelans since the 1980s. More recently, it has been discovered by the rest of the world – and by the cruise lines. There is nothing as grand as a dock for cruise ships, but there is a place to anchor just outside Puerto de la Mar, and it's a short ride ashore by tender boat.

Margarita's main attractions are its sandy and mostly uncrowded coves and beaches (Playa Puerto Cruz on the North Coast is one of the best), its historic churches and some duty-free shopping – particularly in the main town, the Spanish colonial-style Porlamar.

The island was originally two, both with hilly interiors and now connected by a narrow sandbank. The western half (Macanao) is fairly barren and undeveloped. The main sights are in the eastern half, including a colourful waterfront morning market in Porlamar (Boulevard Gomez).

A short drive (about 7 miles/11km) away is the island's oldest settlement and fishing port, Pampatar, which has a well-preserved 17th-century fort (San Carlos Borromeo). Other worthwhile trips include one to Laguna de la Restinga, a national park by the connecting sandbank.

Exploring Willemstad

Be prepared to devote two to three hours to exploring Willemstad, as you'll find plenty to see and do there. Maps are available at the cruise terminal to help you find your way around. First colonised by the Dutch in the 1630s, it is a beautiful town, resplendent with fine examples of 17th- 18th- and 19th-century Dutch and Spanish colonial architecture, some of the best examples of which are to be found on the bay front. Willemstad has been placed on the UNESCO World Cultural Heritage List, with 765 protected monuments and sites.

Smaller ships able to sail past the Queen Emma bridge will bring you alongside at **Otrobanda**, which means "the other side". It is worth exploring in its own right if you enjoy architecture, as its maze of winding streets are flanked by fine Dutch colonial houses. If you want to get straight to where the action is, a short walk across the distinctly wobbly Queen Emma bridge (or a hop on the free ferry which runs when the bridge is open to let ships pass) will get you to **Punda**. This is where you will find the colourful **Floating Market**, lined with boats from Colombia, Venezuela and other islands, selling fresh fish, produce, spices and handicrafts, as well as a variety of duty-free shops.

Just as you come off the bridge, you will see **Fort Amsterdam**, a sandstone waterfront fortress which dates from 1700 and now houses the Governor's Palace. A mid-18th-century church stands nearby.

At one corner of the fort is **Breederstraat**, one of Willemstad's best shopping streets and gateway to the main shopping district, where you can buy everything from Delft pottery and clogs to Italian silk scarves and ties, Swiss watches, Portuguese embroidery, Japanese electrical goods, Indonesian clothing, locally made black coral jewellery and, of course, deep-blue Curaçao liqueur.

Map on page 314

If you didn't reach the town by sailing up the channel, you can do the next best thing – stand in the main street and watch ships sail serenely past the shops and houses at the end, creating the illusion that they are plunging up a street at the crossroads.

BELOW: colourful buildings in Otrobanda.

Map on page 314

For some island flavour try Curaçao liquer.

BELOW: snorkelling at Lagun in the northwest.
RIGHT: the magnificent Hato Caves.

Museums and sites

Not far from the market, on van Brandenburgstraat, is the **Maritime Museum** (daily 9am–4pm, closed some Sundays; entrance fee; tel: 5999-465 2327), which has some fascinating exhibits, including 16th-century maps, 17th-century ship models and multi-media displays, plus a café and gift shop. The museum has its own ferry which gives harbour tours on Wednesday and Saturday afternoon.

Also within walking distance of the Queen Emma Bridge (on Van Leeuenhoekstraat) is the **Curaçao Museum** (Mon–Fri 9am–noon, 2–5pm, Sun 10am–4pm; entrance fee), a 19th-century military hospital set in pleasant shady grounds, which now holds colonial antiques and artefacts of the region's Caiquetio tribes, as well as a collection of paintings.

To explore further afield, hire a taxi and take a look at Curaçao's cactus-rich, Spaghetti Western-style countryside (approximately US$30 an hour for a party of four). Top attractions within an hour's drive include the 4,500-acre (1,820-hectare) **Christoffel National Park ❻** (Mon to Sat 8am–4pm, Sun 6am–3pm; entrance fee; tel: 5999-864 0363), where nature-lovers can glory in rare orchids and cacti, abundant birdlife and the sight of wild goats, donkeys and iguanas.

Its underwater equivalent is the **Curaçao Seaquarium ❼** (tel: 5999-461 6666), which features more than 350 species of sealife, including giant turtles, 20-ft (6-metre) sharks and moray eels, some of them in touch tanks. Four times a day there is a guided tour and a feeding display. There is also an underwater observatory, a semi-submarine and an "Animal Encounters" facility where experienced swimmers can mix with stingrays, angelfish and parrotfish. In the "Shark Encounter" enclosure, visitors can swim on one side of a clear plexiglass screen in close proximity to the sharks swimming on the other side. For these encounters, however, reservations must be made 24 hours in advance. The only white-sand beach on Curaçao is close to the Seaquarium, so, if you are a sun-worshipper you may like to spend some time here.

Curaçao is one port of call where you really don't need to take a ship's excursion, as you will easily find most places on your own or in a cab. If you like organised exploration, however, you could take a 3½-hour tour which includes the Seaquarium and a trip on the submarine, as well as a visit to the **Senior Curaçao Liqueur Factory** (Mon–Fri 8am–noon, 1–5pm; free; tel: 5999-352 6461). Here, you may learn that the liqueur was discovered by accident. The Spaniards planted orange trees on the island in the 16th century, then found the climate was unsuitable. The oranges were bitter and inedible, but the peel, when dried, exuded an aromatic oil. Combined with exotic spices, this produced the liqueur, which went into commercial production in the late 19th century.

There are three-hour island tours to the **Hato Caves ❽**, which have a mirror-smooth underground lake and stunning rock formations, but you can also visit them independently. Or you could spend three hours going to **San Jofat**, an exclusive waterfront development where members of the Dutch royal family have holiday homes; then join a boat to go snorkelling, which is a good way of seeing some of the fascinating little bays and inlets that line Curaçao's coast. ❑

✸ INSIGHT GUIDES
TRAVEL TIPS

CONTENTS

Getting Acquainted

The Caribbean

Area: The Caribbean embraces several groups of islands. The Lesser Antilles include the Windward Islands (Barbados and St Lucia, for example) and the Leeward Islands (the Virgin Islands and Antigua). The Netherlands Antilles, off the coast of Venezuela, include Aruba, Curaçao and Bonaire.

The Greater Antilles is an archipelago of larger islands, including Cuba, Hispaniola, the Cayman Islands and Jamaica. To the north of this area, the Bahamas archipelago spans 500 miles (900 km) from the eastern, Atlantic coast of Florida to the edge of the Caribbean Sea, although cruise itineraries widely include the Bahamas in "Caribbean" itineraries.

Language: Languages commonly used on the islands include English, French, Dutch, Spanish, and various versions of patois.

Time Zones: All of the islands except Trinidad and Tobago are in the Atlantic Time Zone, which is one hour later than Eastern Standard Time and four hours earlier than Greenwich Mean Time. When the United States goes onto Daylight Saving Time, the islands do not change, so during this time of year, time in the eastern part of the US is identical to Island time. Trinidad and Tobago are both in the Eastern Time Zone which is the same as the eastern US during Standard Time.

Currency: There are 11 official currencies:

Bahamian Dollar (B$): Bahamas.
Barbados Dollar (BDS$): Barbados.
Cayman Dollar (CI$): Cayman Islands.
Cuban Peso ($): Cuba.
Dominican Peso (RD$): Dominican Republic.
Eastern Caribbean Dollar (EC$): Dominica, Grenada, Montserrat, St Kitts and Nevis, St Lucia, St Vincent and the Grenadines, Anguilla, Antigua and Barbuda.
Euro (€): Martinique, Guadeloupe, St Martin, St Barthélemy, Saba, St Eustatius, Bonaire, Curaçao, and St Maarten.
Jamaican Dollar (J$): Jamaica
US Dollar (US$): The US and British Virgin Islands.
Trinidad and Tobago Dollar (TT$): Trinidad and Tobago.

Electricity: Different islands run on different electrical currents:
110–120V/60 cycle (US current): Bahamas, US Virgin Islands, British Virgin Islands, Aruba, St Maarten (Dutch side), Trinidad and Tobago. Also Belize, Honduras, and Mexico.
110V/60 cycle: Cuba, Domincan Republic.
110–130V/50 cycle: Anguilla, Bonaire, Barbados, Curaçao, Jamaica
220–230V/60 cycle: St Kitts and Nevis, Montserrat, Antigua and Barbuda.
220–240V/50 cycle: Bonaire, Curaçao, Dominica, Grenada, St Barthélémy, Saba, St Eustatius, St Martin (French side), Guadeloupe, Martinique, St Lucia, and St Vincent and the Grenadines.

Climate

The principal characteristic of the Caribbean's climate is the relative lack of temperature change from season to season. The islands' proximity to the equator means that seasonal temperature changes are limited to less than 10°F (6°C). An added bonus is the trade winds, which bring regular, cooling breezes to most of the islands.

Year round, temperatures average around 80°F (27°C) throughout the region. During the winter (December to March) – which is peak season for tourists – night-time lows can drop to about 60°F (16°C), with daytime highs reaching as much as 90°F (32°C).

Rainfall varies, ranging from around 20 inches (50 cm) a year in Curaçao up to 75 inches (190 cm) a year in Grenada. Rainfall is generally heaviest during October and November, though June is wettest in Trinidad and Tobago. Hurricanes can strike from June to October. The "dry" period, coinciding with the peak tourist season: December to April or May.

HURRICANES

Hurricanes are one of the most damaging and dangerous phenomena affecting the Caribbean. Devastating hurricanes have included Ivan in 2004, which caused damage to 90 per cent of buildings in Grenada and left more than 30 people dead. The storm also hit Grand Cayman, Jamaica and St Vincent; Hugo in 1989 which affected the Leeward Islands; Luis in September 1995, which pounded Antigua, St Martin, and nearby islands; and Marilyn a month later, which caused flooding in Antigua but most damage to the US Virgin Islands. In 1998 Hurricane Georges caused devastation throughout the Caribbean, although Puerto Rico was most severely affected.

Hurricanes usually occur between July and October, although visitations have been known in June and November, and the "hurricane season" stretches from the beginning of June to the beginning of November, when some islands celebrate with a Hurricane Deliverance Day. The average lifespan of a hurricane is eight to ten days.

In summer months, weather-pattern disturbances are common all over the tropics. It is from these that tropical depressions and then tropical storms develop, which can bring gales of up to 73 miles (117 km) per hour and heavy rains. A hurricane warning is issued when the storm reaches winds of at least 74 miles (119 km) per hour and high water and storm surges are expected in a specific area within 24 hours. Warnings will identify specific coastal areas where these conditions may occur.

Would-be cruisers should not be deterred by the thought of hurricanes. Cruise itineraries are designed to avoid bad weather and a ship's captain will always put passenger safety first. Cruise ships are built to withstand bad weather and all modern vessels are fitted with stabilisers (fins under the water level) to reduce the pitch and roll of the ship.

Carnival

Carnival is celebrated at different times on different islands, with the dates falling roughly into three main groups:

● On Trinidad and Tobago, Dominica, Dominican Republic, St Thomas, Aruba, Bonaire, Curaçao, St Lucia, Martinique, Guadeloupe, Haiti, St Martin (French side), and St Barthélemy, Carnival preserves an association with Easter, being celebrated (on all of these islands except St Thomas) in the period leading up to and sometimes including Ash Wednesday. On St Thomas, the Cayman Islands, Jamaica and Puerto Rico, the celebration occurs after Easter.

● On Curaçao, Bonaire, Puerto Rico, St Maarten, St Vincent, Anguilla, St John, Barbados, Grenada, the British Virgin Islands, Antigua, Saba, St Eustatius, Cuba, and Nevis, Carnival takes place in June, July, or early August. On these islands, Carnival is often held in association with the "August Monday" holiday, which marks the end of the sugar cane harvest and the freeing of slaves in the British islands in 1834.

● On St Kitts, Montserrat, the Bahamas and St Croix (in the USVI), Carnival takes place in December and early January, in conjunction with the Christmas season.

● On St Maarten (Dutch side), Carnival takes place in late April, coinciding with the Dutch Queen's birthday celebrations on April 30.

● Cruises can be timed to coincide with the big festivals. *

It is better to cruise outside hurricane season if the thought is off-putting, although there is virtually no "low" season in Caribbean cruising, as many big lines operate year-round.

Public Holidays

Christmas Day and New Year's Day are public holidays, but otherwise holidays vary from island to island. See under individual island listings for specific dates.

Planning the Trip

Passports and Visas

Cruise passengers should not be surprised when they part with their passport at check-in and only see it again when the cruise is over. This is common practice. Ships are cleared by customs and immigration in every port before passengers may disembark and they will be allowed ashore without their passports, but must have a copy of the document or other photo ID. Anyone wishing to visit a casino ashore may, however, need to temporarily retrieve their passport from the purser's desk.

Instead of passports, passengers carry a cruise ship ID card. This is swiped and checked every time the cardholder leaves the ship. On more modern ships, it doubles as a room key and a charge card. Most importantly, it tells the crew whether or not the passenger is on board when the ship is about to depart.

All luggage is X-rayed by cruise lines before boarding, and passengers are required to walk through a security gate every time they return to the ship. Security is tighter than it was pre-11 September, 2001 and visitors are rarely allowed on board nowadays.

For travel in and around the Caribbean islands – except Trinidad and Tobago, Barbados, or Cuba – it is not always necessary for US or Canadian citizens to bring their passports, although it is recommended (re-entry to the US is almost impossible without a passport). US travellers must, however, have some proof of citizenship – a birth certificate, naturalisation card, voter registration card or affidavit. Canadian citizens travelling without passports should carry a birth certificate as proof of citizenship. Citizens of both countries should also have a form of photo ID.

Citizens from outside North America need to carry a passport. All travellers going to – or even passing

through – Trinidad and Tobago, or Cuba must have passports.

Visas are usually required only of visitors from Eastern Europe and Cuba. In addition all travellers must have, upon entering the islands, a return or onward ticket, and adequate funds to support themselves for the duration of their stay.

Cruise passengers arriving via a US gateway city such as Miami, or Puerto Rico, do not need a visa if their country is part of the US Visa Waiver Scheme. Since 11 September, 2001, however, US visa rules have been tightened so it is advisable to check. Travellers from countries participating in the US Visa Waiver Program (VWP) must have a machine-readable passport to enter the United States. If you are a citizen of any of the countries involved check with the passport issuing authority in your home country that your passport is still valid.

US TRAVELLERS

For US travellers returning to the United States from the USVI, there are a number of importation options. Each individual can bring back up to US$1,200 worth of purchases duty-free. Travellers may also send home an unlimited number of packages valued at US$50 or less, provided not more than one such package is posted to any one person in a single day. If you exceed your US$1,200 limit upon returning to the States, the first US$600 worth of merchandise in excess is assessed at a flat duty rate of 10 per cent.

Visiting Cuba

All visitors entering Cuba must show a passport which is valid for at least 6 months beyond the date of arrival in the country. In addition, most visitors must show a tourist card (tarjeta de turista), issued by the Cuban consulate directly or, more commonly, through a travel agent or cruise line. US citizens are not allowed to travel to Cuba under normal circumstances but many do, entering via Jamaica or Canada and using a tourist card.

JEWELLERY AND ART

US law allows the importation, duty-free, of original works of art. Because of concessions made to developing countries, jewellery made in the Caribbean may qualify as original art, and thus be duty-free. If you purchase jewellery, be sure to obtain a certificate from the place of purchase stating that the jewellery was made in the islands. To make sure that the articles you want to bring back fall into this category, contact the US Customs Service for further details.

Duty-free Allowances

Travellers arriving in the Caribbean are generally allowed to bring in the following duty-free items:
● personal effects.
● a carton of cigarettes or cigars, or 8 oz (225 g) of tobacco.
● one bottle (one litre) of alcohol.
● a "reasonable" amount of perfume.

PETS

Cruise ships do not allow pets, with the exception of *QE2*, which has a kennel on board.

FIREARMS

The importation of firearms, including air pistols and rifles, is prohibited.

Health

Health Hazards

All cruise ships have a doctor and nurse on board (the exception being cargo ships or private yachts carrying fewer than 12 people, which are not required to have a doctor). Facilities vary from ship to ship but a doctor should be able to treat most ailments, including heart attacks and appendicitis. Seriously ill passengers may be stabilised until the ship arrives in port, or airlifted off. There will always be a fee for consulting the ship's doctor, although many ships hand out sea-sickness tablets free of charge. Passengers should, however, bring their own supplies of any

medication they use, as the ship's doctor will not be able to provide it.

The main (though small) health risk to travellers on land in the Caribbean is infectious hepatitis or Hepatitis A. Although it is not a requirement, an injection of gamma globulin, administered as close as possible before departure, gives good protection against Hepatitis A. In addition, make sure you observe scrupulous personal hygiene, wash and peel fruit, and avoid contaminated water (drink bottled water if you are unsure).

Sun Protection

To a traveller who is not adjusted to the tropical sun, 80–90°F (27–32°C) may sound "just like summer temperatures back home". Don't be fooled. The sun in the tropics is much more direct than in temperate regions and is even stronger at sea as it reflects off the water.

Bring a high-factor sunscreen and wear it whenever you go out. For starters, expose yourself for only brief periods, preferably in the morning or late afternoon when the sun's rays are less intense. You can increase your sunning time each day, but avoid sitting in the sun for long periods because of the danger of sunburn and skin cancer. Always use high factor protection on small children and be sure to reapply sunscreen after a dip in the pool or sea. Try to keep babies cool and always in the shade. Bring a brimmed hat and a pair of good quality sun glasses, especially if you plan to do any extended hiking, walking, or playing in the midday sun.

Drinking Water

In undeveloped areas away from resorts, it is best to avoid drinking tap water, especially after hurricanes, when water supplies can become contaminated. In these areas, stick to bottled water, and avoid ice in your drinks.

Drinking water on cruise ships is heavily chlorinated and while safe, does not taste good to most people and also explains why cruise ship tea and coffee is so strange tasting. All ships provide bottled water, although many charge for it.

Insects

Mosquitoes are generally only a nuisance in port in the evening. To combat mosquitoes, pack a plentiful supply of insect repellent. Dengue-carrying mosquitoes bite during the day and present a small risk. The only area which usually carries a malaria risk is Hispaniola, more in Haiti than the Dominican Republic.

Immunisation

No immunisations are required for travellers to the Caribbean, unless the traveller is coming from an infected or endemic area. However, it is a good idea to have a tetanus shot if you are not already covered, and possibly gamma globulin *(see Health Hazards)*. Check with a Public Health Department or other source before travelling, just to make sure there are no precautionary steps to take.

Insurance

Though you are unlikely to have to claim, you should always arrange comprehensive travel insurance to cover both yourself and your belongings. Your own insurance company or travel agent can advise you on policies, but shop around since rates vary. Make sure you are covered for baggage or document loss, trip cancellation, emergency medical care and repatriation, and accidental death.

Aids

Aids presents a serious risk in the Caribbean among all sectors of the population. The risk of catching Aids from an unsterilised needle is negligible but passengers wishing to travel with their own set of needles should pack them in their hold baggage or they may be confiscated.

Money Matters

A range of currencies is used in the islands. Whatever the official currency, the US dollar and sometimes the British pound are readily accepted throughout the islands and are the most practical to bring, although you will usually lose out on the exchange rate if paying in sterling. In addition, major credit cards and traveller's cheques are welcome when settling on-board bills and at most major hotels, restaurants and shops. On some of the French and Dutch islands, the euro is the preferred currency, although the US dollar is accepted on many.

In November 2004 the US dollar ceased to be legal currency in Cuba. Instead, travellers must use "convertible pesos". If Cuba is on your itinerary make sure you have plenty of pesos, because changing US dollars inside the country will incur a 10 per cent commission charge. Credit cards and travellers' cheques from US banks are not accepted.

If you are bringing US dollars or pounds sterling, it is a good idea to check around before converting your currency, especially if you are on a limited budget. Try to get price quotes in both the local currency and the currency you are carrying. Then check the applicable exchange rate. You may find you can save some money by making purchases in whichever currency gives you greater value.

Currency on board most ships is the US dollar, although P&O, Fred Olsen and Cunard's Caronia use sterling. Exchange rates on ships are not competitive; use a local bank in port instead.

BUSINESS HOURS

The siesta is alive and well in the Caribbean, and throughout the region small shops close for a couple of hours in the early afternoon, when the sun is at its hottest. As a result, business hours of some small shops generally follow this pattern: shops open early, usually by 8am, certainly by 9am. They begin closing for siesta at noon or a little before, though in some areas, shops may stay open until 1pm. This can be inconvenient if the ship only has a brief stay in port, so time shopping expeditions accordingly. Business resumes about 2 hours later – 2pm in most places – with shops remaining open until 6pm. Again, there is some variation; on a few islands, closing time may be as early as 4pm. On Saturday, most shops are open in the morning, and many have full afternoon hours as well. Sunday is generally a day of rest.

Duty free complexes whose *raison d'etre* is to serve cruise passengers do not tend to take a siesta at all.

On the larger islands, such as Barbados, Trinidad and Tobago, shops generally do not close for extended periods in the afternoon.

BANKING HOURS

Banks are normally open Mon–Fri 8 or 8.30am–noon. Many banks also have afternoon opening hours, especially on a Friday. A few banks open on Saturday mornings. As US dollars, credit cards, and travellers' cheques are widely accepted in the islands, visitors need not worry about finding a money exchange facility immediately upon arrival. You can also use your credit and debit cards to withdraw cash from ATMs (Automatic Teller Machines). Before you leave home, make sure you know your PIN number and find out which ATM system will accept your card. See under individual islands for variations in bank opening hours, and for locations of ATM machines. Some ships now have ATMS on board but read the small print very carefully as charges for using them are almost always punitive.

Getting There

Once you have decided on the cruise that you want, talk to a travel agent, tourist board or airline company to determine the most efficient way to get to the starting point of your cruise.

Passengers wishing to extend their cruise can usually arrange an "open jaws" return, for example, flying into Miami and out of Barbados.

Taxes

There are several taxes that may come as a surprise during your travels in the Caribbean:

The **government room tax** is charged on all hotel room bills and generally averages 5–10 per cent of the total bill.

The **departure tax** is normally around US$10–15, but can be as high as US$25 in certain islands. It is payable upon departure from each of the islands. Remember to keep enough cash to pay the departure tax, usually required in the local currency.

A cruise price may not always include **port taxes**, so double check before buying as these can amount to well over US$140 (£100) for a week's cruise. Port taxes are paid to the cruise line before the cruise, not in individual ports.

CRUISE LINES

Carnival Cruise Lines, US: 3655 NW 87th Avenue, Miami, FL 33178, tel: 800-327 9501. UK: Carnival House, 5 Gainsford Street, London SE1 2NE, tel: 020-7940 4466; www.carnival.com.
Large, modern fleet offering value-for-money cruises in a lively environment. Passengers are mainly Americans and are of all ages.

Celebrity Cruises, US: 1050 Caribbean Way, Miami, FL 33132, tel: 800-722 5941; UK: Addlestone Road, Weybridge, Surrey KT15 2UE, tel: 0800 018 2020/2525 www.celebrity.com

Costa Cruises, US: World Trade Center, 80 SW Eighth Street, 27th Floor, Miami, FL 33130-3097, tel: 800-447 6877/954-266 5600. UK: 5 Gainsford Street, London SE1 2NE, tel: 020-7940 4499; www.costacruises.co.uk.
Italian-run subsidiary of Carnival Corporation. Fleet of mixed-age (including some large) modern ships ideally suited to Caribbean cruising. Passengers are mainly Italian and American and are of all ages.

Cunard Line, US: 24305 Town Center Drive, Santa Clarita, CA 91355, tel: 800-728 6273; UK: Richmond House, Terminus Terrace, Southampton SO14 3PN, tel: 0845 071 0300; www.cunardline.com.
Subsidiary of Carnival Corporation with two ships, QM2 and QE2. QM2 and its smaller sister QE2 carry an international mix of passengers, particularly on their regular trans-atlantic runs.

Disney Cruise Line, US: Disney Cruise Vacations, Guest Communications, PO Box 10238, Lake Buena Vista, FL 32830-0238; tel: 800 951 3532 www.disneycruise.disney.go.com
Two ships operating short cruises around the Caribbean. Attracting all ages and nationalities; superb for families but also appealing to adults.

Fred Olsen Cruise Lines, Fred Olsen House, White House Road, Ipswich, Suffolk IP1 5LL, tel: 01473 742424; www.fredolsen.co.uk
Three ships appealing to a mainly British market. Comfortable rather than the height of luxury and with a very loyal following.

Holland America Line, US: 300 Elliot Avenue West, Seattle, WA 98119, tel: 206-281 3535. UK: 77–79 Great Eastern Street, London EC2A 3HU, tel: 020-7940 4466; www.hollandamerica.com
Subsidiary of Carnival Corporation. Large fleet of elegant ships appealing mainly to Americans in the older age bracket, although the Caribbean generally attracts younger people.

Mediterranean Shipping Cruises, US: 6750 North Andrews Avenue, Fort Lauderdale, FL33309; tel: 954-772 6262; www.msccruises.com. UK: Walmar House, 296 Regent Street, London W1B 3AW, tel: 020-7637 2525; www.msccruises.co.uk
Italian-owned cruise line. Lively, value-for-money ships appealing to all ages and nationalities.

Norwegian Cruise Line, US: 7665 Corporate Center Drive, Miami, FL 33126, tel: 305-358 6670. UK: 1 Derry Street, London W8 5NN, tel: 0845 658 8010; www.uk.ncl.com. Large, pioneer of Freestyle Cruising, with all ships offering an informal setting and a wide choice of dining options. Appeals mainly to Americans, a good mix of ages, including families.

Ocean Village, UK: Richmond House, Terminus Terrace, Southampton, SO14 3PN, tel: 0845 358 5000; www.oceanvillageholidays.co.uk.

P&O Cruises, US: c/o Princess Cruises, 24305 Town Center Drive, Santa Clarita, CA 91355-4999, tel: 800-252 0158 (California only); 800-421 0522; 213-553 1770. UK: Richmond House, Terminus Terrace,

Southampton SO14 3PN, tel: 0845 355 5333; www.pocruises.com
British sister company of Princess Cruises. Large, modern ships appealing to a mainly British market. Particularly suited to families.

Princess Cruises, US: 24844 Avenue Rockefeller, Santa Clarita, CA 91355 California, tel: 1-800-774 62377; UK: Richmond House, Terminus Terrace, Southampton SO14 3PN, tel: 0845 355 5800; www.princesscruises.com.
American arm of P&O. Large, luxurious, modern ships with broad appeal across all ages.

Royal Caribbean International/ Celebrity Cruises, US: 1050 Caribbean Way, Miami, FL 33132, tel: 800-327 6700; 305-539 6000. UK: Royal Caribbean House, Addlestone Road, Weybridge, Surrey KT15 2UE, tel: 0800-018 2020 (Royal Caribbean); 0800-018 2525 (Celebrity), www.celebritycruises.com
Sister cruise lines, of which Celebrity is the more upmarket. Both operate a large, luxurious, modern fleet. RCI in particular appeals to families and has some of the world's largest ships, based in the Caribbean year-round.

Seabourn Cruise Line, US: 6100 Blue Lagoon Drive, Suite 400, Miami, FL 33126, tel: 305-463 3000. UK: Richmond House, Terminus Terrace, Southampton SO14 3PN, tel: 0845-070 0500; www.seabourn.com
Elegant yacht-ships cruising the smaller Caribbean islands. All-inclusive and very upmarket.

Silversea Cruises, US: 110 Broward Blvd., Fort Lauderdale, FL 33301, tel: 800-722 9955. UK: 77–79 Great Eastern Street, London EC2A 3HU, tel: 0870-333 7030; www.silversea.com
Elegant, luxurious-ships cruising the smaller Caribbean islands. Excellent European-style service and cuisine; appeals to mainly North Americans but there is a good mix of nationalities.

Star Clippers, US: 4101 Salzedo Avenue, Coral Gables, FL 33146, tel: 305-442 1611. UK: c/o Fred Olsen, Fred Olsen House, White House Road, Ipswich, Suffolk IP1 5LL, tel: 01473 292229; www.starclippers.com
Romantic sailing cruises on elegant clipper ships. International appeal.

Windjammer Barefoot Cruises, US: 1759 Bay Road, Miami Beach, FL 33139-1413, tel: 305-672 6453, 800-327 2601; www.windjammer.com
Informal sailing cruises on tall-masted ships.

Windstar Cruises, US: 300 Elliott Avenue West, Seattle, WA 98119, tel: 206-281 3535. UK: Carnival House, 5 Gainsford Street, London SE1 2NE, tel: 020-7940 4488.
www.windstarcruises.com
Luxurious yachts with a glamorous appeal, which travel partly under sail.

CARGO SHIPS

For the traveller in search of something out of the ordinary, a cargo ship offers a different type of cruise: comfortable cabins for only a handful of passengers (evening meals are generally taken with the officers) on a working cargo ship. Geest "banana boats", for example, leave Southampton on a round trip lasting 25 days, calling at Antigua, Barbados, Dominica, Grenada, Guadeloupe, Martinique, St Kitts, St Lucia, St Vincent and Trinidad. Enquiries to the following specialist travel agents:

UK

Atlantis Cruising, 16 Brook Parade, Chigwell, Essex IG7 6PF, tel: 020-8559 9007; www.ecruise.co.uk
Cargo Ship Voyages Ltd (agents for Geest), Hemley, Woodbridge, Suffolk, IP12 4QF, tel: 01473 736265.
Mundy Cruising, 5th Floor, Quadrant House, 80–82 Regent Street, London W1B 5JB, tel: 020-7734 4404; www.mundycruising.com

USA

Cruise Locators, 5101 E. La Palma, Suite , Anaheim, CA 92807, tel: 800-955 7447, www.cruiselocators.com
Freighter World Cruises, 180 South Lake Avenue, Pasadena, CA 91101, tel: 818-449 3106.

One of the largest online agencies is www.cruise.com; in the US tel: 888-999 2783.
For online discounts and access to specialist travel agents in the US visit: www.cruisecompete.com.

Tourist Information

Addresses of on-island tourist offices, and representative offices in other countries can be found in the listings for individual islands. In addition, you can visit www.doitcaribbean.com, the website of the Caribbean Tourism Association, or contact the following offices for any enquiry about the islands within the region:

Caribbean Tourism Association
Canada: Taurus House,512 Duplex Avenue, Toronto M4R 2E3; tel: 416-485 8724; Email: ctotoronto@caribtourism.com
UK: 42 Westminister Palace Gardens, Artillery Row, London SWIP IRR; tel:020-7222 4335; Email: cto@carib-tourism.com;
USA: 80 Broad Street, 32nd Floor, New York, NY 10004; tel: 212-635 9530; Email: ctony@caribtourism.com

What to Wear

Cruising in the Caribbean can mean bringing two different wardrobes, one for the cruise and one for any overland travel afterwards.

Some cruise lines, inspired by Norwegian Cruise Line's informal "Freestyle" cruising, have done away with compulsory formal nights, although Cunard, Fred Olsen, Costa, P&O, Seabourn, Celebrity and Holland America Line are just a few that do have gala nights. Dress code for evenings on board is usually:

Casual: smart casual wear but no shorts or vests.

Informal: trousers and smart shirt/jacket for men; cocktail dress for women.

Formal: tuxedos for men; evening dress for women.

A week's cruise will generally have one or two formal nights and a mixture of casual and informal on the other nights.

For shore excursions and extended holidays, "casual" is the word in the Caribbean. Light cotton dresses, trousers, skirts, shorts, and blouses for women, and informal trousers, shorts and comfortable open-necked shirts for men should make up the majority of your wardrobe. The breezes are cooler at night during the winter, so visitors are advised to bring a light jacket or cotton sweater, just in case. Men should bring a jacket and tie, especially if they plan to visit any casinos – most of them (and some of the fancier restaurants and hotels) require at least a jacket for the evening. For the feet, light sandals are appropriate and comfortable on the beach and around town. A light raincoat, or an umbrella, is useful in case of sudden showers. For those planning walks or hikes in the mountains and rainforests, a pair of sturdy walking shoes is essential.

Swimsuits and other beach attire are definitely not appropriate around town. When you venture from beach or poolside into town, cover up – a simple T-shirt and a pair of shorts will do the trick. By following this rule, you will show respect for the standards of many island residents.

Nude or topless (for women) bathing is prohibited everywhere except for Guadeloupe, Martinique, St Martin, St Barthélemy, and Bonaire. Guadeloupe, St Martin, and Bonaire have at least one designated nudist beach.

Getting Married

There are several ways to get married on a cruise. Most unusual is the old-fashioned notion of being married at sea by the captain. This is rarely done nowadays as the country of registry of many ships does not recognise marriage at sea. Moreover, the captain can be held legally liable for marrying a couple not actually entitled to wed.

At Sea

Princess Cruises' *Star*, *Grand*, *Coral* and *Golden Princesses* are registered in Bermuda and the captain can legally perform weddings at sea, although even the basic package starts at around US$1,500. Weddings are only carried out on sea days and must be booked well in advance.

In Port

More common is being married on the ship while it is in port, with couples bringing their own priest or rabbi on board. Many ships have wedding chapels, although these tend to veer towards the kitsch, or appear to be dismal, unromantic afterthoughts in ship design, in which case a prettier spot on deck can be used. Princess, Carnival and Holland America will all arrange weddings on board.

Another option is to get married in one of the ports of call and have either a honeymoon, or a reception, or both at sea. Cruise lines are always happy to arrange private functions and usually do them very well. There are endless options for getting married ashore if you arrange it independently but Carnival, Princess and Disney Cruise Line will all organise a shoreside wedding with a cruise, often using one of their private islands for the ceremony. P&O offers free honeymoon packages if you cruise within 30 days of the wedding. These include flowers, champagne, chocolates, three formal portrait photographs, stationery for thank-you notes, a surprise gift, and an on-board credit amount.

● For a detailed description of every aspect of the cruising experience, plus money-saving tips and exhaustive reviews of more than 250 cruise ships, we recommend the *Berlitz Guide to Ocean Cruising & Cruise Ships* by Douglas Ward, published annually.

Practical Tips

Telecommunications

Telephoning from a ship's satellite system is extremely expensive, at up to US$12 per minute. It is much cheaper to make calls from a land line in port, or even from a mobile phone with a roaming agreement.

Public phonecards in several denominations are available from Cable and Wireless on those islands from which the company operates. Residents of the US and Canada can use AT&T USA Direct public phones with a charge card. Some public phones allow holders of a European charge card, such as a BT Chargecard, to access the home operator.

Calls and faxes may be sent from public calling and fax centres located on many of the islands. Get there early because this a popular and cost effective way to keep in touch with home, for passengers and crew.

North American citizens should be able to use their mobile phones on most Caribbean islands. Europeans will need a tri-band phone and network availability may be restricted to the larger islands.

A growing number of locations have internet cafes. Almost all ships, too, offer internet access although charges vary enormously. The cheapest way to stay in touch via email on board is to use a free web-based service like Yahoo, Hotmail or Fastmail. With these, you only incur a cost for time online. Actually sending and receiving email on a ship via the ship's email address may be charged per email or per kilobyte, and incoming mail is likely to be delivered under your door as a hard copy several hours after it arrives – hardly conducive to speed or privacy.

Travelling with Children

Despite its image as an old people's vacation, cruising can be a perfect family holiday. In the Caribbean, the average age of passengers is younger than elsewhere, and multi-generation groups can be seen on all ships, with plenty of distractions for toddlers, teenagers, parents, and grandparents.

Some ships are more suitable than others for families. The facilities on *Disney Wonder* and *Disney Magic* are superb (with special adult-only areas for those who need a break from children), while Princess, Royal Caribbean and Norwegian Cruise Line all have good children's facilities and entertainment. Among the British cruise lines, P&O is excellent and Cunard's *Queen Mary 2* has the largest nursery at sea, staffed by highly qualified Norland nannies. Parents of toddlers love P&O and Princess ships because they offer a night nursery, providing free care for sleeping infants while the parents relax.

Typical facilities on a modern ship should include air-conditioned children's clubs divided into different age groups, with qualified carers and a suitable ratio of carers to children. Be warned that these clubs may not operate on port days, and that parents cannot both go ashore and leave their children in a club.

Some ships will have children's menus and almost all offer alternative casual dining, so small children do not have to join their parents in the evening in the main dining room. High chairs should be provided. Babysitting can be arranged through the purser's desk and the babysitter is normally paid cash. Baby food is usually available but check first.

The larger the ship, the more there will be to do for children. More than one pool is good, as there will generally be a deck area and pool to which families are steered.

Anyone who does not like the idea of spending their holiday with children would be advised to avoid a big ship in the school holidays.

For staying on, the islands are a perfect holiday destination for a family. Many resorts now offer children's programmes including babysitting facilities; some of the best include Jalousie and Windjammer Landing on St Lucia; Almond Beach on Barbados; and Beaches Negril on Jamaica. Do check, however, as some hotels may not allow children under 12 during the winter high season.

Facilities for Disabled Travellers

Generally speaking, cruising can be an ideal holiday for someone in a wheelchair as most ships provide a relaxing, sociable setting while visiting numerous destinations with minimal hassle. Take the advice of a specialist cruise travel agent before booking and make sure they provide specific information about the facilities on board and the cabin itself. P&O, Princess, Crystal, Celebrity, Royal Caribbean, some Holland America Line ships, Silversea's two larger ships *(Whisper* and *Shadow)* and Radisson's *Seven Seas Mariner* and *Seven Seas Navigator* are especially suited to wheelchair passengers. Cruise ships do not generally provide special facilities for those with hearing difficulties, although Crystal's two ships, the *Queen Mary 2* and some of the Celebrity fleet have special headsets in their cinemas for the hard of hearing. Newer ships have some signage in Braille for the blind.

The quality of cabins for the disabled, however, varies, with passengers complaining of such oversights as lack of low-down mirrors, no panic buttons, a cabin with a wide door but a narrow bathroom door, a lip at the door, and lack of storage space with low rails.

If specially fitted cabins are not available, choose as large a cabin as possible, close to the elevator. When arranging mealtimes, make sure the maitre d' allocates you a table with space for a wheelchair.

Questions to ask when booking:
● Are there any areas of the ship which will be inaccessible?
● Will I be allowed on the ship's tenders?
● Do I need to bring a travelling companion?
● Will there be facilities on shore excursions for a disabled passenger?

When choosing a cruise, pick an itinerary with as few tender ports (where passengers are ferried ashore in small boats) as possible. Wheelchair passengers can use tenders but may be restricted if the sea is choppy.

When it comes to shore excursions, a person's ability to participate depends entirely on their mobility and determination. The Caribbean is not generally geared up to wheelchair users; a common complaint is that the wheels of the chair get stuck in the sand. There are few special facilities such as ramps in public places. However you will find them in modern shopping centres, restaurants, and many resorts, and most excursions can be adapted to accommodate a wheelchair.

The same applies to staying on. Resort hotels may well have a few specially adapted bedrooms or, failing that, ground-floor rooms and minimal steps to public rooms. Booking through a good travel agent is advised.

Religious Services

All the mainstream church denominations can be found on the islands, as well as little-known cults. Attending a local service, perhaps Baptist or Seventh Day Adventist, is a wonderful way to experience an important aspect of Caribbean life, and you will be assured of a warm welcome, as long as you dress smartly and act with decorum and respect. Local tourist offices and free tourist publications should be able to advise times of services.

Interdenominational services are held on most cruise ships, conducted either by the captain or staff captain. Special Jewish charters will usually have a rabbi on board and some offer kosher food.

Tipping

Tipping is a big bone of contention on cruise ships, particularly for Europeans. American passengers live in a tipping culture and tend to be more generous. Tips on a cruise can make a big difference to the cost of the holiday.

What's confusing about tipping is that it is different on every ship, whether it's a matter of stuffing cash in an envelope and posting it into a box, or adding gratuities automatically to each passenger's on-board account.

The recommended amount to tip varies, as do the people who will receive the money. Ships provide guidelines for basic tips (usually to the room stewards and dining room waiters) but are vague about the remainder of the staff, including the maitre d', the wine waiter and the bartender. The important thing is to keep it in perspective. Many cruise lines pay particularly low wages to cabin stewards and dining room waiters, on the assumption that their salaries will be made up with tips, while behind-the-scenes employees like chefs get paid more.

There is a move towards including tips in the cruise price. On Silversea, Seabourn, SeaDream, Radisson Seven Seas, Airtours, Thomson, Crystal and First Choice ships, some or all of the tips are included in the price. Holland America Line and Windstar cruises have a "no tipping required" policy, although tips are not banned. For the British market, Carnival, Disney, and Royal Caribbean allow tips to be pre-paid.

Regardless of tipping policy, ships carrying a lot of Americans usually add a 15 per cent gratuity to the bar bill "for your convenience", a practice many passengers resent. Lines doing this include Carnival, Celebrity, Crystal, Cunard, Disney, Festival, Norwegian Cruise Line, Orient Lines, Princess, Radisson Seven Seas, Royal Caribbean, Royal Olympic, and Star Clippers.

Etiquette

On board, there are only a few etiquette rules to observe. Cruise lines are getting much stricter about smoking, and smokers may well find themselves huddled outside or confined to one cigar lounge. Never throw a lighted cigarette overboard as it can blow back onto the ship and start a fire. Some ships are smoke free, among them *Carnival Paradise*.

Remember, too, that it is forbidden

Hot Tips for Cruisers

Don't feel you have to tip people like the maitre d' or the head waiter unless they have performed a special service for you – ordering a birthday cake or arranging a special menu, for example.

● If the service is poor, don't pay the tip – but at the same time do raise the issue with the hotel manager on board.

● It is good practice to tip your cabin steward extra if you leave your cabin in disarray.

● On some ships, it is forbidden for staff to accept cash tips. If you really want to reward someone, the cruise lines suggest you buy them a small gift instead (although the reality is that they would far prefer cash). If you do give them cash, don't hand it over conspicuously.

● If tips are automatically added to your on-board account, you are perfectly entitled to adjust the amount.

● If you want to do more than tip, a genuine "Thank you" and a letter to the employee's boss is a thoughtful gesture.

to film or record any of the ship's entertainers, for copyright reasons.

On land, common politeness is as desirable on the islands as it is anywhere else. "Please", "Thank you", and a respectful and friendly demeanour will go a long way towards returning the warm welcome you are likely to receive. "Hello", "Goodbye", "Good Morning" and "Goodnight" are always used to friends, family or just to people you might pass on the road. If you need to ask directions or advice always greet the person *before* asking a question. Slow down; life operates on a different timescale in the sleepy Caribbean. Loss of temper, impatience and aggression will not produce results. Two more points: don't take anyone's picture without first asking permission – it is often seen as invasive; and don't drag up shades of colonialism and old B-grade Hollywood movies by referring to island residents as "natives".

Getting Around

By Car

Hiring a car for a day in port is more practical on some islands than others. The US Virgin Islands, for example, are compact, reasonably well signposted and easy to get around. Jamaica is deceptively large, with potholed roads and hectic driving, so not recommended for a self drive car rental; in the Dominican Republic, you'll need a good map and a command of Spanish to stand a chance.

If you want to rent a car, the purser can arrange this in advance so the car is waiting on the dock when the ship comes in, saving valuable time. Otherwise, on islands like Barbados, mini-mokes can be rented at or close to the port for short excursions. You will need a visitor's permit on most islands, which the rental company can arrange for a fee – around US$10.

For longer stays, the islands are well stocked with auto-rental agencies. Travel by car allows great freedom and flexibility to explore the nooks and crannies of the islands, but there are a few things the driver should be aware of. Many of the islands are mountainous, and on all of them roads are narrower than most US and European drivers will be familiar with. Driving may be a little more harrowing than at home; it is not for the faint-hearted. Also, in some areas yearly rainfall is quite light and this allows a film of oil to build up on road surfaces. When it does rain on these roads, they become especially slick, requiring extra caution. All in all, drivers should prepare to drive defensively and with caution, perhaps following the advice of one of the islands' tourist agencies to "sound the horn frequently", especially when approaching bends. Regulations on driving licences vary from island to island – see under the listings for individual islands.

Hiring a motorbike is often an option but apply the same rules as you would at home. Far too many tourists are killed or injured on holiday by riding in swimwear with no crash helmet.

By Taxi

Perhaps the most common means of transport for cruise passengers exploring independently is the taxi. Not only are taxis convenient and, by US or European standards, often quite inexpensive, but taking a taxi also gives you access to the resources of the driver. Where else could you chat with an island expert for the price of a cab ride? Most taxi drivers will gladly help you find things you are looking for, or that you aren't looking for but may be delighted to find. It is usually possible to find a taxi driver who is willing to give you a tour of his or her island and, in some places, drivers are specially trained to do this.

Another positive feature of taxi travel for island visitors is that rates are generally fixed and published. Often, printed sheets with detailed rates are available from points of entry, drivers, and tourist offices. Make sure you agree a rate with the driver before departing and only pay the full fare when you have returned to the ship. Remember that it is your responsibility to get back on time and the ship will not wait for latecomers.

By Bus

Local buses are not really practical for cruise passengers with only a few hours to "do" a destination but for an extended stay, buses are quite inexpensive and have the advantage of allowing travellers to get a small taste of how local residents live. Your hotel, a tourist office, or a police station should be able to supply information on schedules, and fellow riders and drivers are usually friendly and helpful in making sure that bewildered visitors get off at the right stop.

Tour buses (mini and full-sized), vans, jeeps, and "communal taxis" are available on all the islands, for taking groups sightseeing.

Inter-Island Links

Many cruise passengers choose to stay on in the Caribbean after their week or fortnight at sea to island-hop. As you might expect in this region of small-to-tiny islands cut off from one another by the sea, the options for getting around between islands are legion. For the traveller desiring quick transfers (and perhaps the novelty of a ride in a seaplane), there are at least 20 airline companies operating inter-island routes. LIAT is probably the largest and best-known of these, although Dutch Antillean Airlines (ALM) has a monopoly on flights between Aruba, Curaçao, Bonaire, and St Martin.

On the sea, an armada of ferries operates regularly between islands, and there is even a regular run between Aruba, Curaçao and Venezuela. Some of these ferries are the familiar steel-and-smokestack variety, while the inquisitive and adventurous traveller will find hydrofoils, schooners, and other types of sailing vessel plying the waters between islands. El Tigre, for example, is a 20 metre (60-ft) catamaran making a daily run between St Barthélemy and St Martin. It is often possible for travellers to bargain with fishermen and other small boat owners to arrange rides out to the many small islands which lie off the shores of the major islands.

Staying On

If you plan to spend a few pre- or post-cruise days in the Caribbean you can book a hotel direct.

Choosing a Hotel

As there is a variety of currencies in the islands, our price guide (see below) is given in US dollars. See under individual islands for detailed and specific listings.

When writing to a hotel, be sure to complete all mailing addresses, unless otherwise noted, with: (name of island), WI. For full details and reservations (which are recommended), contact the hotel directly by phone, email, or through or a travel agent. Alternatively, try the Caribbean tourist office in your home country, or book online.

ACCOMMODATION PRICE CATEGORIES

Price categories are based on the cost of a double room, for one night:
$ = less than $100
$$ = $100–200
$$$ = more than $200

Choosing a Restaurant

Our price guide (below) is given in US dollars. See individual islands for detailed listings. Reservations are recommended, especially in the winter season; essential at some restaurants.

THE COST OF EATING OUT

Price categories are based on the cost of a meal for one person, excluding drinks:
$ = less than $20
$$ = $20–40
$$$ = more than $40.

Nightlife

Evening entertainment on the islands ranges from relaxing over a leisurely dinner in a restaurant with a veranda facing onto the beach, to frittering your money away in a casino. In between these options are nightclubs, bars, discos, and live music. The larger hotels provide much of the evening entertainment on the islands, including music and dancing both during and after dinner, flashy floor shows usually featuring a limbo dancer, and "folkloric evenings" composed of elements of the music, dance. Travellers with an interest in culture may wish to venture beyond hotel walls in search of steel band, calypso and reggae music, and of bars and clubs frequented by local people.

Nightlife on cruise ships varies from high-tech nightclubs and Broadway-standard shows to a solitary has-been with an electric organ. Bigger, more modern ships tend to have better nightlife and entertainment will be geared to the nationality which predominates on board.

Casinos

The casino is an integral part of any modern cruise ship, with only a tiny minority not offering tables and one-armed bandits.

Ships' casinos are closed in port but open as soon as the ship sails and are often the focal point of activity late at night. Newcomers will often be offered free gambling lessons; cruise lines make a lot of money from casinos.

A number of the islands have casinos, and even some of the region's more relaxed islands have a casino or two. If you do plan to gamble, be sure to bring along appropriate clothes. Dress codes in the casinos tend to be a little more formal than those prevailing elsewhere.

The legal gambling age is 18 on most islands, but on Guadeloupe and Martinique you must be 21. Photo ID will sometimes be required for admittance, and some casinos charge an admission.

Outdoor Activities

Sport

The climate and geography of the Caribbean make the islands perfect for sports enthusiasts, and tourism has helped spark the development of a variety of sports facilities. Following is a list of some of the more popular sporting activities; see listings under individual islands for more information.

WATER SPORTS

Some smaller ships, namely those of Star Clippers, SeaDream Yacht Club, Seabourn, Windstar and Club Med, have a water sports platform which can be lowered from the back of the ship. All of these carry their own equipment. The big cruise lines, namely Royal Caribbean, Norwegian Cruise Line, Princess and Carnival, have private islands where most Caribbean cruises will spend one day. In reality, these "islands" are usually a remote beach where the cruise line has installed water sports equipment and other facilities.

On land, everything from mini Sunfish to two-masted yachts and large motorboats can be hired, either from hotels or from independent beach operators.

Waterskiing is available on most islands and all the necessary equipment may be rented. If you are interested in chartering a yacht, either crewed or bareboat, for a day or a considerable period of time, see Getting There page 324.

Fishing is a popular sport throughout the Caribbean. Most fishing boats can be chartered by the day or half day, and can usually accommodate several passengers. Many will quote rates which are all-inclusive of lunch, drinks, snacks, bait, equipment and any other essential items you might need on your fishing trip.

GOLF

In the Antilles, there are golf courses on Antigua, Aruba, Barbados, British Virgin Islands, Curaçao, Grenada, St Kitts and Nevis, St Lucia, St Martin, the US Virgin Islands, St Vincent and the Grenadines, Guadeloupe, and Martinique. Elsewhere, there are good, often world-class courses. Barbados, Jamaica, Dominican Republic, and the Bahamas have some of the most prestigious courses. Tee times on many courses can be booked in advance through the ship's purser.

TENNIS

Tennis is played on all islands, to varying degrees. Courts are found primarily within the premises of hotels, and arrangements can be made to use these courts even if you are not a hotel guest. Some islands also have private clubs which are open to visitors, and public courts which operate on a "first come, first served" basis. Some ships, including both in the Crystal fleet and P&O's *Aurora*, have paddle tennis courts, which are slightly smaller than a normal court and use softer balls.

HIKING

Rainforests, mountains, waterfalls and gorgeous views await you. Many of the islands have good-sized national parks with prime hiking opportunities (Dominica, Guadeloupe, Grenada, St Kitts, and St John in the US Virgin Islands), and St Lucia's Pitons offer experienced mountain climbers a chance to test their skills. Guides often lead excursions.

Bird-watching

Trinidad and Tobago are noted for their birds. In the US, birdwatching tours are organised by:
Field Guides Incorporated, 9433 Bee Cave Road, Building 1, Suite 150, Austin TX 78733; tel: 512-263 7295; www.fieldguides.com.

Language

Primary Languages

The multiplicity of languages in the Caribbean reflects the region's chequered colonial past. All of the islands use their own patois as well as a whole array of primary languages which include:
• **English**: Anguilla, Antigua and Barbuda, British Virgin Islands, Cayman Islands, Dominica, Grenada, Jamaica, Montserrat, St Kitts and Nevis, St Lucia, St Vincent and the Grenadines, St Maarten, Barbados, Trinidad and Tobago and the US Virgin Islands.
• **French**: Dominica, Guadeloupe, Martinique, St Barthélemy, St Lucia and St Martin.
• **Dutch**: Aruba, Bonaire and Curaçao.
• **Spanish**: Aruba, Bonaire, Curaçao, Cuba, Dominican Republic.
• **Papiamento** is the local language of Aruba, Bonaire and Curaçao. It has evolved from Spanish, Dutch, Portuguese, English, and African and Caribbean languages.

In addition to the languages listed above, Chinese is among the languages spoken on Aruba. English (and, to a lesser extent, other European languages) is spoken in several areas throughout the islands which have a high concentration of foreign travellers, but don't expect everyone to understand you – especially in rural areas and smaller towns. Efforts to communicate with island residents in their own languages are always appreciated.

English is the main language of almost all cruise lines, with the exception of Costa and MSC (Italian); Festival and Royal Olympic (both multi-lingual); Peter Deilmann (German); Aida (German); and Club Med 2 (French).

Further Reading

Cruising publications

Complete Guide to Ocean Cruising & Cruise Ships by Douglas Ward, Berlitz (2006). The industry's bible, it contains detailed, candid reviews of 254 ships, plus impeccable advice.
Porthole, a US-based cruising/lifestyle magazine featuring ships and advice.
Cruise Traveller magazine, advice aimed mainly at the UK market.

History, Economics and Culture

A Short History of the Netherlands Antilles by Cornelius Ch. Goslinga, M. Hijhoff, The Hague (1979).
A Short History of the West Indies by J.H. Parry, P.M. Sherlock and A. Maingot, Macmillan Caribbean, London (1987).
America's Virgin Islands: A History of Human Rights and Wrongs by William H. Boyer, Carolina Academic Press, Durham NC (1983).
Barbados: A History from Amerindians to Independence by F.A. Hoyos, Macmillan Caribbean, London (1978).
The Dominica Story: A History of the Island by Lennox Honychurch, Letchworth Press, Barbados (1975).
Gentlemen of Fortune: The Men who Made their Fortunes in Britain's Slave Colonies by Derrick Knight, F. Muller, London (1978).
Last Resorts, The Cost of Tourism in the Caribbean by Polly Pattullo, Cassell and Latin American Bureau (1996).

Natural History

A Field Guide to Reefs of the Caribbean and Florida by Eugene H. Kaplan, Houghton Mifflin, Boston (1982).
Caribbean Reef Fishes by Dr John E. Randall, T.F.H. Publications, Inc. (1996).
Exploring Tropical Isles and Seas: An Introduction for the Traveler and Amateur Naturalist by Frederic Martini, Prentice-Hall, New Jersey (1984).

The Western Shores

United States

Electricity: 110-115V/60 cycle

Money Matters: The unit of currency is the US dollar ($), which is divided into 100 cents. Credit cards are universally accepted and there are plenty of ATMs. Travellers from outside the US bring US$ travellers' cheques.

Postal Services: Even the most remote towns are served by the US Postal Service. Smaller post offices are limited to business hours (Mon–Fri 9am–5pm), although central, big-city branches may have extended opening times. Stamps are sold at all post offices, plus at convenience stores, gas stations, hotels and transport terminals, usually from vending machines. Postcards mailed from the US are likely to arrive home quicker than those mailed from the islands.

Telecommunications: Payphones are ubiquitous: they are to be found in hotels, restaurants, shopping centres, gas stations and in lighted booths on street corners. They do not usually take more than a quarter (25¢) coin, so invest in a calling card (on sale in visitor information centres and shops) to call long distance. To place a long-distance call within the US, dial 1+area code+local number; to call overseas, dial 011+country

Area Codes

Fort Lauderdale **954**
Galveston **409**
Houston **713**
Miami **305**
New Orleans **504**
Key West **305**
Port Canaveral **321**
Tampa **813**

code+area code+local number. Internet cafes are plentiful – there's one in the Bayside Marketplace at the port in Miami.

Toll-free calls
When in the US, make use of toll-free (no-charge) numbers. They start with 800, 888 or 877.

GETTING AROUND

By Car

A car is by far the best way to get around if you are extending a cruise in the United States. Most rental agencies require that you are at least 21 years old (sometimes 25), have a valid driving licence and a major credit card. Some will take a cash deposit in lieu of a credit card, but this might be as high as $500. Travellers from some foreign countries may need to produce an international licence from their own country. Rental vehicles range from modest economy cars to vans and luxury convertibles.

Be sure to check insurance provisions before signing anything. Cover is usually around $25 per day. You may already be covered by your own car insurance or credit card company, however, so check first.

By Taxi

Taxis are available in all the main tourism centres and wait for passengers at some of the ports. Elsewhere do not hail a passing cab; your hotel should call for you, but otherwise numbers are listed in Yellow Pages. Fares are metered and drivers, like anyone providing a service in the USA, expect a tip – around 10 per cent is usual.

By Bus

The national bus line, Greyhound, as well as a number of smaller charter companies, provide an impressive network of ground travel throughout the country. While some inter-city services include many stops en route, there are also "Express" buses which take in fewer stops.

Reservations and local bus station details are available on 800-231 2222, or at: www.greyhound.com.

FLORIDA

TOURIST OFFICES

Information is available from various outlets in Florida and from:
In the UK
Visit Florida,
Suite 3 Falmer Court,
London Road, Uckfield,
East Sussex TN22 1HN.
Tel: 01825 763633
Fax: 01825 763640.
In the US
Visit Florida,
661 East Jefferson Street, Suite 300
Tallahassee, FL 32301.
Tel: 854-488 5607.
Fax: 850-224 2938.
Website
www.visitflorida.com

PUBLIC HOLIDAYS

1 January: New Year's Day
20 January: M.L. King Jr Day
17 February: Presidents' Day
March/April: Good Friday
26 May: Memorial Day
4 July: Independence Day
1 September: Labor Day
October: (2nd Monday) Columbus Day
11 November: Veterans' Day
27 November: Thanksgiving Day
25 December: Christmas Day

SHOPPING

If you are into kitsch – plastic flamingo ashtrays, canned sunshine, orange perfume and the like – you will find Florida a veritable treasure house. From roadside shacks to massive, futuristic malls, stores carry plenty of traditional souvenirs. And then, of course there are the homegrown souvenirs like citrus fruit that can be shipped home for a small fee. But if you look a little harder, Florida also has an array of quality goods to take home from a trip. There are shops worth seeking that sell designer clothing at factory prices, Haitian art, Art Deco and Florida antiques, Native Indian crafts, and shells that forever smell of the sea. Good buys for European visitors are designer-label jeans, trainers and sportswear at a fraction of the price paid at home.

STAYING ON

Accommodation in Florida ranges from luxury resorts to basic motels, to pretty bed & breakfast inns. Many cruise lines offer special rates at selected hotels as part of a cruise-and-stay package. In Miami, the most popular areas to stay are South Beach (location of the Art Deco hotels), Bal Harbour and Key Biscayne.

WHAT TO EAT

In Florida the range of foods includes diverse flavours and ingredients that reflect the cultural make-up of the state. Here you will find downhome cafeterias, fancy French, take-out Chinese, all-you-can-eat shrimp, kosher delicatessens, dinner show spectacles, Afro-American and Caribbean spicy, fried eggs and grits, Italian spaghetti houses, hearty Nicaraguan, and corner coffee stands.

Meal Prices

Price categories are based on the cost of a meal for one person, excluding drinks:
$ = less than $20
$$ = $20–40
$$$ = more than $40.

Fort Lauderdale

Fort Lauderdale is located in Broward County, which encompasses 3,100 sq. km (1,197 square miles), with 37 km (23 miles) of Atlantic Ocean beach stretching between Palm Beach County on the northern perimeter and Dade County on the southern. It has a resident population of almost 1.6 million, with 150,000 residing in Fort Lauderdale, the largest municipality and the seat of county government. Broward County is bounded on the west by 505,600 acres (204,610 hectares) of Everglades (occupying about ⅔ of the county) and has 300 miles (483 km) of navigable waterways.

ARRIVING BY SEA

The cruise pier is at Port Everglades, the largest cruise port in the world after Miami and home base to several luxury lines. There is very little to do in the vicinity of the port so a taxi or hire car is essential. The downtown area is 10 minutes' drive away.

CALENDAR OF EVENTS

January: Orange Bowl
March: Museum of Art/Las Olas Arts Festival
April: Fort Lauderdale Seafood Festival
May: Pompano Beach Fishing Rodeo; Cajun/Zydeco Crawfish Festival
June/July: Philharmonic "Beethoven by the Beach" Summer Fest
July: Hollywood 4th of July Celebration
September: Las Olas Art Fair
October: Fort Lauderdale International Film Festival
November: Hollywood Jazz Festival

TOURIST OFFICES

In the UK
Greater Fort Lauderdale Convention & Visitors Bureau c/o Ignite Sales and Marketing Ltd,
Broadway House, 21 Broadway, Maidenhead, Berks, SL6 1NJ
Tel: 01628 778863.
Fax: 01628 676798.
In Fort Lauderdale
Greater Fort Lauderdale Convention & Visitors Bureau,
100 E. Broward Boulevard, Suite 200, Fort Lauderdale, FL 33301.
Tel: 954-765 4466.
Local: 800-22 SUNNY.
E-mail: gflcvb@broward.org
www.sunny.org

SHOPPING

Fort Lauderdale is home to Sawgrass Mills Factory Outlet Mall, 12801 W. Sunrise Boulevard, tel: 954-846 2300. Open Mon–Sat 10am–9.30pm, Sun 11am–8pm. This is the largest factory outlet mall in the US, with about 300 stores. Also try Swap Shop of Fort Lauderdale, 3291 Sunrise Boulevard, tel: 954-791 7927. Open Mon–Fri 7.30am–5pm, Sat–Sun

7.30am–6.30pm. Not far from Sawgrass Mills, this is a bargain-hunter's paradise, with rows and rows of stalls selling jewellery, sunglasses, and more at rock-bottom prices. The carnival and free circus is an added attraction. Las Olas Boulevard in town has several good art galleries and restaurants as well as shops.

GETTING AROUND

By Car

Car hire firms at the Port Everglades include Avis, tel: 800-831 2847; Florida Auto Rental, tel: 800-327 3791/954-764 1008; Alamo, tel: 800-327 9633/954-525 4713; Budget, tel: 800-527 0700/954-359 4700. Fun Rentals, tel: 954-389 2000, rents out scooters, 2-person scootcars, bicycles and skates.

By Taxi

Taxis line up at the cruise pier.

By Bus

Public buses service over 410 sq. miles (1,062 sq. km), with 250 buses plus 30 community buses on 40 routes. Tel: 954-357 8400. A free trolley service operates throughout downtown Fort Lauderdale, connecting Broward Performing Arts Center with Las Olas Boulevard boutiques and restaurants. Tel: 954-429 3100.

Intra/Interstate Service is provided by Greyhound Lines. The main bus station is located at 515 N.E. 3rd Street, Fort Lauderdale. Transport-ation between Port Everglades and the station is available by taxi.

By Rail

Rail Passenger Service is provided by Amtrak and Tri-Rail Commuter Line. The nearest passenger station is at 200 S.W. 21st Terrace, Fort Lauderdale and is accessible from either Broward Blvd or the interstate I-95.

Tri-rail, a 67-mile (108 km) commuter railway, connects Palm Beach, Broward and Dade counties with modern double-decker cars. There are six stations in Greater Fort Lauderdale and free shuttle buses connect to the airport and major business and shopping centres. Tel: 800-TRI-RAIL.

Scheduled water taxis also operate on the canals between hotels, restaurants, nightclubs, theatres, shops, beaches, marinas and more. Tel: 954-467-6677.

Links to the Caribbean
Hollywood Airport has comprehensive links to several Caribbean islands. Tel: 954-359 1200. Otherwise, Miami is a short drive down the coast.

STAYING ON

Tropic Seas Resort
4616 El Mar Drive
Lauderdale-by-the-Sea, FL 33308
Tel: 954-772 2555/800-952 9581
A small, comfortable, 1950s motel on the beach just north of Fort Lauderdale with 16 rooms, pool, shuffleboard, and barbecue. **$$**
Marriott's Harbour Beach Resort
3030 Holiday Drive, FL 33316
Tel: 954-525 4000/800-222 6543
www.marriott.com
A high-rise seafront resort with pool, cabanas, tennis courts, health club, shopping and windsurfing. **$$$**
Riverside Hotel
620 E. Las Olas Boulevard, FL 33301
Tel: 954-467 0671/800-325 3280
www.riversidehotel.com
In the downtown shopping district, this historic hotel has antique-furnished rooms, pool and restaurants. **$$$**

Hotel Prices

Price categories are based on the cost of a double room, for one night:
$ = less than $100
$$ = $100–200
$$$ = more than $200.

WHERE TO EAT

Mark's Las Olas
1032 E Las Olas Boulevard
Tel: 954-463 1000
www.chefmark.com
One of the finest restaurants in the city, Mark's is known for its New Florida cuisine, with dishes like crispy squid, marinated quail, and lump crab cakes. The menu changes daily. **$$–$$$**

SHORE ACTIVITIES

Excursions
Everglades swamp safaris by buggy, airboat and kayak; Butterfly World in Coconut Creek; dolphin "encounters"; riverboat dinner cruises; a scenic Riverwalk, linking downtown attractions; shopping at Sawgrass Mills; day trips to the Bahamas; Stranahan House (museum); Delray Beach for historic buildings and cool restaurants; Morikami Museum (Japanese museum with tranquil gardens); palm tree gardens at the Fairfield Tropical Garden.

Best Beaches
Hollywood, Dania Beach, Fort Lauderdale, Pompano Beach and Deerfield Beach all offer excellent facilities.

Water Sports
For a look at the coral reefs contact **Glassbottom Boat Tours** tel: 954-467 6000.
Club Nautico at Pier 66 Marina rents out powerboats for diving, snorkelling and cruising, tel: 954-523 0033.
Action Sportfishing, tel: 954-423 8700, arranges fishing charters for all standards.
Captains Yacht Charters, tel: 954-941 6794. Charters luxury motor yachts, sport-fishing boats and sailboats.

Key West

Key West is located at the very end of the offshore islands scattered off the tip of Florida, the Keys. It is 159 miles (260 km) from Miami.

ARRIVING BY SEA

Ships dock at Mallory Square, in the heart of Old Town, or at The Mole pier, linked to Old Town by a five-minute train ride. Some ships tender, with drop-offs at Mallory Square.

CALENDAR OF EVENTS

March: Historic Seaport Music Festival
June: Florida Keys Tropical Fruit Fiesta
July: Hemingway Days Festival
October: 10-day Annual Fantasy Fest
November: Pirates in Paradise, Historic Seaport

TOURIST OFFICES

Florida Keys and Key West Visitors' Bureau,
PO Box 1146, FL 33041,
Tel: 800-252 5397.

SHOPPING

The souvenir, fashion, art and general kitsch shops located all along Duval Street sell lots of Hemingway and fishing memorabilia; also some great art, surf gear and clothing.

GETTING AROUND

By Car
It is not worth hiring a car in Key West as everything is within walking distance. Scooters and bicycles are can be hired at shops on Duval Street.
Further afield, the drive along the Overseas Highway is famous; first built atop the remains of tycoon Henry Flagler's Overseas Railroad, 193 miles (310 km) of bridges string the low-lying Keys together.

By Bus and Trolley
The Old Town Trolley operates from Mallory Square. For journeys out of Key West, Greyhound Lines makes numerous scheduled stops between Miami International Airport and the Keys, including Key Largo. Tel: 800-454 2487/305-296 9072. The Keys Shuttle offers a door-to-door service from Fort Lauderdale and Miami International airports to Key Largo and other points in the Keys. Call 24 hours ahead to book. Tel: 888-765 9997/ 305-289 9997.

Links to the Caribbean
Key West has its own airport for mainly domestic services. The nearest big international airports are Miami and Hollywood/Fort Lauderdale, with regular services to the Caribbean.

Hotel Prices

Price categories are based on the cost of a double room, for one night:

$ = less than $100
$$ = $100–200
$$$ = more than $200.

STAYING ON

In contrast to the big, glitzy resorts found along the coast in mainland Florida, hotels in Key West tend to be small and quaint.

Curry Mansion Inn
511 Caroline Street, FL 33040.
Tel: 305-294 5349/800-253 3466.
www.currymansion.com
A grand Victorian-style mansion turned into a charming 28-room inn with pool and lush gardens. **$$$**

Island City House Hotel
411 William Street, FL 33040.
Tel: 305-294 5702/800-634 8230.
www.islandcityhouse.com
Off the main strip, this tropical garden hotel has 24 suites with kitchens, swimming pool and Jacuzzi. **$$$**

Pier House Resort & Caribbean Spa
1 Duval Street, FL 33040.
Tel: 305-296 4600/800-327 8340.
www.pierhouse.com
A luxury 142-room resort that feels like it's on its own island, with pools, private beach, bars and cabanas. **$$$**

Southernmost Motel
1319 Duval Street, FL 33040.
Tel: 305-296 5611/800-354 4455.
www.southernmosthotel.com
A comfortable motel with rooms, pool and full-service concierge. **$$–$$$**

WHERE TO EAT

Blue Heaven
729 Thomas Street.
Tel: 305-296 8666.
www.blueheavenkw.com
A one-time bordello where Ernest Hemingway supposedly gambled on cockfights, Blue Heaven is now a trendy art gallery-cum-eatery serving tasty tropical food. Nouveau Island cuisine. **$–$$**

Pisces Seafood Restaurant
1007 Simonton Street.
Tel: 305–294 7100.
www.pisceskeywest.com
An intimate and elegant setting with classic French/tropical specialities like lobster in cognac sauce and shrimp in mango butter. Reservations. **$$$**

Kelly's Caribbean Grill
301 Whitehead Street.
Tel: 305-293 8484.
A combination art gallery and family restaurant, Kelly's serves great Caribbean and American food. **$$**

Louie's Backyard
700 Waddell Avenue.
Tel: 305-294 1061.
www.louiesbackyard.com
Fine American and Caribbean cooking in a romantic, seaside setting with old Key West ambience. Reservations are advisable. **$$$**

Mangia, Mangia Pasta Café
900 Southard Street.
Tel: 305-294 2469.
www.mangia-mangia.com
A classic, family-run eatery with excellent homemade pastas, fish and chicken dishes. **$–$$**

SHORE ACTIVITIES

Excursions

Art galleries on Duval Street; street entertainment at sunset in Mallory Square; tall ships in the Historic Seaport; Ernest Hemingway's home & museum; golf; dolphin "encounters"; day sailing trips.

Best Beaches

The Fort Zachary Taylor State Historic Site beach is clean and shaded by pines. Smathers Beach is good for water sports.

Water Sports

Dolphin encounters can be arranged with **Captain Seaweed Charters**, tel: 305-872 7588. The *Yankee Freedom II* provides daily ferry service from Key West to the Dry Tortugas National Park and Fort Jefferson, including lunch and snorkel gear, tel: 305-294 7009. There are also numerous day sails and deep-sea fishing charters. For windsurf equipment and sailing lessons, contact **Bump and Jump** on tel: 305-664 9494.

Miami

Greater Miami is a sprawling metropolis in south-east Florida made up of over 30 municipalities, covering some 2,000 sq. miles (5,180-sq. km). The main area of interest to the visitor is South Beach with its famous Art Deco architecture.

ARRIVING BY SEA

The Port of Miami is the largest cruise port in the world and is the home base for giants such as Royal Caribbean and Norwegian Cruise Line. The port is just a five-minute ride from downtown and Miami Beach. For general information on the port, call 305-371 7678.

CALENDAR OF EVENTS

February: South Miami Arts Festival; Miami Film Festival; Chinese New Year
February/March: Carnaval Miami (Caribbean-style carnival celebrations)
March: St Patrick's Day celebrations
October: Hallowe'en celebrations
November: Veterans' Day celebrations
December: Annual King Mango Strut (street parades, carnival)

TOURIST OFFICES

In the UK
Greater Miami Convention and Visitors' Bureau,
PO Box 633, Hayward's Heath,
West Sussex RH16 2WU
Tel: 01444 443 355
In Miami
Greater Miami Convention and Visitors' Bureau,
701 Brickell Avenue, Suite 2700
Miami, Florida 33131
Tel: 305-539 3000/800-933 8448
Fax: 305-539 3113

SHOPPING

Best shopping areas include Bal Harbour Shops, 9700 Collins Avenue, Bal Harbour, tel: 305-866 0311. Open Mon–Fri 10am–9pm, Sat 10am–7pm, Sun noon–6pm. Bayside Marketplace, 401 Biscayne Boulevard, tel: 305-577 3344 is a speciality shopping and entertainment complex in downtown

Miami. Open Mon–Thurs 10am–10pm, Fri–Sat 10am–11pm, Sun 11am–9pm. Loehmann's Fashion Island, 18711 Biscayne Boulevard, tel: 305-932 0520 is great for discounted designer wear. Open Mon–Fri 10am–9pm, Sun noon–6pm. Also try Coconut Grove for fashion and the shops of South Beach for fashions and sportswear.

GETTING AROUND

By Car

Car hire firms at the Port of Miami include Avis, tel: 800-831 2847 and Alamo, tel: 305-633 6076.

By Taxi

Taxis in Miami tend to be expensive, and you usually have to telephone in advance for pick-up.

Public Transport

There are three forms of short-distance public transport. Metrorail is a 21 mile (34-km) elevated railway, with stops roughly once every mile; Metromover is a series of little cars on an elevated track extending from the downtown area; and Metrobus has 60 routes throughout the metropolis.

Links to the Caribbean

Miami International Airport is the state's largest in total passenger numbers and airlines. It is also a major jumping-off point for direct flights to the Caribbean and South America.

As well as various US airlines operating services to the main gateway airports in the Caribbean, there are numerous smaller regional carriers such as Caribbean Star, Cayman Airways and LIAT linking the islands to Miami, as well as the main Caribbean airlines like BWIA, Bahamasair and Air Jamaica.

STAYING ON

Bay Harbor Inn
9660 E. Bay Harbor Drive, FL 33131.
Tel: 305-868 4141.
www.bayharborinn.com
Handy for the upmarket Bal Harbour shops and the all-night parties in the Art Deco District of South Beach. **$$**

Cardozo Hotel
1300 Ocean Drive, FL 33139.
Tel: 305-535 6500/800-782 6500.
www.cardozohotel.com
An oceanfront Art Deco hotel in the heart of historic South Beach, with 43 beautifully decorated rooms. **$$–$$$**
Hotel Cavalier
1320 Ocean Drive, FL 33139.
Tel: 305-604 5000/800-OUTPOST.
Well-run Art Deco beauty in South Beach on the ocean. Fine restaurants and bars nearby. **$$–$$$**
Clay Hotel and Hosteling International
1438 Washington Avenue, FL 33139.
Tel: 305-534 2988.
www.clayhotel.com
A hotel and very popular 200-bed youth hostel with dormitory-style rooms and kitchen facilities in the Art Deco District. **$**

Meal Prices

Price categories are based on the cost of a meal for one person, excluding drinks:
$ = less than $20
$$ = $20–40
$$$ = more than $40.

WHERE TO EAT

Joe's Stone Crab
11 Washington Avenue, South Beach.
Tel: 305-673 0365.
Miami's best-known restaurant. The stone crabs are delicious but the wait is always long (and no reservations allowed). Serving lunch and dinner. No lunch Mondays. Open for lunch and dinner mid-Oct–mid-May. Open for dinner only mid-May until end of July. **$$$**
Pacific Time
915 Lincoln Road, South Beach.
Tel: 305-534 5979.
A rotating menu of Pacific/Asian dishes such as grouper in ginger sauce and tempura sweet potatoes. **$$$**
News Café
800 Ocean Drive, South Beach.
Tel: 305-538 6397.
Ultra-hip brunch spot; perfect for hanging out on a Sunday morning before boarding your cruise ship. **$**

SHORE ACTIVITIES

Excursions

Miami Seaquarium; architecture in Coral Gables; shops and restaurants in Coconut Grove; Little Havana (Eighth Street) for the Cuban Museum and the El Credito cigar factory; water sports; fishing; beaches; walking tours of the Art Deco buildings in South Beach.

Best Beaches

South Beach is huge, with every facility under the sun from water sports to volleyball and rollerblading; there is a gay beach area at 12th Street. Haulover Beach Park has a nudist area. Hobie Beach and Windsurfer Beach are good for water sports.

Water Sports

For fishing trips try:
Sailaway Yacht Charter Consultants
15605 S.W. 92nd Avenue, Miami, FL 33157.
Tel: 305-253 7245.
www.1800sailaway.com
Day and week yacht charters.
Action Charters
MiaMarina at Bayside Marketplace, 401 Biscayne Blvd, Pier 5, Slip 11, Miami, FL 33132.
Tel: 305-361 2131.
www.actioncharters.com

Port Canaveral

Port Canaveral is the departure point for Disney Cruise Line, Royal Caribbean, and Carnival, among others. Located at the northern end of Florida's Space Coast 35 miles (56 km) east of the Orlando attractions, this 72-mile (116-km) stretch of Atlantic shore is primarily composed of the cities Titusville, Cocoa Beach, Melbourne and Palm Bay.

ARRIVING BY SEA

Ships dock at Port Canaveral, north of Cocoa Beach and close to the Kennedy Space Center. The best way to get around is by car, although there are taxis at the port.

CALENDAR OF EVENTS

March: Florida Marlins' Spring Training; TICO Warbird Air Show (next best thing to a shuttle launch); Port Canaveral SeaFest (food festival).
April: Melbourne Art Festival.
November: Space Coast State Fair; Space Coast Birding and Wildlife festival.

TOURIST OFFICES

Florida's Space Coast Office of Tourism,
2725 Judge Fran Jamieson Way #B-105, Viera, FL 32940.
Tel: 321-637 5483/800-936 2326.
www.space-coast.com

SHOPPING

Main Street Titusville, Olde Cocoa Village and downtown Melbourne offer the best souvenir and knick-knack shops, while the best beach and surf shop is the Ron Jon Surf Shop, claiming to sell "everything under the sun".

GETTING AROUND

By Car

Hire companies at or near the port include Avis, tel: 321-783 3643 and Budget, tel: 321-784 0634.
Taxis wait at the port.

By Bus/Rail

A beach trolley service runs from Port Canaveral to 13th Street in Cocoa Beach Mon–Sat 7am–9pm and Sun 8am–5pm.

Links to the Caribbean

Orlando, a 50-minute drive away, is the nearest large international airport, served by all the main US carriers and offering links to the Caribbean islands and the Bahamas. There are various small and charter-only airfields along the Space Coast.

STAYING ON

Best Western Cocoa Beach
5600 N Atlantic Avenue,
Cocoa Beach, FL 32931.
Tel: 321-783 7621/800-962 0028.
www.bestwesterncocoabeach.com
Resort hotel right on the beach with plenty of facilities for all the family. **$$**
Radisson Resort at the Port
8701 Astronaut Boulevard, FL 32920.
Tel: 321-784 0000.
www.radisson.com
Just a mile from the cruise terminal with a shuttle service. **$$**
The Resort on Cocoa Beach
1600 N. Atlantic Avenue,
Cocoa Beach, FL 32931.
Tel: 321-783 4000/866-469 8222.
www.vrivacations.com
Luxury resort on the beach with two-bedroom units, ideal for families. **$$$**
Space Shuttle Inn
Kennedy Space Center,
3455 Cheney Highway (Route 50),
Titusville, FL 32780.
Tel: 321-269 9100.
www.spaceshuttleinn.com
Offers special pre- and post-cruise packages, including admission to the Kennedy Space Center. **$**

Hotel Prices

Price categories are based on the cost of a double room, for one night:
$ = less than $100
$$ = $100–200
$$$ = more than $200.

WHERE TO EAT

The area is famous for seafood: lobster, scallops, crayfish, shrimp, fish and crab, as well as specialities including octopus, fried frog legs, alligator and shark. Local desserts include mango pie and "astronaut ice cream" (replica of the freeze-dried dessert that went to the moon).

Flamingo's Restaurant
Radisson Resort At The Port,
8701 Astronaut Boulevard,
Cape Canaveral, FL.
Tel: 321-784 0000.
Fine dining close to the port. **$$**

Florida's Seafood Bar & Grill
480 West Cocoa Beach Cswy,
(Hwy. 520), Cocoa Beach, FL
Tel: 321-784 0892.
Famous for seafood, particularly oysters. **$$**

SHORE ACTIVITIES

Excursions

Merritt Island, home of Kennedy Space Center, a huge exhibit of the history of space travel with spectacular IMAX films and "astronaut encounters". To see an actual launch, get a Launch Viewing Opportunity Ticket through the KSC Visitor Complex, tel: 321-449 4444 or www.kennedyspacecenter.com. Walt Disney World at Orlando is an hour's drive, 0870 24 24 900. Merritt Island National Wildlife Refuge, tel: 321-861 0667, has numerous hiking trails; shops and restaurants at Cocoa Village; also try deep-sea fishing.

Best Beaches

Cocoa Beach is one of the most popular tourist areas, known for its clean beaches and seafood restaurants. Canaveral National Seashore is more remote, with 24 miles (29 km) of wetlands offering good bird- and wildlife-watching.

Water Sports

Water sports gear is available to hire from all the main beaches. Surfing, snorkelling, sailing and deep-sea fishing are all popular, and there are several surf festivals during the year.

Tampa

Tampa is a small city by US standards, with 300,000 inhabitants, situated on the semitropical Gulf of Mexico. It is one of the fastest-growing cruise ports in the US.

ARRIVING BY SEA

Cruise ships dock at the Port of Tampa in the Channel District downtown, just in front of the Florida Aquarium and the Channelside entertainment centre. There are shops in the immediate vicintiy.

CALENDAR OF EVENTS

January: Black Heritage Festival
February: Gasparilla Pirate Festival
March: Gasparilla Festival of the Arts;
Apollo Beach Manatee Arts Festival
4 July: Freedom Festival
October: Hallowe'en celebrations
November: Cigar Heritage Festival

TOURIST OFFICES

In Tampa
Tampa Bay Convention and Visitors
Bureau,
400 N. Tampa Street, Ste. 2800,
Tampa, FL 33602,
Tel: 813-223 1111.

SHOPPING

Among the best buys are designer
clothes and cigars. Old Hyde Park
Village is an outdoor-style shopping
mall and there are plenty of shops in
the Channelside complex and in
Centro Ybor. University Mall
combines well with a visit to Busch
Gardens.

GETTING AROUND

By Car

Car rental agencies in Tampa include
Enterprise Rent-A-Car, situated right in
the cruise terminal, tel: 813-740
9293; U Save Auto Rental, tel: 813-
287 1872

By Taxi

Taxis cannot be hailed on the street –
you have to pick one up at a rank or
call in advance. United Cab, tel: 813-
253 2424, or Yellow Cab, tel:
813-253 0121.

By Trolley

A trolley service connects the uptown
and downtown areas. Telephone 813-
254 4278 for more information.

By Rail

Amtrak offers slow, but leisurely,
services from America's Midwest,
Northeast and South – and connecting
services from points west – to certain
Florida cities. There are daily services
from New York City to Tampa on the
Silver Star.

Links to the Caribbean

Tampa International Airport (tel: 813-
870 8700) links to many US cities
and has international flights to Europe
and the Caribbean.

STAYING ON

Hilton Garden Inn
1700 E. Ninth Avenue, FL 33605.
Tel: 813-769 9267/800-221 2424.
http://hiltongardeninn.hilton.com
The first hotel built in historic Ybor
City in a hundred years. Now visitors
can spend the night and enjoy a
"cooked-to-order" breakfast. **$$**
Hyatt Regency Tampa
211 North Tampa Street, FL 33602.
Tel: 813-225 1234.
http://tamparegency.hyatt.com
A modern high-rise hotel in the heart
of downtown Tampa; 517 rooms, pool
and exercise room. **$$–$$$**
Saddlebrook Resort
5700 Saddlebrook Way,
Wesley Chapel.
Tel: 813-973 1111, 800-729 8383.
www.saddlebrook.com
This 480-acre (194-hectare) resort
has golf, wide green spaces, 45
tennis courts, fitness centre, spa, and
a half-million gallon pool. **$$$**
Tahitian Inn
601 S. Dale Mabry Highway,
FL 33609.
Tel: 813-877 6721/800-876 1397.
www.tahitianinn.com
A comfortable hotel with spa, gym,
swimming pool and cafe. **$–$$**

WHERE TO EAT

Bern's Steak House
1208 S Howard Avenue,
Tel: 813-52 2421.
Prime cuts of beef, organic
vegetables, and a vast wine menu.
Reservations recommended. **$$$**
Crawdaddy's
2500 Rocky Point Drive.
Tel: 813-281 0407.
A funky hang-out much favoured by
locals that serves up fried alligator
and all sorts of other regional
delicacies. **$$$**
Donatello
232 N. Dale Mabry Highway, Tampa.
Tel: 813-875 6660.
A quiet atmosphere, attentive staff

and northern Italian food makes for a
fine meal. Choose anything from
linguine to lobster or veal. **$$–$$$**
Shula's Steak House
4860 W. Kennedy Blvd,
Tel: 813-286 4366
Named for a well-known former
football coach, and themed with
football memorabilia, Shula's serves
a predictable but tasty diet of steaks
and more steaks. **$$–$$$**

Meal Prices

Price categories are based on the
cost of a meal for one person,
excluding drinks:
$ = less than $20
$$ = $20–40
$$$ = more than $40.

SHORE ACTIVITIES

Excursions

The waterfront, with its spectacular
aquarium and Channelside
entertainment complex, including an
IMAX cinema and Pop City; historic
Ybor City, once a Cuban settlement,
with handsome architecture and great
atmosphere; Salvador Dali Museum;
Duck Tours (amphibious sightseeing
vehicles seating around 28); African
theme park, Busch Gardens, one of
Florida's main attractions; the
Manatee and Aquatic Center at the
zoo; Museum of Science and
Technology, including the Gulf Coast
Hurricane Chamber; canoeing on the
Hillsborough River, alligators and all.

Best Beaches

Clearwater Beach, famous for its soft
sand and lined by smart hotels.
Indian Rocks beach if you haven't got
much time. St Pete's Beach for water
sports.

LOUISIANA

New Orleans

● *At the time of going to press the city and port were recovering from damage caused by Hurricane Katrina. Ships homeported in New Orleans were temporarily relocating to nearby ports.*

Located on the Mississippi Delta by the Gulf of Mexico, New Orleans is a vibrant, colourful city with a mixture of Cajun, French and Spanish cultures. Famous for its food, its jazz and blues, its attitude, and most of all, for its Mardi Gras celebrations, the city is increasingly popular as a starting point for Caribbean cruising.

ARRIVING BY SEA

Cruise ships dock at the port, next to the Ernest N. Morial Convention Center. Taxis wait at the port, or you can walk into town.

CALENDAR OF EVENTS

February/March: Mardi Gras – several days of exuberant celebration.
Spring: International Jazz and Heritage Festival
4 July: Go 4th on the River – Independence Day Celebrations.
October: Hallowe'en celebrations are becoming a major event with mask-wearing and eye-popping costumes
Year-round: Jazz and blues events throughout the city

TOURIST OFFICES

New Orleans Metropolitan Convention and Visitors Bureau,
1520 Sugar Bowl Drive
New Orleans, LA 70112.
Tel: 504-566 5011/800-672 6124.
www.neworleanscvb.com
The New Orleans Welcome Center at 529 St Ann Street in Jackson Square is run by the tourist commission and provides maps, brochures, and advice.

SHOPPING

Things to buy include antiques, vodou dolls, vintage clothing, Mardi Gras souvenirs, jazz and blues music, packaged spices, and cookbooks. Royal Street in the French Quarter is the best place to find local colour; the Riverwalk Shopping Center is near the port. Magazine Street is great for antiques, crafts and second-hand books.

GETTING AROUND

By Car

Don't hire a car for a day stop – walk or use the streetcar instead. For longer stays, try: Alamo Car Rental, New Orleans International Airport, tel: 504-469 0532; Avis Car Rental, tel: 504-464 9511. Anyone planning to hire a car should note that driving, and especially parking, in the French Quarter is not easy. Streets are narrow and often congested; cars parked illegally are towed away swiftly, and it is expensive to retrieve them.

By Taxi

Taxis can be hailed on the street and operate on a meter system.

By Bus

Public buses run 6am–6.30pm. For schedules, tel: 504-818 1077.

By Streetcar

The streetcar is by far the best way to get around. The sightseeing excursion from Canal Street to Carrollton and back is just over 13 miles (21 km), takes about 1½ hours, and is a bargain at $1.25. The Riverfront Line is also good for sightseeing. Timetables are available at the Regional Transit Authority (RTA) office: 2817 Canal Street, tel: 504-248 3900. A VisiTour pass, available for one-day or three-days, allows unlimited on-and-off privileges for the streetcars and buses.

Links to the Caribbean

All the main American airlines serve New Orleans, including Delta, United and American, with regular links to Caribbean gateways such as Fort Lauderdale, Miami, and Orlando.

Hotel Prices

Price categories are based on the cost of a double room, for one night:
$ = less than $100
$$ = $100–200
$$$ = more than $200.

STAYING ON

International House
221 Camp Street,
New Orleans, LA 70130.
Tel: 504-553 9550.
www.ihhotel.com
Trendy, boutique-style hotel in the French Quarter. **$$**
Le Pavillon
833 Poydras Street,
New Orleans, LA 70112.
Tel: 504-581 3111.
www.lepavillon.com
Elegant and palatial surroundings located near the French Quarter. Facilties include fitness centre, pool, formal and casual dining. **$$**
Bienville House Hotel
320 Decatur Street,
New Orleans, LA 70130.
Tel: 504-529 2345.
www.bienvillehouse.com
Close to the river in the French Quarter. Intimate hotel with pretty courtyard, outdoor pool and rooms with balconies. **$$**

WHERE TO EAT

New Orleans' extraordinary range of food includes everything from haute cuisine and Bananas Foster to blackened catfish and Creole sole. Other local favourites are: red beans and rice, kidney beans stewed with salt pork, ham hocks, onions and garlic; jambalaya, a version of the Spanish paella, with either seafood or meat; gumbo (spicy soup, originally with okra); crayfish; King Cake (small pastries); *beignet* doughnuts; café au lait with chicory.

Alex Patout's
720 St Louis Street, French Quarter.
Tel: 504-525 7788.
Fax: 504-525 7809.
The chef-owner comes from a long line of Cajun culinary artists in South

Louisiana. His stylish restaurant showcases seafoods enhanced by exotic sauces and seasonings. Reservations advised for dinner; closed for lunch on weekends. **$$$**

Antoine's
713 St Louis Street, French Quarter.
Tel: 504-581 4422.
Fax: 504-581 3003.
This well-known French Creole restaurant has been run by the same family since 1840. Famous dishes such as Oysters Rockefeller originated at Antoine's. Sensational dishes, especially the Baked Alaska. **$$$**

Camellia Grill
626 S. Carrollton Avenue, Uptown.
Tel: 504-866 9573.
A New Orleans institution, the Camellia is famed for its burgers, waffles, chilli and delicious pastries. Sometimes there is a wait. **$**

Café du Monde
French Market; other outlets around town. Go local with a chicory café au lait and home-made *beignets*. **$**

Emeril's
800 Tchoupitoulas Street.
Tel: 504-528 9393.
Fax: 504-558 3925
Elegant, very popular, serving creole cuisine with a nouvelle twist. **$$$**

Gumbo Shop
630 St. Peter Street,
New Orleans, LA 70116.
Tel: 504-525 1486.
Traditional and contemporary creole cuisine served in a 1795 building with lovely garden patio. Bar, 30 wines by the glass and its own cookbook. **$$$**

Meal Prices

Price categories are based on the cost of a meal for one person, excluding drinks:
$ = less than $20
$$ = $20–40
$$$ = more than $40.

SHORE ACTIVITIES

Excursions

French Quarter for cafes, bars, galleries and markets; Jackson Square for historic buildings, museums, antiques, art galleries, perfume shops, sidewalk cafes and tearooms; French Market; Bourbon Street; New Orleans City Park; elegant homes in the Garden District; D-Day Museum; swamp adventures in the Bayou; steamboat cruises. If you're overnighting, don't miss the jazz and blues clubs.

Haunted History Tours, tel: 504-861 2727; www.hauntedhistorytours.com
For vodou, cemetery, vampire, Hallowe'en and ghost tours.

SPORTS

Lake Pontchartrain is ideal for fishing, hiking and canoeing. The wider area of Pontchartrain Basin is known for its rivers, bayous, swamps and hardwood forests. There are several golf courses around the city.

TEXAS

Galveston and Houston

The two main ports for Texas are Galveston and Houston. A financial hub and bustling port, Houston is one of the nation's largest cities, with a population of 1.95 million. The island of Galveston, 1½ hours away, is the city's principal beach resort. One of the South's most significant cities by the end of the 19th century, Galveston was devastated in a matter of hours by the fierce 1900 hurricane.

ARRIVING BY SEA

Galveston

Ships dock at the Port on Pier 25, which is adjacent to the historic Strand District.

Houston

The cruise terminal is on Galveston Bay on the Houston Ship Channel at the main container port for the city. Downtown is 25 minutes' drive and the airport is about 45 minutes away.

CALENDAR OF EVENTS

February: Mardi Gras, Galveston; Houston Livestock Show & Rodeo
April: Houston International Festival; WorldFest: Houston International Film Festival

May: Cinco De Mayo Celebration Galveston Historic Homes Tours
June: Juneteenth Celebration (blues, gospel and jazz)
September: Fiestas Patrias Mexican festival
December: Dickens on the Strand, Galveston

TOURIST OFFICES

In the US
Texas State Board of Tourism,
P.O. Box 5064, Austin, TX.
Tel: 512-462 9191/800-452 9292

In Galveston
Galveston Island Visitor Information Center, 2428 Seawall Boulevard.
Tel: 713-425 4753: www.galveston.com

In Houston
Greater Houston Convention & Visitors Bureau, 901 Bagby, Houston, TX 77002.
Tel: 713-437 5200/800-4-Houston
www.houston-guide.com

SHOPPING

Galveston

Browse the boutiques and shops in the Strand, which is also good for antiques.

Houston

The Galleria, Houston's largest and best-known retail mall, has 320 stores and is visited by more than 16 million people annually. The oldest shopping district is the River Oaks Shopping Center. Also try Rice Village for a huge mixture of stores, from funky fashions and crafts to big names.

GETTING AROUND

By Car

For a day visit, Galveston is easily walkable and Houston has good public transport. For longer stays, Houston is the best place to rent a car.

By Taxi

Taxis need to be called in advance; you can't just hail one on the street. All cabs are metered. In Houston, United Cab, tel: 713-699 0000 or Yellow Cab, tel: 713-236 1111; in Galveston, Busy Bee, tel: 409-762 6666 or Yellow Cab 409-763 3333.

By Bus

Houston has an excellent bus system in the Metropolitan Transit Authority.

By Rail

Amtrak's Sunset Limited train line runs through Houston between Orlando and Los Angeles. The Houston Amtrak station is at 902 Washington Ave, just north of downtown. For information, call 800-USA RAIL/800-872 7245.

Links to the Caribbean

Hobby Airport or George Bush Intercontinental Airport in Houston both have regular connections to the Caribbean and to many USA destinations. The services of the major airlines such as American, Continental and Delta, are conveniently supplemented by smaller ones such as Southwest, Chaparral, Texas and Muse.

Hotel Prices

Price categories are based on the cost of a double room, for one night:
$ = less than $100
$$ = $100–200
$$$ = more than $200.

STAYING ON

Whatever your budget, you should be able to find a suitable place to spend the night in Texas. In addition to independently owned hotels and motels in every price range, there are also chains and historic inns.

Galveston

Flagship Hotel
2501 Seawall Blvd, TX 77550.
Tel: 409-762 9000.
Fax: 409-762 1619.
www.flagshiphotel.com
Nautically themed hotel on a pier stretching 1,000 ft (300 metres) out to sea. **$$$**
Gaido's Seaside Inn
3802 Seawall Blvd, TX 77550.
Tel: 409-762 9625.
Fax: 409-765 9285.
With motel-style units, many with sea view. Also a tiered flower garden. **$$**

Hotel Galvez
2024 Seawall Blvd, TX 77550.
Tel: 409-765 7721.
Fax: 409-765 5623.
Historic seafront hotel run by the Wyndham chain. With a sauna and whirlpool. **$$$**
The Tremont House
2300 Ship's Mechanic Row, TX 77550.
Tel: 409-763 0300.
Fax: 409-763 1539.
Historic, European-style Wyndham hotel, near the Strand. **$$**

Houston

Springhill Suites Houston
Astrodome, 1400 Old Spanish Trail TX 77054.
Tel: 713-796 1000.
Fax: 713-796 8055.
Marriott hotel with pool and restaurant. **$$**
Comfort Inn Brookhollow
4760 Sherwood Lane, 77092.
Tel: 713-686 5525.
Fax: 713-686 5365.
Small inn with outdoor pool and breakfast included in the price. **$$**
Courtyard by Marriott
3131 West Loop South, 77027.
Tel: 713-961 1640.
Fax: 713-439 0989.
Whirlpool/spa and workout facilities, near the Galleria. **$$**
The Houstonian Hotel, Club and Spa
111 North Post Oak Lane, 77024.
Tel: 713-680 2626.
Fax: 713-680 2992.
www.houstonian.com
In wooded grounds. Spa, pools and tennis courts, jogging tracks. **$$$**
Hyatt Regency Houston
1200 Louisiana Street, 77002.
Tel: 713-654 1234.
Fax: 713-951 0934.
http://houstonregency.hyatt.com
Downtown hotel with 977 units. Recent US$15 million facelift. **$$$$**

WHERE TO EAT

Don't plan on dieting while in Texas: Texans love food, and a visit wouldn't be complete without sampling a good portion of it. State favourites include barbecue, chicken-fried steak (an inexpensive steak covered with batter, fried and served with gravy), pecan pie and, of course, Tex-Mex food.

Meal Prices

Price categories are based on the cost of a meal for one person, excluding drinks:
$ = less than $20
$$ = $20–40
$$$ = more than $40.

Galveston

Christie's Beachcomber
401 Broadway.
Tel: 409-762 8648.
Popular beach spot, home-style cooking, buffet. **$$**
Clary's
8509 Teichman Road, off I-45.
Tel: 800-278 0771.
www.galveston.com/clarys/
Longtime family-owned seafood haven. **$$$**
Fisherman's Wharf
Pier 22 adj. the Elissa.
Tel: 409-765 5708.
Patio dining overlooking the port. **$$**
Ocean Grill Restaurant
2227 Seawall Blvd.
Tel: 409-762 7100.
www.galveston.com/oceangrill
Mesquite-grilled seafood, in a simple restaurant by the water. **$$**

Houston

Benihana of Tokyo
9707 Westheimer Road.
Tel: 713-789 4962.
Also at 1318 Louisiana.
Tel: 713-659 8231.
www.benihana.com
Communal dining, sushi, teppanyaki and Japanese specialties. **$$**
Billy Blues Bar & Grill
6025 Richmond near Fountainview.
Tel: 713-266 9294.
Five-storey landmark, barbecue and live blues. **$$**
The Brownstone
2736 Virginia Street (at Westheimer).
Tel: 713-520 5666.
Fax: 713-520 7001
www.brownstone-houston.com
Long-established favourite. Elegant surroundings, opulently decorated. Top-notch food, too. **$$$**

Dessert Gallery
3200 Kirby Drive.
Tel: 713-522 9999.
www.dessertgallery.com
Sara Brook's sexy desserts plus
furniture as art; open late on
weekends, lunch specials. **$**

SHORE ACTIVITIES

Excursions
Houston: Six Flags AstroWorld and
WaterWorld theme parks; Splashtown
water park; Space Center Houston;
Houston Zoo; Museum District;
shopping at The Galleria mall.
Galveston: day trips include the
newly restored beach at 10th Street;
Victorian mansions, shops,
restaurants and bars of the Strand
district; Moody Gardens, a fabulous
interactive natural history exhibition
with designs by NASA; Haak vineyard;
Big Reef Nature Park; local history at
the Texas Seaport Museum.

Best Beach
Galveston, at 10th Street, there are
sunloungers, umbrellas, water
sports, and food vendors on the
beach.

MEXICO & CENTRAL AMERICA

Cozumel, Playa del Carmen and Costa Maya

The Yucatán is a huge, low-lying
peninsula jutting out into the
Gulf of Mexico in the Caribbean.
Rich in antiquities and with fabulous
beaches, world-class diving and a
developed tourism infrastructure, the
area is one of the main destinations for
cruise ships in the western Caribbean.
Ports of entry include Cozumel Island,
nearby Playa del Carmen, a purpose-
built resort 12 miles (19 km) away on
the mainland and Puerto Costa Maya,
a port to the south, on the Costa
Maya, stretching southwards from
Cancún. The most popular shore
excursions are visits to the Mayan
antiquities, which operate from all of
these, although each has its own local
attractions.

ARRIVING BY SEA

Cozumel
Cruise ships dock at the Cozumel
International Pier, a ten-minute drive
from downtown. A ferry makes the
journey to Playa del Carmen
throughout the day, taking around 45
minutes. Some ships dock at Punta
Langosta, closer to downtown San
Miguel. Puerto Costa Maya, a 15-
minute cab ride, is also used, and
finally, large ships may anchor
offshore on a busy day.

Playa del Carmen
Usually a tender port.

Puerto Costa Maya
Cruise ships dock at the new pier.
Most onward transport from here is
with organised shore excursions.
Good access to Cozumel as well as to
Cancún and Playa del Carmen.

PUBLIC HOLIDAYS

6 January: Día de Los Reyes (Day of
the Kings).
17 January: Día de San Antonio Abad
5 February: Constitution Day
24 February: Flag Day
21 March: Birthday of Benito Juarez
April: Santa Samana (pre-Easter Holy
Week)
1 May: Labour Day
3 May: Día de la Cruz (Day of the
Cross)
5 May: Cinco de Mayo
16 September: Independence Day
12 October: Día de la Raza (Columbus
Day)
20 November: Revolution Day
(Anniversary: Revolution of 1910–17)
1 December: Inauguration Day
25 December: Christmas Day

CALENDAR OF EVENTS

Equinox Seasonal Event: **March 21** and
September 21, when a clever illusion
created by the ancient Maya causes a
snake-shaped shadow to fall on the El
Castillo pyramid at Chichén-Itzá.
February/March: Carnival of Cozumel
September: San Miguel Arcangel
Fiesta (Cozumel). Huge festivities in
homage to San Miguel, Cozumel's
patron saint.

2 November: All Souls' Day – Day of
the Dead
12 December: Feast Day of the Virgin
of Guadalupe

MONEY MATTERS

The unit of currency is the Mexican
peso. Banks are open Mon–Fri
9am–4.30pm. The safest and
easiest way to bring money to
Mexico is as dollar travellers'
cheques from a well-known issuer,
in fairly large denominations.
They can be cashed in banks.
If you are bringing cash, the
best place to change your money
is a bank or a *casa de cambio*
(money exchange). You can also
change money at hotels. American
Express will cash personal cheques
for card-holders. Avoid carrying
large amounts of cash; Mexican
pickpockets are efficient.
Major credit cards are widely
accepted in tourist areas but
for public markets and many
smaller, less expensive hotels,
restaurants, and shops you will
have to pay cash.

TOURIST OFFICES

Mexican Government Tourist Offices
(MGTO) are located:
In the UK
Wakefield House, 41 Trinity Square,
London EC3N 4DJ.
Tel: 020-7488 9392.
Fax: 020-7265 0704.
In the US
400 Madison Avenue, Suite 11C,
New York, NY 10017,
Tel: 212-308 2110.
Fax: 212-308 9060.
1880 Century Park East, Suite 511,
Los Angeles, California 90067.
Tel: 213-282 9112.
Fax: 310-282 9116.
5975 Sunset Drive, Suite 305, South
Miami, Florida 33143
Tel: 786-621 2909.
Fax: 786-621 2907.
In Canada
2 Bloor Street West, Suite 1502,
Toronto, Ontario M4W 3E2
Tel: 416-925 0704.
Fax: 416-925 6061.
1 Place Ville Marie, Suite 1931,

Montreal, Quebec H3B 2C3
Tel: 514-871 1103.
Fax: 514-871 3825.
In the Yucatán
The State of Yucatán has a tourist office at Mérida airport (tel: 994 61300) and another in downtown Mérida (corner of calles 60 and 57, tel: 992 49290. In Campeche, the office is on Avda Ruis Cortinex in the Plaza Moch Cuoch (tel/fax: 988 66767). For Chetumal tourist office, tel: 983 20855; fax: 2983 5073.

Websites
www.visitmexico.com
www.cozumelonline.com

POSTAL SERVICES

Post offices usually stay open all day (only mornings on Saturdays) but mail deliveries are slow, and when receiving mail it is safest to have it sent to your hotel. Mail sent to post offices to be picked up (within 10 days) should be addressed to Lista de Correos. Cards and letters to the US cost 2 pesos; to Europe 3 pesos.

TELECOMMUNICATIONS

The country code is 52. The area code for Cozumel is 987; Playa del Carmen's is 984. Mexico's telephone company, Telmex, has installed Ladatel phones in all but the remotest spots in the country. To use one you'll need a phone card, available at newsstands and convenience stores for 30, 50 or 100 pesos. You can make both local and long-distance calls with these cards, if you have enough credit left (shown automatically when you insert the card in the phone). Occasionally you'll even find a coin-operated machine that takes a peso or 50 centavos, but these are exclusively for local and reverse-charge calls. Most hotels also have fax machines, and you may be able to use their facilities. Do note, however, that fax services can be very expensive.

There are numerous internet cafes in both Playa del Carmen and Cozumel.

SHOPPING

It doesn't get much better than Mexico. Look for beautiful ceramics, woodwork, masks, gourd bowls, wooden trays and fine lacquerware; hand-made bird cages; mahogany and cedar furniture; wooden musical instruments; basketware; palm-leaf mats; Panama-style hats; hammocks; rugs; wool, and cotton clothing; embroidery; jewellery. Remember to bargain in markets.

Cozumel's San Miguel and Playa del Carmen have decent shopping. Many cruise lines offer excursions to the huge resort of Cancún specifically for shoppers. In Calica and along the Costa Maya, opportunities are more limited although there are vendors everywhere.

In Playa del Carmen, Avenida 5 and Puerto Antigua are the main shopping areas for handicrafts. Cozumel has a great flea market. Plaza del Sol is just a few minutes' walk from the pier. Duty-free shopping is available in Cancún – look for silver, gold, Kahlua liqueur, traditional Mexican arts and crafts, and hand-rolled cigars.

GETTING AROUND

By Car
You will need a four-wheel drive or a jeep to explore the inland antiquities independently. If you've only got a day, it's better to go on a guided tour. Car hire agencies in Cozumel include: Smart Rent a Car, tel: 872 5651; Hertz, tel: 872 0151; National Car Rental, tel: 872 3263

By Taxi
Cozumel: from Punta Langosta, walk downtown. Otherwise, taxis line up at the International Pier.
Playa del Carmen: taxis line up at the ferry dock.
Puerto Costa Maya: taxis line up at the pier but it is better to take a shore excursion on a day visit as there's not much nearby.

By Ferry
Ferries run between Cozumel and Isla Mujeres, and the Yucatán Peninsula. The latter are mainly passenger ferries, travelling short distances.

There is little in the way of public transport at Playa del Carmen or on the Costa Maya.

Links to the Caribbean
Aeromexico and Aerocaribe operate a comprehensive network of domestic flights, while Aeromexico serves cities all over the world. Short hops around the Caribbean, however, are usually via Miami or Fort Lauderdale.

STAYING ON

There's a huge choice of hotels, from big resorts and tower blocks (in Cancún) to smaller, friendlier inns.

Hotel Prices

Price categories are based on the cost of a double room, for one night:
$ = less than $100
$$ = $100–200
$$$ = more than $200.

Cozumel
Casa del Mar
Carr. a Chankanaab Km 4.
Tel: 872 1900.
Fax: 872 1855
www.casedelmarcozumel.com
Great swim-up bar, on-site dive shop for top diving facilities, and pier. **$$$**
Meliá Cozumel
Costera Nte. 5.8.
Tel: 872 9870.
www.somelia.com
Secluded setting on a very long beach. Golf course. All-inclusive. **$$$**
Safari Inn
Avda Rafael Melgar, between calles 5 and 7 Sur, San Miguel.
Tel:-872 0101.
A prime budget choice for a pleasant room, adjoining dive-shop premises and offering diving packages. **$**
Scuba Club
Carretera Chankanaab Km 1.5.
Tel: 872 0853/872 1800/872 1822.
www.scubaclubcozumel.com
Expert staff make this a favourite with divers. Rate includes meals. **$$$**

Tamarindo Bed & Breakfast
Calle 4 Norte 421.
Tel: 872 3614.
www.cozumel.net/bb/tamarind
Downtown, simple, colourful, friendly,
and very comfortable. **$**

Playa del Carmen
La Posada del Capitán Lafitte
Carretera Puerto Juárez-Tulum Km 62.
Tel: 873 0212.
www.capitanlafitte.com
Cluster of cabañas with air-
conditioning or ceiling fans. Beautiful
beach. Breakfast, dinner and tips
included. **$$$**

Maroma
Carretera Cancún–Tulum Km 51.
30 minutes south of Cancún airport.
Tel: 872 8200.
www.maromahotel.com
A luxurious secluded resort in a
former coconut plantation. Rate
includes breakfast. **$$$$**

Mosquito Blue
Quinta Avenida, between calles 12–14.
Tel: 873 1335/1336.
www.mosquitoblue.com
Cosy hotel at the north end of Playa,
about two blocks from the beach.
Restaurant, pool. **$$–$$$**

Royal Hideaway
Lote Hotelero No 6, Desarollo Playacar.
Tel: 873 4500; US Tel: 800-999 9182.
www.royalhideaway.com
Upscale, all-inclusive resort with many
amenities. **$$$**

WHERE TO EAT

Alongside the usual Mexican
specialities are some tasty local
dishes such as *poc-huc* (marinaded
pork), *pollo pibil* (chicken baked in a
pit), and red snapper stuffed with
vegetables.

Cozumel
La Choza
Calle R. Salas 198 and Avda 10 Norte.
Tel: 872 0958.
www.lachozarestaurant
Some of the best home-cooked
Mexican food in town. **$$**

Las Palmeras
Avda Juárez and Avda Rafael Melgar.
Tel: 872 0532.
Very popular spot for good eating and
people-watching. **$$**

Prima
Calle Rosado Salas 109.
Tel: 872 4242.
Trattoria serving pizzas, including the
Chicago black-pan variety, and
excellent north Italian dishes. **$–$$**

SHORE ACTIVITIES

Excursions
From all three ports
Coach or flightseeing excursions to
Chichen Itza, 100 miles (161 km)
west of Cancún, including a walking
tour of the temples and pyramids;
Tulum ruins (beautiful coastal
location) and Xel-Ha Lagoon; Sian
Ka'an Biosphere Reserve, just south
of Tulum. The Coba Mayan ruins
excursion includes a short hike;
shopping trips to Cancún.

From Cozumel
Day trip around the island, including
San Gervasio ruins deep in the
jungle; Chankanab Nature Park with
jungle trails, a botanical garden with
more than 300 plant species;
Archaeological Park; Cozumel Island
Museum; El Cedral, the oldest Maya
structure on Cozumel; Punta
Celarain, a lighthouse with amazing
views; Punta Sur ec987-o-park with
lagoon, mangrove jungles, white
sand beaches and reefs, and electric
bikes for hire.

From Costa Maya
Off-road jeep safaris through the
jungle; Kohunlich Mayan ruins;
Chacchoben Mayan ruins and
museum tour.

From Playa del Carmen
Xcaret environmental/adventure park,
built along caverns, tunnels and
underground rivers for tubing,
snorkelling, hiking, diving and more.

Best Beaches
Cozumel: Playa San Francisco has a
wide variety of water sports and
restaurants. Also try Playa Mac, Playa
del Sol, Playa Azul, Playa Palancar.
Playa Chen Rio is quieter.
Puerto Costa Maya: There's a beach
club right by the port, with facilities for
everyone including the disabled.

Water Sports
The Mayan coast is one of the
Caribbean's best-known areas for
snorkelling and scuba diving.

From Cozumel
Spend the day exploring Chankanaab
National Park on Cozumel Island or
take the ferry over to Xel-Ha.
Snorkelling trips at both destinations
are widely available. Dive tours are
offered to San Francisco and Palancar
– two of the most popular dive sights
on the island.

From Playa del Carmen
Reef snorkelling or boat trip to
Akumal where there's a sunken
Spanish ship.

Belize

South of Mexico and east of
Guatemala, Belize is best known for
its 185-mile (300-km) coral reef. Back
on the mainland, the coastal and
northern areas of Belize are flat and
hot, mostly made up of mangrove
swamps and lagoons that provide the
spawning environment for marine life.
Further inland, rising to around 3,000
ft (915 metres) above sea level, the
vast central and southern regions are
covered by tropical pine, hardwood
forests and rainforests.

ARRIVING BY SEA

Only small ships can moor up in Belize
City, the main port of call. Others use
tenders. The main points of interest
are outside Belize City but the Belize
Tourism Village, which has over 50
shops, restaurants and tour desks, is
a short hop by water taxi from where
the tenders drop off.

PUBLIC HOLIDAYS

1 January: New Year's Day
9 March: Baron Bliss Day
March/April: Good Friday; Holy Saturday; Easter Sunday; Easter Monday
1 May: Labour Day
24 May: Commonwealth Day
1 September: St. George's Caye Day
21 September: National Independence Day
12 October: Columbus Day
19 November: Garífuna Day
25 December: Christmas Day
26 December: Boxing Day

CALENDAR OF EVENTS

February: Carnival, held one week before Lent
March: Baron Bliss Day celebrations held nationwide to honour this great benefactor of Belize.
May: Cashew Festival, Crooked Tree Village.
Coconut Festival, Caye Caulker.
June: Día de San Pedro – boats and fishermen are blessed, a special Mass is held and and a fiesta/jump-up follows.
August: International Sea and Air Festival, San Pedro. A festival of music, dance, and foods from Belize, Mexico, and neighbouring countries.

MONEY MATTERS

The Belize Dollar (BZ$) has a fixed rate of exchange of BZ$2 to US$1. Most hotels, resorts, restaurants and tour operators will accept US currency, travellers' cheques or credit cards. Always check which dollar rate is being quoted. Banking hours are Mon–Thurs 8am–1pm, Fri 8am–4.30pm.

TOURIST OFFICES

In Belize
Belize Tourist Board,
New Central Bank Bldg, Level 2,
Gabourel Lane, P.O. Box 325,
Belize City.
Tel: 800-624 0686.
Fax: 223 1943.
www.travelbelize.org
Website
www.belizenet.com

POSTAL SERVICES

Belize provides one of the most economical and reliable postal systems in Central America and the country's stamps are amongst the most beautiful in the world, with their depictions of native flora and fauna. There are postal facilities in the Belize Tourism Village, Belize City. The office is open 8am–noon and 1–5pm (until 4.30pm on Fridays).

TELECOMMUNICATIONS

The country code is **501**. Belize Telecommunications Limited provides service between Belize and the United States and Canada. The BTL main offices are located at the corner of Albert and Church streets in Belize City and the corner of Princess Margaret Drive and St Thomas Street. Phone cards are available at numerous locations. There is an internet centre in the Belize Tourism Village.

SHOPPING

Shopping is not spectacular and many goods are imported. Look for Maya-style pottery and slate carving; native Guatemalan handicrafts; Belizean art and music; Maria Sharps Habanero Salsa, a chilli sauce that comes in three different strengths; Belizean rum or cane spirit. Don't buy black-coral or turtle-shell souvenirs because this encourages their depletion, and it is illegal. Most products can be found in the Belize Shopping Village, a local-style mall in Belize City, built with cruise passengers in mind.

GETTING AROUND

By Car
There are plenty of car rental companies but driving outside Belize City is not recommended. It's easy to get lost, there are a lot of remote areas and roads can be bad. On a day trip, a guided tour is recommended. Car rental agencies in Belize City include: Budget Rent A Car, tel: 223 2435; Safari/Hertz, tel: 223 0886; fax: 223 2158; Smith and Sons, tel: 207 0159.

By Taxi
Taxis are available in towns and resort areas and have green licence plates. There are no meters, so always negotiate the fare before you set off.

By Bus
The least expensive way to get around Belize on a day-to-day basis is by bus. Buses run regular schedules and by other Central American standards, Belizean buses are clean, roomy and efficient, although they do get very full. You can view bus timetables online at www.travelbelize.org.

Links to the Caribbean
The following charter/local scheduled airlines have links domestically, and to the Cayes:
Caribee Air Service, tel: 224 4253; Maya Island Air, tel: 800-521 1247, 226 2435; www.mayaairways.com
Javier's Flying Service, tel: 223 5360, www.javiersflying.bz; Tropic Air, tel: 800-422 3435, www.tropicair.com.
Flights to Belize go through Miami, Dallas, Houston and Los Angeles. The major airlines servicing Belize are American Airlines, Continental, Tropic Air *(see above)*, Maya Island Air *(see above)* and Grupo TACA, tel: 227 7363.

Hotel Prices

Price categories are based on the cost of a double room, for one night:
$ = less than $100
$$ = $100–200
$$$ = more than $200.

STAYING ON

Hotels vary from eco-lodges in the rainforest to simple resorts on the Cayes, as well as business properties and guesthouses in the cities.

Belize Biltmore Plaza
Three and a half miles Northern Highway, Belize City.
Tel: 223 2302.
Fax: 223 2301.
www.belizebiltmore.com
E-mail: sales@belizebiltmore.com
Full service colonial-style hotel situated in a quiet residential

area on the outskirts of Belize City. Ideally located for day trips to the nearby Maya ruins and sanctuaries where endangered creatures roam freely in the wild. **$$$**

Caves Branch Jungle Lodge
PO Box 356, Belmopan,
Cayo District, Belize.
Tel: 820 2800.
www.cavesbranch.com
Located on its own 23,472 hectare (58,000 acre) estate in the heart of the Belize jungle, along the banks of the pristine Caves Branch River. Accommodation ranges from camping to basic cabaña suites. Pool, plus river swimming. **$–$$$**

Sunbreeze Hotel
P.O. Box 14, San Pedro Town,
Ambergris Caye.
Tel: 226 2191/800-688 0191.
Fax: 226 2346.
E-mail: sunbreeze@btl.net
www.sunbreeze.net
39 rooms on a beautiful beach on Ambergris Caye, a 75-minute boat ride or short flight from Belize City. Ideal for the barrier reef. **$$**

WHERE TO EAT

Belize's national dish may be rice and beans, but that doesn't mean that local cuisine stops there. Tropical reef fish, lobster and conch (available in season on the cayes and transported across Belize) are luxurious ingredients for a national cuisine. Conch should not be eaten during the out-of-season months of July, August, and September, since it will have been illegally caught. Belize also offers an exotic range of tropical fruits, especially in the interior. Try a "soursap" milkshake, and ask for whatever other unusual produce is the local favourite. Try to experience some of the smaller Belizean restaurants, which is a good way to meet Belizeans and appreciate their friendliness.

Fort Street Restaurant
4 Fort Street.
Tel: 230 116.
Colonial manor house with veranda. Serves mainly seafood but also local specialities such as smoked chicken and pepper-crusted pork chops. **$$**

JB's Watering Hole
P.O. Box 489, Belmopan.
Tel: 820 2071.
Laid-back hang-out outside Belize City serving nachos, burgers, ribs and local specialities. **$**

The Smoky Mermaid
13 Cork Street, Belize City.
Tel: 223 4759.
Housed in an old colonial house and cooled by sea breezes. Creole, local and international dishes. Fine dining at good prices in a cool, tropical setting. **$$**

Meal Prices

Price categories are based on the cost of a meal for one person, excluding drinks:
$ = less than $20
$$ = $20–40
$$$ = more than $40.

SHORE ACTIVITIES

Excursions

Belize City: Fort George, St John's Cathedral, Bliss Institute, Government House. Main attractions are outside the city: Al Tun Ha Mayan antiquities; Río Frio caves; Crooked Tree Wildlife Sanctuary; Belize River; manatee-spotting trips; swimming with sharks and rays; diving on the reef. Action Belize offers pre-bookable excursions and adventure on cruise ship days for independent travellers. Tel: 250 8884; fax: 765-807 3865; www.actionbelize.com.
Belize World Heritage sites, such as the Blue Hole and the Barrier Reef, are easily accessible.

Ideal starting point for high adventure jungle and caving expeditions, especially cave tubing through 6 miles (10 km) of river caves and abseiling over 300 ft (91 metres) into the abyss.

Best Beaches

Take a boat from Belize City to the Cayes. Ambergris Caye has facilities but is still unspoilt; Laughing Bird Caye is pretty and remote; Glover's Reef Atoll is a great picnic spot.

Diving

At almost 300 km (185 miles) long, the coral reef off Belize is second only to Australia's Great Barrier Reef and is a favourite locale for scuba divers. Three of the four major atolls in the Western Hemisphere are located here, including Lighthouse Reef with its nearly perfectly circular, and highly photographed, Blue Hole. The Hole itself is over 135 metres (450 ft) deep. **Sea Sports Belize** (Tel: 501-223 5505) offers trips to nearby spots as well as charter services to outer cayes and atolls.

Honduras: Roatán

Roatán Island is part of the Bay Islands archipelago, some 48 km (30 miles) off the coast of Honduras in the Mesoamerican Barrier Reef – the second-largest reef in the world. The capital is the small town of Coxen Hole.

ARRIVING BY SEA

Ships dock at Coxen Hole, close to the shops and bars of the West End.

PUBLIC HOLIDAYS

1 January: New Year's Day
March/April: Easter
14 April: America's Day
1 May: Labour Day,
15 September: Independence Day,
3 October: Morazan or Soldiers' Day
12 October: Columbus Day,
21 October: Armed Forces Day
25 December: Christmas Day

MONEY MATTERS

The local currency is the lempira, although the US dollar is widely accepted and easy to exchange.

TOURIST INFORMATION

The best information is provided online by independent websites. Try:
www.roatanonline.com
www.roatanet.com
www.bayislandtourism.com

POSTAL SERVICES

There are postal facilities in Coxen Hole.

TELECOMMUNICATIONS

The dialling code for Honduras is **504**. You can dial direct from some of the larger hotels and from payphones in Coxen Hole.
There is internet access at Internet Cafe, Thicket Mouth Road, J.C. Commercial Center, Coxen Hole. Tel: 445 1241. Fax: 445 1611.

SHOPPING

Hammocks, arts and crafts, wood carvings, and quilts are good buys. Shopping areas include Coxen Hole, the West End, French Harbour and Punta Gorda.

GETTING AROUND

By Car

The island is only about 30 miles (48 km) long and exploration is easy. Consider a moped or bicycle, available in Coxen Hole. Car hire firms: Toyota, tel: 445 1166; Avis, tel: 445 1568.

By Taxi and Bus

Taxis can be hailed in towns – they will sound their horns if they are free. The first place you are likely to find one is a short distance from the ship on the paved road to Coxen Hole. Agree the rate before setting off.
Dark blue minibuses serve the West End – simply wave to stop one. They are cheaper than taxis around town but for a trip further afield, take a private taxi. Pay in local currency.
There's also a water taxi service between West End and West Bay. You can take a water taxi elsewhere, but negotiate the fare first.

Links to the Caribbean

There are direct air services to Roatán from Miami and Houston with TACA, Honduras, tel: 550 8222 or 234 2422. Sol Air also plans to introduce services from Miami and Dallas/Fort Worth. All other flights are via the Honduras mainland.

The ferry, *Galaxy*, travels between the Bay Islands and La Ceiba on the mainland of Honduras, a 1½-hour trip. Tel: 445 1795.

STAYING ON

Accommodation is in attractive villas and beach huts – there are no high rises on Roatán yet.
Coral Gardens Resort
West End, Roatán.
Tel: 445 1428.
Located on Mangrove Bight overlooking the Caribbean Sea. All 22 rooms have ocean views. Superb restaurant and dive centre with dive boats on site. **$$**
Island Pearl
West Bay Beach, Roatán.
Tel/Fax: 978 6955/403 8020.
www.roatanpearl.com
Four charming cottages in romantic setting on West Bay Beach. Beautiful interiors and very peaceful location. Ideal for honeymooners. **$$**
Roatán Vista Villas
Sandy Bay
The Bay Islands, Roatán.
Tel: 445 1498 or in the US 202-342 0191
www.roatanisland.net
Private villas in a beautiful setting on Sandy Bay on Roatán Island, surrounded by hibiscus and banana palms and close to the best dive sites. The owner also rents out beach cottages and studio apartments. **$$**

Hotel Prices

Price categories are based on the cost of a double room, for one night:
$ = less than $100
$$ = $100–200
$$$ = more than $200.

WHERE TO EAT

Beans and rice is the staple diet, although mango-glazed chicken and conch soup are worth a try. Restaurants tend to be basic beach shacks, mainly in fabulous settings, or small establishments in town.

Bite on the Beach
West Bay Beach, Roatán.
Local specialities and cold beers right on the beach where the water taxis dock. Take your snorkel gear along. **$**
Cindy's Island Restaurant
West End (opp. Sueno del Mar dive shop).
Rustic place serving fabulous island food and lobster on the patio. Most of the fish on the menu are caught by Cindy's husband Ed. **$**

Meal Prices

Price categories are based on the cost of a meal for one person, excluding drinks:
$ = less than $20
$$ = $20–40
$$$ = more than $40.

Qué Tal Cafe
Coxen Hole (next to the Casi Todo bookstore).
Tel: 445 1007.
Deli food, fresh fruit, home baking – an ideal place for a light lunch. **$**

SHORE ACTIVITIES

Excursions

An tour of unspoilt Roatán can include a visit to Garífuna fishing villages, the Tropical Treasure Bird Park, with its large colourful parrot collection, Carambola Gardens, or Jonesville, a stilt village. Snorkelling and diving around the spectacular coral reef is popular, so is lazing on the beach. The Institute of Marine Sciences runs dolphin shows and encounters. Visitors can also see the Museum of Roatán, or hike the island's interior.

Best Beaches

Tabyana Beach, a short drive from Coxen Hole, has beautiful white sand and easy access to the barrier reef.

Water Sports

Happy Divers, offers a full range of dives using its own boat and PADI-qualified instructors. Next to Rudy's Restaurant in West End, tel: 445 1794.
For parasailing, scuba diving and fishing, try **Native Sons Water Sports**, tel: 445 4003

Costa Rica

Costa Rica has more than 1,200 km (750 miles) of Caribbean and Pacific coastline. Here you will find every kind of terrain from rain- and cloud-forest-cloaked mountains to savanna and tropical beaches. The capital is San Jose. Costa Rica has made a name for itself recently as a destination for adventure sports and wildlife tours in an eco-friendly setting.

Cruise ships call at Puerto Limón on the Caribbean coast. This is a large, industrial port city with a population of 170,000, known principally as a banana and grain exporting centre. A number of national parks are within easy reach of the town and form the basis of most shore excursions.

ARRIVING BY SEA

Cruise ships dock at Puerto Limón and the majority of passengers are ferried off immediately on excursions.

PUBLIC HOLIDAYS

1 January: New Year's Day
March/April: Easter
11 April: Anniversary of the Battle of Rivas (banks remain open)
1 May: Labour Day
29 June: St Peter and St Paul
25 July: Anniversary of the Annexation of Guanacaste Province
2 August: Our Lady of the Angels (banks remain open)
15 August: Assumption/Mothers' Day
15 September: Independence Day
8 December: Immaculate Conception (banks remain open)
24 December: Christmas Eve (banks remain open)
25 December: Christmas Day
28–31 December: Christmas Holiday

CALENDAR OF EVENTS

March: National Craft Fair, San José
October: Carnival, Puerto Limón
31 December: New Year's Eve

MONEY MATTERS

The currency unit is the colón. The current rate of exchange can be found in the English-language *Tico Times* business pages or the same section of the daily *La Nación*. Cash machines are available in the biggest shopping centres and credit cards are widely accepted. Banking hours are Mon–Fri 9am–3pm. Private banks are a better option for changing dollars and dollar travellers' cheques than state banks, which are terribly slow in exchanging currency (having to wait in line for two or more hours is not uncommon).

TOURIST OFFICES

Costa Rican Tourist Institute (Instituto Costarricense de Turismo), Apdo 506-777 1000, San José, Tel/fax: 506-223 1753, 800-343 6332.
Website
www.visitcostarica.com

POSTAL SERVICES

There are postal and telegraph offices in cities and villages throughout the country, open Mon–Fri.

TELECOMMUNICATIONS

The dialling code is **506**. Some, but not all, payphones support IDD. Dial 001 and then the country code. Public phones require a coin or card deposit before dialling a direct access number. Calls from hotels are very expensive.

Long-distance access numbers include: **British Telecom**: 167; **Canada Telecom**: 161; **AT&T Direct**: 0-800 0 114 114; **US AT&T**: 114; **US MCI**: 162; **US Sprint**: 163.

Internet facilities are available at: **ATEC**, Puerto Viejo de Limón, tel/fax: 750 0188; www.greencoast.com/atec.htm

SHOPPING

There are street vendors everywhere, particularly in the tourist areas. Look for wooden items, including bowls, plates, cutting boards and boxes; leather bags, wallets, and briefcases; woven bags; jewellery; and handmade paper. Coffee and coffee liqueurs also make good souvenirs. Do not buy coral, tortoiseshell items, furs, or alligator or lizard skins.

GETTING AROUND

By Car

By far the best way to get around on a brief visit is to take a shore excursion. For touring the country, a four-wheel drive is recommended. Roads are but can be rough in places. Visitors can drive with an international driving licence. All hire companies have their head office in San José; call first for details of rentals in Puerto Limón. In San José: Adobe Rent-a-Car, Downtown, tel: 258 4242; Europcar, Paseo Colón, between 36th and 38th streets, tel: 257 1158.

By Taxi

Taxis wait at the port when ships call. Always agree the price beforehand. Taxis can represent good value for sightseeing.

By Bus

Buses are operated by private companies which link San José with the principal provincial towns and cities, seaports and tourist areas. With good-quality vehicles and frequent buses, travel around the country is relatively easy.

Links to the Caribbean

Most Latin American carriers fly regularly to San José. The two Costa Rican Airlines, LASCA and Aero Costa Rica, connect with many points in the US and code-share with several US carriers, including Delta, Northwest, and TWA. International airlines serving San José include American, Continental, Iberia, KLM and LTU. American carriers fly from Miami, Atlanta, New York, Dallas, Houston and Mexico City.

STAYING ON

It is advisable to book ahead for the big luxury hotels, especially during high season.

Chalet and Cabinas Hibiscus
Playa Negra, Cahuita,
Puerto Limón.
Tel: 755 0021.
Email: hibiscus@racsa.co.cr
Small hotel on Cahuita beach, with swimming and bike hire. **$**

Oasys del Caribe
Carrer Portete, Puerto Limón.
Tel: 795 0024.
Garden chalets, a restaurant and
pool, 10 minutes from Limón. **$**
Pachira Lodge
PO Box 1818-1002,
San Jose.
Tel: 223 1682/800-644 7488
www.pachiralodge.com.
Pretty lodge in Tortuguero, in 34 acres
(14 hectares) of gardens, 5 minutes
from the park entrance. Buffet-style
meals, fishing and turtle-spotting
tours included. **$$**

WHERE TO EAT

Local specialities have a Caribbean
flavour and include *casado* (rice,
beans, stewed beef, plantains and
cabbage); *Olla de Came* (beef and
plantain soup); and *sopa negra*, a rich
black bean soup. *Agua de sapo* (toad
water) is a refreshment prepared with
lemon juice, molasses, ginger and rum.

Hotel Prices

Price categories are based on the
cost of a double room, for one
night:
$ = less than $100
$$ = $100–200
$$$ = more than $200.

The Red Stripe Cafe
In front of the bus stop of Puerto Viejo
Open daily from 6am for a breakfast
of *gallo pinto* and coffee. Lunch and
dinner menu of soup and fish. **$**
Elenas (Caribbean)
Chiquita Beach, Limón.
Tel: 750 0265.
Live music and satellite TV. A popular
stop on the way to Puerto Viejo. **$$**

SHORE ACTIVITIES

Excursions
Coastal tour with jungle scenery,
handicraft shopping and lunch;
rainforest aerial tramway; hiking in the
Río Dante rainforest with a guide;
canoe excursion along the Tortuguero
Canal to spot wildlife; white-water
rafting; banana plantation visits.

Best Beaches
Cahuita National Park borders the
beaches which give access to the
coastline's only coral reefs. Puerto
Viejo, close to the town, is also a
good bet for a day trip. Tortuguero, to
the north, is only accessible by boat
or plane; turtles, caimans and
manatees can be spotted here. Barra
del Colorado is best for fishing and
has several luxurious fishing lodges.

Sports
Hiking, horse riding, white-water
rafting, canoeing and golf can all be
arranged. Hire scuba and snorkelling
equipment on Cahuita beach.

Venezuela: Isla Margarita

Margarita Island, a 20-ft by 42-ft (32-
km by 67-km) holiday resort off the
north coast of South America, is the
main beach escape for Venezuelans. It
consists of two islands, linked by a
narrow sandspit and a bridge. The
western region is dry and hot, while
the more developed east, where the
main port, Porlamar, is located, is
more mountainous, with rainforest.

ARRIVING BY SEA

An ambitious waterfront market-cruise
port is under construction in Porlamar.
In the meantime, cruise ships arrive in
Guamache (near Margarita's ferry
dock), 30 minutes away by taxi or bus.

PUBLIC HOLIDAYS

1 January: New Year's Day
February/March: Carnival (Monday
and Tuesday before Ash Wednesday)
March/April: Thursday and Friday of
Holy Week (Easter week)
19 April: National Declaration of
Independence
1 May: Labour Day
24 June: St John the Baptist day
5 and 24 July: Signing of National
Independence Act; Birth of Simon
Bolívar (24th)
12 October: Columbus Day
25 December: Christmas Day

CALENDAR OF EVENTS

February: Carnival – before Ash
Wednesday
March/April: Easter – parades and
solemn ceremonies
24 June: St John the Baptist day
14 August: Feast of the Assumption
31 December: New Year's Eve –
traditional festivities

MONEY MATTERS

The unit of currency is the bolivar.
Beware of 5,000 and 10,000 notes;
many are forged. ATMs, too, may have
been tampered with, so beware.
Change money using a Visa or
MasterCard and keep exchange
receipts for conversion of bolivars
back into dollars. Credit cards are
accepted in most tourist destinations.

TOURIST OFFICES

In the US
Venezuelan Tourism Association,
1101 Brickell Ave, #901, Miami,
Florida 33139.
Tel: 577 4214.
Fax: 372 5167
In Venezuela
Corpoturismo, Torre Oeste Piso,
Parque Central, Caracas.
Tel: 507 8815.
Fax: 573 8989.
In Isla Margarita
There is an information booth at the
airport. Hotels are also a good bet.
Websites
www.islamargarita.com
www.margaritaonline.com

POSTAL SERVICES

You can send postcards from Margarita
– there is a post office in Porlamar.

TELECOMMUNICATIONS

The international dialling code is **58**
and the area code for Margarita is
295. Most phones can be used to dial
direct internationally; buy a CANTV
tarjeta (phone card) to use a public
phone. Email is becoming more
commonplace but internet cafes come
and go. There are several in Porlamar
and Playa del Agua.

SHOPPING

Margarita is duty-free, so electronics, jewellery, cosmetics, perfumes, designer clothes and spirits are cheap. Bargain for jewellery and make sure it comes with a guarantee. The main shopping district is Porlamar, which is packed with duty-free outlets.

GETTING AROUND

By Car

Visitors will need an international driving licence. Roads are generally good, although signposting is erratic, and driving at night can be risky. Try Baveca Rent-a-Car, tel: 249 1651.

By Taxi

Taxis can be hailed in towns but are unmetered so negotiate fares before you set off.

By Bus

Buses are cheap, crowded and serve most of the island. Bus stops can vary from driver to driver – this is not a quick way to get around.

Links to the Caribbean

Conferry offers a service for cars and passengers between Margarita and the mainland, tel: 239 8340/8148, www.conferry.com. There are good domestic air connections to Caracas and many charter companies offer day trips by air into southern Venezuela to Canaima for the Angel Falls. Try Aerotuy, tel: 895-632 211; www.tuy.com. Aeropostal also flies to Barbados and Trinidad.

STAYING ON

Accommodation on Margarita tends to be mass market, low-grade hotels, some with all-inclusive packages. Prices are quoted in US$, but payable in bolívars at the exchange rate of the day. When verifying prices, ask if taxes are included – if not, pay 15 per cent more.

Hotel Bella Vista

End of Avda Santiago Mariño, Porlamar. Tel: 261 7222/4157. Fax: 261 2557. www.hbellavista.com. Four-star pioneer of the luxury tourist

hotels, built in the late 1950s. Directly on the beach and adjacent to the prime duty-free shopping area, near main restaurants and night entertainment. **$$$**

La Samanna

Avda Bolívar at Francisco Esteban, Gómez, Urb Costa Azul. Tel: 262 2212. www.lasamannademargarita.com Luxury lodging aimed at clients using the adjoining Thalassotherapy centre. Restaurants, piano bar, shops. **$$$**

La Casona da Chef Huguito

Calle Miranda, San Juan Bautista. Tel/Fax: 0295-259 0040. www.posadachefhuguito.netfirms.com Quiet village near airport and ferry. Large yet cosy complex of apartments, balcony, kitchen; pool and tropical garden, restaurant and bar. Breakfast included. **$$$**

WHERE TO EAT

Cheers

Avda Santiago Mariño. Tel: 261 0957. Spacious (but busy) restaurant, divided into sections. Good food by day; casual, sociable atmosphere at night, with live music; in an area popular for bar-hopping. **$$**

Cocody

Avda Raúl Leoni, sector Bella Vista. Tel: 261 8431. A taste of France in the Caribbean, romantic terrace with tropical atmosphere. **$$$**

Dady's Latino

Avda 4 de Mayo, in the new Jumbo Ciudad Comercial (shopping centre). Tel: 265 9405. Dining by day complete with tuxedoed waiters and table-side preparation. **$$**

La Atarraya de las 15 Letras

Calle San Rafael at Charaima. Tel: 261 5124. Typical margariteña and criolla cuisine. **$**

Margaritaville

Entry beside Señor Frog (Avda Bolivar, C.C. Costa Azul). Large complex of indigenous-style *churuatas* with attractive indoor/ outdoor restaurant, handicrafts shops and more – definitely worth a visit.

Meal Prices

Price categories are based on the cost of a meal for one person, excluding drinks:
$ = less than $20
$$ = $20–40
$$$ = more than $40.

Mosquito Beach Club

Playa Caribe
(1 mile/2 km east of Juan Griego). On the beach where the young and beautiful go to play. The restaurant has seafood, burgers and salads. Changing rooms, showers and sun shades. Lively at night, with music and dancing. Bilingual staff. **$$**

SHORE ACTIVITIES

Excursions

Island tours, day trips to Canaima/Angel Falls, longer trips to the Orinoco Delta, Parque del Agua water park for kids; Los Roques national park; boats to Isla de Coche; Los Frailes islands; boat trips.

Best Beaches

Playa del Agua for facilities and a long, clean strip of sand; Coche Island; Moreno and El Yaque for windsurfing.

Water Sports

For diving trips try **Atlantis Diving Center**, Centro Comercial Turistico, Playa El Agua, Avda 31 de Julio, tel: 249 1325. Windsurfing equipment for hire on Playa del Agua beach and at Moreno.

Horse Riding

For countryside hacks and beach rides, contact Dan and Trudy O'Brien, tel: 249 0558; email: obrien1@casatrudel.com; www.casatrudel.com.

Other Sports

Parapenting and ultra-light aircraft are popular for sightseeing. There are bungee jumps at Playa del Agua and Parguito beaches.

THE CARIBBEAN

Grand Cayman

Grand Cayman is a green, luxuriant island, the largest in the archipelago of three which make up the Cayman Islands, south of Cuba and northwest of Jamaica. The island is famous for its diving, its conservation efforts, and as an offshore financial centre. It is well-developed for tourism and represents a charming, safe port of call that is easy to explore independently. However, in 2004 Hurricane Ivan caused extensive damage and as a result some attractions and services listed here may be affected.

ARRIVING BY SEA

Cruise ships dock in downtown George Town, within easy walking distance of the shops and the beginning of Seven Mile Beach.

PUBLIC HOLIDAYS

1 January: New Year's Day
February/March: Ash Wednesday
March/April: Good Friday, Easter Monday
May: (3rd Monday) Discovery Day
May/June: Whit Monday
June: (Monday following second Saturday) Queen's Birthday
July: (1st Monday): Constitution Day
11 November: Rememberance Day
25 December: Christmas Day

CALENDAR OF EVENTS

January: Underwater film festival
May: Seafarers' festival
October: Pirates' week
October: Annual turtle release

MONEY MATTERS

The unit of currency is the Cayman Islands dollar. US dollars are widely accepted, as are credit cards.

TOURIST OFFICES

In Canada
234 Eglinton Avenue East, Suite 306, Toronto, Ontario M4P 1K5.
Tel: 416-485 1550.
Fax: 416-485 7578.
In Canada, tel: 800-263 5805.
In the UK
Cayman Islands Department of Tourism, 6 Arlington Street, London SW1A IRE.
Tel: 020-7491 7771.
Fax: 020-7409 7773.
In the US
Doral Centre, 8300 N.W. 53rd Street, Suite 103 Miami, FL 33166.
Tel: 305-599 9033.
Fax: 305-599 3766.
3 Park Avenue, 39th Floor, New York, NY 10016.
Tel: 212-889 9009.
Fax: 212-889 9125.
In Grand Cayman
There is a tourist information office at North Terminal cruise ship dock in George Town Harbour. The head office is located at:
The Pavilion, Cricket Square, Elgin Avenue, George Town, P.O. Box 67 GT, Grand Cayman, BWI
Tel: 949 0623; fax: 949 4053.

Websites
www.caymanislands.co.uk
www.caymanislands.ky

POSTAL SERVICES

Branches of the Philatelic Bureau are located in the main post office in George Town and the Westshore branch on West Bay Road. There's also a tiny post office in Hell, which will postmark your cards "from Hell".

TELECOMMUNICATIONS

Modern telephone service is available 24 hours a day, with international direct dialling.
The area code for the Cayman Islands is **345**. CardPhone service is now available at select locations on all three islands. Pre-paid phone cards in values of CI$10, CI$15 and CI$30 can be purchased at the Cable and Wireless main office in Anderson Square in George Town.

Important long-distance access numbers include **AT&T USA DIRECT**: 800-872 2881; **US SPRINT**,888-366 4663 and **MCI DIRECT**: 800-624 1000.
Internet access is available at: Chelsea's Sports Bar & Billiards, tel: 949 8042
Cable & Wireless (CI) Ltd, tel: 949 7800; fax: 949 5472.

SHOPPING

Good things to buy in Grand Cayman include jewellery, antiques, old maps, perfumes, cosmetics, gemstones, local paintings, rugs, sculpture and rum cakes. You'll find everything you need in George Town, and volcanic gifts and gimmicks at Hell.

GETTING AROUND

By Car

Driving is on the left. Drivers must be at least 25. The island is easy to get around by car, scooter or bicycle. Car hire firms include Dollar Rent a Car, tel: 949 4790/0700; Sunshine Car Rentals, tel: 949 3858.

By Taxi

Taxis are available the cruise dock and there's a sign showing current rates.

By Bus

The bus terminal is located adjacent to the public library on Edward Street in downtown George Town and serves as the dispatch point for buses to all districts. There are 38 mini-buses operated by 24 licensed operators, serving eight routes. Daily service starts at 6am from the depot.
The system uses colour-coded logos displayed on the front and rear of buses to identify routes. Licensed buses are identified by blue licence plates. Tel: 945 5100.

Inter-Island Links

Cayman Airways, (in Miami), the Cayman Islands' national flag carrier operates jet services (on 737-200 aircraft) between Grand Cayman and Miami, Tampa, Houston and Kingston (Jamaica). It also operates jet services from Grand Cayman to Cayman Brac.
Tel: 949 8200.

Island Air operates four daily scheduled flights between Grand Cayman, Cayman Brac and Little Cayman. Day trips and private charters are also available, tel: 949 5252; fax: 949 7044.

STAYING ON

Hotels range from small guest houses and beach villas to large resorts.

Annie's Place
282 Andrew Drive,
Snug Harbour, Grand Cayman.
Tel: 945 5693.
Fax: 945 4547.
E-mail: ampm@candw.ky
A select guesthouse within four blocks of Seven Mile Beach. Designer-furnished rooms, en-suite bathrooms. Dine in a formal dining room or a relaxed area off the courtyard. **$$**

Treasure Island Resort
269 West Bay Road,
Grand Cayman.
Tel: 949 7777.
Large casual resort. All rooms have a private patio or balcony, air-conditioning, ceiling fan, satellite TV, direct-dial telephones and an in-room safe (for an extra charge). **$$**

Hotel Prices

Price categories are based on the cost of a double room, for one night:
$ = less than $100
$$ = $100–200
$$$ = more than $200.

Westin Casuarina
West Bay Road SMB, Grand Cayman.
Tel: 945 3800.
US Reservations: 800-WESTIN
www.westincasuarina.com
Large hotel on Seven Mile Beach with luxurious rooms. Tropical gardens with waterfalls and fountains, freshwater pools, whirlpools, restaurants with indoor and outdoor seating, 24-hour room service, swim-up pool bar, a dive shop and luxury spa. **$$$**

WHERE TO EAT

There's a good range of cafes, bars, and restaurants – many specialising in seafood.

Meal Prices

Price categories are based on the cost of a meal for one person, excluding drinks:
$ = less than $20
$$ = $20–40
$$$ = more than $40.

Chicken! Chicken!
West Shore Center, West Bay Road.
Tel: 945 2290.
Caribbean wood-roasted chicken, salads, and homemade Caribbean-style cornbread. **$**

Cracked Conch by the Sea
West Bay, George Town.
Tel: 945 5217.
www.crackedconch.ky
Famous for fresh seafood and "jerk" dishes, also turtle, conch, charbroiled steaks, chicken, pastas, salads and Caribbean wraps.

Grand Old House
Waters Edge, Old Plantation House, George Town.
Tel: 949 9333/547 0658.
www.grandoldhouse.com
Elegant lunch dining featuring Caribbean fusion specialities. **$$$**

SHORE ACTIVITIES

Excursions
Relax on Seven Mile Beach, or see the volcanic rocks at Hell, less than a mile away is the Cayman Turtle Farm. An island tour can also include a trip to Queen Elizabeth II Botanic Park or the Pedro St. James historic monmument. A boat trip that always gets booked up is to Stingray City to feed the stingrays.

Best Beaches
Seven Mile Beach has everything – space, restaurants, water sports, snorkelling and clean sand.

Water Sports
For diving, try Bob Soto's

(tel: 800-262 7686/345-949 2022; www.bobsotoreefdivers.com). The Cayman Islands has superb wall dives and wrecks. Equipment for other sports can be rented by the day on Seven Mile Beach.

Golf
There are three golf courses: Safehaven; Britannia; and the Sunrise Family Golf Centre.

Jamaica

A vibrant island rich in culture and colour, situated 90 miles (145 km) south of Cuba and 100 miles (161 km) west of Haiti, Jamaica is a large, fertile island cloaked in dense rainforest, the long spine of the Blue Mountain range at its centre. The main resorts are located along the north coast.

ARRIVING BY SEA

Cruise ships dock at Ocho Rios and Montego Bay.

Ocho Rios
The cruise terminal is located on the edge of town and has telephones, toilets, an information desk and outside, a taxi rank.

Montego Bay
Cruise ships dock at the multimillion dollar Freeport complex, on a spit of reclaimed land to the west of the bay. Most ships run a shuttle service for the 20-minute journey into town; failing this, there will be a long line of willing taxi drivers outside the terminal.

PUBLIC HOLIDAYS

1 January: New Year's Day
February/March: Ash Wednesday
March/April: Good Friday, Easter Monday
23 May: Labour Day
1 August: Emancipation Day
6 August: Independence Day
October (3rd Monday): National Heroes' Day
25 December: Christmas Day
26 December: Boxing Day

CALENDAR OF EVENTS

March: Gospel spring festival
March/April: Carnival is Jamaica's biggest festival. Held the week after Easter in Kingston and Chukka Cove. the week after Easter.
June: Ocho Rios jazz festival
July: International Reggae Day and Reggae Sumfest
August: Breadfruit festival
October: Port Antonio Marlin Tournament
November: Film and music festival

MONEY MATTERS

The currency is the Jamaican dollar (J$). US dollars are widely accepted, with change given in Jamaican dollars. Credit cards are widely accepted, too, and there are exchange facilities in all the main tourist areas.

TOURIST OFFICES

In Canada
303 Eglinton Avenue E, Suite 200, Toronto, Ontario M4P 1L3.
Tel: 416-482 7850.
In the UK
1–2 Prince Consort Road, London SW7 2BZ.
Tel: 020-7224 0505.
In the US
1320 South Dixie Highway, Suite 1101, Coral Gables, FL 33146.
Tel: 305-665 0557.
In Jamaica
Cornwall Beach, P.O. Box 67, Montego Bay.
Tel: 876-952 4425.
Ocean Village Shopping Centre PO Box 240, Ocho Rios.
Tel: 974 2582.

Website
www.visitjamaica.com

POSTAL SERVICES

There are postal facilities in Ocho Rios and Montego Bay centre.

TELECOMMUNICATIONS

Jamaica's dialling code is **876**. International cables and inland telegrams can be sent from most hotels and post offices. Direct international telephone service operates 24 hours a day. There are internet cafes and calling offices in Ocho Rios and Montego Bay.

SHOPPING

Local crafts include "Annabella" boxes made of wood and painted, or otherwise adorned by hand; pimento-filled Spanish jars; beautiful hand-embroidered linens with motifs of birds and flora; silk and cotton hand-painted or batiked in daring colours; wood carvings; paintings; and excellent pottery/ceramics. Lignum vitae, an extremely hard and heavy wood, with a dark-to-black centre and light-to-yellow edge, is used in a lot of the carvings, some excellent, and it makes very useful and unusual chopping boards. Also look for Reggae to Wear clothing, Jamaican fragrances (White Witch, Pirate's Gold, Khus Khus, Jamaica Island Lyme and Jamaica Island Bay Rum) and handmade soaps in unusual fragrances (cerasee and mint, mint and bay, ortanique). A special favourite is Starfish Aromatic Oils' Blue Mountain coffee candle, which can permeate your kitchen with the aroma of freshly brewed coffee. Rums and liqueurs, reggae music, Blue Mountain coffee and cigars also make good souvenirs.

In Ocho Rios, visit the craft market on Main Street and shops on Pineapple Place. Harmony Hall has a good selection of the best island crafts. In Montego Bay, there are shops all along Gloucester Avenue.

GETTING AROUND

By Car

Driving is on the left. To hire any vehicle, visitors may use a driving licence (valid for at least 12 months) for up to a 3-month period. Drivers must be at least 25 years of age to hire a car and must post a bond to meet insurance regulations with cash, major credit card, or travellers' cheques. Service stations are open daily and will only accept cash. Distances are long between the main attractions and roads are potholed. It is not worth hiring a car for a day visit. Take an excursion or a taxi instead. Many visitors do, however, hire cars for an extended stay. Hire companies include Island Car Rentals, tel: 929 5875; Rainbow Car Rental & Tours, tel: 974 7114

By Taxi

Taxis wait at the cruise terminals and have predetermined rates between one location and another. All cabs have red PPV plates (Public Passenger Vehicle) along with ordinary licence plates.

By Bus

Limousines, air-conditioned coaches, and local bus services connect all villages, cities and towns. The buses are a colourful, if time-consuming way of exploring the island.

By Air

Air Jamaica Express operates from Montego Bay and Kingston to all areas in Jamaica with landing fields, on a daily basis. For more information call 876-922 4661, email: www.airjamaica.com.

Inter-Island Links

Air Jamaica, tel: 800-523 5585, flies all over the world. Locally, Cayman Airways, tel: 345-949 8200, serves the Cayman Islands; Copa, tel: 800-234 2672 or 800-231 0856 flies to Panama, Colombia, Peru and Ecuador; Cubana, tel: 345-949 4606, flies to Havana; Air Jamaica Express, tel: 876-923 8680 or 800-523 5585, serves Santo Domingo, Grand Cayman, Belize; and BWIA, tel: 876-929 4231/3, flies from Kingston to Antigua, Barbados, Port of Spain, St Maarten and St Lucia.

STAYING ON

Jamaican hotels range from small inns to some of the finest resorts in the Caribbean.

Ocho Rios

Sand Castles
Main Street, Ocho Rios.
Tel: 800-284 3515.
www.sandcastlesochorios.com
Large child-friendly resort with restaurant, pool and kids club. Self catering or full board options. **$$$**

Sandals Dunn's River
Mamme Bay, Ocho Rios.
Tel: 972 1610/1612.
Fax: 972 1611.
www.sandals.com
Large, luxury couples-only all-inclusive resort. Part of a chain with a reputation for good service. Another branch of Sandals at Main Street. **$$$**

Hotel Prices

Price categories are based on the cost of a double room, for one night:
$ = less than $100
$$ = $100–200
$$$ = more than $200.

Montego Bay Area

Coral Cliff Hotel
165 Gloucester Ave, Montego Bay.
Tel: 952 4130.
Fax: 952 6532.
A 22-room colonial-style hotel with a pool, restaurant and bar overlooking the bay. One mile from town and two minutes from Doctor's Cave Beach. **$$**

Half Moon Resort
Rose Hall, Montego Bay.
Tel: 953 2211.
Fax: 953 2731.
www.halfmoon-resort.com
Lavish resort on a beautiful 400-acre (162-hectare) estate, with a mile-long white sand beach. An 18-hole championship golf course, golf academy, tennis and water sports. **$$$**

WHERE TO EAT

Ocho Rios

Evita's Italian Restaurant
Eden Bower Road.
Tel: 974 2333.
Authentic Italian food with house specialities Rasta Pasta, Pasta Viagra and Jerk Spaghetti. Fresh homemade pasta. Try the "Jamaican Bobsled" for dessert. A popular restaurant overlooking Ocho Rios. **$$**

The Mug Restaurant
On the Ocho Rios Highway,
St Ann's Bay.
Tel: 972 1018.
A pleasant place for lunch on the water's edge. Fish, conch and other Jamaican favourites. **$$**

The Ruins
Da Costa Drive, Ocho Rios.
Tel: 974 8888/4729.
A waterfall cascades 40 ft (12 metres) into pools surrounding the dining terrace. Jamaican and international cuisine with traditional island recipes. **$$$**

Montego Bay Area

Belfield Restaurant
Barnett Estate.
Tel: 952 2382.
Step back in time to enjoy fine Jamaican cuisine in a restored sugar mill on the 3,000-acre (1,200-hectare) Barnett Estate. **$$$**

Nikita's
Doctor's Cave Beach Hotel,
Gloucester Avenue.
Tel: 952 7838.
Centrally located. Upscale Italian restaurant. Open daily. **$–$$$**

The Pelican
Gloucester Avenue.
Tel: 952 3171.
A longtime favourite of locals and visitors as well, for its hearty Jamaican food, especially breakfast. Popular American dishes too. Good value. **$$**

Meal Prices

Price categories are based on the cost of a meal for one person, excluding drinks:
$ = less than $20
$$ = $20–40
$$$ = more than $40.

SHORE ACTIVITIES

Excursions

From Ocho Rios
One of the islands most visited attractions is Dunn's River Falls; you can tour the working Prospect Plantation or lunch at Harmony Hall, formerly a great house and now an art gallery and restaurant. Nature lovers can drive through lush Fern Gully or see the pretty Shaw Park Gardens, Coyaba River Garden and Museum, or take a rural cycling tour. Overlooking Ocho Rios is Firefly, Noel Coward's beautiful house, open to the public.

From Montego Bay
There are historic walking tours of the town, better known for duty-free shopping. There are also guided tours of the great houses: Rose Hall and Greenwood. Take a relaxing river rafting trip along the Martha Brae.

Best Beaches

Ocho Rios Area
James Bond Beach Club, Oracabessa.
Tel: 726 1630. Open 9am–6pm, closed for clean-up on Mondays except public holidays. Entrance fee. Water sports; Jet Ski Safari, three magnificent white-sand beaches ring this private peninsula, 20 minutes from Ocho Rios. Restaurant/bar; marina facilities.

Montego Bay Area
Doctor's Cave Beach, with its white-sand and clear-water believed to be fed by mineral springs. Open 8.30am–6.30pm daily. Entrance fee. Tel: 952 2566; www.doctorscavebathingclub.com. Rose Hall Beach Club: with volleyball, other games and water sports. Two bars and restaurant. Entrance fee. Tel: 953 9982.

Port Antonio Area (for longer stays)
Portland's beaches are incomparable; those at Frenchman's Cove and Dragons Bay are considered among the finest in the world. Boston Beach is popular for bathing, and the waves are high enough for surfing.

Water Sports

There are hire facilities at all the main beaches, including Doctor's Cave and James Bond Beach.

Horse Riding

Chukka Cove, 11 miles (7 km) west of Ocho Rios (tel: 972 2506; www.chukkacaribbean.com), has extensive polo facilities. But for day visitors, the most popular activity is countryside and beach rides of varying length by horse. Lessons available.

Golf

Jamaica is home to several excellent courses: two of the most prestigious are Half Moon (tel: 953 2211) and Tryall (tel: 956 5681 or 956 5662 ext 202). Book tee times well in advance, either through the ship's purser or directly.

Bermuda

Bermuda is not strictly a Caribbean island; it is 600 miles (965 km) east of Cape Hatteras (North Carolina) on America's east coast. The fish-hook-shaped British territory consists of seven islands linked by bridges, and measures 22 miles (35 km) in length and 21 sq. miles (54 sq. km). The widest point is 2 miles (3 km) across.

ARRIVING BY SEA

In Hamilton, the cruise pier is downtown within easy walking distance of the shops. In St George, ships dock at the pier on Kings Square, again, an easy walk.

PUBLIC HOLIDAYS

1 January: New Year's Day
March/April: Good Friday; Easter Monday
24 May: Bermuda Day
June: (3rd Monday) Queen's Birthday
July/August: (Thursday before first Monday) Cup Match Day; also the second day of the cup match, Somers Day (Friday after Cup Match Day)
September: (1st Monday) Labour Day
11 November: Remembrance Day
25 December: Christmas Day
26 December: Boxing Day

CALENDAR OF EVENTS

January/February: Bermuda Festival: 6-week international arts festival

February: Annual street festival: music, crafts and fashion show
April: Agricultural show
April/May: Open houses and gardens: homes and gardens open to visitors every Wednesday afternoon.
June: Queen's birthday parade
November: Remembrance Day

MONEY MATTERS

Legal tender is the Bermuda dollar (Bd$) which is divided into 100 cents. It is pegged to the US dollar. US currency is generally accepted at par in shops, restaurants and hotels, with many cashiers returning change to visitors in US dollars.

Travellers' cheques in US dollars are accepted everywhere. Major credit cards, too, are welcome in most hotels, shops and restaurants. Banking hours are Mon 9.30am–4pm, Tues–Thurs 8.30am–4pm, Fri 8.30am–4.30pm.

All banks close Sat, Sun, and public holidays. Major branches have ATMs.

TOURIST OFFICES

In the UK (European representative)
Bermuda Tourism,
36 Southwark Bridge Road,
London SE1 9EU.
Tel: 020-8410 8188.
In the US
675 Third Avenue, 20th Floor, New York, NY 10017.
Tel: 212-818 9800.
Fax: 212-983 5289.
Email: fdesk@bermudatourism.com
In Bermuda
Global House, 43 Church Street, Hamilton MH 12.
Tel: 292 0023.

Website
www.bermudatourism.com

POSTAL SERVICES

Postcards, stamps and letters can be bought or mailed from picturesque Perot's Post Office on Queen Street in Hamilton. The main post office for Bermuda is located on the corner of Church Street and Parliament Street in Hamilton.

TELECOMMUNICATIONS

The dialling code for Bermuda is **441**. Calling cards can be used at most payphones. There are several internet cafes in Hamilton and on Water Street and York Street in St George. Dialling access codes are:
AT&T: 800-872 2881
MCI: 800-888 8000 (C&W); or 800-888 8888 (TBI)
Sprint: 800-623 0877

SHOPPING

Things to buy include Outerbridge sherry pepper sauce; Hortons black rum cake; Bermuda spirits (Black Seal Rum, Silver Label Light Rum, Rum Swizzle, Bermuda Gold, Banana Liqueur, Bermuda Triangle); cashmeres, linens, woollens, tartan, silk scarves and walking sticks, Wedgwood, Royal Crown Derby and other fine china and porcelain.

Most shops are open Mon–Sat 9am–5.30pm. Some shops, however, open at 9.15am and may close at 5pm, so it's wise to enquire first. On Sundays, almost nothing is open.

GETTING AROUND

By Car

Driving is on the left. The speed limit is 20 mph (35 kph). Speeding is rare and no one honks their horn, except in greeting. There is no private car hire, although mopeds can be rented.

By Taxi

Taxis may be hired by the hour, day, or mile (a day is considered to be six consecutive daylight hours). Rates are the same for any number of passengers, up to a maximum of six, for normal transport and general sightseeing. All taxis are metered and the tariff is fixed by law. If a taxi sports a blue flag, it belongs to a qualified tour guide – a good way to see the island.

By Bus

Buses are frequent and good, with comprehensive schedules (they almost always run on time), but a complicated fare system. The island is divided into 14 zones of about 2 miles (3 km) each, with different fares charged according to how many zones are crossed. You must have the exact fare. Books of tickets (called tokens) are available from the bus terminal on Church Street, Hamilton, next to City Hall, or from any post office.

Links to the Caribbean

Bermuda can be reached in less than two hours from the East Coast of North America and in less than seven hours from the UK. There are also direct services from Canada.

STAYING ON

Bermuda has plenty of deluxe hotels as well as small guesthouses and cottage colonies – usually a complex of luxury private bungalows built around a main clubhouse – with pool, bar, restaurant and a spa.

Hotel Prices

Price categories are based on the cost of a double room, for one night:

$ = less than $100
$$ = $100–200
$$$ = more than $200.

Hamilton

Fairmont Hamilton Princess
76 Pittsbay Road, Hamilton CM CX.
Tel: 295 3000.
Fax: 295 1914.
E-mail: hamilton@fairmont.com
Located near downtown Hamilton, the Princess is a grand hotel in the old tradition. Access to the Fairmont Southampton Princess facilities. $$$
Little Pomander Guest House
16 Pomander Rd, Paget PG05.
Tel: 236 7635.
Fax: 236 8332.
www.littlepomander.com
On Hamilton Harbour, a short walk from the Bermuda National Trust headquarters. Delightful rooms. $$

St George

Aunt Nea's Inn at Hillcrest
St George GE BX.
Tel: 297 1630.
Fax: 297 1908.
www.auntneas.com
A lovely bed-and-breakfast tucked away in one of St George's picturesque alleys, a short stroll from Kings Square. $$

Meal Prices

Price categories are based on the cost of a meal for one person, excluding drinks:

$ = less than $20
$$ = $20–40
$$$ = more than $40.

WHERE TO EAT

For a small place Bermuda has a variety of dining experiences, ranging from casual Bermudian eateries to elegant Continental restaurants. Be warned: dining out is expensive.

Hamilton

M.R. Onions
Par-la-Ville Road, Hamilton.
Tel: 292 5012.
Bermudians proudly call themselves "Onions", after an erstwhile export. Seafood, steaks; local specialities. $$
The Spot
6 Burnaby Street, Hamilton.
Tel: 292 6293.
A breakfast and lunch "spot", jammed at lunchtime with business people and shoppers. light meals, burgers and sandwiches. No credit cards. $
Spring Garden Restaurant and Bar
19 Reid Street, Hamilton.
Tel: 295 7416.
Hidden in a small, shaded courtyard, this bar and restaurant serves tasty Barbadian cuisine, including specialities such as flying fish. $–$$
Rosa's Cantina
121 Front Street, Hamilton.
Tel: 295 1912.
The island's only Tex-Mex place, Rosa's has burritos, fajitas, quesadillas and Texas-style steaks, as well as Mexican beers, sangria, margaritas and a balcony overlooking Front Street. $$

SHORE ACTIVITIES

Excursions

In Hamilton you can visit the Cathedral or Fort Hamilton, and fit in a shopping trip for good duty-free items. There is also the botanical gardens and a guided walking or cycling tour of the 18-mile (29-km) Railway Trail. Wander the alleys of historic St George or tour the island by scooter. Visit the Ocean Discovery Centre, Royal Naval Dockyard, or art galleries in St George.

Best Beaches

Horseshoe Bay Beach; Church Beach (for snorkelling); Tobacco Bay; Elbow Beach (for the famous pink sand).

Water Sports

Most ships call April to November, when parasailing, scuba-diving and snorkelling; windsurfing, rowing and yachting can all be arranged. take a glass-bottomed boat tour to observe Bermuda's active marine life; moonlight sails through the Great Sound, or pirate parties on secluded islets.

Horse Riding

There is one main riding centre offering trail rides in Bermuda: Spicelands, Middle Road, Warwick (tel: 238 8212).

Responsible Cruising

Visitors can take some initiatives to protect the Caribbean way of life and the environment:

- Disembark in every port.
- Check out tours available at the quaysides.
- Use local restaurants or cafés.
- Buy locally made souvenirs.
- Visit museums and churches.
- Hire a guide to show you around.
- Only take photos of people with their permission.

Eastern Caribbean

The Bahamas

The Bahamas is an archipelago of over 700 islands starting 60 miles (97 km) off the eastern coast of Florida and stretching southeast for 560 miles (900 km) to the edge of the Caribbean Sea. Just over 30 of the islands are inhabited and 20 are well developed for tourism. Cruise ships call at Freeport in Grand Bahama and Nassau on the island of New Providence. Although Nassau and Paradise Island account for less than two per cent of the land area in the Bahamas, they are home to 60 per cent of Bahamians.

ARRIVING BY SEA

Nassau
Ships line up at the huge dock in the centre of Nassau, a short walk to the shops and the Straw Market. To get to Paradise Island, take a taxi from the port or walk over the toll bridge.
Grand Bahama Island
Ships dock at the Lucayan Harbour Cruise Facility, which lies 65 miles (105 km) east of West Palm Beach, and west of Freeport.

PUBLIC HOLIDAYS

1 January: New Year's Day
March/April: Good Friday; Easter Monday
May/June: Whit Monday
June: (1st Friday) Labour Day
10 July: Independence Day
August: (1st Monday) Emancipation Day
12 October: National Heroes Day
1 November: Bahamas Day
25 December: Christmas Day

CALENDAR OF EVENTS

April: Gospel Festival
June: Junkanoo
September: Atlantic Superboat Challenge (international powerboating)
November: Bahamas Music Festival
December/January: Junkanoo

MONEY MATTERS

The unit of currency is the Bahamian dollar. US dollars and credit cards are widely accepted.

TOURIST OFFICES

In Canada
121 Bloor Street East, Suite #1101, Toronto, Ontario M4W 3M5.
Tel: 416-968 2999.
Fax: 416-968 0724/6711.
In the UK
Bahamas House, 10 Chesterfield Street, London W1J 5JL.
Tel: 020 7355 0800.
Fax: 020 7491 9459.
In the US
11400 West Olympic Boulevard, Suite #204, Los Angeles, CA 90064.
Tel: 310-312 9544.
Fax: 310-312 9545.
150 East 52nd Street, 28th Floor (North), New York, NY 10022.
Tel: 212-758 2777.
Fax: 212-753 6531/242-832 0796.
In the Bahamas
The Bahamas Ministry of Tourism, PO Box N-3701, Nassau.
Tel: 302-2000.
Fax: 302 2098.
Nassau/Paradise Island Promotion Board,
1st Floor S.G. Hambros Building, Southern Entrance, Nassau.
Tel: 322 8381
Grand Bahama Island Tourism Board, Freeport International Bazaar, PO Box F-40251, Grand Bahama
Tel: 352 8044.
Fax: 352 2714.
Website
www.bahamas.com
www.grand-bahama.com

POSTAL SERVICES

Post offices on Nassau/Paradise Island are located at Cable Beach, Carmichael Road, Clarence A. Bain, Elizabeth Estates, Fox Hill, Grants Town, Nassau International Airport and Shirley Street. In Freeport the post office is downtown, on Explorer's Way. Main post offices usually open Mon–Fri 8.30am–5.30pm and Sat 8.30am–12.30pm.

Shopping

With no sales tax and low tariffs, the Bahamas can be a bargain-hunter's delight. Some merchants sell imported goods at prices 30 to 50 percent lower than in the US, but compare the prices of goods at home before you go.

Bay Street in Nassau offers the biggest and best selection of shops. For fine china, crystal and figurines, visit Treasure Traders, Little Switzerland and John Bull. The largest selection of French perfumes are at Lightbourne's, the Perfume Shop and the Perfume Bar. Several stores, like Colombian Emeralds, sell fine gems. For guaranteed Bahamian-made goods, try Bahamian T'ings (cards, art work and pottery) and The Plait Lady (straw work). Balmain Antiques sells fabulous old maps of the Caribbean.

Finally, there is the open-air straw market selling handwoven goods. Bargain here, but not at other Bay Street establishments.

TELECOMMUNICATIONS

The dialling code is **242**. The telephone system is sophisticated, with high-speed internet access, roaming agreements with many US cellular networks and international direct-dialling all over the world.

Nassau has two internet cafes, in East Bay Street Shopping Centre and in Chippies Wall Street Cafe.

GETTING AROUND

By Car
Driving is on the left and an international licence is required. Most car hire firms are based at the airport

but the following have offices downtown: A1 Rent a Car, tel: 377 5520; Hertz, tel: 377 8684/352 9250. Alternatively, hire a scooter

By Taxi

You can call a cab or hail one on the street. Cab stands are also located at most large hotels. Cabs are metered and surcharges often apply for more than two persons and extra luggage.

By Bus

Buses are also called "jitneys" and run daily until around 8pm. They are reliable, but can be crowded.

Inter-Island Links

Several international airlines serve Nassau from the US mainland, with other connections from Europe. Internal flights are operated by Bahamasair, which links 16 islands in the chain using a "hub and spoke" system via Nassau, which means all flights connect over Nassau. For a group of people, private charter can be cost effective. Try: **Airstream Ltd**, tel: 356 6666; **Caribbean Aviation**, tel: 328 6539/377 3317; **Four Way Charter**, tel: 377 5751.
Inter-island ferries are operated by Bahamas FastFerries from Nassau to Eleuthera and mail boats carry passengers from Nassau to Freeport.

STAYING ON

Accommodation in the Bahamas ranges from intimate inns and cottages to huge resort and casino complexes.

Nassau/Paradise Island

Atlantis
P.O. Box SS-6333, Paradise Island.
Tel: 363 2000/3000.
www.atlantis.com
Massive mega-resort with restaurants, bars, cinema, casino and shows, golf, tennis and ocean theme park. **$$$**

Compass Point Resort
West Bay Street, Cable Beach.
Tel: 327 4500; 800-633 3284 (US)
Fax: 327 2407.
www.compasspointbahamas.com
One- and two-bedroom colourfully decorated cottages, studio cabañas, and a three-bedroom penthouse, minutes from the airport. **$$$**

Dillet's Guest House
PO Box N-204, Nassau.
Tel: 325 1133.
Fax: 325 7183.
www.islandeaze.com
Simple, family-owned Bahamian home transformed, with Internet access. **$$**

Graycliff Hotel
West Hill Street,
P.O. Box N-10246, Nassau.
Tel: 322 2796.
Fax: 326 6188.
www.graycliff.com
Georgian-style hotel in a 260-year old mansion. The only 5-star restaurant in The Bahamas. The Graycliff Cigar Company is next door. **$$$**

Grand Bahama Island

Our Lucaya
Royal Palm Way, Lucaya, Grand Bahama
Tel: 373 1444.
Fax: 373 8804.
www.ourlucaya.com
Large, luxury family resort with good beach. Opposite Port Lucaya marketplace. **$$$**

Price categories are based on the cost of a double room, for one night:
$ = less than $100
$$ = $100–200
$$$ = more than $200.

WHERE TO EAT

Fish turns up for dinner, lunch and even breakfast, with snapper and grouper being the most common.
Seafood favourites include turtle steaks, crayfish, grouper, conch (pronounced "conk") and the delicious clawless Bahamian lobster. Among the top incarnations are cracked conch, for which the conch is pounded until tender, battered and deep-fried; steamed conch (cooked with sautéed onions, peppers, thyme, tomatoes and maybe okra or carrots). Conch chowder is a rich, spicy soup with vegetables; conch salad contains minced raw conch,

Meal Prices

Price categories are based on the cost of a meal for one person, excluding drinks:
$ = less than $20
$$ = $20–40
$$$ = more than $40.

marinated in lime juice, and mixed with chopped onions and peppers.

Bahamian Kitchen
Trinity Place, off Market Street, Nassau.
Tel: 325 0702.
An impressive array of everything from salads to turtle steak cooked to order. Excellent value. **$**

Conch Fritters
Marlborough Street, Nassau.
Tel: 323 8778.
Specialising in its namesake with both American and Bahamian dishes. **$$**

Ferry House Restaurant
Opposite Port Lucaya marketplace, Lucaya, Grand Bahama
Tel: 373 1595.
Simple, but elegant decor. Gourmet seafood and marina views. **$$$**

Pier One Seafood Restaurant
Freeport Harbour, Grand Bahama
Tel: 352 6674.
Steak and seafood; sunset views. **$$$**

SHORE ACTIVITIES

Excursions

Some of Nassau and Paradise Islands attractions include: Government House; Parliament Square and Fort Charlotte; Pirates Museum; Atlantis Resort (special day rates for cruise passengers); Botanical Gardens and dolphin encounters. In Grand Bahama: Garden of the Groves; snorkelling and diving off Deadman's Reef.

Best Beaches

Arawak Cay for peace and quiet; Paradise Island for water sports and the big hotels.

Water Sports

Everything is available here, from Hartley's Underwater Walk (wearing a dive helmet) to snorkelling, sailing, powerboating and windsurfing. For an adventurous day trip to one of the out islands, try Powerboat Adventures, tel: 393 7116/7126; www.powerboatadventures.com For day sailing, call Barefoot Bahamas, tel: 393 0820.

Horse Riding

Happy Trails offers beach and countryside rides, and riding lessons, tel: 362 1820; www.windsorequestriancentre.com.

Cuba

The Republic of Cuba, the largest archipelago in the Western Hemisphere, is over 775 miles (1,250 km) long, 118 miles (190 km) wide at its eastern head to 19 mile (30 km) at its western tail. Neighbouring islands include The Bahamas, Haiti, Jamaica and Key West, Florida. Mountain, desert, rainforest and some 300 beaches make up the island's terrain. Population is 11 million and Havana is the capital.

ARRIVING BY SEA

Cruise ships dock at the waterfront terminal in the heart of Old Havana, a short walk from the city centre.

PUBLIC HOLIDAYS

1 January: Liberation day
19 April: Victory at Bay of Pigs (1962)
1 May: Labour Day
25–27 July: Revolution Day celebrations
8 October: Death of Che Guevara
10 October: Beginning of the War of Independence
25 December: Christmas Day
In addition to these official public holidays, there are innumerable other important dates which are commemorated, including:
28 January: Death of José Martí (1895)

CALENDAR OF EVENTS

January: New Year's Day and Anniversary of the Revolution
February: Carnival in Havana
July: Carnival in Santiago

MONEY MATTERS

The Cuban peso, divided into 100 centavos, is the official currency. US dollars are not legal tender. Cuban pesos are used everywhere.

You can change dollars into pesos legally at Government licensed CADECA booths or illegally on the street with black-market vendors. Credit cards issued outside the US are accepted in tourist outlets. Most bank branches open Mon–Fri 8.30am–3pm.

TOURIST OFFICES

In Canada
2070 rue Université, Bureau 460, Montréal Québec H3A 2L1
Tel: 514-875 8004
Fax: 514-875 8006
In the UK
154 Shaftesbury Avenue, London WC2H 8JT.
Tel: 020-7240 6655.
In Cuba
General tourist information offices do not really exist in Cuba. Instead, there is a whole range of tourism enterprises, whose services sometimes overlap and which concentrate on offering packages or other specific services rather than telling visitors the opening hours of a museum and so on.
Amistur Cuba specialises in political tours and people wishing to see the revolutionary side of Cuba. They can be found at 406 Paseo Street, between 17 and 19 streets, Vedado, Havana. Tel: 7-830 1220/834 4544/833 2374; email: amistur@amistur.cu.
Cubamar Viajes specialises in eco-tourism, bicycle tours and other general sports. They are located at 3rd Street and Malecon, Vedado, Havana. Tel: 7-833 2524; fax: 7-833 3111; www.cubamarviajes.cu

Website
www.cubaweb.cu

POSTAL SERVICES

Every rural town has a post office, and major cities have a central post office with municipal branches. You can buy stamps here for pesos.

Domestic delivery is slow, but faster from city to city than within the same city. Mail to Europe and the Americas arrive a month or more after posting, even when sent via airmail.

TELECOMMUNICATIONS

The dialling code is **53**. Each province has a separate dialling code, for example, the code for Havana is **7**.

The local telephone service is somewhat unreliable. If you must make a call, go to a hotel or a telephone office (signed "Telecorreos" or "Etecsa"). It is not practical to expect to check email on a day visit to Havana; currently the only facilities are in hotel business centres. Visit: www.cubatravel.cu for information.

SHOPPING

Cigars and rum are two of the best gifts to take home from a trip to Cuba – Cohiba is one of the more famous cigar brands. Note that cigars cannot be taken in to the US. Cuban coffee is also excellent; Cubita, Turquina and Hola are the best brands. Also look for Cuban music CDs and pre-revolution books and magazines.

GETTING AROUND

By Car

Cuban highways and secondary roads are fairly well maintained, except for the potholes. Otherwise, driving is safe and Cubans are ever helpful with directions – even though they are often vague when it comes to distances. Rental cars are expensive and visitors should take out maximum insurance cover to allow for scams on the part of the hire company.

Be sure to check the car carefully for damage, including scratches. Draw attention to anything you find, and insist any damages are noted on the paperwork. Cars can be hired through major hotels in Havana and other towns. The main rental companies include: Micar, tel: 7-833 0101/833 0202; Rex, tel: 7-273 9166/69

It is not worthwhile renting a car if you've only got a day – distances are great and there is plenty to see in Havana itself.

By Taxi

Private taxis are a good way to see Havana. The day rate within the city is US$25–$40 (more for a big American gas-guzzler) and it is the same for excursions outside the city. Set a price before you go.

By Bus

Buses, known as *guaguas*, are often slow, crowded, and uncomfortable, but are nevertheless a cheap way to get around the island, as well as a good way to meet Cubans. *Especiales* are faster and more comfortable, but less common.

Inter-Island Links

AeroCaribbean/BahamasAir flies from Nassau to Havana on most days. Other scheduled flights operate from Kingston, Montego Bay, Nassau and Pointe-a-Pitre.

Hotel Prices

Price categories are based on the cost of a double room, for one night:
$ = less than $100
$$ = $100–200
$$$ = more than $200.

STAYING ON

Cuba has a wide and ever-improving range of hotels.

Hotel Acuario

Marina Hemingway, 5a and 248, Barlovento.
Tel: 7-204 7628.
Fax: 7-204 4379.
Sometimes still known by its old name, Jardin de Eden, 98 villas. Rooms with garden or sea view. Water sports centre. **$$**

Hotel Meliá Cohiba

Paseo and Primera, Vedado.
Tel: 7-833 3636.
Fax: 7-833 4555.
Email: melia.cohiba@solmelia.com
Five-star hotel complex on the seafront. Filled with restaurants, cafes, bars, nightclubs and shops.
$$$

Hotel Santa Isabel

Calle Baratillo, Plaza de Armas, Habana Vieja.
Tel: 7-860 8201.
Fax: 7-860 8391.
A renovated former colonial palace, in the heart of Old Havana. A vision in turquoise and stone, with a courtyard. Five-star; popular with the business market. Excellent restaurant. **$$$**

WHERE TO EAT

Most state-run restaurants tend to serve bland, international fare rather than Cuban creole cuisine, although they are improving. Menus can seem monotonous. Fried chicken (*pollo frito*) turns up all the time, while the most common lunch snack served in dollar cafes and restaurants is the ham and cheese sandwich (*sandwich de jamón y queso*).

For an authentic Cuban meal, try the private restaurants or *paladares*, which traditionally consist of a few tables in somebody's home (legally, they can have a maximum of just 12 covers), and have a more congenial atmosphere than state-run restaurants.

El Aljibe

7a between 24 and 26, Miramar.
Tel: 7-204 1583/84.
A fine restaurant in thatched buildings amid tropical gardens. Truly excellent Cuban cooking. **$$**

La Bodeguita del Medio

Calle Empedrado 207, off Plaza de la Catedral.
Tel: 7-867 1374.
Bohemian atmosphere with creole cooking in this old Hemingway haunt.
$$$

El Floridita

On the corner of Obispo and Monserrate, Old Havana.
Tel: 7-867 1300/1.
Havana's most fabled dining spot, and Hemingway's favourite for his daiquiris (the best in town), is elegant but rather dark and overpriced. Main courses include grilled lobster, shrimp flambéed in rum, and turtle steaks. **$$$$**

El Patio

Plaza de la Catedral, Old Havana.
Tel: 7-867 1034.
Go for the fabulous location, in an old colonial palace, rather than the food.

You can eat either on the ground floor, surrounded by palms and serenaded from the grand piano, or upstairs. International menu. **$$$**

Meal Prices

Price categories are based on the cost of a meal for one person, excluding drinks:
$ = less than $20
$$ = $20–40
$$$ = more than $40.

SHORE ACTIVITIES

Excursions

Walking and driving tours of Havana, including the convents of San Francisco and Santa Clara, the cigar factories, Museu de la Revolucion; excursions to Cojimar and the Hemingway Museum (gardens only); beach visits.

Best Beaches

Beaches near the city tend to be dirty and overcrowded. The Playas del Este (eastern beaches) are better – a string of beaches starting some 16 km (10 miles) from the city. But most day visitors to Havana are more interested in the amazing old city than the beach.

Sports

The Hemingway Marina tourist complex (at Santa Fe, 20 minutes by taxi) offers sport fishing and scuba diving. Tel: 7-209 7270/7928. If you are staying on, the beach resorts further afield have good facilities, and will often have qualified instructors for a whole range of sports including waterskiing, sailing, snorkelling, diving, fishing, yachting, as well as basketball, volleyball, squash, tennis and horse riding. A growing number of hotels also have bicycles and mopeds for rent.

Puerto Rico

Puerto Rico, a dependent territory of the USA, is an island facing the Atlantic on the north and the Caribbean on the south. It is the smallest of the Greater Antilles, running 100 miles (160 km) east-west and 35 miles (56 km) north-south. The Cordillera Central, a mountain range whose peaks reach well over 3,000 ft (900 metres), takes up most of the island's area and is surrounded by foothills. To the northeast, odd haystack-shaped limestone formations make up the karst country, a unique and fascinating landscape of rock cones and caves. Puerto Rico is ringed by palm-lined, white-sand beaches and by coral reefs, and is veined with rivers and streams. The island has no natural lakes. San Juan has one of the finest natural harbours in the Caribbean and is the starting point for many Eastern Caribbean cruises.

ARRIVING BY SEA

Ships dock at the port in Old San Juan, near the historic centre.

PUBLIC HOLIDAYS

1 January: New Year's Day
6 January: Three King's Day
11 January: Eugenio María de Hostos' Birthday
22 February: Washington's birthday
22 March: Emancipation Day
March/April: Good Friday
16 April: Jose de Diego's birthday
30 May: Memorial Day
24 June: St John the Baptist day
4 July: US Independence Day
17 July: Luis Muñoz Rivera Day
25 July: Constitution Day
1 September: Labour Day
12 October: Columbus Day
11 November: Veterans' Day
19 November: Discovery of Puerto Rico Day
November: (3rd Thursday) Thanksgiving Day
25 December: Christmas Day

CALENDAR OF EVENTS

Each town has its patron saint's day, which is a celebration not to be missed. See www.gotopuertorico.com for a list of saints' days. The biggest celebrations are on 24 April during the St John the Baptist patron saint festival in San Juan. Also worth a look:
6 January: Three Kings' Day
February: Coffee harvest festival
24 April: St John the Baptist patron saint festival
May: Jazz festival

MONEY MATTERS

The currency is the US dollar. Credit cards are widely accepted and there are ATMs at banks in Old San Juan.

TOURIST OFFICES

In Canada
41–43 Colbourne Street, Suite 301, Toronto, Ontario M5E 1E3.
Tel: 416-368 2680, 800-667 0394. within Canada only
Fax: 416-368 5350.

In Europe
Calle Serrano 1–2 Izq., 28001, Madrid, Spain.
Tel: (34) 91-431 2128.
Fax: (34) 91-577 5260.
toll free from UK: 0800-898920

In the US
666 Fifth Avenue, 15th Floor, New York, NY 10103.
Tel: 800-223 6530.
Fax: 212-586 1212.

In Puerto Rico
Puerto Rico Main Office, La Princesa Bldg. #2 Paseo La Princesa, Old San Juan, P.R. 00902. P.O. Box 902-3960, San Juan, P.R. 00902-3960.
Tel: 787-721 2400/800-866 7827. There is also a tourist office near Pier One at the port.

Website
www.gotopuertorico.com

POSTAL SERVICES

There is a post office in Old San Juan and in Hato Rey. Hotels also sell stamps. Two-day Priority Mail service is available and overnight documents can be sent via Federal Express. United Parcel Service and DHL also have offices here.

TELECOMMUNICATIONS

The dialling code is **787**. Not all payphones have a connection for international calls and calling from a hotel is expensive. There is an internet cafe at the port, on the waterfront.

SHOPPING

The more upmarket shopping areas tend to be concentrated in the Old City and the Condado. Old San Juan has more of a boutique atmosphere of the two. Plaza de Las Américas is the Caribbean's largest shopping mall, in Hato Rey. Puerto Rico is a good place to find interesting jewellery, arts and crafts, cigars, music, leather goods, wooden masks and designer clothes.

GETTING AROUND

By Car

A car is a good idea if you are staying on but not necessary for a day visit. Most car rental companies are based at Condado, a 10-minute taxi ride from the port. Try Charlie Cars, tel: 728 2418 or 800-289 1227 (US)

By Taxi

Taxis wait at the port and can be found all over the city and hailed on the street. They are metered and charge extra for things like suitcases. Cruise passengers are often seen as gullible targets for an increased fare.

By Bus

Local city buses are called *guaguas*; all small yellow trolleys run around the old town and are free.

Inter-Island Links

San Juan airport is a major international hub. International flights are operated by American Airlines, American Eagle, American Trans Air, British Airways, Carnival, Continental, Copa, Delta, Flamenco, Hill Aviation, Iberia, KLM, LASCA, LIAT, Mexicana, Northwest, Sunaire Express, Towers Air, TWA, United and Vieques Air Llink.

Local airlines include American Eagle, Flamenco, and Vieques Air Link, and they have offices either at the Luis Muñoz Marin International Airport, or the Isla Grande Airport.

There are four daily American Eagle flights between San Juan and Ponce. Flamenco Airways flies to Culebra and St Thomas from Fajardo and San Juan. Some charter or inter-island flights leave from the Isla Grande Airport.

STAYING ON

Within the San Juan metro area, major hotel resorts are concentrated in Condado and Isla Verde. These hotels generally have casinos, live entertainment, discotheques, restaurants, bars and sports facilities. For a lot less you can stay in one of a number of guest houses and smaller places throughout Condado or Ocean Park.

El Escenario Guest House
152 San Sebastián,
Old San Juan.
Tel: 721 5264.
Pleasant guest house above a lively bar. This may be Old San Juan's best lodging bargain. Rates include breakfast on the rooftop terrace. **$**

Galeria San Juan
204 Norzagaray,
Old San Juan.
Tel: 722 1808.
Fax: 977 3929.
www.thegalleryinn.com
Art gallery and guest house in a 16th-century mansion restored by sculptor and local personality Jan D'Esopo, whose art is available for purchase. From the house, the artist's sculpture of Christopher Columbus looks towards the sea. **$**

Hotel El Convento
100 Cristo,
Old San Juan.
Tel: 800-468 2779/787-723 9020.
www.elconvento.com
Historic 16th-century convent, converted in the 1960s. An ideal base for exploring Old San Juan. **$$$**

Hotel Prices

Price categories are based on the cost of a double room, for one night:
$ = less than $100
$$ = $100–200
$$$ = more than $200.

Sheraton Old San Juan Hotel
100 Brumbaugh Street,
Old San Juan.
Tel: 721 5100.
The Old City's largest hotel, was built as part of the waterfront expansion. Has a roof-top pool, restaurant and two lounges. **$$$**

Meal Prices

Price categories are based on the cost of a meal for one person, excluding drinks:
$ = less than $20
$$ = $20–40
$$$ = more than $40.

WHERE TO EAT

Local specialities include *frijoles negros* (black bean soup); *arroz con pollo* (chicken with rice); *asopa* (a gumbo soup); and *lechon* (roast suckling pig). The local rum is excellent.

Amadeus
106 San Sebastián,
Old San Juan.
Tel: 722 8635.
Traditional Puerto Rican dinners, fresh seafood and delicious *ceviche* on Plaza San José. The bar is both well-stocked and crowded. **$$**

La Bombonera
259 San Francisco,
Old San Juan.
Tel: 722 0658.
Traditional cafeteria-style bakery. Best place for a cheap, satisfying *arroz con pollo* and coffee with pastry. **$**

Cafe Berlin
407 San Francisco,
Old San Juan.
Tel: 722 5205.
Owned by a German baker, this gourmet vegetarian eatery fronting Plaza Colón has fresh pasta, organic food and a delicious salad bar. **$$**

Chef Marisoll
202 Cristo Street,
Old San Juan,
Tel: 725 7454.
Romantic patio restaurant with contemporary cuisine by award-winning chef. Local food prepared nouvelle-style. **$$$**

Mango's Café
2421 Laurel,
Punta Las Marías,
Old San Juan,
Tel: 727 9328
Delicious Jamaican, Caribbean and Creole food, drinks and music. **$**

SHORE ACTIVITIES

Excursions

Walking around Old San Juan (see Casa Blanca, Mueso de las Americas, the Dominican Convent, San Cristóbal Fortress, the tourist board office, La Princesa, in a former prison on the waterfront, El Morro fort, cellist Pablo Casal's house, La Fortaleza, and walk along the city walls). Shore excursions include the Barcardi rum distillery, hiking in El Yunque rainforest, golf, kayaking, snorkelling and horse riding.

Best Beaches

San Juan as a port is not really a beach destination, although there are beaches at Condado and Isla Verde, a 10-minute taxi ride from the port. Luquillo beach, near the El Yunque national park, is a lovely long stretch of sand with water sports. Pine Beach Grove in Isla Verde is good for surfing, and novice windsurfers will enjoy the usually flat water of the Condado lagoon.

Water sports

The eastern end of the island and on the Puerto Rico Wall to the south are good scuba diving areas. Try Caribe Aquatic Adventures, tel: 281 8858; www.caribeaquaticadventures.com. For fishing, call Captain Mike's Sportfishing, tel: 721 7335.

Golf

There are 18 golf courses on the island, many of them world-class. Try the two Hyatt hotels (www.hyatt.com), or Berwind Country Club, which accepts non-members on certain days, tel: 876 3056.

US Virgin Islands

Located about 40 miles (64 km) east of Puerto Rico, the United States Virgin Islands (USVI) is composed of over 60 islands with a total land area of 136 sq. miles (352 sq. km). The inhabited islands are St Thomas, St Croix and St John.

ARRIVING BY SEA

St Thomas

Cruise ships dock at Havensight, where there are plenty of shops, or Crown Bay. On busy days some cruise ships operate tenders straight into Charlotte Amalie.

St John

Passengers arrive by tender into National Park Dock.

St Croix

Big ships moor in Frederickstad; smaller vessels in Christiansted.

PUBLIC HOLIDAYS

1 January: New Year's Day/Three King's Day
6 January: Martin Luther King Day
February: (3rd Monday) Presidents' Day
31 March: Transfer Day
March/April: Good Friday; Easter Monday
20 June: Organic Act Day
3 July: Emancipation Day
4 July: Independence Day
23 July: Supplication Day
1 November: Liberty Day
November: (last Thursday) Thanksgiving Day
25 December: Christmas Day
26 December: Boxing Day

CALENDAR OF EVENTS

6 December–January: St Croix Christmas Festival
17 March: St Patrick's Day Festival, St Croix
April: (third week) St Thomas Carnival
July: (week of the 4th) St John's Carnival
October: St Croix Music and Arts Festival

MONEY MATTERS

The currency is the US dollar (US$). Normal banking hours are Mon–Thurs 9am–3pm, Fri 9am–5pm. There are ATMs at the dock in Frederickstad on St Croix and in Charlotte Amalie, St John. All major credit cards are accepted on the main islands.

TOURIST OFFICES

In Canada
3300 Bloor Street, Suite 3120, Centre Tower, Toronto, Ontario M8X 2X3.
Tel: 416-233 1414.
In the UK
Molasses House, Clove Hitch Quay, Plantation Wharf, London SW11 3TW.
Tel: 020-7978 5262.
E-mail: usvi@destination-marketing.co.uk
In the US
3460 Wilshire Boulevard, Suite 412, Los Angeles, CA 90010.
Tel: 213-739 0138.
2655 Le Jeune Road, Suite 907, Miami, FL 33134.
Tel: 305-442 7200.
1270 Avenue of the Americas, Suite 2108, New York, NY 10020.
Tel: 212-332 2222.
444 North Capital Street NW,
In USVI
St Thomas: there are two visitors bureaux; one at Tolbod Gade, Charlotte Amalie, another at the Welcome Center, Havensight Dock.
St Croix: 53A Company Street, Christiansted.
St John: located next to the post office in Cruz Bay.

Websites
www.usvi.net
www.usvi-on-line.com
www.usvitourism.vi
www.st-croix.com
www.st-john.com
www.st-thomas.com

POSTAL SERVICES

Post offices can be found in the main towns of the three islands as well as in smaller towns such as Frederiksted.

Shopping

The USVI enjoy a duty and sales tax-free status so that most things are 20–50 per cent cheaper than on the mainland. Wednesday and Friday are the most crowded shopping days, due to the number of cruise ships calling.
St Thomas has the widest choice of duty-free shopping with a large proportion in Charlotte Amalie; Havensight Mall by the cruise terminal and Red Hook on the east coast are shopping malls packed with outlets selling jewellery, watches, cameras, spirits and other duty-free goods. St Thomas also has a selection of handicraft outlets.
St Croix's King's Alley Walk is a shopping area in Christiansted. In St Croix Leap in the west, there are some excellent wood-carvers.
St John has a variety of local arts and crafts. The most popular areas are Mongoose Junction and Wharfside Village in Cruz Bay.

TELECOMMUNICATIONS

The dialling code is **340**. Direct-dial and operator-assisted long-distance calls may be placed from most hotel and pay phones.

If you are using a US credit phone card, dial the company's access number as follows:
AT&T, tel: 800-CALL ATT (225 5288).
MCI, tel: 800-888 8000.
Sprint, tel: 800-877 8000.

Internet facilities are available in Frederickstad, St Croix, and the Havensight Mall, St Thomas.

GETTING AROUND

By Car

Driving is on the left. A US driver's licence is valid in the USVI. Vehicles to rent range from a saloon to a jeep.
St Thomas: ABC Auto & Jeep Rentals, tel: 776 1222; Budget, tel: 776 5774, 800-626 4516 (toll free only when dialled in the country of origin).
St Croix: Avis, tel: 778 9355; Caribbean Jeep & Car Rental, tel: 773 4399.
St John: St John Car Rental, tel: 776 6103.

By Taxi

Taxis can be picked up at the cruise terminals in St Croix and St John. In St Thomas, taxis tend to be shared minibuses or jeeps with fixed fares. Fares are published by the Virgin Islands Taxi Association, but you should negotiate before boarding.

Taxi companies include **St Thomas**: VI Taxi Association, tel: 774 4550. **St Croix**: St Croix Taxi Association, tel: 778 1088.

By Bus

There are regular bus services on St Thomas, St John and St Croix; look for the Vitran bus stop signs. On St Croix buses run every half hour between Christiansted and Frederiksted (17 miles/27 km).

Inter-Island Links

There are airports on St Thomas and St Croix. You can fly between the USVI on Cape Air (tel: 800-352 0714) or Seaborne Airlines (tel: 73 6442). There are regular ferry services from St Thomas (Charlotte Amalie) to St John, Tortola, and Virgin Gorda. Contact Ferry Transportation Services (tel: 776 6282). There is no regular ferry service to St Croix. Local airlines link the USVI with nearby islands: the BVI, Anguilla, and St Martin. Airlines: Air Anguilla, tel: 246-497 8690/776 5789; LIAT, tel: 246-495 1187; American Eagle, tel: 800-433 7300.

STAYING ON

There is a wide choice of hotels, from big resorts to guesthouses.

St Thomas

Mafolie
PO Box 1506, Red Hook, VI 00803.
Tel: 774 2790.
Fax: 774 4091.
www.mafolie.com
A family-run hotel with splendid harbour view. Take the free shuttle to Magen's Bay beach; also a pool. **$–$$**

Island View Mountain Inn
PO Box 1903, St Thomas, USVI 00803.
Tel: 774 4270.
Fax: 774 6167.
www.islandviewstthomas.com
Fantastic views from this guesthouse, on beautiful Crown Mountain. **$–$$**

St Croix

Pink Fancy
27 Prince Street, Christiansted, St Croix, USVI 00820.
Tel: 773 8460.
Fax: 340-773 6448.
www.pinkfancy.com
Old Danish town villa with a fascinating past. Decorated with glitzy memorabilia and antiques. **$$**

Tamarind Reef
5001 Tamarind Reef,
Christiansted, St Croix, USVI 00820.
Tel: 773 4455.
Fax: 773 3989.
www.usvi.net/hotel/tamarind
West Indian-style hotel, fronting the beach. Many rooms have kitchenettes. Water sports facilities. **$$–$$$**

St John

Caneel Bay
PO Box 8310, Great Crux Bay,
St John, USVI 00831.
Tel: 776 6111.
Fax: 693 8280.
www.caneelbay.com
Restored hotel built in the 1950s by Laurence Rockefeller. Situated on a peninsula in the heart of the National Park. Very quiet. Seven beaches. **$$$**

Gallows Point Suite Resort
PO Box 58, Cruz Bay, St John,
USVI 00831.
Tel: 776 6434.
Fax: 776 6520.
www.gallowspointresort.com
Neat wooden houses with fully equipped apartments. **$$$**

WHERE TO EAT

Locally produced fruits and vegetables, and fresh seafood provide the raw materials for island cooks, who create anything from bullfoot soup (what it sounds like) and *fungi* (cornmeal pudding) to French food.

St Thomas

Banana Tree Grille
Bluebeard's Castle, Charlotte Amalie.
Tel: 776 4050.
Elegant dining with a beautiful view across the harbour. **$$**

1829 Government Hill
1829 Government Hill,
Charlotte Amalie.
Tel: 776 1829.
Excellent continental food and service in an historic house. **$$–$$$**

Hervé's
Kongens Gade, Government Hill,
Charlotte Amalie.
Tel: 777 9703.
Excellent French cuisine in a relaxed bistro-style setting. **$$–$$$**

St Croix

The Buccaneer
Gallows Bay, Christiansted.
Tel: 712 2100.
www.thebuccaneer.com
Four restaurants under one hotel roof. Classic Mediterranean specialities, often with a tropical twist. **$$–$$$**

Duggans's Reef
Route 82, Teague Bay.
Tel: 773 9800.
Pasta with a Caribbean touch. Outdoor dining overlooking Buck Island. **$$$**

Tutto Bene
2 Company Street, Christiansted.
Tel: 773 5229.
Excellent pastas with Italian flair. **$$**

St John

Fish Trap
Raintree Inn, Cruz Bay.
Tel: 693 9994.
Fresh fish, chicken and steak. **$$**

Morgan's Mango
Cruz Bay.
Tel: 693 8141.
This seafood and steak restaurant serves imaginative dishes with a Caribbean flavour. **$$**

Meal Prices

Price categories are based on the cost of a meal for one person, excluding drinks:
$ = less than $20
$$ = $20–40
$$$ = more than $40.

Paradiso
Mongoose Junction.
Tel: 693 8899.
Good food in a casual but classy setting and tasty Italian dishes. **$–$$**

SHORE ACTIVITIES

Excursions
St John: Paradise Point Tramway for great views (opposite the Havensight Mall); Annaberg Sugar Plantation; hiking trails; beaches and water sports.
St Thomas: St Peter Great House; Kon-Tiki party cruises; Kayak Marine Sanctuary; Coral World marine park (underwater observatory); Atlantis submarine; sea plane excursions; day trips to St John; duty-free shopping in Charlotte Amalie
St Croix: Historic Christiansted; Estate Whim Plantation Museum; Buck Island National Park (for snorkelling); cycling; water sports

Best Beaches
St John: Trunk Bay (snorkelling trail); Hawksnest.
St Thomas: Magen's Bay, Sapphire, Coki for water sports; trips to St John.
St Croix: Sandy Point; Cane Bay for snorkelling; Hotel on the Cay for soft sand and water sports.

Golf
St Thomas has a championship course with beautiful views – Mahogany Run (tel: 777 6250; www.mahoganyrungolf.com). **St Croix** has two 18-hole courses – Carambola (tel: 778 5638; www.golfvi.com) and Buccaneer (tel: 773 2100; www.thebuccaneer.com).

Hiking
Two-thirds of **St John** is a US National Park so there are many trails to choose from. The National Park Visitors' Centre in Cruz Bay is open

daily 8am–4.30pm, tel: 776 6201. Reef Bay Trail (tel: 776 6201 ext 238) is a lovely downhill hike passing a ruined sugar mill and a spectacular beach. Book in advance.

Diving

Some of the finest diving in the Caribbean is to be found in the USVI.
On **St Thomas**, a particularly lively spot is Coki Beach which specialises in beginners. Coki Beach Dive Club, tel: 340-775 4220; www.cokidive.com. Try Chris Sawyer Diving Center, Red Hook, tel: 340-777 7804; www.sawyerdive.vi. Magen's Bay, Sapphire and Coki Beach all have water sports equipment for hire.
On **St John**, located in Wharfside Village, Cruz Bay, is Low Key Water sports, a PADI facility offering daily diving from beginners to advanced, and kayaking (tel: 340-693 8999; www.divelowkey.com). There is an underwater snorkelling trail off Trunk Bay; Cinnamon Bay and Salt Pond Bay also have good snorkelling. Windsurfing equipment can be hired at Cinnamon and Maho Bay.
St Croix has amazing underwater scenery at Cane Bay, where a dramatic wall drops off thousands of feet very close to the shore. Try Dive Experience, tel: 340-773 3307, www.divexp.com, or Cane Bay Dive Shop, tel: 340-773 9913, www.canebayscuba.com. Sailing equipment is available at Hotel on the Cay.

St Martin/St Maarten

At the top of the Lesser Antilles, between Anguilla and St Kitts, lies the island of St Martin. Shared by France in the north and the Netherlands (Sint Maarten) in the south, the 37-sq. mile (96-sq. km) island is a popular cruise, vacation and shopping spot. St Martin is rolling and green, and Pic du Paradis (the highest point) rises to only 1,390 ft (420 metres). Residents and visitors can move freely between the two parts of the island.

ARRIVING BY SEA

On the French side, ships tender passengers to the centre of Marigot's seafront. On the Dutch side, the cruise pier is in the centre of Philipsburg. On busy days, some ships tender passengers to the town centre.

PUBLIC HOLIDAYS

St Maarten
30 April: Coronation Day
1 May: Labour Day; Ascension Day
May/June: Whit Monday
11 November: St Maarten Day
15 December: Kingdom Day
25 December: Christmas Day

St Martin
1 January: New Year's Day
March/April: Easter Monday
1 May: Labour Day
8 May: VE Day; Ascension Day
May/June: Whit Monday
Late May: Slavery Abolition Day
14 July: Bastille Day
21 July: Schoelcher Day
15 August: Feast of the Assumption
1 November: All Saints' Day
11 November: St Martin Day
25 December: Christmas Day

CALENDAR OF EVENTS

St Maarten
Mid April: Carnival

St Martin
Before Lent: Carnival
Easter: Easter Parade
14 July: Bastille Day

MONEY MATTERS

The euro is the official currency but US dollars are also universally accepted. Normal banking hours are Mon–Fri 8.30am–3pm. Several banks have ATMS.

TOURIST OFFICES

In Canada
French Government Tourist Office, 1981 Ave McGill College, Suite 490, Montreal, Québec H3A 2W9.
Tel: 514-288 2026.

French Government Tourist Office,
30 St Patrick Street, Suite 490,
Toronto, Ontario M5T 3A3.
Tel: 416-593 6427.
Sint Maarten Tourist Office,
703 Evans Avenue, Suite 106,
Toronto, Ontario M9C 5E9.
Tel: 416-622 4300.
In the UK
French Government Tourist Office,
178 Piccadilly, London WIJ 9AL.
Tel: 09068-244 123.
E-mail: info-uk@franceguide.com
In the US
St Martin Tourist Bureau,
675 Third Avenue,
New York, NY 10017.
Tel: 212-475 8970.
E-mail: sxmtony@msn.com
French West Indies Tourist Board,
444 Madison Avenue,
New York, NY 10022.
Tel: 900-990 0040.
E-mail: info@francetourism.com
French Government Tourist Office,
9454 Wilshire Boulevard,
Los Angeles, CA 90212.
Tel: 310-271 6665.
E-mail: fqto@qte.net
Sint Maarten Tourist Office,
675 Third Avenue, Suite 1806,
New York, NY 10017.
Tel: 212-953 2084/800-786 2278.
In St Martin
Port de Marigot, 97150 Marigot, St
Martin.
Tel: 590-875721
In St Maarten
Imperial Building, Vineyard Office Park,
#33 W.G. Buncamper Road, St.
Maarten.
Tel: 599-542 2337.

Websites
www.caribbean.co.uk
www.franceguide.com
www.st-martin.org
www.st-maarten.com

POSTAL SERVICES

In Marigot, the main post office is on
Rue de la Liberté, with branches at
Baie Nettle, Howell Center, Grand
Case and Quartier d'Orleans.

In Philipsburg, calls and telegrams
are sent through the Landsradio
central office in the Pondfill section of
town, between Loodsteeg and Market

Street. The Philipsburg post office is
behind the Landsradio building, with
another branch at Juliana airport.

TELECOMMUNICATIONS

The dialling code for the Dutch side is
599-54; for the French side: **590**.
Direct-dial overseas calls can be made
from most phones, including pay
phones; large hotels can send and
receive faxes and e-mail.
There is an internet cafe on Front
Street in Philipsburg.

SHOPPING

The French side is best for designer
clothes, perfumes, chocolate, cigars,
wine; good bargains on the Dutch side
include duty-frees, electronics and
spirits. For duty-free goods head for
Front Street, Philipsburg, and Rue de
la République and Marina Porte la
Royale, Marigot.

GETTING AROUND

By Car
Driving is on the right. Foreign
licences are accepted. Hire
companies operating on the island
include:
Dutch side: Cannegie Car Rental,
Front Street, Philipsburg,
tel: 599-542 2497.
French side: Avis, Bellevue,
tel: 590-875060.

By Taxi
Taxis are available in the centres of
both towns. Wait either at the pier or
where the tenders drop off. There are
no metres, but there are fixed charges
so check the price before you start.

By Bus
Buses travel regularly from
6am–midnight between Philipsburg
and Marigot, as well as on other
principal routes. Ask at the tourist
office about island tours by minibus.

Inter-Island Links
Destinations linked with St Maarten by
local airlines include Barbados, Trinidad
and Tobago, Martinique, St Barthélemy,
Anguilla, BVI, St Kitts, Curaçao, Aruba,
Bonaire, St Thomas, Saba, St

Eustatius, and Jamaica. Inter-island
airlines include: Winair, tel: 599-545
4273; LIAT, tel: 599-545 2403.
A ferry from Marigot serves Anguilla
(on the hour, 7am–5pm, 20-minute
journey time), there is also a ferry from
both Philipsburg and Marigot to St
Barthélemy. *Voyager I & II* run between
St Martin, St Barths and Saba. See:
www.voyager-st-barths.com

STAYING ON

Hotels on St Martin/St Maarten are
not cheap, especially during the
peak winter season. Both the French
and Dutch sides have small
guesthouses, apartments and villas,
which can be rented at weekly or
monthly rates.

Hotel Prices

Price categories are based on the
cost of a double room, for one
night:
$ = less than $100
$$ = $100–200
$$$ = more than $200.

St Maarten
Divi Little Bay Beach Resort
PO Box 961, Philipsburg, NA.
Tel: 542 2333.
Fax: 542 4336.
www.divilittlebay.com
Large resort on Little Bay, with hilltop
and beachfront rooms. **$$$**
Pasanggrahan Royal Inn
15 Front Street, Philipsburg, NA.
Tel: 542 3588.
Fax: 542 2885.
www.pasanhotel.com
Small, atmospheric, colonial hotel
with pool. **$–$$**
La Vista Hotel
PO Box 2086, NA.
Tel: 544 3005.
Fax: 544 3010.
Small, Antillean-style resort on Pelican
Point near to the beach. **$$–$$$**

St Martin
Hévéa
163 Blvd de Grand Case 97150, FWI.
Tel: 875685.
Fax: 878388.
Intimate colonial-style inn. **$–$$**

Le Meridien
Anse Marcel, BP 581, 97150, FWI.
Tel: 876700.
Fax: 873038.
www.lemeridien.com
A hotel consisting of two parts:
L'Habitation and Le Domaine. With a
spa and marina. **$$$**
La Samanna
PO Box 4077, 97064, FWI.
Tel: 876400.
Fax: 878786.
www.lasamanna.com
Exclusive resort with plenty of
facilities. **$$$**

Meal Prices

Price categories are based on the
cost of a meal for one person,
excluding drinks:
$ = less than $20
$$ = $20–40
$$$ = more than $40.

WHERE TO EAT

On both sides, traditional French
cooking and spicy Caribbean cuisine
are available; the French side tends to
have more gourmet restaurants, and
offers the option of a short hop
across to Anguilla for lunch.

On the Dutch side, options include
Dutch favourites such as pea soup and
sausages and Indonesian *rijstaffel*, a
banquet of up to 40 dishes.

St Maarten

Chesterfields
Great Bay Marina, Philipsburg.
Tel: 542 3484.
Seafood and pasta overlooking the
water. Popular watering hole for
yachties. **$$**
Pasanggrahan Royal Inn
15 Front Street, Philipsburg.
Tel: 542 3588.
International cuisine in fine colonial-
era beachfront hotel. **$–$$**
Wajang Doll
167 Front Street, Philipsburg.
Tel: 542 2867.
Indonesian food on the waterfront. **$$**

St Martin

La Brasserie de Marigot
11 Rue du Général de Gaulle, Marigot.
Tel: 879443.
French Caribbean cooking with a French
ambience; pavement tables. Take-out
also available. **$$**
Le Cottage
97 Blvd de Grand Case.
Tel: 290330.
French creole cuisine prepared by a
French chef. Good wines. **$$$**
The Rainbow
176 Blvd de Grand Case.
Tel: 875580.
Caribbean-style seafood. **$$**
Le Santal
Nettle Bay Beach, near Marigot.
Tel: 875348.
This restaurant is internationally
renowned as one of the best in the
Caribbean. French. **$$$**

SHORE ACTIVITIES

Excursions

St Maarten: Snorkelling and diving
(book in advance for the wreck dive) at
Proselyte Reef; duty-free shopping;
regatta in the America's Cup yachts
(often organised as a shore excursion);
art galleries in St Philipsburg; day trips
to Marigot and Anguilla.
St Martin: Beach at Grand Case, 20
minutes from Marigot; fruit, spice and
fish market in Marigot on Wednesday
and Sunday; butterfly farm; trip to
Philipsburg for duty-free shopping; day
trip to Anguilla.

Best Beaches

St Maarten: Orient Beach for water
sports; Baie Rouge for nude/topless
sunbathing
St Martin: Mullet Bay; Cupecoy Beach
for privacy in shelter of caves and cliffs

Water Sports

Diving, snorkelling, windsurfing and
sailing can be arranged from all the
main beaches.

Southern Caribbean

British Virgin Islands

Located at the top of the Lesser
Antilles, near the US Virgin Islands and
Anguilla and a short hop from Puerto
Rico, the British Virgin Islands (BVI) are
made up of over 50 islands, cays, and
rocks. The largest, Tortola, at 12 miles
(19 km) long and 4 miles (6 km) wide,
has the highest elevation in the BVI, at
1,760 ft (540 metres). It is also a
popular offshore financial centre.

ARRIVING BY SEA

Larger ships arrive in Tortola and tender
off Road Harbour, Road Town. Smaller
ships also tender off the islands of
Virgin Gorda and Jost van Dyke.

PUBLIC HOLIDAYS

1 January: New Year's Day
March: H. Lavity Stoutt's Birthday (1st
Monday); Commonwealth Day (2nd
Monday)
March/April: Easter; Good Friday;
Easter Monday
May/June: Whit Monday
June: (2nd Monday) Queen's Birthday
1 July: Territory Day
21 October: St Ursula's Day
14 November: The Prince of Wales'
Birthday
25 December: Christmas Day
26 December: Boxing Day

CALENDAR OF EVENTS

March/April: Easter Festival; Virgin
Gorda Carnival.
End May: BVI Music Festival.
End June/beginning July: Bacardi HIHO
International windsurfing competition.
August: Tortola's week-long Carnival
commemorating slave emancipation.

The official holidays are first Monday, Tuesday, and Wednesday of August.

MONEY MATTERS

Currency is the US$. Banking hours are 9am– 2pm, although some banks are open until 3 or 4pm. There are banks in Road Town (Tortola) and Spanish Town (Virgin Gorda).

TOURIST OFFICES

In the UK
British Virgin Island Tourist Board, 15 Upper Grosvenor Street, London W1K 7PJ.
Tel: 020-7355 9585.
Fax: 020-7355 9587.
In the US
British Virgin Islands Tourist Board, 1270 Broadway, Suite 705, New York, NY 10001.
Tel: 212-696 0400.
Fax: 212-563 2263.
E-mail: ny@bvitouristboard.com
3450 Wilshire Boulevard, Suite 1202, Los Angeles, CA 90010.
Tel: 213-736 8931.
Fax: 213-736 8935.
Email: la@bvitouristboard.com
3400 Peachtree Road NE, Suite 1735, Lennox Towers, Atlanta, Georgia 30326.
Tel: 404-467 4741.
Fax: 404-467 4342.
Email: at@bvitouristboard.com
In the British Virgin Islands
P.O. Box 134, Wickhams Cay, close to the Crafts Market, Road Town, Tortola
Tel: 494 3134.
Fax: 494 3866.
E-mail: bvitor@bvitouristboard.com
Virgin Gorda Yacht Harbour.
Tel: 495 5181.

Websites
www.britishvirginislands.com
www.bvitouristboard.com
www.bviwelcome.com

POSTAL SERVICES

The main post office on Tortola is on Main Street (take the lane off Waterfront Drive at the Ferry Dock).

TELECOMMUNICATIONS

The dialling code is **284**. International phone calls may be made from most phones, and some will take phone cards. Most hotels are able to send faxes or e-mails. Also available is AT&T USA Direct Service: 800–872 2881. There is an internet cafe at Data Pro in Road Town.

SHOPPING

An assortment of shops, including duty-free, line Tortola's Main Street in Road Town. The most famous of these is Pusser's Company Store which, in addition to its own rum, sells clothes, antiques, and all things nautical. There are also branches in Soper's Hole Wharf in the west and Leverick Bay in Virgin Gorda. The waterfront Crafts Alive Market sells locally made products. BVI Apparel has factory outlets selling clothes and gifts at low prices at Soper's Hole, Baugher's Bay and Road Town. Dive BVI Ltd stocks diving equipment. On Anegada, Pat's Pottery & Art features items all made on the island. Don't miss the eccentric Sunny Caribbee Herb & Spice Company in Road Town for lotions, herbs and spices.

GETTING AROUND

By Car
Driving is on the left. A temporary BVI driving licence is required. It can be obtained through the rental agency (for about US$10) on presentation of your valid driving licence. Advance booking is recommended in peak season. Cars can be rented in Road Town, close to the docks. Car rental firms include: **Avis**, Road Town, (opposite the Botanic Gardens). Tel: 495 4973; **International Car Rentals**, Road Town. Tel: 494 2516.

By Taxi
Taxis are easy to find on the BVI. They stop if hailed on the road, and wait at the cruise terminal. They have fixed prices, but check the fare before starting a journey. On Virgin Gorda, small lorries with benches run a reasonably-priced shuttle service between the main tourist points.

Inter-Island Links

By Air: There are good connecting flights from the international airports on St Martin and Puerto Rico; smaller airlines connect the BVI with the US Virgin Islands and Tortola with Anegada:
Air Sunshine: tel: 495 8900; in the US: 800-327 8900.
Air St Thomas, tel: 495 5935.
American Eagle, tel: 495 2559.
Carib Air, tel: 787-791 1240.
Gorda Aero Services, tel: 495 2271.
LIAT, tel: 495 1187, 495 2577.
Winair, tel: 494 2347.

By Ferry: Timetables are available in hotels, at the tourist board, and in *Welcome* magazine.
There are regular services from: Road Town, Tortola to Spanish Town, Virgin Gorda, and Peter Island; West End, Tortola to Jost Van Dyke; Beef Island, Tortola to North Sound and Spanish Town, Virgin Gorda (North Sound Express); Road Town, Tortola and West End to St Thomas and St John (both USVI); Virgin Gorda to St Thomas (USVI). There is also a free ferry from Beef Island, Tortola to Marina Cay (from Pusser's).

Hotel Prices

Price categories are based on the cost of a double room, for one night:
$ = less than $100
$$ = $100–200
$$$ = more than $200.

STAYING ON

It is easier to find a four or five-star deluxe hotel on the BVI than a budget guesthouse. However, there are five camp grounds, three on Anegada, one at White Bay on Jost Van Dyke, and one at Brewer's Bay on Tortola. There are also villas for rent (on a weekly or monthly basis). Some of the smartest hotels are on the outer islands.

Tortola

The Moorings – Mariner Inn
Road Town, Tortola, BVI.
Tel: 494 2332.
Basic rooms with kitchenettes. There

Hotel Prices

Price categories are based on the cost of a double room, for one night:

$ = less than $100
$$ = $100–200
$$$ = more than $200.

are dockside moorings and facilities for bareboat charters. **$$**

Prospect Reef Resort
Road Town, Tortola, BVI.
Tel: 494 3311.
Fax: 494 5595.
www.prospectreef.com
Large complex set around a marina west of Road Town, good facilities for yachting and water sports. **$$–$$$**

Sebastian's on the Beach.
Apple Bay, Tortola, BVI.
Tel: 495 4212, 800-335 4870.
www.sebastiansbvi.com
Friendly, informal place right on the beach, especially popular with young set and surfers. Caribbean dishes in a restaurant overlooking the bay. **$–$$**

Virgin Gorda

Biras Creek Hotel
North Sound, Virgin Gorda, BVI.
Tel: 494 3555.
Fax: 494 3557.
www.biras.com
Thirty-two luxury suites with breathtaking views over the Atlantic and the North Sound. Excellent sports facilities, pool, quiet sandy beach, and restaurant. **$$$**

The Bitter End Yacht Club and Resort
North Sound, Virgin Gorda, BVI
Tel: 494 2746, 800-872 2392; VHF Channel 16.
www.beyc.com
A maritime atmosphere. Hillside villas. Good water sports facilities (wind-surfing, sailing and diving). The waterfront bar and restaurant have barbecues in the evenings. **$$$**

Outer Islands

Anegada Reef Hotel
Setting Point, Anegada, BVI.
Tel: 495 8002.
Fax: 495 9362.
www.anegadareef.com
A perfect place to relax, 18 rooms; mooring facilities, dive shop. **$$–$$$**

White Bay Villas
White Bay, Jost Van Dyke, BVI.
Tel: 410-571 6692, 800-778 8066.
Fax: 410-571 6693.
www.jostvandyke.com
Six timber cottages on one of the best beaches in the Caribbean, next to the Soggy Dollar bar. **$$**

WHERE TO EAT

American, European and Caribbean creations, such as fungi (cornmeal pudding) and roti (curry wrapped in a thin chapati). Seafood, tropical fruits and vegetables are fresh and plentiful.

Look for the BVI Restaurant Guide (with map), a free annual publication available at the tourist board, which details restaurants, opening hours, prices and dress codes.

Tortola

Callaloo
Overlooking Prospect Reef Lagoon.
Tel: 494 3311.
International and creole-style gourmet cuisine. **$$$**

C & F Restaurant
Purcell Estate, Road Town.
Tel: 494 4941.
A cosy family place, serving local cuisine, especially seafood. Popular with locals and visitors alike. **$$**

Mrs Scattacliffe's
Carrot Bay.
Tel: 495 4556.
Homely atmosphere. The chef cooks mainly with home-grown vegetables. Specialties include soursop sherbert, coconut bread and papaya soup. Reservations necessary. **$**

Virgin Gorda

The Lobster Pot
Fischers Cove Beach..
Tel: 495 5252.
A romantic place serving Caribbean seafood, steak and chicken. **$$**

Meal Prices

Price categories are based on the cost of a meal for one person, excluding drinks:

$ = less than $20
$$ = $20–40
$$$ = more than $40.

The Mad Dog
The Baths.
Tel: 495 5830.
Small casual bar serving tasty sandwiches. **$**

Jost Van Dyke

Foxy's
Great Harbour.
Tel: 495 9258.
Buzzing with life, especially on the during the Friday and Saturday evening barbecues. Salads, grilled fish and chicken. Snack lunches on weekdays. Mainly seafood or *rotis* for dinner. **$**

SHORE ACTIVITIES

Excursions

Sailing, snorkelling, and beach day trips are the best reasons to visit the BVI. Other excursions include shopping in Road Town; hikes in Sage Mountain National Park (Tortola); day sailing trips to Virgin Gorda and Jost van Dyke and mini-regattas.

Sailing

The BVI is one of the best sailing areas in the Caribbean. Most cruise ship companies organise sailing trips or mini-regattas as excursions. International yacht charters such as **The Moorings**, **Stardust** or **Sun Sail** have branches on Tortola, for day hire, or a longer crewed or bareboat charter. Yachts are usually rented on a weekly basis. Check with the BVI tourist board, or see *Welcome* magazine for a comprehensive listing of small charter companies.

Water Sports

There is good snorkelling on the rocky edges of many beaches, such as Smuggler's Cove, Tortola or Deadman's Beach, Peter Island. Norman Island, with the nearby rocks called "the Indians", is worth a visit.

Apple Bay, Cane Garden Bay, and Josiah's Bay are popular windsurfing beaches on Tortola; there are also good conditions in Trellis Bay. Boardsailing BVI has lessons for beginners and sailing classes (tel: 495 2447); best in November

The wreck of the RMS *Rhone*, which lies west of Salt Island is the most popular dive site in the BVI and is also a marine park. The reefs around Anegada have been badly damaged by too many divers and heavy anchoring. Diving has now been banned to allow the reef to recover, and to establish a marine park there. Dive operators in the BVI include: Dive BVI, tel: 495 5513; fax: 495 5347; www.divebvi.com; Dive Tortola, tel: 494 9200; www.divetortola.com.

Bonefish and marlin sport fishing tours can be arranged through the Anegada Reef Hotel, tel: 495 8002; fax: 495 9362.

Antigua

Antigua lies in the central region of the Lesser Antilles, between St Barts, St Kitts and Nevis, Montserrat, and Guadeloupe. The island is relatively dry and flat, with the highest point, Boggy Peak at 1,330 ft (405 metres). Together with Barbuda and Redonda, (not covered in this book), Antigua is part of an independent nation within the British Commonwealth.

ARRIVING BY SEA

Cruise ships dock at Heritage Quay, in the centre of St Johns, or Deepwater Harbour, a three minute taxi ride away.

PUBLIC HOLIDAYS

1 January: New Year's Day
2 January: Carnival Last Lap
March/April: Easter; Good Friday; Easter Monday
May: (1st Monday) Labor Day
May/June: Whit Monday
June: (2nd Saturday) Queen's birthday
July: (1st Monday) V.C. Bird Day; Caricom Day.
August: (1st Monday and Tuesday) Carnival
October: (1st Monday) Merchants' Day (shops closed)
1 November: Independence Day
25 December: Christmas Day
26 December: Boxing Day

CALENDAR OF EVENTS

April: Antigua Sailing Week – a regatta with international participants held in late April.
International cricket.
July/August: Carnival – a 10-day festival starting the last week in July and culminating on the first Monday and Tuesday in August – in memory of the abolition of slavery.
October: Jazz Festival.

MONEY MATTERS

The currency is the EC dollar; US dollars are also widely accepted. Major credit cards are accepted in most restaurants and shops. Most of the major banks are located in High Street, St John's. Banking hours vary but are generally 8am–1pm and 3pm–5pm Monday–Thursday; 8am–12pm and 3pm–5pm Friday; the Bank of Antigua opens 8am–noon Saturday. Several banks have ATMs, located at Woods Shopping Center, St John's; the Royal Bank of Canada, Market Street and High Street, St John's. There is a branch of Antigua Commercial Bank in Codrington, Barbuda. There is also a branch of American Express at Antours, Long Street, St John's.

TOURIST OFFICES

In Canada
60 Avenue Clair East,
Suite 304,Toronto,
Ontario M4T 1N5.
Tel: 416-961 3085.
Fax: 416-961 7218.
In the UK
Antigua House,
15 Thayer Street,
London W1M 5LD.
Tel: 020-7486 7073.
Fax: 020-7486 1466.
In the US
610 5th Avenue,
Suite 311,
New York, NY 10020.
Tel: 212-541 4117.
Fax: 212-541 4789.
In Antigua
PO Box 363, Thames Street,
St John's.
Tel: 268-462 0480.

Website:
www.antigua-barbuda.org

POSTAL SERVICES

The main post office in St John's is on Long Street.

TELECOMMUNICATIONS

The international dialling code is **268**. Local and long-distance calls can be made from most telephones or from the offices of the Cable and Wireless telephone company on St Mary Street in St John's, and the Yacht Marina Office in English Harbour. Here you can also buy phone cards for payphones, send faxes and use the Internet. There is another 24-hour office near Clare Hill in northern Antigua, and an internet cafe on Redcliffe Street, Redcliffe Quay .

SHOPPIING

Heritage Quay and Redcliffe Quay in St John's are popular because of their proximity to the cruise terminal. There are duty-free shops and a market. Harmony Hall art gallery exhibits the work of Caribbean artists at Brown's Bay, near Freetown (tel: 975 4222). The market in St John's is good for local produce, such as the Antigua Black pineapple, reputed to be the sweetest in the world.

GETTING AROUND

By Car

Driving is on the left. Drivers require a a local driving permit, available for a fee (US$20) at any police station or car hire office if you present a valid driving licence. Some roads outside St John's are narrow and potholed with no pavement, so beware. Rental agencies: Avis, tel: 462 2840; Hertz, tel: 481 4440; Dollar Rent-a-Car, tel: 462 0362; Budget, tel: 462 3009; National, tel: 462 2113.

By Taxi

Taxis wait at the cruise terminals. Fares are posted at the cruise ship terminal, airport, tourist office, and in hotels. Agree a price before starting your journey. Many Antiguan taxi drivers are also qualified tour guides.

Inter-Island Links

Cruise ships do not generally call at Barbuda but for anyone staying on, the island is just 10 minutes away from Antigua by air. There is also a helicopter service to Montserrat, Caribbean Helicopters, tel: 460 5900. Antigua has direct air connections from Europe, USA and Canada, and frequent links with most Caribbean islands. Try: LIAT, tel: 480 5601; BWIA, tel: 462 1260; Carib Aviation, tel: 462 3147; Caribbean Star Airlines, tel: 480 2561; Air St Kitts/Nevis, tel: 465 8571.

STAYING ON

Antigua has luxury resort hotels, villas, guesthouses and apartments.

Admiral's Inn
Nelson's Dockyard,
PO Box 713, St John's.
Tel: 460 1027.
Fax: 460 1534.
www.admiralsantigua.com
Small, traditional hotel in a restored building at English Harbour. **$–$$**
Long Bay Hotel
Long Bay.
Tel: 463 2005.
Fax: 463 2439.
Family-owned and operated since 1966. Rooms cottages and a villa. Good water sports and beach. **$$$**
Jolly Harbour Resort
PO Box 1793, St John's.
Tel: 462 3085.
Fax: 462 7772.
Large hotel and villa complex with leisure amenities, yacht marina and a wide range of water sports. **$$–$$$**

Hotel Prices

Price categories are based on the cost of a double room, for one night:
$ = less than $100
$$ = $100–200
$$$ = more than $200.

Meal Prices

Price categories are based on the cost of a meal for one person, excluding drinks:
$ = less than $20
$$ = $20–40
$$$ = more than $40.

WHERE TO EAT

There are some delicious local dishes worth trying, such as pepper-pot, conch or chicken with rice and peas. Alternatively visitors can taste some of Antigua's international cuisine – French, Italian and Vietnamese.
The Admiral's Inn
Nelson's Dockyard.
Tel: 460 1027.
This traditional hotel-restaurant has West Indian cuisine. The outdoor terrace is pleasant. **$$**
Harmony Hall
Brown's Bay, near Freetown.
Tel: 460 4120.
A delightful lunch spot (and hotel) overlooking the old sugar mill and the bay; Italian dishes served on the terrace of a plantation-style house which includes an art gallery and craft shop. **$$–$$$**
Pizzas on the Quay (Big Banana Holding Co.)
Redcliffe Quay, St John's.
Tel: 462 6979.
Great pizzas and pasta. Popular at lunchtime. **$**
Calypso
Amaryllis Hotel, St John's.
Tel: 462 8690.
www.amaryllishotel.com
Good local food, with plenty of fish and seafood. **$$**
Shirley Heights Lookout
Shirley Heights, Nelson's Dockyard.
Tel: 460 1785.
Elegant restaurant in a renovated 18th-century house. Steel pan band livens things up on Thursday and Sunday evenings. **$$–$$$**

SHORE ACTIVITIES

Excursions

The museum at Nelson's Dockyard; open air market on Saturdays in St John's; Harmony Hall art gallery;

cricket matches at Antigua Recreation Ground in St John's; barbecue and steel band every Sunday at Shirley Heights Lookout Restaurant (from 3pm, not to be missed).

Water Sports

Sailing can be arranged through Nicholson Yacht Charters, tel: 800-662 6066, or Sun Yacht Charters, St John's, tel: 800-772 3500, 207-236 9611. If you prefer the rum'n'sun and loud music approach, try a trip on the *Jolly Roger* pirate ship from Redcliffe Quay, St John's, tel: 462 2064. For windsurfing, lessons and equipment, contact Windsurf Antigua, tel: 462 9463.
Several hotels have dive shops. Dive operators include: Dive Antigua, Rex Halcyon Cove, Dickenson Bay, tel: 462 3483; Jolly Dive, Club Antigua, tel: 462 7245; Dockyard Divers, Nelson's Dockyard, tel: 460 1178; Dive Runaway, Runaway Beach Club, tel: 462 2626.

Best Beaches

There is one beach for every day of the year on Antigua. Fort James, Dickenson Bay, Runaway Bay are only 5-10 minutes by taxi from St John's; Leper Colony Beach is accessible by four-wheel drive only.

Golf

There are golf courses at Cedar Valley Golf Club, tel: 462 0161 (18-hole) and the Harbour Club, Jolly harbour, tel: 462 8830 (short 18-hole).

Horse Riding

Riding tours are available at Spring Hill Riding Club, Falmouth Harbour, Antigua, tel: 460 2700.

St Kitts and Nevis

The two-island nation of St Kitts and Nevis lies toward the northern end of the Leeward Island chain, in the vicinity of St Martin, Antigua and Montserrat. The volcanic origin of these islands is apparent in their mountainous landscape.

ARRIVING BY SEA

Cruise ships dock at Port Zante terminal in Basseterre, St Kitts, a short walk from the centre of town. There are shops and restaurants at the terminal.

PUBLIC HOLIDAYS

1 January: New Year's Day
2 January: Carnival Last Lap
March/April: Good Friday, Easter Monday
4 May: Labour Day
August: (1st Monday) Emancipation Day (2nd Monday); Culturama Last Lap
16 September: National Heroes Day
19 September: Independence Day
25 December: Christmas Day
26 December: Boxing Day

CALENDAR OF EVENTS

Mid–late June: St Kitts Music Festival.
July–first Monday in August: Culturama – carnival and arts festival on Nevis.
September: Independence celebrations.
Mid-December–early January: Carnival.

MONEY MATTERS

The currency on both islands is the Eastern Caribbean dollar (EC$); US dollars are also widely accepted. Banks are open Monday–Thursday 8am–2pm and Friday 8am–4pm. There are many local and international banks, but none are open on Saturday. There are ATMS at several banks.

TOURIST OFFICES

In Canada
133 Richmond St West, Suite 311, Toronto, Ontario M5H 2L3.
Tel: 416-368 6707.
E-mail: canada.office@stkittstourism.kn
In the UK
10 Kensington Court, London W8 5DL.
Tel: 020-7376 0881. E-mail: uk-europe.office @stkittstourism.kn

In the US
414 East 75th Street, New York, NY 10021.
Tel: 212-535 1234.
E-mail: info@stkittstourism.kn
In St Kitts and Nevis
Pelican Mall, Basseterre, St Kitts.
Tel: 465 4040/2620.Main Street, Charlestown, Nevis. Tel: 469 7550.
www.stkitts-tourism.com

POSTAL SERVICES

There are two post offices, located on Bay Road in Basseterre and Main Street in Charlestown. Opening hours: St Kitts: Mon–Tues 8am– 4pm, Wed–Fri 8am– 3.30pm. Nevis: Mon–Fri 8am–3.30pm.

TELECOMMUNICATIONS

The dialling code is **869**. Direct-dialled international calls may be made from any telephone by dialling 1, and operator-assisted calls may be made by dialling 0. Credit card calls, fax, Internet, e-mail, beeper and cell phone services are also available. Offices are located at:
St Kitts: Cayon St, Basseterre, tel: 465 2219 (open 7.30am–6pm weekdays, 7.30am–1pm Saturday, and 6–8pm Sunday and public holidays).
Nevis: Main Street, Charlestown, tel: 469 5294.
There are Internet cafes in the TDC Mall and the Pelican Mall in St Kitts.

SHOPPING

For local colour, don't miss the market in Basseterre (Saturday morning). For colourful clothing, look for imaginative batik prints whose fabrics are often made from locally-grown cotton. Try: Caribelle Batik workshops in Romney Manor, St Kitts. Kate Design for paintings, pottery and printed silk. Shops are at Rawlins Plantation, Basseterre, and Charlestown.

GETTING AROUND

By Car

Driving is on the left. Visitors must present a valid national or international licence at the Traffic Department or the Fire Station, along with a small fee to obtain a temporary licence. Branches of the Traffic Department are located at the police stations in Basseterre on Cayon Street and Charlestown on Island Road. Car hire agencies include: Avis, South Independence Square, Basseterre, St Kitts, tel: 465 6507. Caines, Princes Street, Basseterre, St Kitts, tel: 465 2366.

By Taxi

Taxis wait at the cruise terminal. Tariffs are fixed, but confirm the fare before starting out.

By Bus

Small minibuses are reliable and cheap but they rarely travel the usual tourist routes.

Inter-Island Links

St Kitts is linked by air with many islands including Puerto Rico, Antigua, Barbados, St Martin, Anguilla, St Barths, Saba, St Eustatius, USVI, BVI, Grenada, and St Lucia.
Nevis is linked with USVI, St Barths, Anguilla, Antigua, and St Martin. Airlines serving the routes to and from St Kitts and Nevis include: Winair, tel: 465 0810; LIAT, tel: 465 2286; Carib Aviation, tel: 465 3055; Nevis Express, tel: 469 9755/4756; Caribbean Star and Caribbean Sun, tel: 465 5929.
An air taxi and a ferry, run daily between Basseterre, St Kitts and Charlestown, Nevis. Journey time is 30–45-minutes Tickets can be purchased at the ferry terminal.

STAYING ON

Hotels in St Kitts and Nevis are generally small, some are converted plantation houses and sugar mills. St Kitts and Nevis also have cottages, apartments and condominiums.

St Kitts

Frigate Bay Resort
P.O. Box 137, St Kitts.
Tel: 465 8935.
Fax: 465 7050.
www.frigatebay.com
Overlooking Frigate Bay. Guests are exempt from green fees. **$$$**

Hotel Prices

Price categories are based on the cost of a double room, for one night:
$ = less than $100
$$ = $100–200
$$$ = more than $200.

The Golden Lemon
Dieppe Bay, St Kitts.
Tel: 465 7260.
Fax: 465 4019.
www.goldenlemon.com
Beautifully decorated and restored 17th-century inn and villas about 15 miles (24 km) from Basseterre. **$$$**
Rawlins Plantation Inn
P.O. Box 340, St Kitts.
Tel: 465 6221.
Fax: 465 4954.
www.rawlinsplantation.com
A former plantation great house converted into an elegant inn with cottages set in tropical gardens. **$$$**

Nevis
Hurricane Cove Bungalows
Oualie Beach, Nevis.
Tel/Fax: 469 9462.
www.hurricanecove.com
Wooden bungalows perched on a bluff overlooking Oualie Beach, with views of The Narrows and St Kitts. **$$–$$$**
Nisbet Plantation Beach Club
Newcastle, Nevis.
Tel: 469 9325.
Fax: 469 9864.
www.thereefs.com/nisbet
Lovely rooms and cottages on the site of an 18th-century oceanside coconut plantation. **$$$**

WHERE TO EAT

St Kitts and Nevis have restaurants specialising in West Indian, Creole, French, Indian, and Chinese food. In addition to the ubiquitous fresh seafood, the most distinctive feature of local cuisine is the abundance of fresh vegetables from the islands' volcanic soil. Breadfruit, eggplant (aubergine), sweet potatoes, and okra all appear on island plates.

St Kitts
Ballahoo
The Circus, Basseterre, St Kitts.
Tel: 465 4197.
West Indian seafood and fruit drinks are served in this popular meeting place with scenic views. **$$$**
The Golden Lemon
Dieppe Bay, St Kitts.
Tel: 465 7260.
www.goldenlemon.com
Acclaimed for its Continental and Caribbean dishes. Reservations required. **$$$**

Nevis
Nisbet Plantation Beach Club
Newcastle, Nevis.
Tel: 469 9325.
Lunch and Sunday barbecue on the beach; formal dining in the great house. **$$–$$$**
Unella's Bar and Restaurant
Charlestown, Nevis.
Tel: 469 5574.
Fresh seafood and waterfront views. **$–$$**

Meal Prices

Price categories are based on the cost of a meal for one person, excluding drinks:
$ = less than $20
$$ = $20–40
$$$ = more than $40.

SHORE ACTIVITIES

Excursions
Historic tours of St Kitts; Romney Manor batik workshops; Black Rocks at Sandy Bay (lava formations); views and battlegrounds on Brimstone Hill; day trips to nearby Nevis, six minutes by air or 45 minutes by ferry.

Best Beaches
Banana Bay and Cockleshell Bay for peace and quiet; Turtle Beach and Frigate Beach for water sports; Friars Bay for snorkelling.

Water sports
Strong currents make swimming on the Atlantic side of the islands dangerous. Swim safely on the calmer Caribbean side. For diving, try: Kenneth's Dive Shop, Newtown Bay Road, Basseterre, tel: 465 1950; Pro-Divers, Turtle Beach, tel: 466 3483; St Kitts Scuba, Bird Rock, tel: 465 1189.

Hiking
Both islands have lush rainforests and hilly terrain. A particular thrill is the hike down into the crater of an old volcano on Mount Liamuiga in St Kitts. On Nevis, Eco-Tours Nevis (tel: 469 2091) organises guided hikes, including an Eco-Ramble.

Golf
Frigate Bay Golf Course is an 18-hole championship course in St Kitts, a 9-hole golf course is at Golden Rock (tel: 465 8103). Nevis has an 18-hole course attached to the Four Seasons Resort (tel: 469 1111).

Dominica

Dominica is located in the middle of the gracefully curving Antillean chain, between Guadeloupe and Martinique. Measuring 15 miles (25 km) wide by 29 miles (46 km) long, Dominica is blessed with dramatic mountainous scenery. It is also the only island where Caribs have survived and maintained traditional crafts, such as canoe carving.

ARRIVING BY SEA

The main cruise terminal is in the capital, Roseau, in the centre of the town's waterfront. Some ships berth at Portsmouth in the north but may have to tender in.

PUBLIC HOLIDAYS

1 January: New Year's Day
March/April: Good Friday; Easter Monday
1 May: Labour Day
May/June: Whit Monday
August: (1st Monday) August Monday
3 November: Independence Day
4 November: Community Service Day
25 December: Christmas Day
26 December: Boxing Day

CALENDAR OF EVENTS

February/March: Carnival is held on the Monday and Tuesday preceding Ash Wednesday.
Late June: Dive Fest is an annual watersports festival.
End of October/early November: Creole Day – Independence day festivities (national costume is worn).
October (last weekend): World Creole Music Festival is a three-day event.

MONEY MATTERS

The currency is the Eastern Caribbean dollar (EC$). US dollars are accepted in some places, although change will be given in EC$. Banking hours are usually Mon–Thurs 8am–2pm, Fri 8am–4pm. First Caribbean, Barclays, the Royal Bank of Canada, and the Bank of Nova Scotia are the main commercial banks, all with branches in Roseau. There are ATMs, including one at the Royal Bank of Canada, Bay Street.

TOURIST OFFICES

In the UK
Dominica High Commission,
1 Collingham Gardens,
London SW5 OHW.
Tel: 020-7370 5194/5.
In the US
Dominica Tourist Office,
110–64 Queens Blvd, PO Box 427,
Forest Hills, NY 11375-6347.
Tel: 718-261 9615.

Website
www.dominica.dm

POSTAL SERVICES

The main post office is at the Bay Front, Roseau (open 8am–4pm Mon–Fri).

TELECOMMUNICATIONS

The dialling code is **767**. Cable and Wireless provides the telecommunications service at Mercury House, Hanover Street, Roseau. Phonecards are available from Cable and Wireless, some shops and hotels. In Roseau, there is a bank of telephones on the pier, but they are credit card phones with the option of making reverse charge calls to the US. Cellular services are also provided by Orange and AT&T. Internet cafes are located on the bay front and on King George V Street.

SHOPPING

While Dominica cannot compete with other ports of call for the range of duty-free luxury goods, it has crafts that are unique to the island, such as Indian reed baskets, which provide a direct link to Venezuelan culture. These can be bought in Carib Territory or from Tropicrafts on the corner of Queen Mary Street in Roseau. Caribana, at 31 Cork Street, showcases local painters, sculptors, and jewellers.

GETTING AROUND

By Car

Driving is on the left. The speed limit in built-up areas is 20 mph (32 kph). Roads in Dominica are twisting and narrow, with steep gradients; surfaces vary from excellent to pot-holed.
Jeeps can be rented at the cruise pier from Budget, Avis and local operators. You need a national or international driving licence and a local visitor's permit, available from the police traffic department (High Street, Roseau), from the police station or airport, or from a car rental company. Hire companies: Avis, tel: 800-882 8471; Budget, tel: 449 2080; Island Car, tel: 255 6844.

By Taxi

Taxis wait at the cruise terminal and will conduct private round-the-island tours. Official drivers should have number plates beginning with the letter H or HA. On fixed routes the fares are set by the government. Settle on a price before your journey.

By Bus

Minibuses are the local form of public transport, from early in the morning to nightfall. They run mainly to and from Roseau. There are no fixed timetables; buses leave when they are full. In Roseau there are various departure points depending on the destination. There are frequent services to villages around Roseau, but making a round trip in one day from Roseau to more remote communities can be a problem. Allow plenty of time to get back to the ship if you are using public transport.

Inter-Island Links

There are no direct flights from Europe to Dominica. Connections with Dominica are made with the regional airline, LIAT, from neighbouring Caribbean islands, including Antigua, Guadeloupe, and Martinique. American Eagle flies daily from San Juan, Puerto Rico (with connections to the US). The main airport is Melville Hall. LIAT occasionally also uses the smaller Canefield Airport, close to Roseau.
LIAT, tel: 448 2421.
American Eagle, tel: 448 0628.
Caribbean Star, tel: 448 2181.
A regular, efficient ferry service connects Dominica with Guadeloupe (to the north); Martinique and St Lucia (to the south). For tickets contact: L'Express des Isles, Whitchurch Centre, Roseau. Tel: 448 2181.

STAYING ON

Most accommodation is concentrated around Roseau.

Anchorage Hotel.
P.O. Box 34, Roseau.
Tel: 448 2638.
Fax: 448 5680.
www.anchoragehotel.dm
Long-established, family-run hotel, just south of Roseau. **$$**
Cherry Lodge Guesthouse
20 Kennedy Avenue, Roseau.
Tel: 448 2366.
Rooms in a traditional building, with wooden verandah. **$**
Fort Young Hotel
P.O. Box 519, Roseau.
Tel: 448 5000.
Fax: 448 5006.
www.fortyounghotel.com
Built over an 18th-century French fort overlooking the sea, Dominica's smartest hotel still displays its original battlements. Swimming pool; pleasant atmosphere. **$$$**

Meal Prices

Price categories are based on the cost of a meal for one person, excluding drinks:
$ = less than $20
$$ = $20–40
$$$ = more than $40.

WHERE TO EAT

Fresh fruit juices, made with tamarind, guava, sorrel, grapefruit, are one of the delights of Dominican cuisine, along with specialities such as "mountain chicken" (a large frog endemic to Dominica); crab backs and *titiri* (fritters made of tiny fish). Other more rustic Dominican dishes include saltfish, ground provisions (*dasheen*, yam, sweet potato, cous-cous), *callaloo* (young shoots of the *dasheen*) soup. Rouseau, rather than Portsmouth, is the place for eating out.

Callaloo
King George V Street, Roseau.
Tel: 448 3386.
Dine on the upstairs verandah. **$$**
Coconut Beach
Picard Beach, Portsmouth.
Tel: 445 5393.
Overlooking the twin peaks of the Cabrits National Park. The view is finer than the seafood and creole fare. **$$**
La Robe Creole
3 Victoria Street, Roseau.
Tel: 448 2896.
The capital's smartest restaurant in a stone townhouse, with a delicious variety of authentic creole dishes. **$$$**
The Mousehole Snackette
Victoria Street, Roseau.
Tel: 448 5000.
Snack bar serving fresh fruit juice, creole pastries, lunchtime *rotis*, codfish, bakes, and other local specialties. Next to La Robe Creole. **$**

SHORE ACTIVITIES

Excursions

Excursions are offered from both Roseau and Portsmouth but given the logistics, passengers are usually restricted to just one trip.
    In Roseau you can visit the marketplace, Botanical Garden, cathedral and the Dominica Museum. Outside town there are trips to Trafalgar Falls; island tours; guided hiking trails of varying difficulty; the Morne Diablotin National Park, home to an endangered species of Amazonian parrot (access by four-wheel drive vehicle); boat trips on the Indian River; tours of the Carib Territory, for traditional crafts and culture. Portsmouth provides easy access to the Carib territory and the unspoilt Cabrits National Park.

Best Beaches

Hampstead Beach on the northern coast is one of the finest, with white sand and palms, and sheltered Macousheri Bay and Coconut Beach near Portsmouth; accessible by four-wheel drive vehicle, Turtle Beach and Pointe Baptiste (unsafe for swimming due to Atlantic rollers and currents).

Water Sports

Dominica has whale-watching trips organised by local operators, and some of the best diving in the Caribbean, with steep 1000-ft (300 metre) drop-offs, hot springs, pinnacles and walls. Dive sites are concentrated along the west coast. The deep waters make local expertise essential for diving excursions. Operators offer a variety of packages for beginners and experienced divers. An annual Dive Fest in July, has diving, kayaking, swimming, fishing, snorkelling, sunset cruises. Approved dive operators who also provide snorkelling gear, include:
Anchorage Dive Center, tel: 448 2638; fax: 448 5680; Dive Castaways, tel: 449 6244; fax: 449 6246; Dive Dominica, tel: 448 2188; fax: 448 6088.

Horse Riding

High Ride Adventures, Soufrière, tel: 448 6296.

Martinique

Located south of the Tropic of Cancer, Martinique, a French overseas *département*, is a 420-sq mile (1,050-sq.km) island belonging to the Windward Islands group in the Lesser Antilles.

ARRIVING BY SEA

Cruise ships dock in the capital, Fort-de-France, at two places: the old dock in Tourelles, 1.5 miles (2 km) from the town centre, around 15 minutes' walk, and at Pointe Simon, 600 yards (549 meteres) from the nearest shops.

PUBLIC HOLIDAYS

1 January: New Year's Day
February: Carnival
March/April: Easter Sunday; Easter Monday
22 May: Slavery Abolition Day
14 July: Bastille Day
21 July: Schoelcher Day
15 August: Assumption Day
1 November: All Saints Day
11 November: Armistice Day
25 December: Christmas Day

CALENDAR OF EVENTS

March: International Sailing Week.
April: Aqua Festival (Festival of the Sea).
1–30 May: Le Mai de St Pierre (festivities in commemoration of the eruption of the Pelée volcano).
June: Jazz at Leyritz Plantation Estate.
July: Fort-de-France Cultural Festival; International Bicycle Race; Crayfish Festival in Ajoupa Bouillon.
August: Yawl sailing race.
November: Biennial International Jazz Festival or the International guitar festival (alternate years).
December: Rum Festival, Musée du Rhum, St James Distillery.

MONEY MATTERS

The local currency on Martinique is the Euro (€), but US dollars (US$) are also accepted. Most major credit cards are accepted throughout the island and there are banks with ATMs in the town centre.

TOURIST OFFICES

In Canada
Martinique Tourist Office,
2159 rue Mackay,
Montreal, Quebec H3G 2J2.
Tel: 514-844 8566.
Fax: 514-844 8901.

Maison de la France,
1981 Ave McGill College, Suite 490,
Montreal PQ 3A2 2W9.
Tel: 514-288 4264.
Fax: 514-845 4868
In the UK
Maison de la France,
178 Picadilly, London W1V OAL.
Tel: 09068 244 123 (premium line).
In the US
Martinique Promotion Bureau,
444 Madison Avenue,
16th Floor, New York, NY 10022.
Tel: 212-838 7800.
Fax: 212-838 7855.
In Martinique
Rue Ernest Deproge, 97200 Fort-de-
France.
Tel: 596-63 79 60; fax: 73 66 93.
Maison du Tourism Verte, 9 Boulevard
du General de Gaulle, 97200 Fort-de-
France.
Tel: 63 18 54; fax: 70 17 61.

Website
www.martiniquetourism.com

POSTAL SERVICES

There are post offices in all of the
main towns. Hotels, tabacs and other
shops also sell stamps.

TELECOMMUNICATIONS

The dialling code for Martinique is
596. Direct-dialled telephone calls can
be made from public payphones and
hotels. The larger hotels also have fax
facilities. Telegrams, faxes, and
phones calls can be made from post
offices. Internet facilities are available
at Le Web Cybercafe, 4 rue Blenac,
Fort-de-France

SHOPPING

Many shops are outposts of French
chains. Good buys include jewellery,
cosmetics, and French fashions. The
the main shopping streets are rue
Victor Hugo and rue de la Republique.
There is a mall, The Galleria, a short
taxi ride from town, with a French
supermarket and fashion stores.

GETTING AROUND

By Car

A current driving licence is required to
rent a car for 20 days or less. Visiting
drivers should have at least one
year's driving experience. Budget car
rental has an office at the cruise
terminal and Avis is in Fort-de-France.

By Taxi

Taxis wait at the cruise terminal but
are unmetered and expensive.

Inter-Island Links

Airlines connecting Martinique to
Antigua, Barbados, Dominica,
Grenada, Guadeloupe, Puerto Rico, St
Lucia, St Martin, St Vincent, and
Trinidad include: Air Caraibe, tel: 51
17 27; Air Saint-Martin, tel: 51 57 03.
Jet Aviation Service, tel: 51 57 03
and LIAT, tel: 0590-21 1393.
Ferries link Martinique to Dominica,
Guadeloupe and St Lucia: Caribbean
Express Des Iles, tel: 63 12 11.

Hotel Prices

Price categories are based on the
cost of a double room, for one
night:
$ = less than $100
$$ = $100–200
$$$ = more than $200.

STAYING ON

Martinique has a wide selection of
accommodation, including attractive,
smaller places which form the Relais
Créoles group of hotels.
Hotel Baie du Galion
Presqu'île de la Caravelle Tartane,
97220 Trinité.
Tel: 58 65 30.
Fax: 58 25 76.
www.hotelbaiedugalion.com
On Caravelle peninsula near
numerous bays and coves. **$–$$**
La Malmaison
7 rue de la Liberté, 97200 Fort-de-
France.
Tel: 63 90 85.
Fax: 60 03 93.
Pleasant rooms overlooking the
Savannah Park. Good service. **$**

Marouba Club
Le Coin, 97221 Carbet.
Tel: 78 00 21.
Fax: 78 05 65.
www.marouba.mq
Situated in a tropical park on the edge
of a volcanic sand beach. Excellent
facilities and activities. **$$–$$$**
Leyritz Plantation
Bourg, 97218 Basse Pointe.
Tel: 78 53 92.
Fax: 78 92 44.
www.plantationleyritz.com
A restored 18th-century sugar
plantation. Creole cuisine. **$–$$**

WHERE TO EAT

Familiar French dishes are given an
twist by the use of tropical fruits,
vegetables, and seafood. Visitors will
find plenty of spicy Caribbean
specialities. Restaurant hours are
usually noon–3pm and 7–10pm.
La Belle Epoque
97, route de Didier, Fort-de-France.
Tel: 64 41 19.
Serves French and Creole food.
Closed Sat noon and Sun. **$$**
Le Fromager
Route de Fond Denis, St Pierre.
Tel: 78 19 07.
Serves Creole specialities. **$$**
Le Mareyeur
Pointe des Nègres, Fort-de-France.
Tel: 61 74 70.
Creole and seafood specialities. **$$**

SHORE ACTIVITIES

Excursions

Shopping in duty-free outlets, markets
and Galleria shopping mall for French
designer outlets; La Savane botanical
gardens in Fort-de-France; Macouba
fishing village; St Pierre for the
waterfront and Muse Volcanologique;
for the beaches take a ferry trip to
Pointe du Bout (25 minutes).

Best Beaches

Pointe les Salinas (for divers); Anse
Mitan and Anse-a-l'Ane.

Water Sports

Popular areas for water sports include
Tartane (Trinité), Robert, Schoelcher,
and St Pierre. In the south, scuba
diving, water skiing, jet skiing, surfing

and windsurfing, sailing and canoeing are all available. Contact:
Agi Cat Club, Immeuble Sarde N55, Pointe du Bout, 97229 Les Trois-Ilets, tel: 66 03 01; fax: 66 03 24.
Loisirs Nautiques, 97227 Ste Anne. Tel: 6 76 48. Fax: 76 77 64.
Ship Shop, Carenantilles – Ancienne Usine du Marin, 97290 Marin, tel: 74 70 08; fax: 74 78 22. Sub Diamond Rock, Pointe la Chery, 97223 Diamant. Tel/Fax: 76 10 65.
Tropicasub, La Guinguette, BP 10 Quartier Mouillage, 97250 St Pierre. Tel: 78 38 03. Fax: 52 46 82.

Golf

Martinique Golf and Country Club, 97229 Les Trois-Ilets, tel: 68 32 81; fax: 68 38 97. An excellent 18-hole championship course.

Guadeloupe

South of Antigua and north of Dominica, toward the centre of the Lesser Antilles, lies Guadeloupe, part of a French archipelago which also includes the islands of St Barthélemy, St Martin, Les Saintes, La Désirade, and Marie Galante.

ARRIVING BY SEA

Cruise passengers arrive at centrally located Pointe-à-Pitre, which, along with Basse-Terre, is one of the island's two main towns. The Centre Saint-John Perse, a commercial area, is 5 minutes' walk from town centre.

PUBLIC HOLIDAYS

1 January: New Year's Day
February/March: Ash Wednesday
March/April: Easter
May 1: Labour Day
May 8: VE Day
May 27: Abolition Day
May (variable): Ascension Day
May (variable): Whit Monday
14 July: Bastille Day
21 July: Schoelcher Day (emancipation)
15 August: Assumption Day
1 November: All Saints Day
11 November: Armistice Day
22 November: Ste Cecilia Day
24 December: Christmas Eve

25 December: Christmas Day
26 December: Young Saints Day; Children's Parade
31 December: New Year's Eve

CALENDAR OF EVENTS

February: Carnival
May: Fête de la Musique Traditionnelle in Ste Anne.
November: (first Saturday) Creole Music Festival, at Pointe-à-Pitre.

MONEY MATTERS

The local currency is the euro (€), but US dollars (US$) are also accepted at some establishments. Most major credit cards are accepted. There are also banks with ATMs.

TOURIST OFFICES

In Canada
French Tourist Office,
1981 Avenue McGill College, Suite 490, Montréal H3A 2W9.
Tel: 514-844 8566.
Fax: 514-844 8901.
30 St Patrick Street, Suite 700, Toronto M5T 3A3.
Tel: 416-593 4723.
Fax: 416-979 7587.
In the UK
French Tourist Office (Maison de la France),
178 Piccadilly, London W1 0AL.
Tel: 020-7629 2869.
Fax: 020-7493 6594.
In the US
French Tourist Office,
444 Madison Avenue, New York, NY 10022.
Tel: 212-757 1125.
In Guadeloupe
Office du Tourisme de la Guadeloupe, 5 Square de la Banque, BP 422, 97163 Pointe-à-Pitre.
Tel: 590-82 09 30.
Office du Tourisme, Basse-Terre.
Tel: 590-81 24 83/81 61 54.
Office Municipal de St-François.
Tel: 590-88 48 74.

POSTAL SERVICES

In Pointe-à-Pitre, post offices are located on Boulevard Hanne and Boulevard Légitimus.

TELECOMMUNICATIONS

The international dialling code is **590**. Long-distance telephone calls can be made from payphones and most hotels, which also have fax facilities. Main post offices have telegram, fax, and phone.

SHOPPING

Best buys are bolts of fabric, arts and crafts, French designer clothing and perfume. There are shops at the Centre St-John Perse and the Cora Center in Bas-du-Fort. Good markets include the Marche St Antoine, Marche de la Danse and the Place Gourbeyre flower market by the cathedral.

GETTING AROUND

By Car

A valid driving licence is sufficient to rent a car for 20 days or less. Drivers should have at least one year's driving experience. Pointe-à-Pitre and Pôle Caraïbes airports have car rental agencies, but they are expensive. Mopeds are also available for hire.

By Taxi

Taxis are available at the cruise terminal but they are expensive; not all routes have pre-fixed rates. Drivers usually only speak French.

Inter-Island Links

Air links with neighbouring islands are available with the following airlines:
Air Guadeloupe, tel: 590-83 02 23.
Air Caraibes, tel: 590-21 13 34.
Air Saint-Martin, tel: 590-21 12 89.
Air Martinique, tel: 590-21 30 40.

STAYING ON

Accommodation on Guadeloupe varies from large luxury resorts to small family-run guesthouses and campgrounds. Hotels are concentrated around Gosier, Grande-Terre.

Grande-Terre

Sofitel Auberge De La Veille Tour
Montauban, Gosier.
Tel: 590-84 23 23.
Fax: 84 33 43.
www.sofital.com
Luxury hotel in an authentic 18th-

century windmill, set in a 7-acre (3-hectare) park. Sea views. **$$$**
Hotel La Toubana
Ste Anne.
Tel: 88 07 74.
Fax: 88 38 90.
Cottages surrounded by lush tropical gardens, with spectacular vistas of the south coast and offshore island, a pool, private beach and a popular French and creole restaurant. **$$**

Basse-Terre

Le Jardin Malanga
L'Hermitage, Trois-Rivières.
Tel: 92 67 57.
Fax: 92 67 58.
A beautifully renovated 1927 great house and three spacious guest houses with lush gardens and hillside views of Les Saintes. Perfect location, for exploring the Chutes du Carbet. **$**

Hotel Prices

Price categories are based on the cost of a double room, for one night:
$ = less than $100
$$ = $100–200
$$$ = more than $200.

WHERE TO EAT

Guadeloupe's cuisine mirrors its many cultures. The local creole specialities combine the finesse of French cuisine, the spice of African cookery, and the exoticism of East Indian and Southeast Asian recipes. Fresh seafood appears on most menus.

Grande-Terre

Le Roi de la Langouste at Chez Honoré
Anse à la Gourde, St François.
Tel: 88 52 19.
Creole specialties and clawless lobster. **$**
Chez Prudence (Folie Plage)
Anse Bertrand.
Tel: 22 11 17.
Creole cuisine. **$–$$**
Le Relais du Moulin
Ste Anne.
Tel: 88 23 96.
Hotel restaurant serving creole specialties. **$–$$**

Meal Prices

Price categories are based on the cost of a meal for one person, excluding drinks:
$ = less than $20
$$ = $20–40
$$$ = more than $40.

Basse-Terre

Le Karacoli
Deshaies.
Tel: 28 41 17.
Creole cuisine on the beach. Open lunchtimes only. **$–$$**
Restaurant du Domaine de Severin
La Boucan, Ste Rose.
Tel: 28 34 54.
Creole cuisine. **$–$$**
Le Ti'Racoon
Parc Zoologique – Route des Deux Mamelles, Bouillante.
Tel: 98 83 52.
French and creole specialties. **$–$$**

SHORE ACTIVITIES

Excursions

Shopping in Pointe-a-Pitre; trips along the dramatic coastline at Pointe des Chateaux; La Soufriere volcano and national park; diving and snorkelling at the Cousteau Underwater Park in Basse-Terre; day trips to Marie-Galante island; water scooter tours of the mangroves; deep-sea fishing; hiking.

Best Beaches

Anse Carot on Marie-Galante; Gosier and Ste-Anne; Pointe des Chateaux has snack bars, scenery, but rough seas. In town, try Plage du Bourg.

Water Sports

Day sailing trips are run from Marina Bas du Fort, Gosier (tel: 90 92 98). For scuba diving, contact:
Aux Aquanautes Antillais, Plage de Malendure, Bouillante, tel: 98 87 30.
Tropical Sub, tel: 28 52 67.
Plaisir Plongée Caraïbe, Chez Guy and Christian, Pigeon, Bouillante, tel: 98 82 43.
There is good snorkelling at Cousteau Underwater Park on the Golden Corniche (a popular cruise excursion), with glass bottomed boat trips.

St Lucia

St Lucia lies at the southern end of the Lesser Antilles between Martinique and St Vincent. The island is 27 mile (43 km) long and 14 miles (22 km) wide and has been independent since 1979. It is volcanic in origin, as can be seen from its hot sulphur springs, mountainous terrain, fertile soil, and the landmark peaks of the Pitons.

ARRIVING BY SEA

Cruise ships dock at the efficient Pointe Seraphine cruise terminal in downtown Castries, two minutes walk from the shops.

PUBLIC HOLIDAYS

January 1–2: New Year's Celebrations
February 22: Independence Day
March/April: Easter; Good Friday
May 1: Labour Day
August 1: Emancipation Day
August 30: Feast of St Rose de Lima
October 17: Feast of La Marguérite
December 13: National Day
December 25: Christmas Day
December 26: Boxing Day

CALENDAR OF EVENTS

February/March: Carnival (the two days leading up to Ash Wednesday).
May: St Lucia Jazz Festival.
October: Thanksgiving Day; Jounnen Kweyol Entenasyonnal (International Creole Day).

MONEY MATTERS

The currency is the EC dollar, although US dollars are also accepted in most places as are credit cards and traveller's cheques. There are foreign exchange facilities in Castries.

TOURIST OFFICES

In Canada
St Lucia Tourist Board,
8 King Street East, Suite 700,
Toronto, Ontario M5C 1B5.
Tel: 416-362 4242.
Fax: 416-362 7832.

In the UK
1 Collingham Gardens,
London, SW5 0HW.
Tel: 0870 900 7697.
Fax: 020-7431 7920.
In the US
St Lucia Tourist Board,
800 Second Ave., Suite 400J, 9th
Floor, New York 10017.
Tel: 212-867 2951/2950.
Fax: 212-867 2795.
In St Lucia
St Lucia Tourist Board,
PO Box 221, Sureline Building, Vide
Bouteille, Castries.
Tel: 758-452 4094.
Fax: 758-453 1121.

Website
www.stlucia.org

POSTAL SERVICES

The main post office in Castries is in
Bridge Street, while most towns have
a small post office. General opening
hours are 8.30am–4.30pm Mon– Fri.

TELECOMMUNICATIONS

The dialling code for St Lucia is **758**.
Long-distance calls can be made and
faxes sent from most hotels. However,
the service provided at the Cable and
Wireless offices (Bridge Street,
Castries) is more reliable and less
expensive; you can buy phonecards
for public payphones there too.
    There are Internet facilities in the
Cable and Wireless office,
Gablewoods Mall, Castries.

SHOPPING

Pointe Seraphine on the waterfront in
Castries is a duty-free complex selling
perfume, china, crystal, designer-wear
and locally-made arts and crafts.
Castries Market is worth a look, if only
for the fruit and vegetables and crafts.
Gablewoods Mall is open daily
9am–9pm.

GETTING AROUND

By Car

Driving is on the left. Visiting drivers
must obtain a temporary driving
permit, valid for 3 months, by

presenting a current driving licence at
the police station (Bridge Street,
Castries), or car rental company, with
a small fee of around EC$20. Cars
and four-wheel drive vehicles are
available to rent at the port; a four-
wheel drive is best for places such as
the Sulphur Springs volcano. Contact:
Avis, tel: 451 6976;
Ben's West Coast Jeeps and Taxis,
tel: 459 5457/7160;
Budget, tel: 452 0233;
Cool Breeze Jeep-Car Rental, tel: 454
7898;
Hertz, tel: 452 0680.

By Taxi

Taxis line up at the dock. The prices
are fixed for set routes, but check at
the tourist office booth close to the
taxi rank. Negotiate a rate for island
tours before setting out.

By Bus

Travelling by bus in St Lucia is cheap
and it can be fun. Minibuses run to and
from the main towns throughout the
day, but are less reliable at night. Allow
plenty of time as travel can be slow.

Inter-Island Links

LIAT flights from George F. L. Charles
Airport, just outside the centre of
Castries, connect St Lucia to islands
including Antigua, Dominica, Grenada,
Barbados, St Kitts and Nevis, St
Vincent and Trinidad. There is also a
high-speed catamaran service,
Caribbean Express, to neighbouring
Martinique, Guadeloupe, and
Dominica.

Hotel Prices

Price categories are based on the
cost of a double room, for one
night:
$ = less than $100
$$ = $100–200
$$$ = more than $200.

STAYING ON

St Lucia has a wide choice of
accommodation, from vast all-
inclusive resorts and luxury hotels, to
intimate inns and guesthouses.

Anse Chastenet
PO Box 7000,
Soufrière, St Lucia, WI.
Tel: 459 7000.
Fax: 459 7700
www.ansechastenet.com
Sought-after honeymoon hotel in the
lee of the Pitons peaks. Luxurious
rooms with open side and excellent
views. Black sand beach. **$$–$$$**
Green Parrot Hotel
Castries, The Morne.
Tel: 452 3399.
Fax: 453 2272.
Comfortable rooms in a practical hotel
situated about 3 miles (5 km) outside
the main town of Castries. **$–$$**
Jalousie Plantation
PO Box 251, Soufrière.
Tel: 456 8000.
Fax: 459 7667.
www.thejalousieplantation.com
Luxury hotel in a dramatic setting,
encircled by a banana plantation,
between the twin peaks. Sports
facilities and a helicopter pad. **$$$**

Meal Prices

Price categories are based on the
cost of a meal for one person,
excluding drinks:
$ = less than $20
$$ = $20–40
$$$ = more than $40.

WHERE TO EAT

Specialities include pumpkin soup and
soufflé, flying fish, *poile dudon* (a
chicken dish), pepperpot, green fig
(banana) and saltfish, conch and
tablette (a sweetmeat made of
coconut).

Chez Paul
next to Derek Walcott Square,
Castries.
Tel: 451 3111.
Sophisticated French-creole cuisine,
sometimes with an Asian influence.
$$–$$$
The Coal Pot
Vigie Marina, Castries.
Tel: 452 5566.
International and Caribbean
specialities from a French chef. **$$**

Dasheene Restaurant and Bar
Soufrière, Ladera Resort.
Tel: 459 7323.
Classy blend of international and creole cuisine; excellent mountain views and impeccable service. **$$$**
Jimmie's
Vigie Cove, Castries.
Tel: 452 5142.
Delicious Caribbean cuisine. Fish specialties. **$$–$$$**

SHORE ACTIVITIES

Excursions
Sightseeing trips to the Pitons; Diamond Falls, Mineral Baths and Sulphur Springs; rainforest walks; Pigeon Island National Park; deep sea fishing. If you're staying on, don't miss the the weekly street party at Gros Islet – the Friday night jump-up.

Best Beaches
Anse Cochon and Anse Chastanet for snorkelling; Pigeon Island for white sandy beaches, good facilities, water sports, and the Pigeon Island Museum. A lot of cruise passengers go to Choc Bay, a short drive from the cruise terminal; Vigie, near Castries, is also clean and pretty, although it is near the airport and can be noisy.

Water Sports
There are many places offering water sports on the island from sailing, surfing, and water-skiing to diving and deep-sea fishing. Most sail charter companies are based in Marigot Bay and Rodney Bay. For more details contact: Moorings St Lucia, Marigot Bay. Tel: 451 4357. Sun Sail Stevens, Rodney Bay. Tel: 452 8648.
For deep-sea fishing day and half day trips, contact: Captain Mike, tel: 452 7044.
For diving and snorkelling, contact: Anse Chastanet Dive Centre, tel: 459 1354.

Horse Riding
Visitors can tour the island on horseback, along the beaches or through St Lucia's lush countryside. Contact: International Riding Stables, Gros Islet, tel: 452 8139.

Golf
There are two courses on the island, a public one at the Cap Estate, tel: 450 8522; a private one at Sandals St Lucia Resort, tel: 452 3081.

Barbados

The most easterly island in the Caribbean, Barbados lies 100 miles (160 km) outside the Antillean curve, directly east of St Vincent. This 21 by 14-mile (33 by 22-km) coral limestone island is divided into 11 parishes; its population enjoys one of the Caribbean's highest standards of living.

ARRIVING BY SEA

The cruise port is about one mile outside Bridgetown. Taxis wait at the terminal and there are shops directly outside.

PUBLIC HOLIDAYS

1 January: New Year's Day
21 January: Errol Barrow Day
March/April: Easter; Good Friday; Easter Monday
28 April: Heroes Day
1 May: Labour Day
May/June: Whit Monday
August: (1st Monday) Emancipation Day; Kadooment Day
30 November: Independence Day
25 December: Christmas Day
26 December: Boxing Day

CALENDAR OF EVENTS

January: Windsurfing championships; jazz festival; regional cricket series.
February: The Holetown Festival.
March: Holder's Season (opera).
April: Oistins Fish Festival; Congaline street festival.
May: Gospelfest; The Mount Gay Regatta.
June: Harris Paints Sailing Regatta.
July: Crop Over festival begins.

MONEY MATTERS

The currency is the Barbados dollar. US dollars are also widely accepted and goods are often labelled with a price in US dollars, so check which currency is being quoted before making a purchase. It is not permitted to export BDS dollars.
Money can be changed at banks and hotels. Traveller's cheques in US dollars and major credit cards are widely accepted.
ATMs (Automatic Teller Machines) are available in most banks around the island. Banks are open 8am–2pm Mon–Thurs; 8am–1pm, 3–5pm Fri.
VAT at 15 per cent is added to most goods and services, so check to see whether the price includes VAT. Restaurants and hotels add a 10 per cent service charge, but it is normal to add another 5 per cent as a tip.

TOURIST OFFICES

In Canada
5160 Yonge Street, Suite 1800, North York, Toronto, Ontario M2N GL19..
Tel: 416-512 6569.
Fax: 416-512 6581.
In the UK
263 Tottenham Court Road,
London W1P 9AA.
Tel: 020 7636 9448.
Fax: 020 7637 1496.
In the US
800 2nd Avenue,
New York, NY 10017.
Tel: 212-986 6516.
800–221 9831.
Fax: 212-573 9850.
3440 Wilshire Boulevard, Suite 1215, Los Angeles, California 90010.
Tel: 213-380 2198.
Fax: 213-384 2763.
In Barbados
Harbour Road, Bridgetown.
Tel: 246-427 2623.
Fax: 246-426 4080.
There is an office at the cruise terminal (tel: 246-426 1718); an information kiosk is at Cave Shepherd, Broad Street.

Websites
www.barbados.org

POSTAL SERVICES

The main post office is in Cheapside, Bridgetown (open 8am–5pm Mon–Fri). Each parish has its own post office and stamps can also be bought in bookshops and hotels.

TELECOMMUNICATIONS

The dialling code is **246**. It is simple to phone abroad with a phonecard from a public payphone. Cards to the value of BDS$10–BDS$60 are available from hotels and local stores. There are several Internet centres in Bridgetown, including in the Cave Shepherd department store.

SHOPPING

Look for local crafts, cigars, pottery and rum. Bridgetown has several art galleries. Visitors can shop duty-free in some outlets; always carry a cruise ID card. In Bridgetown, the main shopping area is Broad Street. Pelican Village (arts, crafts, and cigars in chattel houses) is just outside the cruise terminal (closed Sunday).

GETTING AROUND

By Car

Driving is on the left and roads are good, if narrow outside Bridgetown.

A visitor's driving licence is available from car rental companies and most police stations for a fee. Rental companies have a choice of cars, including mini mokes (beach buggy-style vehicles): Contact: Auto Rentals, tel: 428 9830; Courtesy Rent-a- Car, tel: 431 4160. Sunny Isle Motors, tel: 419 7498; Corbin's Car Rentals, tel: 427 9531; National Car Rental, tel: 426 0603; Coconut Car Rentals, tel: 437 0297.

By Taxi

Taxis wait at the cruise terminal and in town. Agree a fare before setting off.

Inter-Island Links

There are frequent flights and boat trips to nearby islands such as St Vincent and the Grenadines, St Lucia, and Grenada. For details, contact: Chantours, Plaza 2, Sunset Crest, St James, tel: 432 5591.; Grenadine Tours, Hastings Plaza, tel: 435 8451; Caribbean Safari Tours, Ship Inn, St Lawrence Gap, tel: 427 5100;

Windward Lines, Hincks Street, Bridgetown, tel: 431 0449; Trans Island Air (TIA), Grantley Adams Airport, tel: 418 1654; fax: 428 0916; LIAT, Grantley Adams Airport, tel: 428 0986.

Hotel Prices

Price categories are based on the cost of a double room, for one night:
$ = less than $100
$$ = $100–200
$$$ = more than $200.

STAYING ON

Barbados is a natural place in which to extend a cruise holiday as so many cruises start and finish here.

Most of Barbados's expensive hotels line the west coast – also known as the Platinum Coast – with less expensive ones located along the south-east coast.

Renting a villa or an apartment is a good alternative to a hotel. Rental agencies include:

Karibik Barbados Tours, St Lawrence Gap, Christ Church, tel: 428 3172; Alleyne, Aguilar and Altman, St James, tel: 432 0840; Bajan Services, St Peter, tel: 422 2618.

West Coast

Cobblers Cove
Road View, St Peter.
Tel: 422 2291.
Fax: 422 1460.
www.cobblerscove.com
Elegant luxurious hotel built in country house style on a lovely white sand beach. Friendly staff. **$$$**

Coral Reef Club
Holetown.
Tel: 422 2372.
Fax: 422 1776.
www.coralreefbarbados.com
Luxury accommodation including cottages set in beautiful gardens. **$$$**

Little Good Harbour
Shermans, St Peter.
Tel: 439 3000.
Fax: 439 2020.
www.littlegoodharbourbarbados.com
Luxurious suite-hotel in traditional style. Casual, elegant restaurant. **$$$**

Inn on the Beach
Holetown, St James, Barbados, WI.
Tel: 432 0385.
Fax: 432 2440.
Air-conditioned apartments overlooking the beach. **$$**

South Coast
Casuarina Beach Club
Dover, Christ Church.
Tel: 428 3600.
Fax: 428 1970.
www.casuarina.com
Beach hotel in a beautiful palm garden. **$$**

Silver Sands
Christ Church.
Tel: 428 6001.
Fax: 428 3758.
www.silversandsbarbados.com
Off the beaten track, with basic rooms and apartments; good windsurfing. **$$**

Southeast Coast
The Crane
St Philip.
Tel: 423 6220.
Fax: 423 5343.
www.thecrane.com
A traditional colonial-style hotel on atop a cliff. An extensive expansion and modernisation is ongoing. **$$$**

WHERE TO EAT

Local specialities include flying fish cutters (breaded flying fish in a bun) for lunch; red snapper, hot saltfish cakes, pickled breadfruit and pepperpot, often accompanied by rice and peas, macaroni pie, plantain, sweet potato, or yam. Among the usual fast food, look out for roti, a savoury pocket of curried chicken, prawn, beef or potato.

Bridgetown and West Coast
The Mews
2nd Street, Holetown, St James.
Tel: 432 1122.
Superb seafood dishes. Live jazz on Friday night. A good after-dinner rendezvous spot. **$$$**

Lone Star
Holetown beach.
Tel: 419 0599.
Cool beach hangout serving pasta to caviar. **$–$$$**

Olive's Bar and Bistro
2nd Street, Holetown.
Tel: 432 2112.
Simple food with a Caribbean and
Mediterranean flavour. **$$**
Waterfront Cafe
The Careenage, Bridgetown.
Tel: 427 0093.
Traditional Bajan specialties and
creole cooking served up to the sound
of live music. **$$**

South Coast
Carib Beach Bar
2nd Avenue, Worthing, Christ Church.
Tel: 435 8540.
Fish and beach barbecues, popular
with the locals. **$$**

Meal Prices

Price categories are based on the
cost of a meal for one person,
excluding drinks:
$ = less than $20
$$ = $20–40
$$$ = more than $40.

SHORE ACTIVITIES

Excursions
Visit the art galleries and shop in
Bridgetown; tour St Michael's
cathedral; the Garrison; Mount Gay
Rum distillery tour; self-drive tours by
mini-moke to the north and east
coasts; Welchman Hall Gully nature
reserve; Harrison's Cave; Andromeda
Gardens; Earth Works Pottery; Animal
Flower Cave in the north; Cherry Tree
Hill for views of the Atlantic coast;
Atlantic beaches; *Jolly Roger* party
cruises; cricket matches at Kensing-
ton Oval; day trips to the Grenadines.

Best Beaches
Holetown for people-watching and
great food; Brighton Beach next to the
cruise terminal; Bathsheba for wild
Atlantic scenery; Crane Beach.

Water Sports
Most water sports are available at the
hotels along the west and south
coasts. Equipment can be hired at
Brighton Beach.
There are several wrecks to explore

and excellent visibility for divers and
snorkellers. Try: Underwater Barbados,
tel: 426 0655; West Side Scuba
Centre, tel: 432 2558; Heatwave, tel:
429 9283; Hightide Water sports, tel:
432 0931/228 3322; Atlantis
Adventures, tel: 436 8929.
Mount Gay Regatta is the highlight
of the yachting season in May or June.
Small sailing boats, such as a Sunfish
or Hobie Cat, can be rented by the
hour along the south and west coast
beaches. Sailing trips around the
island can include lunch, snorkelling,
or a moonlight cruise. For private
charters contact: Tiami Catamaran
Sailing Cruises, tel: 430 0900; Limbo
Lady, tel: 420 5418; Cool Runnings,
tel: 436 0911.
Body surfing is good along the
southeast coast, you can rent boards
on the beach at The Crane. The best
surfing around the island is in an area
known as the Soup Bowl at Bathsheba
on the Atlantic Coast, but beware of
the strong currents. Contact: the
Barbados Surfing Association at
Coconut Court Hotel, Hastings, Christ
Church, tel: 427 1655 for details.
There is excellent windsurfing to be
had at the southernmost point of the
island at Silver Sands and Silver Rock.

Nightlife

Barbados is lively at night,
especially on the south coast:
After Dark, Gateways, St Lawrence
Gap. Tel: 435 6547. Three discos
in one. Local hangout.
The Boatyard, Bay Street,
Bridgetown. Tel: 436 2622. Live
bands every evening except
Monday and Wednesday.
The Casbah, Baku Beach. Tel: 432
2258. Sophisticated nightclub on
the west coast.
Harbour Lights, Bay Street,
Bridgetown. Tel: 436 7225. An
open-air nightclub on the beach.
Top live bands at weekends.
The Ship Inn, St Lawrence Gap. Tel:
435 6961. Top local bands, seven
nights a week.
The Waterfront Cafe, The
Careenage, Bridgetown. Tel: 427
0093. Live music nightly with jazz on
Thursday, Friday, and Saturday.

Contact: the Windsurfing Association
at Silver Rock Hotel, Silver Sands,
Christ Church, tel: 428 2866.

St Vincent and The Grenadines

At the bottom of the Antillean curve,
near St Lucia, Barbados, and
Grenada, is an 18 by 11-mile (30 by
18-km) island, with a chain of 32
islets to the south. St Vincent, the
large island, is mountainous, with
volcanic ridges rising to over 4,000 ft
(1,200 metres). The Grenadines vary
in size from 7 sq. miles (18 sq. km) to
mere dots in the ocean, their terrain
is mountainous and flat, surrounded
by glistening sand and clear waters.

ARRIVING BY SEA

Cruise ships dock at the cruise
terminal in Kingstown, the capital of
St Vincent. The jetty is 5–10 minutes'
walk from the town centre.

PUBLIC HOLIDAYS

1 January: New Year's Day
March/April: Easter; Good Friday;
Easter Monday
May/June: Whit Monday
7 July: Caricom Day
July (early): Carnival Tuesday
August: (1st Monday) August Monday
27 October: Independence Day
25 December: Christmas Day
26 December: Boxing Day

CALENDAR OF EVENTS

February: Mustique Blues Festival.
Easter: Bequia Regatta, boat races
and festivities; Easterval, a weekend
of music, culture and boat races on
Union Island.
July: Carnival.
Late July/early August: Canouan
Yacht Races and festivities.
Late November: Petit St Vincent Yacht
Races and evening festivities.
16–24 December: Nine Mornings –
parades and dances in the days
leading up to Christmas.

MONEY MATTERS

The currency is the EC dollar, which is tied to the US dollar. US dollars can be used in most places and major credit cards are accepted in most hotels and restaurants. In restaurants and hotels the standard service charge is 10 per cent. Where no service charge has been added, a tip of 10 per cent is appreciated. International banks with local branches include Barclays in Kingstown (tel: 456 1706) and Bequia, and CIBC in Kingstown (tel: 457 1587).

TOURIST OFFICES

In Canada
333 Wilson Avenue, Suite 601,
Toronto, M3H 1T2,
Tel: 416-633 3100.
E-mail: svgcan@home.com
In the UK
10 Kensington Court,
London W8 5DL.
Tel: 020-7937 6570.
E-mail: svgtourismeurope@aol.com
In the US
801 Second Avenue,
New York, NY 10017.
Tel: 212-687 4981/800-729 1726.
E-mail: svgtony@aol.com
In St Vincent and the Grenadines
Ministry of Tourism, Cruise Ship Terminal, Kingstown, St Vincent
Tel: 784-457 1502.
E-mail: tourism@caribsurf.com
There are also branches at the E. T. Joshua Airport, tel: 458 4379; on Bequia, tel: 458 3286 and Union Island, tel: 458 3286.

Websites
www.bequiasweet.com
www.vincy.com
www.svghotels.com
www.svgtourism.com

POSTAL SERVICES

The post office in Kingstown is on Halifax Street. Open 8.30am–3pm Mon–Fri, 8.30–11.30am Sat.

TELECOMMUNICATIONS

The dialling code is **784**. Long distance calls, telegrams, and telex services are available at the Cable and Wireless office in Kingstown, on Halifax Street.

SHOPPING

St Vincent and Bequia are good places to find colourful batiks; locally-made art and crafts, such as straw baskets and wood carvings; goatskin drums; stamps; and fresh fruit from the market in Kingstown.

GETTING AROUND

By Car

Driving is on the left. You will need an international licence or a local licence (EC$40) which can be arranged at the Police Station in Bay Street, Kingstown, or the Licencing Authority in Halifax Street. Car hire is expensive and cars have limited access to some areas. A jeep is the best bet. Car rental companies on St Vincent include Avis, tel: 456 4389; David's Auto Clinic, tel: 456 4026; Rent & Drive, tel: 457 5601. On Bequia:Phil's Rental Service, tel: 458 3304.

By Taxi

Taxi fares are fixed but check with the driver first to avoid misunderstandings. Taxis and minibuses are also available on Bequia and Union Island.

By Bus

Local minibuses on St Vincent tend to be busy and noisy, but they are also cheap. Allow plenty of time to get back to the port if using public transport.

Inter-Island Links

St Vincent is linked by air with other islands including Barbados, Trinidad, St Lucia, Martinique and Grenada. Petit St Vincent, Palm Island and Mustique, all private islands, are also accessible with permission.
Inter-island ferries are cost effective. Schedules can be erratic, so check departure times. Contact: Admiralty Transport, Port Elizabeth, Bequia, tel: 458 3348.
Airlines operating local flights: Air Caribe, tel: 458 4528; LIAT, tel: 457 1821; Mustique Airways, tel: 458 4380; SVG Air, tel: 457 5124; Trans Island Air (TIA), tel: 485 8306/8440.

STAYING ON

Apart from St Vincent and Bequia, three islands are given over entirely to upscale holiday resorts: Young Island, just 200 yds (183 metres) off St Vincent's shore, Palm Island, and Petit St Vincent in the Grenadines.

St Vincent

Cobblestone Inn
P.O. Box 867, Upper Bay Street, Kingstown.
Tel: 456 1937.
Fax: 456 1938.
www.thecobblestoneinn.com
In an 19th-century arrowroot warehouse, this quiet hotel has two restaurants; one on the roof. **$$**
Umbrella Beach Hotel
Villa, St Vincent.
Tel: 458 4651.
Fax: 457 4930.
Basic, but clean accommodation on the beach opposite Young Island. **$**
Young Island Resort
P.O. Box 211, St Vincent.
Tel: 458 4826.
Fax: 457 4567.
www.youngisland.com
Exclusive, luxurious resort situated on its own small private island. **$$$**

Bequia

Frangipani
Admiralty Bay, Bequia.
Tel: 458 3255.
Fax: 458 3824.
Simple accommodation, in an old chandlery. Tastefully decorated rooms and a popular hotel bar. **$–$$**

Other Grenadines Islands

Firefly Inn
Mustique.
Tel: 488 8414.
Fax: 488 8514.
www.mustiquefirefly.com
Tiny, informal, but elegant hotel, in a

lovely position on Mustique. Book well in advance. **$$$**

Palm Island Beach Club
Palm Island.
Tel: 458 8824.
Fax: 458 8804.
www.palmislandresorts.com
Exclusive all-inclusive resort surrounded by white sand beach. Water sports. **$$$**

Petit St Vincent (PSV)
Petit St Vincent.
Tel: 458 8801.
Fax: 458 8428.
www.psvresort.com
A delightful resort hideaway ideal for peace and privacy. **$$$**

WHERE TO EAT

Spicy Caribbean cuisine predominates with continental and American fare also available. A variety of exotic fruits and vegetables, and an abundance of lobster and other fresh seafood enrich St Vincent's cooking. Try something unusual, such as barbecued goat or fresh shark.

St Vincent

Bounty
Egmont Street, Kingstown.
Tel: 456 1776.
Snacks and sandwiches at the place where locals go for their lunch. **$**

Cobblestone Inn
Upper Bay Street, Kingstown.
Tel: 456 1937.
Fax: 456 1938.
Rooftop restaurant serving Caribbean food and hamburgers. **$$**

Ocean Allegro
Villa Harbour.
Tel: 458 4972.
Excellent service, food and beach views, with occasional salsa nights. **$$$**

Lime Restaurant & Pub
Villa Harbour.
Tel: 458 4227.
Caribbean dishes in an informal setting. Fresh seafood specialities. **$$**

Bequia

Whalebones
Port Elizabeth.
Tel: 458 3233.
Caribbean food with an emphasis on seafood; an atmospheric setting. **$$**

Mustique

Basil's Bar
Britannia Bay.
Tel: 458 4621.
Well-known bar built over the water. A popular haunt of the rich and famous. Good seafood dishes. **$$$**

Meal Prices

Price categories are based on the cost of a meal for one person, excluding drinks:

$ = less than $20
$$ = $20–40
$$$ = more than $40.

SHORE ACTIVITIES

Excursions

Hiking La Soufriére volcano (a tough, full day walk) or Mount St Andrew (gentler, with amazing views); Trinity Falls and Baleine (reach the waterfall, by boat); Montreal tropical gardens; day sailing trips; snorkelling in Tobago Cays; beaches and water sports on Canouan; eating out on Bequia.

Best Beaches

Villa, just south east of Kingstown; Young Island, offshore near Villa; and smaller Grenadines islands. Small ships may tender off one of these.

Water Sports

Divers will find a range of sponges, corals, fish, exciting marine life, and a number of sunken wrecks. Operators include: Dive St Vincent, Young Island Dock, tel: 457 4714; Bequia Dive Adventures, Admiralty Bay, tel: 458 3826; Dive Canouan, Tamarind Beach Hotel, tel: 458 8044; Dive Mustique, Cotton House Hotel, tel: 456 4777; Grenadines Dive, Union Island, tel: 453 3133. To organise bare boat sailing or a yacht with a crew contact: Barefoot Yacht Charters, P.O. Box 39, Ratho Mill, St Vincent, tel: 456 9526; Grenadine Escape, P.O. Box 836, Villa, St Vincent, tel: 457 4028; Passion Day Charters, Bequia, tel: 458 3884; Sunsail, PO Box 133, Ratho Mill, St Vincent, tel: 458 4308.

For sportfishing trips try: Blue Water Charters, Aquatic Club, Villa, St Vincent tel: 456 1232/458 4205; Crystal Blue Charters, Indian Bay, St Vincent, tel: 457 4532.

Grenada

Grenada is the most southerly of the Windward Islands, lying toward the bottom of the Lesser Antilles chain. The island is mountainous and volcanic, with the highest point, Mount St Catherine, reaching 2,755 ft (840 metres). Two smaller, islands are dependent territories: Carriacou and Petit Martinique. Grenada is known for its nutmeg and spice production, hence the nickname, "Spice Island".

● *At the time of going to press Grenada was recovering from the effects of Hurricane Ivan, As a result limited attractions may be available.*

ARRIVING BY SEA

Cruise ships dock in St George's at the cruise ship dock on Carenage Road, a 10-minute stroll around the Carenage from the shops and museums.

PUBLIC HOLIDAYS

1 January: New Year's Day
7 February: Independence Day
March/April: Easter; Good Friday; Easter Monday
1 May: Labour Day
31 May: Whit Monday
June: Corpus Christi
August: (1st Monday/Tuesday) Emancipation Days
August: Carnival
25 October: Thanksgiving Day
25 December: Christmas Day
26 December: Boxing Day

CALENDAR OF EVENTS

January: Spice Island Fishing Tournament. Annual La Source Grenada Sailing Festival.
Late April: Annual Carriacou Maroon Music Festival.
May/June: Spice Jazz Festival.
June: Fisherman's Birthday is celebrated in Gouyave at the end of the month.

August: The second weekend in August is Carnival time in Grenada; Rainbow City cultural festival, Grenville.

MONEY MATTERS

The currency is the East Caribbean (EC) dollar (EC$), tied to the US dollar. US dollars are also widely accepted. Banks open 8am–3pm Monday–Thursday, 8am–5pm on Friday. They close for lunch 1–2.30pm. Most banks are in St George's, but there are branches in Grenville, Gouyave, Sauteurs, and Carriacou.

TOURIST OFFICES

In Canada
Grenada Tourism Office,
439 University Avenue, Suite 920,
Ontario M5G 1Y8.
Tel: 416-595 1339.
In the UK
Grenada Tourism Office,
1 Collingham Gardens,
Earls Court, London SW5 0HW.
Tel: 020-7370 5164.
In the US
Grenada Tourism Office,
820 Second Avenue, Suite 900D,
New York, NY 10017.
Tel: 212-687 9554.
In Grenada
Grenada Board of Tourism,
Burn's Point, PO Box 293, St George's.
Tel: 473-440 2279.
There is also an information booth in the cruise terminal.

Websites
www.interknowlege.com/grenada
www.grenadagrenadines.com

POSTAL SERVICES

The main post office is on Lagoon Road, south of Carenage, St George's. Open 8am–3.30pm Mon–Thurs, 8am–4.30pm Fri.

TELECOMMUNICATIONS

The dialling code is **473**.
International calls, faxes, and telexes can be made from the Cable and Wireless offices on the Carenage (open 7.30am–4.30pm Mon–Fri, 7.30am–1pm Sat,

10am–noon Sun). Grenada has direct-dial services and credit card calls can be made to Europe, and to North America via AT&T and MCI using the access codes: MCI: 800-888 8000; AT&T: 800-872 2881. Internet access available at the Carenage Cafe, Otway Building, Carenage, St George's.

SHOPPING

Look out for packets of spice, jams, syrups, candy, rum, even jewellery made from nutmeg. Also batik and screen-printed items. Spices and oils are available from Arawak Islands factory on Upper Belmont Road, tel: 444 3577/3566. Don't miss the Grande Anse Craft and Spice Market, 5 minutes from the harbour.

GETTING AROUND

By Car
Driving is on the left. Some roads are in poor condition, especially in the mountains. Drivers must be over 21 and have a valid licence as well as a local permit (available from the central police station). There is a good choice of rental firms, but cars can be difficult to obtain, particularly in high season and during Carnival. Rental companies include: Avis, tel: 440 3936; Budget, tel: 440 2778; Maitlands, tel: 444 4022; McIntyre Bros Ltd, tel: 444 3944/1550; Y&R Rentals, tel: 444 4448; Martin Bullen, Carriacou, tel: 443 7204.

By Taxi
Taxis are available at the cruise ship dock and on the Carenage in St George's. They are not metered and there are no fixed charges, so agree the fare with the driver before setting off. Taxi drivers can be hired by the hour or day for sightseeing tours. Allow a day for a tour of Grenada.

By Bus
Grenada has an inexpensive and comprehensive bus network, but buses are normally crowded.

By Bicycle
Bicycles can be hired from Ride Grenada (tel: 444 1157). The island's mountainous terrain,

tropical climate, and sometimes erratic road conditions should be borne in mind if visitors plan to tour the island on two wheels.

Inter-Island Links
LIAT, St Vincent Grenada Air (SVG Air) and Airlines of Carriacou connect Grenada with Carriacou (6–8 flights daily). LIAT also provides services to all eastern Caribbean destinations. LIAT, tel: 440 2796/5428. Airlines of Carriacou, tel: 440 2898, 444 1475. SVG Air, tel: 444 3549. Carriacou can also be reached by schooners, most of which depart in the morning from the Carenage, returning the following day. The journey takes about four hours; with loud music and refreshments.

STAYING ON

Many of Grenada's expensive hotels are dotted around the southern tip of the island, especially along the Grand Anse beach. Guesthouses tend to be rudimentary and there are also plenty of self-catering apartments.

Hotel Prices

Price categories are based on the cost of a double room, for one night:
$ = less than $100
$$ = $100–200
$$$ = more than $200.

Blue Horizons
Cottage Hotel
P.O. Box 41, St George's.
Tel: 444 4316.
Fax: 444 2815.
www.grenadabluehorizons.com
Cottage-style buildings scattered around attractive grounds, with one of the island's best restaurants, La Belle Creole. Guests can use the beach facilities of Spice Island Resort. **$$**
The Calabash
P.O. Box 382, St George's.
Tel: 444 4334.
www.calabashhotel.com
The most prestigious hotel in Grenada, set in beautiful gardens of calabash (gourd) trees just outside St George's at L'Anse aux Epines. **$$$**

La Sagesse Nature Centre
P.O. Box 44, St George's.
Tel: 444 6458.
Fax: 444 6458.
www.lasagesse.com
An small, informal guesthouse on a spectacular beach. In St David's, away from the tourist strip. Good food, but some distance from St George's. **$$**

Spice Island Beach Resort
PO Box 6, Grand Anse, St George's.
Tel: 444 4258.
Fax: 444 4807.
www.spicebeachresort.com
Beautiful beach location, some rooms with private pool. All-inclusive option. Ideal for water sports.**$$$**

Carriacou
Silver Beach Resort
Hillsborough, Carriacou.
Tel: 443 7337.
Fax: 443 7165.
Small and relaxed hotel, situated on an idyllic grey sandy beach. Self-catering option, or eat in the good seafood restaurant. **$**

WHERE TO EAT

Grenada's colonial past has endowed the island with an interesting mix of British and French influences. The emphasis tends to be on seafood, but there are many local delicacies worth sampling. Callaloo soup made from dasheen leaves (like spinach) is excellent, as are traditional pepperpot, a stew of almost every possible ingredient, and *lambi* (conch). Game sometimes appears on tourist menus, although some may prefer not to experiment with armadillo, iguana, or manicou. Spices, especially nutmeg, are another favourite, delicious in rum punches.

Coconut Beach
Grand Anse.
Tel: 444 4644.
Excellent French-creole cooking with occasional live music in a beachside setting. **$$**

Morne Fendue Plantation House
St Patrick's.
Tel: 442 9330.
A Grenadian institution. Serves lunch only. Reservations essential.**$$**

Nutmeg
Carenage, St George's.
Tel: 440 2539.
A great place for lunch, overlooking the harbour. Simple food and deservedly famous rum punches. **$**

SHORE ACTIVITIES

Excursions
Markets, shopping, Georgian architecture and three historic forts in St George's; Grand Etang National Park for hiking and nature trails; Dougaldston Spice Estate; Gouyave Nutmeg Processing Station (tours); Morne Fendue Plantation House; Sauters for Carib's Leap, where the the Caribs leapt to their deaths rather than surrender to the French; Clabony Sulphur Pond, with healing properties; River Antoine Rum distillery.

Best Beaches
Grand Anse is just outside St George's, a two-mile stretch of soft white sand with bars, restaurants, shops, and water sports. La Sagesse is quieter with good hiking in the area; good swimming and again, fewer crowds at Levera Beach and Bathway Beach.

Water Sports
Grenada and Carriacou have a good range of diving sites, including the Caribbean's biggest wreck, *Bianca C*, which sank outside St George's in 1961. There are spectacular reefs. Grand Anse beach has dive companies, as does Carriacou. Contact: Carriacou Silver Diving, tel: 443 7882; Dive Grenada, tel: 444 1092; Scuba World, tel: 444 3684.
   Windsurfing and waterskiing facilities are available on Grand Anse beach. The Secret Harbour Hotel rents snorkelling equipment and also organizes windsurfing, yacht charters, and speedboat outings. Contact:

Grenada Yacht Services, tel: 440 2508; Moorings' Club, tel: 444 4439; Spice Island Marina, tel: 444 4257; Grenada Yacht Services (tel: 440 2508) organize deep-sea fishing trips.

Horse Riding
Contact: The Horseman (tel: 440 5368) for lessons or trail riding.

Trinidad and Tobago

The most southerly Caribbean island, Trinidad lies 7 miles (11 km) off the coast of Venezuela. With an area of 1,864 sq. miles (4,660 sq. km). Together with Tobago, which lies 21 miles (34 km) to the northeast, Trinidad forms an independent nation within the British Commonwealth. Trinidad's highest point is at Cerro del Aripo (3,080 ft/930 metres). The smaller island, Tobago has lush vegetation and beautiful beaches.

ARRIVING BY SEA

Cruise ships dock in the centre of Port of Spain, the capital of Trinidad, within easy walking distance of the shops.

PUBLIC HOLIDAYS

1 January: New Year's Day
30 March: Spiritual Baptist Liberation Day.
March/April: Easter; Good Friday; Easter Monday; Indian Arrival Day
June (variable): Corpus Christi.
19 June: Labour Day
1 August: Emancipation Day
31 August: Independence Day
24 September: Republic Day
October/November (variable): Divali
25 December: Christmas Day
26 December: Boxing Day

CALENDAR OF EVENTS

February/March: Hosay, the Muslim winter festival with processions, music and dance.
March: Phagwa – Hindu New Year – is celebrated at March full moon.
February/March: Carnival reaches a climax on the Monday and Tuesday before Ash Wednesday, and although not an official public holiday, everything is closed.

March/April: the Tuesday after Easter is the goat race, Buccoo, an important social occasion in Tobago.
Late July: Tobago Heritage Festival
Variable (according to lunar calendar): Eid-ul-Fitr is the Islamic New Year festival; marks the end of Ramadan.
October/November: Diwali, the Hindu Festival of Lights.

MONEY MATTERS

The Trinidad and Tobago (TT$) dollar is the main currency on both islands. Most hotels, restaurants and shops accept major credit cards. Several banks in Port of Spain have ATMs. The only banks on Tobago are in Scarborough, the capital.

TOURIST OFFICES

In Canada
The RMR Group Inc,
Taurus House, 512 Duplex Avenue,
Toronto M4R 2E3.
Tel: 416-485 8724.
Fax: 416-485 8256.
In the UK
Mitre House, 66 Abbey Road, Bush Hill Park, Enfield, Middlesex EN1 2QL.
Tel: 020-8350 1099.
Fax: 020-8350 1011.
In the US
Sales Marketing and Reservations Tourism Services (SMARTS),
7000 Blvd. East, Guttenberg,
New Jersey 07093.
Tel: 201-662 3403.
Fax: 201-869 7628.
In Trinidad
TIDCO (Tourism and Industrial Development Company of Trinidad and Tobago Limited),
10–14 Phillips Street, Port of Spain.
Tel: 623 6022/1932/4.
Fax: 623 3848.
In Tobago
TIDCO,
Unit 24, Tidco Mall,
Sangster's Hill, Scarborough.
Tel: 639 4333/3151.
Fax: 639 4514.

Websites
www.VisitTNT.com
www.tidco.co.tt

POSTAL SERVICES

There are post offices in most main towns. Surface mail can take several weeks to arrive. Opening hours are Monday–Friday 8am–4pm.

TELECOMMUNICATIONS

The dialling code is **868**. A phonecard is recommended for long-distance calls, some of which must be made through the operator. Telegrams and faxes can be sent from hotels or post offices. There are several Internet centres in Port of Spain.

SHOPPING

Trinidad and Tobago are best for handicrafts, batik, rum, clothing and duty-free goods such as cigarettes and computers (carry your cruise ship ID to qualify for duty free prices). Frederick Street, Queen Street, Charlotte Street and Henry Street are the main shopping areas. For a good selection of local calypso and soca music try Rhyner's Record shop on Prince Street, Port of Spain.

GETTING AROUND

By Car

Driving is on the left. Visitors wishing to rent a car must be at least 21 years old and possess a valid driving licence. Car rental companies include: Auto Rentals, Piarco Airport, tel: 669 2277; Econo-Car Rentals, Cocorite, tel: 622 8074/2359,
For bicycles: Baird's Rentals Ltd, Crown Point and Scarborough, Tobago, tel: 639 2528.

By Taxi and Bus

Any form of public transport is referred to as a taxi. Taxis are available at the town centre. Fares are fixed. Route taxis (minibuses) run along set routes and have fixed fares. Maxi taxis travel greater distances than route taxis.

Inter-Island Links

There is a ferry service between the two islands, except on Saturday. The crossing from Port of Spain to Scarborough takes about 6 hours. BWIA and Inter-Island Express connect the two islands by air, the journey takes 20 minutes and there are eight flights per day. Flights get booked up on public holidays.

Hotel Prices

Price categories are based on the cost of a double room, for one night:
$ = less than $100
$$ = $100–200
$$$ = more than $200.

STAYING ON

Choose Trinidad for nightlife and Tobago for chilling out.

Trinidad

Asa Wright Nature Centre and Lodge
Blanchisseuse Road, Arima,
Tel: 667 4655.
Fax: 667 0493.
www.asawright.org
Inn for nature lovers, in an isolated location in the Northern Range. Full board only. **$$$**
Laguna Mar Beach and Nature Hotel
Paria Main Road, Blanchisseuse.
Tel: 628 3731.
Fax: 628 3737.
www.lagunamar.com
Small guesthouse close to the beach and Marianne River. **$–$$**
Johnson's
16 Buller Street, Woodbrook, Port of Spain.
Tel: 628 7553.
Friendly bed-and-breakfast in a central location. Relatively quiet. **$–$$**
Hilton Trinidad
Lady Young Road, St Ann's, Port of Spain.
Tel: 624 3211.
Fax: 624 4485.
www.hilton.com
Central location, plenty of amenities and live shows in the evening. **$$$**

Tobago

Arnos Vale Hotel
Plymouth.
Tel: 639 2881.
Fax: 639 3251.
www.arnosvalehotel.com
Picturesque, quiet location

surrounded by luxuriant vegetation.
Small beach. **$$$**

Blue Waters Inn
Batteaux Bay, Speyside.
Tel: 660 2583.
Fax: 660 5195.
www.bluewatersinn.com
Favoured by divers in a remote location
on the northwest coast. **$$–$$$**

Rex Turtle Beach Hotel
Great Courland Bay, Scarborough.
Tel: 639 2851.
Fax: 639 1495.
www.rexcaribbean.com
Pleasant hotel on a beautiful wide
beach. Mostly English clientele. **$$**

WHERE TO EAT

Trinidad and Tobago are multicultural
societies with a broad range of culinary
influences, including African, Indian,
Chinese and French. Staples are fresh
seafood, vegetables and fruit.

Trinidad

Hong Kong City
86A Tragarete Road, Port of Spain.
Tel: 622 3949.
Chinese specialties with a creole
twist. **$**

Aspara
13 Queen's Park East, Port of Spain.
Tel: 623 7659.
Restaurant with authentic North Indian
cuisine. **$**

Surf Country Inn
Blanchisseuse.
Tel: 669 2475.
International and Caribbean cuisine
with north coast views. Sunday is
popular with the locals. **$–$$**

Meal Prices

Price categories are based on the
cost of a meal for one person,
excluding drinks:
$ = less than $20
$$ = $20–40
$$$ = more than $40.

Tobago

Black Rock Café
Black Rock.
Tel: 639 7625.
Pretty verandah restaurant with local
dishes, steaks, and seafood. **$–$$**

Bonkers
At the Toucan Inn, Storebay Local
Road, Crown Point.
Tel: 639 7173.
Dependable local dishes and the best
cocktails on the island. **$–$$**

Jemma's Seaview Kitchen
Speyside.
Tel: 660 4066.
Top-rate island cuisine, served in a
cheerful tree house by the sea. **$**

Hiking

Walking is a good way to explore
the islands and see the fabulous
flora and fauna. Always travel with
an experienced guide. For details
contact: **The Forestry Division**,
Long Circular Road, Port of Spain.
Tel: 622 4521/622 7476; **Trinidad
and Tobago Field Naturalists' Club**,
The Secretary. 1 Errol Park Road,
St Ann's. Tel: 625 3386/645 2132
(evenings and weekends);
**Chaguaramas Development
Authority Guided Tours**, tel:634
4227/4364; **Pioneer Journeys**, Pat
Turpin, Man-O-War Bay Cottages,
Charlotteville. Tel: 660 4327.

SHORE ACTIVITIES

Excursions

Shopping, Botanic Gardens; stroll
along Brian Lara Promenade in Port of
Spain; Gasparee Caves (by boat); rum
distillery tours; hiking at Blanchisseuse; manatee spotting at Navira
Swamp; Pointe-a-Pierre Wildfowl Trust;
Asa Wright Nature Centre; cricket
matches at the Oval; Carnival
celebrations. Little Tobago Bird
Sanctuary; hiking up Pigeon Peak;
snorkelling and diving at Buccoo Reef.

Best Beaches

Maracas on Trinidad for surfing; Las
Cuevas (one hour from Port of Spain)
for peace and quiet. On Tobago,
Pigeon Point, Store Bay, Mount Irvine,
and Speyside, where the reefs are
less damaged than Buccoo.

Water Sports

The best diving and snorkelling can be
found among the exciting reefs around
Tobago and its neighbouring islands.

Dive operators on the island work with
beginners and experienced divers. For
more details contact: Scuba
Adventure Safari, Crown Point, tel:
660 7767; Man Friday Diving,
Charlotteville, tel/fax: 660 4676; Dive
Tobago, Pigeon Point, tel: 639 0202.

Aruba and Curaçao

Aruba and Curaçao are the most
westerly of the Lesser Antilles and
they are are flat and dry, with an
average annual rainfall of only 20
inches (50 cm). Many species of
cactus grow here, as well as the
strange Watapana (or Divi-Divi) tree,
whose top always inclines to the
southwest in line with the prevailing
northeast trade winds.

Together with Bonaire (not covered
in this book), Aruba and Curaçao form
the ABC Islands which, along with St
Maarten, St Eustatius, and Saba,
belong to the Netherlands Antilles and
are thus a part of the Kingdom of the
Netherlands.

ARRIVING BY SEA

Aruba

Cruise ships dock next to Seaport
Mall in the centre of Oranjestad, the
capital, 5 minutes' drive from the
nearest beaches.

Curaçao

There are two piers: the Curaçao
mega-pier, used by bigger ships, and
the Curaçao Cruise Terminal. Both are
a short walk from Willemstad.

PUBLIC HOLIDAYS

1 January: New Year's Day
25 January: G.F. Betico Croes
Birthday
18 March: Aruba Day
March/April: Good Friday; Easter
Monday
30 April: Rincon Day; Queen's Day
(celebrating birthday of Queen Beatrix
of Netherlands)
1 May: Labour Day; Whit Monday
20 May: Ascension Day
2 July: Curaçao Flag Day
25 December: Christmas Day
26 December: Boxing Day

CALENDAR OF EVENTS

January: Carnival on Curaçao; Aruba Carnival.
October: Aruba Music Festival.

MONEY MATTERS

The official currency on Aruba is the Aruban florin, although the US dollar, is accepted virtually everywhere. Curaçao uses the Netherlands Antilles florin (NAf), also known as the Netherlands Antilles guilder.

TOURIST OFFICES

Aruba

In Canada
Aruba Tourism Authority,
5875 Highway #7, Suite 201,
Woodbridge, Ontario L4L 1T9.
Tel: 905-264 3434.
Fax: 905-264 3437.
E-mail: ata.canada@aruba.com
In Europe
Aruba Tourism Authority,
Schimmelpennincklaan 1, 2517 JN
The Hague, The Netherlands.
Tel: 70 3566220.
Fax: 70 3604877.
E-mail: ata.europe@aruba.com
Aruba Tourism Authority, Unit D,
The Saltmarsh Partnership,
The Copperfields,
25 Copperfields Street,
London SE1 0EN.
Tel: 020 7401 8961/7928 6100.
In the US
Aruba Tourism Authority,
1000 Harbor Blvd,
Weehawken, NJ 07087.
Tel: 201-330 0800.
Fax: 201-330 8757.
E-mail: ata.newjersey@aruba.com
Aruba Tourism Authority,
1 Financial Plaza, Suite 136,
Ft. Lauderdale, FL 33394.
Tel: 954-767 6477.
Fax: 954-767 0432.
E-mail: ata.florida@aruba.com
In Aruba
Aruba Tourism Authority,
172 L.G. Smith Boulevard,
Oranjestad.
Tel: 823777.
Fax: 834702.

Websites
www.aruba.com
www.cruisearuba.com
www.visitaruba.com

Curaçao

In Europe
Curaçao Tourist Bureau Europe,
Vastland 82-84,
3011 BP Rotterdam, Holland.
Tel: 31-10 414 2639.
E-mail: ctbenl@wirehub.nl
In the US
The Curaçao Tourist Board,
475 Park Avenue, Suite 2000,
New York, NY 10016.
Tel: 212-683 7660.
Fax: 212-683 9337.
E-mail: curacao@ix.netcom.com
The Curaçao Tourist Board,
330 Biscayne Boulevard,
Miami, FL 33132.
Tel: 305-374 5811.
Fax: 305-374 6741.
In Curaçao
Tourism Development Bureau,
PO Box 3266, Pietermaai 19,
Willemstad.
Tel: 461 6000.
Fax: 461 2305.

Websites
www.curaçao-tourism.com
www.curaçao.com

POSTAL SERVICES

The main post offices are in the centre of Oranjestad and Willemstad.

TELECOMMUNICATIONS

The dialling code for Aruba is **297** and for Curaçao **59 99**. Local and long-distance calls can be made from hotels or from the telephone offices in or near the post offices, or from the offices of Setel, Setar, and Telbo, from where faxes and telegrams can also be sent. Aruba and Curaçao have Internet cafes, there is one in the Royal Plaza Mall, Oranjestad, and at Café Iguana in Willemstad, Curaçao.

SHOPPING

The ABC islands have a range of tax-free shopping outlets. Oranjestad in Aruba is gold mine of designer wear,

jewellery, perfume and local art. The Seaport Mall is right next to the cruise terminal and there's a second mall under the Sonesta Hotel opposite.

Curaçao has great tax-free purchases, shopping malls and interesting boutiques in Willemstad. Look out for Dutch cheeses, flavoured Curaçao liqueur and local art.

GETTING AROUND

By Car

Driving is on the right. To rent a car you must be 21 years of age and in possession of a valid national driving licence. Car rental firms will deliver to and collect from the cruise terminals in Aruba and Curaçao. In Aruba, rent a four-wheel drive vehicle if you want to explore the interior. Rental companies include: Budget, Aruba, tel: 5828600; Tropic Car Rental, Aruba; tel: 5930788; Avis, Curaçao, tel: 9-461 1255; fax: 9-461 5253; Budget, Curaçao, tel: 9-868-3466.

By Taxi

Taxis are available for hire at the cruise terminals, and other central locations. In addition, on Aruba and Curaçao, public transport is provided by buses and taxis following fixed routes. Always agree the fare before beginning a taxi journey.

Inter-Island Links

Royal Aruban Airlines run scheduled flights between Aruba and Curaçao several times a day.

STAYING ON

High season is from mid-December to mid-April. Prices are lower in summer.

Hotel Prices

Price categories are based on the cost of a double room, for one night:
$ = less than $100
$$ = $100–200
$$$ = more than $200.

Aruba

Amsterdam Manor Resort
252 J.E. Irausquin Boulevard,
Palm Beach.
Tel: 587 1492.
Fax: 587 1463.
www.amsterdammanor.com
Elegant family hotel in the style of a
Dutch canal house. Across from the
beach. **$$**

Coconut Inn
Noord 31.
Tel: 586 6288.
Fax: 586 5433.
www.coconutinn.com
Friendly bed and breakfast with
comfortable rooms. **$–$$**

Hyatt Regency Aruba
85 J.E. Irausquin Boulevard,
Palm Beach.
Tel: 586 1234.
Fax: 586 1682.
www.aruba.hyatt.com
Luxurious mini Las Vegas by the
beach. Casino, aquatic park, artificial
castle ruin, and boutiques. **$$$**

Curaçao

Avila Beach Hotel
Penstraat 130, Willemstad.
Tel: 461 4377.
Fax: 461 1493.
www.avilahotel.com
Tastefully extended former governor's
residence with antique furniture. **$$**

Curaçao Marriott Beach Resort and
Emerald Casino, John F. Kennedy
Boulevard, Piscaderbaai.
Tel: 736 8800.
Fax: 462 7502.
Luxury hotel, Dutch-Caribbean
architecture, beach. **$$$**

Habitat Curaçao
Coral Estate, Rif Saint Marie.
Tel: 864 8304.
Fax: 864 8464.
www.habitatcuracaoresort.com
Colourful complex with simple
cottages and suites for divers. **$$**

Price categories are based on the
cost of a meal for one person,
excluding drinks:
$ = less than $20
$$ = $20–40
$$$ = more than $40.

WHERE TO EAT

Both islands have Indonesian,
Chinese, French, Spanish and Italian
restaurants. Specialities include
seafood dishes. Cornmeal bread, goat
stew, hearty soups, grilled fish and
filled patties (*pastechi*) are all popular
local dishes. Splash out on a *rijstaffel*
Indonesian banquet, where up to 40
small dishes are served.

Aruba

Chez Mathilde
Havenstraat 23, Oranjestad.
Tel: 583 4968.
French cuisine in a renovated 19th-
century house. **$$$**

Papiamento
Washington 61, Oranjestad.
Tel: 586 4544.
European and local cuisine in an old
villa. **$$$**

Curaçao

Bistro Le Clochard
Riffort, Otrabanda.
Tel: 462 5666.
Gourmet cuisine with French-Swiss
accents. Delightful location on the
Sint Anabaai. **$$$**

Indonesia
Mercuriusstraat 13, Willemstad.
Tel: 461 2606.
Excellent Javanese cuisine. **$$**

Jaanchie's
Westpunt.
Tel: 864 0126.
A congenial garden restaurant, known
for its fish soup and other seafood
specialities. **$**

SHORE ACTIVITIES

Excursions

Aruba: Half day jeep safaris into the
desert-like interior; duty-free shopping
in Oranjestad; snorkelling on the
wreck *Antilla*; visits to the Natural

Bridge; catamaran snorkelling tours;
butterfly farm tours.
Curaçao: Museum and synagogue
tours; art galleries, the floating
market in Willemstad; Ostrich and
Game Farm; Landhuise Chobolobo
(liqueur factory); Amstel Brewery
tours; Seaquarium underwater
observatory.

Best Beaches

Aruba: Palm Beach and Eagle Beach,
5 to 10 minutes by taxi from the port;
Baby Beach in the south for soft sand
and snorkelling.
Curaçao: Seaquarium Beach; Playa
Port Mari for snorkelling; Caracas Bay
Island for activities from horse riding
to kayaking.

Water Sports

Both islands have diving in clear
water. Dive operators: Aruba Pro Dive,
Oranjestad, tel: 825520;
fax: 877722; Underwater Curaçao,
Willemstad, tel: 461 8100; Ocean
Encounters, Lions Dive Hotel, tel: 461
8131.
Snorkelling gear, windsurf boards
and Hobie Cats can be hired at most
beaches.

Cycling and Hiking

The flat, but rugged terrain of the ABC
Islands is ideal for cycling. For details
of mountain bike rentals and tours
contact: Pablito Big Rental,
Oranjestad, tel: 878655.
At a more leisurely pace, hiking is
the best way of studying the islands'
remarkable flora and fauna, especially
through the National Parks.

Golf

Courses include:
Tierra del Sol, tel: 860978, an 18-
hole golf course in the north west of
Aruba. The Curaçao Golf Club in
Emmastad is open to non-members.

Private Cruise Islands

Each major cruise line has a private island (in reality, usually one beach reserved exclusively for the cruise line on certain days, apart from Disney's Castaway Cay, which is wholly-owned by the cruise line). These are used for private beach days and all facilities are provided, from a restaurant to rest rooms, hammocks, water sports equipment and entertainment. The bonus of these beaches is that local hawkers are usually prevented from hassling passengers and the equipment is of a reliable standard. The disadvantage is that 2,000 passengers on one beach can stretch facilities and there is little chance of getting away from it all in a big group.

Most islands can be accessed by tender. There are usually extra charges although passengers can use their ship's ID cards for making purchases. Expect to sign waiver forms for any hired equipment, and strict safety controls on all sports, for example, passengers may not be allowed even to snorkel alone.

Great Stirrup Cay

NORWEGIAN CRUISE LINE

The first private island to be developed. Located at Bertram's Cove, in the Bahamas, with white sand, offshore coral reefs and shade from palm trees. Snorkelling equipment, foam floats, inflatable rafts, pedalos, kayaks and small sailing boats available for day hire. Hammocks available. Limbo dancing, beach games and lunchtime barbecue. There's also hiking (you can walk to the lighthouse) and volleyball.

Princess Cays

PRINCESS CRUISES AND P&O CRUISES

One and a half miles (2 km) of beach front at the tip of lovely Eleuthera, one of the Bahamas out islands, closest to Nassau. The island has shade from palm trees and hammocks to lie in and a coral reef offshore. There is water sports equipment to hire and a beach barbecue, as well as a bar, boutique and a small section where local vendors sell souvenirs and braid hair. Every day a ship is in, there's a colourful Junkanoo (carnival) procession at lunchtime.

Labadee, Haiti

ROYAL CARIBBEAN AND CELEBRITY CRUISES

This is the only private island with any access to local culture. Labadee is in fact on a peninsula, with a pretty beach in a quiet corner of poverty-stricken Haiti, backed by trees that offering plenty of shade. Entertainment includes water sports, beach volleyball, 200-year old ruins to explore (a short walk away) and local tradespeople selling crafts. Snorkelling expeditions to nearby Amiga Island reveal anchors, cannonballs, pottery and other 16th century artefacts on the sea bed.

Coco Cay

Royal Caribbean International's other island. Originally named Little Stirrup Cay, this strip of sand is located within the Berry Island chain of the Bahamas, about 50 miles (80 km) from Nassau. There is a rumour that the grave of the pirate Blackbeard is located here.

There is a sunken plane and a shipwrecked replica of *Queen Anne's Revenge*, Blackbeard's flagship that sunk off North Carolina in 1718. Activities include pirate hunting, snorkelling and scuba diving, jet skiing, parasailing, or paddle boats. Two restaurants serve food all day, one in the shopping village and one on the beach. Access is via tender.

Half Moon Cay

HOLLAND AMERICA LINE

This stunning private island, a former pirate hideout, is visited by Holland America's ships during most of their Caribbean and Panama Canal itineraries.

Only 45 of the island's 2,400 acres (971 hectares) are developed. Activities include a nature trail, volleyball, shuffleboard, basketball, swimming, snorkelling, Scuba diving, kayaking, windsurfing, parasailing, paddle boating, banana boating, sailing, jet skiing, deep-sea fishing and trips on glass bottom boats. Children's activities take place on a special section of the beach and include treasure hunts and the ice cream parlour. In addition, there are two bars and a food pavilion serving barbecue dishes.

Castaway Cay

DISNEY CRUISE LINE

Located 175 miles (282 km) east of Miami, formerly Gorda Cay. Castaway Cay is the only cruise line private island with its own pier; all the others are tender stops. Passengers are transported around by tram, with Disney characters in abundance.

There are three beaches, one for families, one for teens, and one for adults only. The latter includes a bar, hammocks and beach massages. The teen beach has volleyball.

Activities and facilities include paddleboats, kayaking, snorkelling for sunken treasure, tubes and rafts. Cookies Bar-B-Q serves up burgers, hotdogs, ribs, fries and salads. There's even a post office and a shop on this island.

ART & PHOTO CREDITS

Cartographic Editor **Zoë Goodwin**
Cover Design **Tanvir Virdee**
Picture Editor **Hilary Genin**
Picture Research **Britta Jaschinski**

Index

Numbers in italics refer to photographs

A
B
C
D
E
G
H
I
J
a
b
c
d
e
f
g
h
i
k
l

INSIGHT GUIDES

The classic series that puts you in the picture

Alaska
Amazon Wildlife
American Southwest
Amsterdam
Argentina
Arizona & Grand Canyon
Asia's Best Hotels & Resorts
Asia, East
Asia, Southeast
Australia
Austria
Bahamas
Bali
Baltic States
Bangkok
Barbados
Barcelona
Beijing
Belgium
Belize
Berlin
Bermuda
Boston
Brazil
Brittany
Brussels
Buenos Aires
Burgundy
Burma (Myanmar)
Cairo
California
California, Southern
Canada
Caribbean
Caribbean Cruises
Channel Islands
Chicago
Chile
China
Colorado
Continental Europe
Corsica
Costa Rica
Crete
Croatia
Cuba
Cyprus
Czech & Slovak Republic
Delhi, Jaipur & Agra
Denmark

Dominican Rep. & Haiti
Dublin
East African Wildlife
Eastern Europe
Ecuador
Edinburgh
Egypt
England
Finland
Florence
Florida
France
France, Southwest
French Riviera
Gambia & Senegal
Germany
Glasgow
Gran Canaria
Great Britain
Great Gardens of Britain
 & Ireland
Great Railway Journeys
 of Europe
Greece
Greek Islands
Guatemala, Belize
 & Yucatán
Hawaii
Hong Kong
Hungary
Iceland
India
India, South
Indonesia
Ireland
Israel
Istanbul
Italy
Italy, Northern
Italy, Southern
Jamaica
Japan
Jerusalem
Jordan
Kenya
Korea
Laos & Cambodia
Las Vegas
Lisbon
London

Los Angeles
Madeira
Madrid
Malaysia
Mallorca & Ibiza
Malta
Mauritius Réunion
 & Seychelles
Mediterranean Cruises
Melbourne
Mexico
Miami
Montreal
Morocco
Moscow
Namibia
Nepal
Netherlands
New England
New Mexico
New Orleans
New York City
New York State
New Zealand
Nile
Normandy
North American &
 Alaskan Cruises
Norway
Oman & The UAE
Oxford
Pacific Northwest
Pakistan
Paris
Peru
Philadelphia
Philippines
Poland
Portugal
Prague
Provence
Puerto Rico
Rajasthan

Rio de Janeiro
Rome
Russia
St Petersburg
San Francisco
Sardinia
Scandinavia
Scotland
Seattle
Shanghai
Sicily
Singapore
South Africa
South America
Spain
Spain, Northern
Spain, Southern
Sri Lanka
Sweden
Switzerland
Sydney
Syria & Lebanon
Taiwan
Tanzania & Zanzibar
Tenerife
Texas
Thailand
Tokyo
Trinidad & Tobago
Tunisia
Turkey
Tuscany
Umbria
USA: The New South
USA: On The Road
USA: Western States
US National Parks: West
Venezuela
Venice
Vienna
Vietnam
Wales
Walt Disney World/Orlando

INSIGHT GUIDES

The world's largest collection of
visual travel guides & maps